McFeely Li[brary]

George School, Pa.

Presented by

Elbert & Carol Thompson

McFeely Library
george school, pennsylvania

Individuals

and

World Politics

Robert A. Isaak

Duxbury Press

North Scituate, Massachusetts
A division of Wadsworth Publishing Company, Belmont, California

Duxbury Press
A DIVISION OF WADSWORTH PUBLISHING COMPANY, INC.

© 1975 by Wadsworth Publishing Company, Inc., Belmont, California 94002. All rights reserved. No part of this book may be reproduced, stored in a retrieval system, or transcribed, in any form or by any means, electronic, mechanical, photocopying, recording, or otherwise, without the prior written permission of the publisher, Duxbury Press, a division of Wadsworth Publishing Company, Inc., Belmont, California.

Individuals and World Politics was edited and prepared for composition by Katharine Gregg. Interior design was provided by Jane Lovinger and the cover was designed by Patricia Sustendal.

L.C. Cat. Card No.: 75-3563
ISBN 0-87872-094-4

PRINTED IN THE UNITED STATES OF AMERICA

1 2 3 4 5 6 7 8 9 10 — 79 78 77 76 75

To my parents

Robert D. & Margie A.

Contents

Preface

Why are individuals counted for so little in world politics while nation-states and the international system are counted for so much?

In our age of mass politics, it is popular to believe that collectivities, not individuals, determine political actions. Government bureaucracies, multinational corporations, and the masses are often viewed as the main forces that shape political life. However, collectivities alone cannot explain the unusual effectiveness of certain great leaders. Nor can they explain the hero worship of Mao Tse-tung as the great saint of the people or the individual skills of Henry Kissinger, which allow him to make short-term peace agreements in his own image in order to create stability and power for himself and the United States. I think the explanation is that the age of mass politics has hidden heroes, namely, the manipulative elite who are disguised and buried behind the bureaucracies, propaganda, and collectivist political theories.

The danger of not believing that such strong leaders can and do exist in world politics is that the masses of people in the world will be conditioned to believe that political events are inevitable, that history makes history, not men, and that individual human beings are no longer responsible for their own political actions. The age of mass politics has become a totalitarian age because of the willingness of groups of people to give in to and support individual extremists in times of crisis when people are led to believe that no one can solve problems, much less control political reality. The repressed longing for leadership among the masses leads to the efficient control of people in totalitarian dictatorships. Existing freedoms and responsibilities are cashed in for promised goods and the mindless comforts of social control.

This primer on world politics assumes that individuals do matter and introduces basic principles and theories of international relations through the experiences of great world leaders in the twentieth century. In contrast to most books introducing international politics this one assumes that mere abstract theories, which begin from the global viewpoint of the international system, are not as meaningful to human beings as principles that grow naturally out of the concrete, everyday experiences of people who happen to become involved in world politics. Systems talk is dehumanizing if it doesn't start with flesh and bones. The human focus should be upon the people caught in tension between local, national, and international political systems that frustrate them.

Of course not all people are equally significant for world politics. The question then becomes how do certain everyday individuals get pulled increasingly into international relations to the point of becoming great world leaders? In answering this question, I had to choose from the vast array of influential individuals of many backgrounds in our era. The basic criterion became, which human beings introduced a new principle of international politics in our century through their ideas and political actions? I have then traced these individuals from their everyday origins to their peaks of success in world politics in order to uncover the principles that moved them and helped them to move the world. Each political portrait is followed with a section explaining in detail the principles of world politics that are involved. Finally, I have summarized the present and future implications of these principles.

The advantage of choosing recent historical figures as a point of departure is that the reader can grasp world politics through another human being's experience and through his distinctive culture and upbringing. He can get a feel for a leader's political consciousness and the principles that served him so well but that also frequently caused him to make mistakes. For such great political leadership often fluctuates betweeen genius and madness, between a selfless concern for ideals and others and a self-consuming megalomania.

Such exposure to the basic principles of world politics is particularly international in that it is viewed through the perspectives of an Indian, a Russian, a Chinese, an American, a German, a Frenchman, a Swede, and a Jewish-German immigrant to the United States. Not accidentally the reader is plunged into many of the major historical events of our times: the Russian and Chinese Revolutions, World Wars I and II and their settlements, the nonviolent national movement in India, the creation and frustrations of the Common Market, the American diplomacy in Vietnam and the Middle East, the American-Soviet detente, and the relaxation of tensions between the Western world and the People's Republic of China. By reliving international politics with its major actors, it is possible to learn principles and theories by example. In so doing we may come to understand the potential and limits of the individual to affect events in world politics that shape the future of all people.

Every human being examines world politics from a point of view, hidden or revealed. It would be superhuman to see the subject from all points of view simultaneously, to be totally objective. Therefore, a scholar in the social sciences has an obligation to bring his point of view and basic assumptions out into the open at the outset of his work. My point of view is humanistic and my basic assumption is that the most meaningful vision of world politics for most people is one that stems from the specific viewpoints of other individuals. In my opinion, that is why most people are fascinated by biographies, particularly those of great historical figures, and why psychoanalysis, psychohistory, and even simulation approaches have become increasingly popular with students and social scientists. As Harold Lasswell wrote in 1930 in his famous *Psychopathology and Politics*, "Political science without biography is a form of taxidermy." Perhaps we have been stuffed with system theories and nation-state abstractions long enough.

Of course to take a humanistic point of view does not guarantee a humanistic result. A great man may begin with the assumption that individuals can have an impact on world affairs only to become a megalomaniac and dehumanize his country and the world with a greedy dictatorship. A different kind of danger results when idealists believe that wars begin only in the minds of men and blind themselves to social and historical factors that condition men into world war before they know what is happening. The paradigm of this book holds that actual power in world politics is based upon the needs and nature of human beings, the social facts of political life, and the limits of nationalism and historical opportunity.

Individuals do not stand alone. They are crucibles of their political culture and social class. My focus is upon the tensions between the individual needs and values of great leaders and the particular social facts which frustrate them. International politics is defined here as the attempt of certain groups of men to solve the tensions between the needs of their own people and the social facts of others and the world. The individuals that I examine are all leaders of groups, and my assumption is that their leadership is not the result of mere chance but is due in part to certain personality factors and historical opportunities. In the concluding chapter, when all eight figures are considered together, some surprising similarities that exist between their needs, values, social situations, and historical opportunities become clear.

Nor are the principles of world politics that I have chosen accidental. I used the recent Princeton survey of the areas most frequently taught in world politics courses as a basis for selecting concepts and individuals. Part One introduces the reader to the basic principles of the book. Part Two discusses the needs and nature of political men (Gandhi), the use by leaders of interest groups and class situations (Lenin), and their ability to transform such needs, values, and social facts into an effective ideology in order to organize movements, revolutions, and nation-states (Mao Tse-tung). Part Three examines nation-states that are already formed and illustrates how leaders manipulate them with ideas of total peace (Wilson) and total war (Hitler). Of course history outmaneuvers those leaders in the end, but we can learn much from their extreme examples, their successes, and their failures. Finally Part Four introduces the principles of international integration, organization, and diplomacy that have become so important in our era through the experiences of de Gaulle, Hammarskjöld, and Kissinger.

This book does not claim that individuals are the sole causes or independent variables of action in world politics. They are rather the cutting edge of a complex, many-faceted process of social action. But individuals give us a way to see the world meaningfully without getting thoroughly lost or alienated in a jungle of social and historical factors or theoretical abstractions. Psychology, socioeconimics, politics, and history come together in the flesh and blood of one human being in a specific situation with whom we can momentarily identify, if only to criticize and reject him as a model in the end. The hope here is to bring the complexities of world politics to life through other lives.

This endeavor does not attempt to provide comprehensive histories of the lives of the leaders considered nor of the events surrounding their stories. Rather it should be viewed as an interconnected series of eight colored snapshots, each taken from a particular angle chosen by the author to highlight certain principles. Any other writer would have shot the pictures differently. We are how we see things. And part of the human dilemma is that each of us is partially blind, a fact, however, that gives us some claim to uniqueness. The reader will have to try to make up for my blind spots with his own eyes. Earlier readers who did, helping to improve the mosaic that follows, include Arpad von Lazar of The Fletcher School of Law and Diplomacy, Robert Tomasek of The University of Kansas, Ralph Hummel of The John Jay College of the City University of New York, Edwin Fedder of the University of Missouri at St. Louis, Thomas Millington of Hobart and William Smith Colleges, David McLellan of Miami University, Geoffrey Field of the College at Purchase of the State University of New York, Herbert Kaskoff and Thomas Massucci, my graduate assistants, and Bob Gormley and his publishing group at Duxbury Press.

R.A.I.

PART ONE

Understanding World Politics

The very same principle that influences a bully to break the windows of a whore who has jilted him, naturally stirs up a great prince to raise mighty armies, and dream of nothing but sieges, battles and victories.

DEAN SWIFT

A Tale of a Tub

Great world leaders prove everyday that individuals do matter in international politics. Leaving nothing to chance, they break beyond existing social reality and use a few basic principles of world politics as tools to move the world. By slipping into the shoes of the great political figures of our era we can see how some men move beyond their backyard existences, transform their nations into their own images, and change the rules according to which the game of nations is played. World politics becomes alive when we encounter it through the lives of others who experienced it. And, who knows, we may even be able to apply their recipes for political action to our own needs and problems.

If the world were merely a dice game, if Chance were always king, neither free will nor great men would exist. But experience teaches us that some men know how to throw the dice or move in their direction better than others. From China Mao Tse-tung manipulated international ping-pong games to announce to the world that China was officially ready to join the superpowers as an equal in the game of nations. American diplomat Henry Kissinger slipped secretly in and out of Vietnamese, Chinese, and Middle Eastern capitals to make suprizing agreements from what many thought to be hopeless situations. These are certainly no ordinary men. Yet their beginnings were suprisingly ordinary.

Mao Tse-tung was raised from a peasant family and was once just one of many revolutionary students. When Kissinger first came to the United States from Nazi Germany, he worked during the day squeezing the acid out of brush bristles in a Manhattan shaving brush factory and went to school at night. While ordinary people might well have taken such situations for granted, leaving things to chance, these individuals did not. Great world leaders come into being by opposing chance, by taking nothing for granted, and by using ideas and action to impose their wills upon others.

In the political games of everyday life, the odds aren't equal for everyone. Great world leaders constantly seek to better their odds by controlling their own lives and those of others, by breaking out of the patterns of everyday routine, and by living for ideas beyond their own selfish needs. Whether they use their power for good or evil is secondary to the fact that they exist and often hold our existence and fate in their hands. Such leaders become historical facts. They become history in so far as human will makes a difference. Yet in their becoming also resides their downfall, as philosopher Friedrich Nietzsche noted: "What is great in man is that he is a bridge and not an end: what can be loved in man is that he is an *overture* and a *going under*."

The basic motivation of great world leaders is the need to change the world and to sacrifice themselves to principles which they become. Gandhi became militant nonviolence in India; Lenin became Russian Communism; Hitler anti-Semitism and German superiority; Hammarskjöld world peace through a United Nations with teeth. Such world leaders must be able, as Hammarskjöld put it, "to exist for the future of others without being suffocated by their present." They live for a vision beyond themselves, yet most could be caught uttering the words of the Greek poet Kazantzakis: "I'm the kind who likes to grasp his dream like flesh."

And dreams they are. More important than the great leaders are the inevitable limits that frustrate them and are their final undoing. Kissinger struck that tragic chord of history when he wrote, "I believe there is the tragedy of a man who works very hard and never gets what he wants. And then I believe there is the even more bitter tragedy of a man who finally gets what he wants and finds out that he doesn't want it." The historical conditions or social facts that frustrate human needs and dreams include existing social values, such as nationalism; other personalities, such as enemies; social institutions, such as social class; political institutions, such as legislatures; and existing rules of the game, such as he who has most force wins. Nationalistic values haunted Hammarskjöld; enemies murdered Gandhi; social class differences frustrated Mao; legislatures stymied Wilson; and the very principle of survival of the fittest that brought Hitler to power caused his ultimate defeat.

Shakespeare wrote, "Some are born great; some achieve greatness; and some have greatness thrust upon 'em." World politics is not merely the biographies of great men; it is the story of the necessities or conditions that make them possible. If politics is defined as the attempt to solve tensions between human needs and social facts, Everyman cannot understand the principles of world politics behind great leaders without being acquainted with three kinds of necessities they all faced: the needs and nature of human beings, the social facts of political life, and the limits of nationalism and historical opportunity.

Mohandas Gandhi symbolized the needs and nature of political man in India by refusing to satisfy his basic physiological needs in order to force British officials into submission by fasting and gain independence for his country. If he had been wrong about the good nature of the British he might have starved to death or have been executed. By understanding the repressive social facts or conditions of traditional Russian society, Nikolai Lenin successfully led the vanguard of the Russian Revolution. Without understanding such social facts, Lenin might have been forced to flee from Russia with his ideals unfulfilled, as did his opponent Alexander Kerensky. Understanding the psychological power of nationalism and when to seize historical opportunity enabled Adolf Hitler to consolidate his power in Germany and initiate the greatest war of all time. However, not recognizing the limits of the power of German nationalism nor the limits of his opportunity led Hitler to blind acts of willpower and ultimate defeat.

Men like Gandhi, Lenin, and Hitler helped to determine the fate not only of their own nations but of the entire world as we know it today. Each provided a model solution for other men to follow in international politics: Gandhi, the principle of nonviolent civil disobedience; Lenin, pragmatic realism of elitism in revolution; and Hitler, an ideology of nationalism and unyielding willpower. Examples such as these indicate that in world politics there is no escape. The alternative to power is impotence, and those who opt out of the political game must resign themselves to seeing it decided by others. To view world politics as merely the outcome of **historical determinism** is inaccurate and robs man of all hope and **self-determination**. On the other hand, to see world politics as the outcome of man's free will alone encourages him to become a god or beast and blinds him to the limits of his human condition. As Albert Camus noted, there is no Truth, only truths. No single theory will ever cover all international situations. To understand the tensions of international relations, the tensions between man's free will and historical determinants, the best we can do is to sketch the assumptions without which those various views of world politics could not exist. Then by briefly sampling different case studies of great world leaders, each of us may be better able to select the appropriate truth to apply to the international problems of his own rapidly changing world.

The Needs and Nature of Everyman

Everyman is born into the world with **needs**. Such needs include bodily needs, security, love, self-esteem, and self-actualization, listed in order of priority according to psychologist Abraham Maslow.* In a world of scarcity and deprivation human beings cannot survive or remain human without becoming political. **Politics** is social action that helps men to solve the tension between their needs and social facts.

*Beginning with the most basic needs, Abraham Maslow's empirically grounded need hierarchy is defined as follows: (1) physiological needs: food, water, rest; (2) security needs: physical and psychic security; (3) love needs: warmth, affection, inclusion; (4) self-esteem needs: positive evaluation of the self by the self and others; (5) self-actualization needs: fulfilling one's highest potential, superior perception of reality, increased spontaneity and creativity, increased identification with the human species. See A. Maslow, *Motivation and Personality* (N.Y.: Harper and Row, 1954).

A classic tale told by philosopher Jean Jacques Rousseau illustrates the role of human needs and human nature in political problem solving. A long time ago five hungry men who had just learned the rudiments of speech and communication came together. Previously each had been able to satisfy his needs on his own without creating any social relationships, but their world had been hit by hard times. Scarcity and deprivation prevailed. So the five men realized they had a choice: cooperate or die. They decided to create a social relationship to solve the tension between their mutual hunger and the social fact of a scarcity of food. They formed a plan to capture a stag, one-fifth of which would satisfy the hunger need of each man. In standing at their posts to carry out the plan, however, one man spotted a hare that would be just enough to satisfy his own hunger. He deserted his post to catch the hare and allowed the stag to escape.

This simple story has profound implications. The moral seems to be that even when men get together to cooperate for mutual interests, they cannot trust each other. The man who deserted the community was thinking more about his short-term hunger need than his long-term security need. In the future when he could find no hares, he could hardly expect his former comrades to include him in their hunting ventures. Moreover, upon perceiving his desertion it is likely that they might become angry enough to track him down and kill him. By becoming obsessed with his lower-level hunger needs, he might have sacrificed the satisfaction of higher-level needs such as security. On the other hand, if all five men were actually starving to death, he might have been foolish to jeopardize his life in the present for some utopia in the future by letting the hare escape.

Everyman constantly finds himself in similar dilemmas. By trying too hard to satisfy one need he may prevent another from being satisfied; but by not trying he may end up with no satisfaction whatsoever. Man's perception of the tension between his needs or between needs and social facts is **political consciousness**. Acting out of this consciousness is politics.

Ordinary men do politics when they become so aware of the tension created by their frustrated needs that they act together to change existing social facts, that is, existing values, personalities, institutions, and rules of the political game, in order to create conditions more likely to solve their problems. Great world leaders begin doing ordinary politics like everyone else but get carried away into doing **international politics**. They become leaders of national groups. International politics is the attempt of certain groups of men to solve the tensions between the needs of their own people and the social facts of others and the world.

International politics goes on within as well as between nations. When a group of people identifies itself culturally as a people, say "the Nodnicks," and comes into tension or conflict with a different people, say "the Dudnicks," a minor kind of international politics is taking place. Anti-Nodnickism within The Big City is just as bad as Anti-Americanism or Anti-Sovietism within the world at large. For example, in New York City, a group of Inner Slobovians can cause an international incident by kidnapping the Outer Slobovian ambassador to the United Nations. International politics always begins at home, at somebody's home. It does not refer to mere global abstractions out there somewhere with no relation to the here and now of our cozy domestic lives. Rather world politics begins with the tension problems that arise when a French exchange student comes to an American school, when a son is drafted into the army—or volunteers, when you buy a bottle of Italian wine rather than an American product, when one of your relatives derives great joy from a biased war movie that makes fun of a typical German, Russian, or Chinese soldier. Our national images are formed at home, and our international relations with others begin as soon as our national values interact or conflict with those of a different heritage, whether in school, on television, on the street, or in a foreign country.

In a complex world like ours, to be able to view a political situation without distortion is hard, perhaps impossible. In that sense all human beings may be somewhat pathological. For at times all of us perceive the world through static snapshots and are too rigid to grasp the quick changes of the complex reality we are experiencing. We see the world through our upbringing, through our culture, and through our nation. Our sight is colored and limited by our experience just as the language we speak is the skin of that experience. Disliking uncertainty and ambiguity, we sometimes grasp quickly for a simple explanation that will momentarily rescue us from our anxiety. Such thinking is particularly true of our anxiety about foreign people, languages, and cultures. *They* should speak *our* language, we think. There is a natural human tendency to oversimplify reality and reject ambiguity by reverting to stock responses we have learned from our national culture. Although our universal human needs may be the same as those of foreigners, our human nature has been nationalized.

Human nature is not an unchangeable law, totally good or totally bad, but is a result of the interaction of a specific individual's needs with his heritage and environment. All of us are culturally biased. Our individual values and the ways we try to satisfy our needs are colored and limited by the social facts of our specific spot on the earth. Individual personality develops out of the tension between human needs and social facts. Philosopher Jean Paul Sartre said, "We only become what we are by the radical and deep-seated refusal of that which others have made us."

The Social Facts of Political Life

Since the time when Antigone broke the law and disobeyed the king to bury her brother, people have found that their needs and values have been frustrated by **social facts**. Social facts are existing man-made conditions that frustrate or satisfy human needs. When over a period of time men act out social relationships that they have created to satisfy needs, such relationships become routines or institutions or "social facts." Continuing

Rousseau's story, if the five hungry men met every Wednesday to go hunting, forming a Stag Club, a simple social relationship would be transformed into an institution or social fact of political life.

Although such a social fact may satisfy the needs of the five hungry men for a while, eventually their arrangement may become outdated and frustrate more needs than it satisfies. Suppose that five hungry women come along and are denied membership to the club because of a male chauvinist admissions policy. Finding their needs frustrated by social facts, the women might rebel by refusing to satisfy the men's sexual needs. Humanistic political life involves the continual reform of social facts that no longer serve human needs in a community. In this sense the social relationships that make up society are distinct from the existing social facts or conditions that may no longer be relevant to the needs of such relationships. Social relations are created to satisfy human needs. They are maintained as social facts or institutions as long as they serve their purpose. Then they are discarded and new social facts are created to satisfy new needs. Creation, maintenance, and decay seem to mark the continual cycle of the social facts of political life.

Thus society refers to neither individuals nor institutions alone but to social relationships between people. Historian Arnold Toynbee noted, "In a social structure individuals are merely the *foci* in the network of relationships. . . . A visible and palpable collection of people is not a society; it is a crowd. A crowd, unlike a society, can be assembled, dispersed, photographed or massacred."[1]

At least five types of social facts help to make up a society: existing values, personalities, social institutions, political institutions, and rules of the game. Explanations of all political activity, domestic or international, depend upon how these facts or variables come together in the situation at hand.[2]

Values are what people want. Since people often want more than they need, it is clear that, though values often originate with basic needs, they tend to go beyond them. Take the case of the security need of American foreign policymakers. Although following World War II the United States possessed the greatest military potential in the world, many American leaders wanted more security. One result was that in the name of security interests American planes dropped 7.4 billion tons of bombs on Southeast Asia between 1964 and 1973, many more than were dropped in the whole of World War II. Ironically the excessive bombing and the sacrifice of American lives caused by the desire for security led to an actual decrease in American security as American morale dropped and American public opinion pushed the government to withdraw all American troops from Southeast Asia, reduce troops in the rest of the world, end the draft, and cut the defense budget. By pressing too hard for certain values beyond their actual needs, people can undermine the very goals they are trying to achieve.

In order to create social relationships to solve problems, people must find minimal basic values they can agree on. Each of us is carefully socialized to believe in our society's basic values. Americans are taught to affirm life, liberty, and the pursuit of happiness through individual competition and the accumulation of property. The Japanese, in contrast, are taught to subordinate individual interests to attain harmony within the group in order to achieve happiness. Social values are goals defined for individuals by others in society. Only by becoming politically conscious of such values can one modify them.

The characteristics that an individual brings to bear in his face-to-face social relationships constitute his personality. The focal point of personality is the ego, the conscious expression of the tension between a person's needs and values and his social world. Psychologist Sigmund Freud claimed that culture results from the tension between an individual's ego and the superego—social values or norms—of his social world and that civilization emerges from the sacrifice of one's ego to the social values of society.[3] The most important political consequence of personality is the conscious will of the individual to solve the tension between his needs and social facts. Personal political competence means competence at self-determination. Each human being yearns to become self-sufficient, to become complete. His ability and style in that attempt define his personality.

Great world leaders develop unusually dynamic personality traits and desire self-determination for their group or people as well as for themselves. They are driven to become the origin of political action rather than the mere pawn of social facts. They adopt and become a cause and seek to change their social world for the sake of needs and values they believe to be important. Self-determination for themselves and their people becomes their passion, their meaning of freedom.

Every human personality is limited by the social and political institutions in which he lives and which limit his freedom. Social institutions are old social relationships set up some time ago to regulate need satisfaction between human beings. The two social institutions most relevant to politics are class and status. Class is how much you have of what there is to get of the social values, how you got it, and what you do with it. Thus the elites of most countries constitute the upper class in terms of possessing more property and privileges than the masses of the middle and lower classes. Status is how much others think you have of what there is to get. In the Chinese Revolution Mao Tse-tung was perceived by others as having a great deal of status even though he did not possess much property. On the other hand, for many years the Shah of Iran did not have much status despite the enormous potential wealth of his oil fields. When he and his colleagues quadrupled oil prices, the financial balance of power in the world shifted drastically. By proving he had class, he gained status and respect everywhere.

Those social institutions most concerned with regulating public tension and conflicts in society are called political institutions. Specifically, political institutions are standard arrangements for administering the solution of typical problems or conflicts of values. They include executive offices, legislatures, courts, departments of state and defense, armies, and political parties.

Which problems are typical in a political community is determined by the existing rules of the game. Rules of the game are the accepted routines according to which politics is normally done in a community. Public laws are formal rules of the game. Traditions, ethical restraints, campaign and fund-raising tactics are informal rules of the game. Two classic types of rules of the game in nations throughout the world are the democratic and the authoritarian. Typical democratic communities are run as if the vote of each participating citizen counted in the decision making of political institutions. On the other hand, typical authoritarian communities are run as if only the decision of the dictator or the ruling elite mattered in political problem solving. The democratic and the authoritarian are both ideal types, that is, abstract intellectual categories used to typify reality and to describe the meaning of its larger patterns. In real life, there is much authoritarianism on the part of the elites in democracies and much concern about how the masses will react in authoritarian dictatorships.

Significantly, authoritarian types of governments often have the advantage over more diffuse democratic governments in foreign policy making. This aspect of American democracy led the poet Robert Frost to observe: "There are two games—checkers and giveaway. We have been giving away to Germany, to Japan, to China, etc., etc., etc. I want checkers for a change."

If one takes all five types of social facts together, values, personality, social institutions, political institutions and rules of the game, one can derive a person's potential power in social relationships.[4] For example, a man is apt to have a great deal of potential power in the United States today if he has White Anglo Saxon Protestant values, an agreeable, dynamic personality, an upper-class family background, a job as a Senator, and maximizes his values in the competitive rules of the American game of negotiation and compromise. Specific patterns of social conduct that provide the basis for potential power are called roles.

Social and political organizations are usually structured in hierarchies or triangles of authority, with the roles of the elite with the greatest power potential at the top and the roles of the mass at the bottom. Role potency, or the potential power of a particular role, is determined in most cases by the number of people affected by the decisions of the person who occupies that role. The roles with greatest potency in world politics are those heads of states and corporations and foreign policymakers who make peace and war and economic decisions that affect the lives of millions of people.

Whether or not potential power is turned into actual power depends upon the combination of perceived situational opportunity, personal decision making, and self-determination. These are the crucial components of political man. Power is a social relationship between people in which some have more of their needs satisfied than others. To know how and when to jump in and out of the right social roles at the right times is one of the key prerequisites to great political leadership. Otto von Bismarck demonstrated this ability in uniting Germany under his leadership in the nineteenth century. He escaped a subservient civil servant job before it dried him up and managed to obtain an ambassadorship in Prussia and used that role carefully for ten years to prepare himself and other people for his assumption of the most powerful role of all, chancellor of a united Germany.

Limits of Nationalism and Historical Opportunity

People like Bismarck who fill foreign policy decision-making roles are in a position of power that enables them to define the national interest in international political relationships. National interest refers to needs or values of a national community identified by the elite as being most critical for their people in specific international situations. The Greek historian Thucydides noted, "Identity of interests is the surest of bonds whether between states or individuals."

To understand the notion of national interest it is necessary first to understand the **nation-state**, that heavy-handed social reality that colors our upbringing and limits our vision of the world. The philosopher Friedrich Nietzsche wrote some bald truths about the nation-state which he called "The New Idol":

> State? What is that? Well then, open your ears to me, for now I shall speak to you about the death of peoples.
>
> State is the name of the coldest of all cold monsters. Coldly it tells lies too; and this lie crawls out of its mouth: "I, the state, am the people" . . .
>
> It is annihilators who set traps for the many and call them "state": they hang a sword and a hundred appetites over them.
>
> Where there is still a people, it does not understand the state and hates it as the evil eye and the sin against customs and rights . . .
>
> All-too-many are born: for the superfluous the state was invented.
>
> Behold, how it lures them, the all-too-many—and how it devours them, chews them, and ruminates! . . . It would use you as bait for the all-too-many . . .
>
> State I call it where all drink poison, the good and the wicked; state, where all lose themselves, the good and the wicked; state, where the slow suicide of all is called "life" . . .

> Only where the state ends, there begins the human being
> who is not superfluous . . .[5]

Nietzsche's negative view of the state is due to the tendency of elites to make it into a religious object so that they can more easily manipulate the masses for their own narrow goals. Similarly have many scholars of the "realist" school of world politics become so infatuated with the abstract nation-state, its power and its rules, that they have dehumanized international relations, losing sight of individuals and human needs in the process. The world for these so-called realists becomes an inevitable battleground between the national interests of greedy nation-states. The differences between good and bad leadership within specific states is rarely discussed by those who take the nation-state viewpoint on international politics.

However, because it is the most powerful social fact of international life, the nation-state cannot be ignored. The development of the nation-state is the key to understanding the rules of the game according to which politics is played in the world today, for the world is made up of a system of nation-states. It must only be remembered that individuals create nation-states and maintain their interests. Nation-states are not inevitable machines that operate without human origin or control.

When a group of people organize social relationships on a particular territory so that cooperative agreements or laws can be decided upon, reviewed, and carried out they create a state. A **state** is an organization given the **legitimacy**, or the recognized legal authority, to govern over power relationships of a particular territory. The people who make up the sociocultural world controlled by the state are called the **nation**. If the people constituting the nation recognize the authority of the state as legitimate, this relationship is called a nation-state, and it is the most powerful form of social relationship men have yet created.

Revolutions occur when some of the people making up a nation no longer recognize the state or organization governing their lives as legitimate. This is why the elite controlling a state is often willing to use any means to maintain its legitimacy, from everyday lying, to ideological propaganda, to the declaration of needless wars. Elites often use the myth of **sovereignty** to maintain their legitimacy. Sovereignty is where legitimacy lies in a nation-state. Monarchs in monarchies trace sovereignty to themselves: "I am the state." Members of democratic elites in democracies trace sovereignty to the people: "We represent the people." Both claims are myths, or frozen cultural beliefs, used by elites to manipulate the masses for their own ends.

The dominant myth of our times is the myth of the nation-state itself or nationalism. **Nationalism** is the belief that a particular nation-state merits Everyman's ultimate loyalty and constitutes his ultimate solution. Each of us is brought up to think of nationalism as patriotism: my country right or wrong. Dr. Samuel Johnson's observation is rarely quoted by schoolteachers: "Patriotism is the last refuge of a scoundrel."

Nationalism is the secular religion of the modern era and is cultivated by political elites to maintain their legitimacy and to give them a psychological basis for powerful ideological tools such as propaganda. As a myth it has tremendous symbolic power, rooted in the symbols of a common territory, language, heritage, and sociocultural world.

• When believers in nationalism come into contact with people from other countries the result is ethnocentrism. **Ethnocentrism** is an excessive attachment to the sociocultural world and life-style of one's own people: my culture right or wrong. A typical example is the religious belief in the American way of life preached by many Americans traveling abroad, or by those who refuse to go abroad arguing that they must see their own country first. Ethnocentrism is etched into the subconsciousness of each human being through his upbringing and can only be modified if he develops international political consciousness: perhaps some cultures are more suited than mine for fulfilling certain of my needs. Attitudes resulting from nationalism and ethnocentrism lead to psychological and ideological rigidity, which, in turn, breed international conflict and war. As often as not Pogo was right: "We have met the enemy and he is us."

Naturally ethnocentrism is not a sickness suffered by Americans alone. People all over the world are nationalistic, ethnocentric, and narrow-minded. A classic example of such widespread ethnocentrism is given by the poet and adventurer Antoine de Saint-Exupéry in his famous book *The Little Prince*:

> I have serious reason to believe that the planet from which the little prince came is the asteroid known as B-612.
>
> This asteroid has only once been seen through the telescope. That was by a Turkish astronomer, in 1909.
>
> On making his discovery, the astronomer had presented it to the International Astronomical Congress, in a great demonstration. But he was in Turkish costume, and so nobody would believe what he said.
>
> Grown-ups are like that . . .
>
> Fortunately, however, for the reputation of Asteroid B-612, a Turkish dictator made a law that his subjects, under pain of death, should change to European costume. So in 1920 the astronomer gave his demonstration all over again, dressed with impressive style and elegance. And this time everybody accepted his report.[6]

Nationalism, ethnocentrism, and the elitist view of the national interest are colored by the stage of development of the nation at hand. History reshapes the interactions between basic needs—physiological, security, love, self-esteem, and self-actualization—and existing social facts—values, personalities, social institutions, political institutions, and rules of the game—of each national culture just as the shaking of ·a kaleidoscope reshuffles the colors of its reality. The ways in which national leaders use self-determination to solve the tensions between national needs and social facts as they see them are subtly limited by this developmental process.

Nation-states, like all other social relationships, go through developmental phases of creation, maintenance, and decay.[7] That is, organized social relationships, like nation-states, are created when people get together to satisfy common needs and to solve common problems. To the extent that those social relationships are successful in meeting the needs for which they were created they are maintained and become cultural routines and institutions. However, institutionalized relationships tend to become rigid and bureaucratic, cut off from the original needs they were created to serve. Decay sets in, old routines break down, and rebellions and revolutions result. Then another group of individuals gets together to solve human problems by creating new social relationships, renewing the old nation-state, or creating an entirely different one. All national leaders have their historical opportunities limited by the developmental phases of creation, maintenance, or decay in which they find their nation-states. Their individual power to satisfy their own needs and those of their people depends upon their ability to accurately perceive those limited opportunities and to make the most of them.

Such national opportunities depend not merely upon the internal conditions of a leader's nation-state, but upon the dynamic relationships existing between his people or nation and others. In trying to negotiate for means to satisfy the needs of his people on the world stage, the leader's potential power depends upon the potential power of his entire people as a collective unit, and that power is often measured by the extent to which the nation's needs have already been met, especially in the areas of economic and military security. Accordingly, a few nations are perceived to be great powers but most are not. Among the great powers are superpowers who alone possess sufficient nuclear weaponry and economic development to literally place their peoples in another world of development.

Nevertheless, middle range national powers give their leaders more room for movement than might be imagined. Through careful regional organization, developing oil producing nations suddenly find their financial powers amazingly strengthened when their leaders are shrewd enough to cooperate and to sense how much their rich customers will bear. Likewise, by organizing into regional bargaining blocs, like the European Common Market, leaders of middle range powers can create common tariffs and policies that make them more competitive with the great powers economically. By playing the superpowers against each other and knowing when they will not use their nuclear weapons, leaders of smaller nations, like Fidel Castro of Cuba and Anwar Sadat of Egypt, often outmaneuver national leaders with much greater potential power, although in Secretary of State Henry Kissinger they may have met their match.

The Humanist Perspective

This book attempts to present a humanist theory of world politics. A theory is a way of grasping reality and working within it. Its success depends on whether it is meaningful in the real world, whether it takes the facts into account, and whether it works.

Every human being moves through life with theories in his head that color his vision, whether he knows it or not. A story is told about a drunk who is asked why he is looking under a certain streetlight for a key. "Because there is more light here," he replies. Each of us has his own idea of where to look for the most light to explain everyday reality as we experience it. Without such notions we could not distinguish the significant from the insignificant. Everything would be flat, meaningless, and uninteresting.

Most of us take our theories or interpretations of life for granted, not questioning them or examining them consciously. We move through life drunk with habit, at least as long as the habit seems to work for us. At times we even come to believe we really have a handle on 'The Truth.' We come to believe in our own objectivity.

Alas we are not superhuman and are not capable of seeing all points of view and facts simultaneously. We are small, partially blind human beings with biases and fantasies. Sociologist Max Weber wrote, "There is no absolutely 'objective' scientific analysis of . . . 'social phenomena' independent of special and 'one-sided' viewpoints according to which . . . they are selected, analyzed and organized for expository purposes. . . . All knowledge of cultural reality . . . is always knowledge from *particular points of view.*"[8] We all begin with colored viewpoints and the least we can try to do is to be honest about it and spell them out.

This book is written from the humanist point of view. It begins with individual human beings and their needs.

Traditionally the study of world politics has been approached from either the nation-state or global viewpoint. That is, rather than looking at the politics of the world through the eyes of individuals, these theories began from the collective viewpoint of the interests and power of a particular nation-state or from the global viewpoint, which treated the world as a huge system of interaction and power balances. Such approaches are necessarily abstract and are deliberately dehumanizing, for they seek to obliterate the individual and the unique for the sake of the general and normal rules.

Realism and Scientism

Those who take the power and interest of the nation-state as their basic assumption in world politics call themselves "the realists." The most popular exponent of realism, Hans Morgenthau, has argued that human nature and society have objective laws that can be discovered and used to calculate rational interests and power balances in the world for each nation-state.[9] He does not define politics in terms of human needs but merely as a struggle for power. The power struggle between nations supposedly leads naturally and inevitably to an equilibrium or balance of power system that is self-regulatory.

> It will be shown in the following pages that the international balance of power is only a particular manifestation of a general social principle to which all societies composed of a number of autonomous units owe the autonomy of their component parts; that the balance of power and policies aiming at its preservation are not only inevitable but are an essential stabilizing factor in a society of nations; and that the instability of the international balance of power is due not to the faultiness of the principle but to the particular conditions under which the principle must operate in a society of sovereign nations.[10]

In that statement, Morgenthau assumes not only that a system of necessary relationships exists out there, but that the system is based upon an inevitable principle of a tendency toward stabilization. Morgenthau's principle is a matter of faith and cannot be disproved. Such an inevitable principle falls into the same category in which Professor W.G. Runciman placed doctrinaire versions of Marxism, Freudianism and Catholicism: "It is what is sometimes described as the 'closed' character of all three systems which renders them immune to evidence in a way that a theory in the natural sciences never can be. It is not that the holder of such a belief may never change his mind, but that if he does the process is better described as 'conversion' than by either the ice-cream model ('he decided he didn't like it after all') or the natural science model ('his evidence failed to confirm his hypothesis')."[11]

The difficulty with the realist approach is not only that it focuses upon the abstraction of the nation-state, but that its static view of human nature and the so-called inevitable balance of power make the approach unscientific. To combat the parochialism of the traditional nation-state or realist approach to world politics, a group of social scientists created an alternative theory or paradigm in the 1950s called behavioralism, which claimed to be more scientific by focusing upon all behavior in the entire global system of world politics. The basic thrust of the behavioralists in international politics also attempts to establish an equilibrium or system stability. However, their approach and method are different.

Rather than assuming that there is an inevitable law of nature that determines the objective nature of man and the inevitable balance of power through conflict and compromise, the behavioralists begin to gather all kinds of facts about the international system hoping to derive theories and test hypotheses scientifically from the data. Many feel it is more scientific to turn data into numbers and statistics when they can.[12] The advantages of the behavioralist movement are that it forces social scientists to become more interdisciplinary and more precise and to focus upon human behavior from an international perspective. Like traditional realism, behavioral scientism often focuses more on system stability than on human beings and their needs.[13] It, too, becomes dehumanizing for trying too hard to be objective, general, and scientific.

Scientific Humanism

There is at least one other major approach to international politics in addition to the realist nation-state approach and the behavioralist systems approach. It is the idealistic humanistic approach. While the realist position assumes that man is basically selfish and aggressive and therefore focuses upon balance of power relationships, the idealistic humanists went to the other extreme arguing that man is basically good and that war begins because of imperfect social or educational systems that corrupt him. The idealistic position is as much a matter of faith as realism and focuses most of its efforts upon reforms of the nation-state or international system through international organization or other means. Not only is idealistic humanism often wishy-washy, but it, too, assumes a static view of human nature and therefore focuses on the higher levels of the nation-state and global system.[14]

The critical question becomes Is a humanist approach to world politics possible that avoids naive idealism, that takes the power realities of existing nation-states into account, and that can utilize the scientific method to analyze world politics from the individual to the global level without losing the focus upon man and his needs? One possible answer to this question is to begin the study of world politics with individuals, their values, and needs and to examine the tensions between human needs and social conditions scientifically in order to derive useful explanations of foreign policy decision making, peace, and war in the world at large. In short, by focusing upon the psychosocial tensions of people interacting with other people in the world arena, the scientific bases of psychology, biology, economics, sociology, and political science can be integrated with the humanistic interests of history, philosophy, and political theory to eventually arrive at a comprehensive explanation of human behavior in world politics.

This book begins with individuals who affected world politics and attempts to derive general principles that guided their behavior. The approach assumes that the subject of international relations is most meaningful if it is explored from an individual's viewpoint. Only by beginning with a coherent human world-view can world politics be humanized. The importance of nation-states and the international system as a whole is not denied, but such abstractions and conditions depend for their meaning upon a human perspective that gives them value or significance. The critical focus for international politics should be upon the tensions between nation-states and historical conditions on the one hand and the needs and values of human beings on the other.

Human beings can look at world politics from the viewpoint of individuals, from the viewpoint of nation-states, and from the viewpoint of the international system. Your viewpoint determines what your focus will be, what facts you will stress, and what conclusions you are likely to draw. This book assumes that the most human way to approach world politics is to begin with actual human lives, with biographies and intentions, with personal successes and failures in doing world politics. Nation-state and global factors are taken into account, but only as social facts and historical situations that aid or frustrate particular human beings in their effort to satisfy their own needs and those of their people. Abstract principles of world politics are meaningful in a human sense only to the extent that they are embodied with flesh and blood and are tested in actual historical experience.

Moreover, the nation-state and systems approaches to world politics can easily stimulate a belief in man's powerlessness. National and global complexities are made to appear so overwhelming that one loses sight of what a single individual can do. Whether individuals use great power for good or evil purposes is another question. A humanist theory does not guarantee humanistic results, although it does tend to pinpoint human responsibility for success and failure. Furthermore, the humanist perspective highlights the ways in which great political personalities have created effective strategies to mediate between their own needs and the needs and opportunities of societal, national, and international politics. We can learn from their examples without adopting them as models. Perhaps we will be able to create a more humanistic world politics by knowing enough about their mistakes to avoid them. Their blindness may sharpen our sight. And their examples of effective willpower may shake us out of our powerlessness long enough to go out and help the world, our nation, and ourselves.

Notes

1. Arnold Toynbee, *A Study of History* (New York: Oxford University Press, 1972), p. 43.

2. See Robert A. Isaak and Ralph P. Hummel, *Politics for Human Beings* (North Scituate, Mass.: Duxbury Press, 1975).

3. Sigmund Freud, *Civilization and Its Discontents*, standard ed., trans. James Strachey (New York: W.W. Norton & Co., 1961).

4. See Kalman Silvert, *Man's Power* (New York: Viking Press, 1970).

5. Friedrich Nietzsche, *Thus Spoke Zarathustra* in *The Portable Nietzsche*, trans. Walter Kaufmann (New York: Viking Press, 1972), pp. 160-163.

6. Antoine de Saint-Exupéry, *The Little Prince* (London: William Heinemann, Ltd., 1960), p. 13.

7. For various interpretations of the creation, maintenance, and decay developmental phases of nations, cultures, and civilizations, see Oswald Spengler, *The Decline of the West*, trans. C. Atkinson (New York: Random House, Modern Library, 1965); Toynbee, *A Study of History*; Pitirim Sorokin, *Social and Cultural Dynamics* (New York: Bedminster Press, 1937); Isaak and Hummel, *Politics for Human Beings*.

8. See " 'Objectivity' in Social Science and Social Policy," in Max Weber, *The Methodology of the Social Sciences*, trans. Henry A. Finch and Edward A. Shils (New York: Free Press, 1949), p. 72 and p. 81.

9. Hans Morgenthau, *Politics Among Nations*, 4th ed. (New York: Alfred A. Knopf, 1967).

10. Ibid., p. 161.

11. W.G. Runciman, *Social Science and Political Theory* (Cambridge, England: Cambridge University Press, 1965), p. 162. This discussion of the individual versus the nation-state and global system approaches is explored more deeply in Robert A. Isaak, "The Individual in International Politics: Solving the Level-of-Analysis Problem," *Polity 7*, no. 2 (1974).

12. See J. David Singer, ed., *Quantitative International Politics* (New York: Free Press, 1968). For a history of the development of the behavioral paradigm in world politics, see Arend Lijphart, "The Structure of the Theoretical Revolution in International Relations," *International Studies Quarterly* 18, no. 1 (March 1974); 41-74.

13. This systems stability bias of behavioralism is demonstrated in Isaak and Hummel, *Politics for Human Beings*.

14. For a comparison of idealistic humanism in international politics with the realist approach, see E. H. Carr, *The Twenty Years Crisis, 1919-1939* (New York: Harper Torchbooks, 1964; originally published in London by Macmillan, 1939). See also Kenneth Waltz, *Man, the State and War* (New York: Columbia University Press, 1954) and Klaus Knorr and James Rosenau, eds., *Contending Approaches to International Politics* (Princeton, N. J.: Princeton University Press, 1969).

PART TWO

Ideology, Revolution, and Nation-Making

When our individual interests and prospects do not seem worth living for, we are in desperate need of something apart from us to live for. All forms of dedications, devotion, loyalty and self-surrender are in essence a desperate clinging to something which might give worth and meaning to our futile, spoiled lives. Hence the embracing of a substitute will necessarily be passionate and extreme. We can have qualified confidence in ourselves, but the faith we have in our nation, religion, race or holy cause has to be extravagant and uncompromising.

ERIC HOFFER

The True Believer

Having examined the individual, human origins of world politics, needs and values, we now proceed in Part Two to discuss human nature and personality formation in the creation of ideology, revolutionary movements, and nation building. In Part Three we turn to the question of the theoretical extremes of total peace and total war in nations already established. Finally, in Part Four we complete our examination with the global, international phenomena that structure world politics in our era, such as international integration, international organization, law, and national diplomacy. Each concept is introduced through the background and everyday life of an individual who eventually became the living embodiment of that concept.

Part Two illustrates the human need to sacrifice oneself for a cause. In times of social crisis Gandhi, Lenin, and Mao Tse-tung politicized a spiritual longing that led to the formation of powerful ideologies, revolutionary movements, and nation-states. These men were all successful, charismatic revolutionaries and nation makers. Each represents a different strategy for developing countries and a theory of modernization and consolidation of national power under different conditions. Future leaders of less developed countries may learn from these experiences in their own efforts to create bases of national power in order to help satisfy the needs of their people. The details of each leader's family upbringing, education, jobs, and development of political consciousness illustrate how these men began like ordinary people and then used their potentials to satisfy their needs and values by creating ideologies and going into national and international politics.

CHAPTER 1

The Needs and Nature
of Political Man — Gandhi

> Man does not live by
> bread alone. Many prefer
> self-respect to food.
>
> MOHANDAS GANDHI

Mohandas Gandhi was a man who used truth to force others to submit to their own humanity. As his biographer Louis Fischer wrote, "Gandhi was a unique person, a great person, perhaps the greatest figure of the last nineteen hundred years." The shrewd little Indian symbolized all the needs of man: hunger, sex, security, love, self-esteem, and self-actualization. By denying himself the satisfaction of his lower needs for the sake of his higher principles, Gandhi fasted the British government into submission and helped to bring independence to India with a minimum of bloodshed and violence. His tactics of nonviolent resistance helped him to change his part of the world in his own time and to provide a model for political movements in ours. Martin Luther King was just one of many leaders who learned from Gandhi how to use the noble motives buried in the needs and nature of men for political change with worldwide implications.

For many Gandhi became a saint. First, however, he was a man. Normal need deprivation motivated Gandhi to become a man. Deliberate, abnormal need deprivation brought Gandhi the power to become a leader of men in world politics. He was one of those rare individuals who helped to reform the world by beginning the reform with himself.

Gandhi's life illustrates the role an individual can play in the politics of the world. His development began typically, but ended atypically. Like Everyman he attempted initially to solve the tensions between his personal needs and social facts. Unlike Everyman, however, he became politically aware of great tensions between some of his needs, and these tensions drove him to restrain himself from satisfying lower needs for the sake of higher ones. He sought self-actualization in the outside world through self-determination for his people. By deliberate example Gandhi became a symbol of the higher needs and nature of man. In doing so he demonstrated that self-discipline and nonviolent resistance can be used effectively to gain independence for a nation that is repressed by "civilized," Western colonial rule. From the global point of view, he proved that an individual's values and behavior can matter a great deal in national and international politics.

Mohandas Gandhi (right) with his brother Laxmidas in 1886. *Wide World photo.*

I. Gandhi: A Political Portrait

Personality, Consciousness, and Society

Gandhi was born in 1869 in the seacoast town of Porbandar northwest of Bombay. The facts of his sociocultural world had a profound impact on the early development of his personality. His father was the prime minister of Porbandar. His grandfather had held a similar position. He, therefore, inherited a family background of political awareness and local participation in government. In terms of social class, he was born into the Bania **caste**, which was a division of the ancient third-ranking Vaisyas, or the merchant class. The name Gandhi signified grocer, though the political activity of the family had raised the Gandhis' status beyond that of mere tradesmen.

Gandhi learned to be practical from his father who "had no education, save that of experience." From his mother he inherited religious devotion. She was deeply religious, going to the temple and fasting regularly. Later Gandhi combined religious belief with pragmatism to create a powerful political ideology of humanistic nationalism.

Gandhi was the fourth and last child of his father's fourth and last wife. The child, however, was the future Mahatma of whom Albert Einstein predicted that in generations to come, no one would ever believe that such a person had lived.

As a boy, Gandhi was not particularly remarkable. Although his father wanted to groom him to take over the family premiership of their small principality, the boy was more deeply influenced by the religious attitudes of his mother and her strict views on sex, alcohol, and tobacco. At school he stumbled over the multiplication table and failed to master the mouth organ. His ears stuck out and he was shy. He participated in typical pranks, like stealing money from the servants to buy tobacco, and even contemplated suicide with a friend by eating seeds of a poisonous plant. He thought better of dying so young, however, and ate just enough seeds to save face without hurting himself. The thought of suicide ultimately resulted in both of the boys giving up smoking cigarettes and stealing the servants' pennies for the purpose of smoking. Later another friend tempted him to eat meat (his family being vegetarian) which he eventually rejected, but not before he had tried to reform the friend. Thus, even in boyhood, Gandhi was quickly exposed to the tensions between personal needs and desires, on the one hand, and the restrictive social facts of his cultural and religious upbringing on the other.

Great world leaders are born into tension between human needs and social facts like anyone else. Physical needs, security needs, and love needs are supported and frustrated by mothers, fathers, and the social world to help shape their personalities. Unlike ordinary people their awareness of such tensions is often acute and creates a drive towards political action to resolve them. As Seneca noted, a great step towards independence is a good-humored stomach.

During his first year in high school a British school inspector came around to test the students. Gandhi misspelled one English word out of five—kettle. The inspector indicated that he should copy the correct spelling from his neighbor so the school record would not be spoiled. Gandhi refused but still maintained his respect for the inspector, noting later that he was by nature blind to the fault of elders. Here one can already note that, as Gandhi's consciousness developed in awareness of tensions between his personal integrity and social pressures, he was able to find unusual explanations and compromises that permitted him to maintain his own values, while at the same time respecting the right of other people to hold opposing viewpoints.

At thirteen Gandhi was married by traditional family arrangement. The two girls chosen for him earlier had died. Later he disapproved of child marriage, although he maintained the relationship with his wife, Kasturbai, for sixty-two years until her death. His marriage soon stimulated intense carnal desire and jealousy. He later noted that the odd social facts or traditions of his sociocultural world saved him from himself:

> Along with the cruel custom of child marriages, Hindu society has another custom which to a certain extent diminishes the evils of the former. Parents do not allow young couples to stay long together. The child-wife spends more than half her time at her father's place. Such was the case with us. That is to say, during the first five years of our married life (from the age of thirteen to eighteen), we could not have lived together longer than an aggregate period of three years. We would hardly have spent six months together when there would be a call to my wife from her parents. Such calls were very unwelcome in those days but they saved us both . . . [1]

Gandhi's marriage soon made him conscious of the tensions between his various needs and the social facts that made it impossible for him to satisfy all of his needs. His desire tormented him and brought him feelings of guilt. When he was sixteen, he helped his mother and an old servant nurse his sick father, giving him medicine and massaging his legs at night. At that time he thought his highest need was to fulfill his daily duties to his father. His desire intervened, however. The night his father died Gandhi had intercourse with his pregnant wife which was against his religion and the rules of medical science he had been taught. When the child was born it lived no more than three or four days. Gandhi was deeply ashamed and never forgave himself.

The intensity of his early sensual experience later led Gandhi to abstain from sensual indulgence. His guilt over eating meat became a motive for strict vegetarianism. His distracting sexual drives later led to a vow of celibacy, which his wife accepted. The strong influence of the Hindu religious work, *Bhagavad-Gita* (a poem of 700 stanzas) even led him to dispossess himself of all property. He was convinced that "The only thing that can be possessed at all is non-possession, not to have anything whatsoever. Or . . . a willing surrender." [2] To find oneself is to become independent of "outside," material things and to give in to one's true nature. Through self-sacrifice and self-control Gandhi molded his personality to become a vessel for man's highest human need: service to his fellow men. "We thus arrive at the ideal of total renunciation and learn to use the body for the purposes of service so long as it exists, so much so that service, and not bread, becomes with us the staff of life. We eat and drink, sleep and awake, for service alone. Such an attitude of mind brings us real happiness . . ." [3]

Gandhi's reform of himself was a slow process. He experienced many failures and frustrations on the way. After high school he went for a short while to Samaldas College, which he found to be difficult. At a friend's urging he decided to go to England. He wanted to study medicine and become a doctor. His brother recalled that their father objected to the dissection of bodies and wanted Gandhi to become a lawyer. His family reluctantly gave him permission to go after he took three vows for his mother's sake: not to touch wine, women, or meat in Britain. So he went to England, to study law, even though he became an outcaste for going, for according to the caste system he would compromise his religion by being obliged to eat and drink with Europeans! [4] Gandhi spent almost three years in England, easily earning his law degree and spending most of his time on religious and vegetarian experiments and trying to "ape the English gentleman."

In addition to the *Gita*, two other books strongly influenced Gandhi throughout his life: Leo Tolstoy's *The Kingdom of God is Within You* and John Ruskin's *Unto This Last*. Gandhi later summarized Ruskin's teachings which had guided him politically and personally:

1. That the good of the individual is contained in the good of all.

2. That a lawyer's work has the same value as the barber's, inasmuch as all have the same right of earning their livelihoods from their work.

3. That a life of labor—the life of the tiller of the soil and the handicraftsman—is the life worth living. [5]

In creating his personal and political philosophy, Gandhi combined those principles with the principle of **ahimsa**, the doctrine of nonviolence, which he first clearly noted in an experience before his father's death. At the time Gandhi was fifteen and stole a link from his brother's gold armlet to buy cigarettes. After the crime he could not bear the guilt and decided to confess to his father and seek adequate punishment. Since his father was a strict and demanding parent, Gandhi believed it was not in his father's nature to forgive easily, although he did not fear corporal punishment. He didn't have the courage to talk with his father directly and so handed the sick man a letter recording his crime. The old man broke into tears as he read his son's confession, moving Gandhi to weep with him. Gandhi perceived his father's grief as a sign of love and forgiveness, "an object lesson in Ahimsa" that freed his own spirit of hatred and aggression. The belief in nonviolence helped Gandhi escape his constant feeling of guilt and need for punishment, and he became determined to teach it to other Indian people so that they could benefit from his experience. Psychologist F. Lowtzky claims that the experience in nonviolent dependence upon his father later led Gandhi to see England as the Indian people's father to be treated with respect and nonviolence as well. [6]

Roles, Power, and Ideology

When Gandhi returned to India from England, he failed as a practicing lawyer. In 1893, at age twenty-four, he set sail for South Africa from Bombay. His power to persuade helped him to obtain the only empty berth on the boat, an extra in the captain's own cabin. His mission was to win a lawsuit, make some money, and begin a successful career.

As soon as he arrived in South Africa he took a train. A white man entered his first-class compartment, looked him up and down, disturbed, and went to complain to the officials. They returned and informed him that as a colored man he must move to the third-class compartment. He refused and had to be physically removed from the train by a constable. Gandhi perceived a severe blow to his need for self-esteem as a human being. Lesser men might have swallowed the insult and accepted such repressive social facts. But not Gandhi.

> I began to think of my duty. Should I fight for my rights or go back to India, or should I go on to Pretoria without minding the insults, and return to India after finishing the case? It would be cowardice to run back to India without fulfilling my obligation. The hardship to which I was subjected was super-ficial—only a symptom of the deep disease of color prejudice. I should try, if possible, to root out the disease and suffer hardships in the process. Redress for wrongs I should seek only to the extent that would be necessary for the removal of color prejudice. [7]

As basic bodily, security, and love needs become satisfied, humans long for more, for self-esteem and self-actualization. As unjust social facts force one

to become a slave or to take a stand, man finds his meaning and his
opportunity for greatness in the role he chooses. Albert Camus noted in The
Rebel, "When he rebels, a man identifies himself with other men and so
surpasses himself." Political power begins with esteem for yourself and
others.

~*~*~*~*~*~*~

At that critical moment Gandhi's personality made him politically
conscious of the choice he must make between his own needs and the social
fact of prejudice. Political awareness made him realize that his choice of a
role, or pattern of social conduct resulting from the experience, would have
implications not only for his own integrity and self-esteem but for that of
his people as well. Years later in India Dr. John R. Mott, a Christian
missionary, asked Gandhi what had been the most creative experiences in
his life. In reply Gandhi told the story of how he had been thrown off the
train and had come to his critical decision that night in the Maritzburg
Station.

Within a week of arriving in Pretoria Gandhi summoned all the
Indians in the city to a meeting to "present them a picture of their
condition." Although he had gained some experience in organization by
leading a vegetarian club in England, it was his first public speech.
Typically he stressed the obligations of his own people to reform themselves more than the unjust social facts under which all Indians suffered in
South Africa. Compared to the English, his own people were unsanitary,
and he told them so. He emphasized the necessity of forgetting all
distinctions between Hindus, Moslems, Parsis, Christians, and so forth,
thereby denying ethnocentrism or the claim of superiority on the part of a
certain culture. Furthermore, he advised those who had the leisure to learn
English and immediately began to teach English himself to interested
subjects. For Gandhi was profoundly aware that power is a social
relationship in which those people who know how to play by the existing
rules of the society have most of their needs satisfied. He wished to change
the formal rules or laws in order to end discrimination against Indians on the
basis of skin color. He knew, however, that in terms of existing social facts
his people had to change their informal habits in order to better adapt to
their foreign world. Otherwise, Indians would legally gain potential power
only to lose the actual power to satisfy their needs because they could not
speak English or because their dirtiness would repel the non-Indians. Power
in social relationships depends upon perceiving the rules of the game in the
context of others. Knowing that, Gandhi wanted to be sure the Indians
understood the rules in South Africa—namely, that personal appearance
dominated legislative politics.

Politically speaking, Gandhi did not give up his role of lawyer to
become a practical reformer in South Africa but maintained both roles
simultaneously, living in their tension. Similarly, he perceived that the
position of any Indian as Indian in South Africa would be a complex

combination of roles in tension: Indian as Indian; Indian as British subject; Indian as subservient worker in South Africa; Indian as member of the human race with the right to dignity. Gandhi could not help but sense that his own role as an Indian leader in South Africa was somewhat special. Slowly he gave up lower-level, material pleasures in order to merit this unusual position. His self-purification and "possession of non-possession" prepared him spiritually to become a worthy member of the political elite, ready to sacrifice his life for public service.

As psychoanalyst Erik Erikson put it:

> Gandhi's actualism . . . first of all consisted in his knowledge of, and his ability to gain strength from, the fact that nothing is more powerful in the world than conscious nothingness if it is paired with a gift of giving and accepting actuality. It is not for me to say what this power is; yet obviously it demands the keenest of minds and a most experienced heart, for otherwise it would be crushed between megalomania and self-destruction. As for the rest of mankind, I have an inkling that our response to such a man rests on the need of all men to find a few who plausibly take upon themselves—and seem to give meaning to—what others must deny at all times but cannot really forget for a moment. [8]

The "conscious nothingness" of Gandhi refers to the recurrent virtue in Eastern religions of deliberately losing or leaving oneself to attain a transcendent state of spiritual consciousness. In contrast, Everyman consumes his life in everyday roles, often sacrificing his highest spiritual need for self-esteem and self-actualization for the sake of his lower-level, material and domestic needs. Great political leaders seek out unusual roles of leadership to satisfy their higher needs but sacrifice certain lower-level, material and domestic satisfactions. Great men are always becoming. Everyman resides in being.

After settling the law suit, for which he had come to South Africa, in twelve months, Gandhi prepared to sail home to India and his family. At a farewell party, he was handed a copy of the daily paper which announced that the Natal government had proposed a bill to deprive Indians of their right to elect members of the legislature. Louis Fischer wrote, "Gandhi stressed the necessity of resisting this move. His friends were ready but they were 'unlettered, lame' men, they said, and powerless without him. He consented to stay a month. He remained twenty years fighting the battle for Indian rights. He won."[9] Had Gandhi not chosen to lead his people in their fight for self-determination, thousands of Indians would have suffered much longer under the unjust social facts of South African law and prejudice. Gandhi's efforts assured his people in South Africa: the right of properly dressed Indians to travel first class in trains; laws declaring Hindi and Parsi marriages valid; the abolition of the annual tax on indentured laborers and the end of indentured labor imported from India.

Gandhi's ideology had become such an integral part of him as a man that personal power and political power were one. Ahimsa, the personal belief in nonviolence and love for all living things, flowed naturally into **satyagraha**, the "truth force" of public, nonviolent resistance to effect social change. During his nonviolent struggles for the Indian people in South Africa, those two basic ideological concepts lay behind all of his actions: addressing conferences; drafting memoranda to government ministers; writing letters to newspapers; circulating petitions; demonstrating peacefully; and making many friends among Whites, Indians, and Negroes. He also published two pamphlets: *An Appeal to Every Briton in South Africa* and *The Indian Franchise, An Appeal*. Of these Louis Fischer wrote, " 'Appeal' was the key to Gandhi's politics. He appealed to the common sense and morality of his adversary."[10] Or, as Gandhi put it, "It has always been a mystery to me how men can feel themselves honored by the humiliation of their fellow-beings."[11] The political aim behind satyagraha was justice and equality for all human beings, particularly for those discriminated against in a society.

The term satyagraha originated in a slogan contest Gandhi held in South Africa. He wanted an Indian expression to describe the program of civil disobedience he was leading. The word that won was sadagraha, firmness in a good cause. Gandhi personally changed sadagraha to satyagraha since he preferred the meaning truth force. As a search for justice satyagraha calls for peaceful resistance to political authority on either an individual or mass basis. "The first condition of non-violence," said Gandhi, "is justice all round in every department of life."[12]

As an individual plays with the tensions in his social life to satisfy his needs, he discovers that his higher, spiritual needs force him to become the roles he took on in passing. Such higher level needs are called by many names: self-actualization, self-determination, freedom, peace, and justice. Psychologist Abraham Maslow wrote of such self-actualization needs: "A musician must make music, an artist must paint, a poet must write, if he is to be ultimately at peace with himself. What a man can be, he must be." But to satisfy his ultimate needs, a person must do it with, through, and for others. He not only becomes his part; he becomes his people. Just as he finds himself frozen in roles to hold the tensions of his individual self together, so he also submits to ideologies to keep his collective self in balance.

Erikson noted that Gandhi's view of ahimsa implied not only a refusal to do physical harm but a determination to not violate another person's essence. Gandhi always respected the position and integrity of his opponent, whether another Indian, a South African, or a representative of the British government. He was aware that to violate a person's essence or to wound his self-respect was a form of violence that would encourage counterviolence. The attitude of nonviolence and deep human respect for one's adversary became a powerful ideological tool when it was wedded with satyagraha: the force of an unbending adherence to the truth with justice as its motivation. Erikson wrote, "The truth in any given encounter is linked with the developmental stage of the individual and the historical situation of his group: together, they help to determine the *actuality*, i.e., the potential for unifying action at a given moment."[13] In other words, the ahimsa-satyagraha synthesis worked for Gandhi only because of the religious and nationalistic aspects of the Indian culture that dominated the country at that point in its historical development. The truth of any particular moment in an international political situation is relative to the developmental perspective, or the national viewpoint of the countries involved, and to the personal integrity of the negotiators.

Origins of Militant Nonviolence

World War I followed Gandhi's victory with satyagraha in South Africa. During that period Gandhi organized an ambulance corps, which served the British for a while in the Boer war. Although his own sympathies were with the Boers, he did not think his loyalty to British rule permitted him to enforce his individual convictions. "I felt that if I demanded rights as a British citizen, it was also my duty as such to participate in the defense of the British empire. I held then that India could achieve her complete emancipation only within and through the British Empire."[14]

However, Gandhi was not the same man who had studied law in Britain and failed practicing it in India. Before he won any political battles he had won a personal battle by transforming his living habits into a philosophy of life. While he worked in the Boer war, two ideas became firmly fixed in Gandhi's mind. "First, an aspirant after a life devoted exclusively to service must lead a life of celibacy. Secondly, he must accept poverty as a constant companion through life. He may not take up any occupation which would prevent him or make him shrink from undertaking the lowliest of duties or largest risks."[15]

Even in South Africa Gandhi had not lost touch with India. In 1909 he wrote a small book on Indian **home rule** and maintained contact with leaders in India. He returned to India in 1915, and at the advice of his political guru, Professor G.K. Gokhale, he spent his first year back with his ears open and his mouth shut.

Gandhi's process of self-purification led him to see all political issues as moral ones, just as he linked his own self-determination to the right of self-determination for the Indian people. After visiting the poet Rabindranath Tagore, who first called Gandhi Mahatma, at his school in Bengal,

Gandhi decided to set up his own **ashram** at Sabarmati on the Sabarmati River across from the city of Ahmedabad. This ashram, a settlement of about 200 inhabitants, attempted to be self-sufficient—spinning, weaving, raising its own crops, and teaching in the villages nearby. But as another poet, Sarajini Naidu, said later, "It costs a great deal to keep Gandhi living in poverty," a remark which referred to the heavy support his ashram received from rich Indian merchants.

The first moral and political crisis in the ashram came quickly. A family of **Untouchables** applied to join. The Untouchables were the lowest social class and caste of the Hindu religion, who did all the dirty work and whose very presence was supposed to defile those above them. Gandhi's decision was bold and immediate. He called the outcastes "Harijans," Children of God; named his weekly newspaper *Harijan*; and fought discrimination against the Untouchables for the rest of his life. He immediately met opposition from the conservative social facts of his environment. The rich refused to support him any longer, and his wife revolted against having an Untouchable in her kitchen. However, a rich man finally solved the financial crisis, and Gandhi used his traditional Hindu authority as husband to overrule his wife's wishes. Soon they adopted an Untouchable child as their own.

According to Erikson, Gandhi's leadership in the strike of textile workers in Ahmedabad, 1917-18, was a critical event in his psychopolitical development. Gandhi was nearly fifty years old. It was here that he first used personal, religious fasting for political purposes: a powerful tool that he later used often and that persuaded the mill owners to arbitrate within three days. He had informed the mill owners that he should be treated like a striker, that he was not fasting against them, and that his fast should not be understood as a form of blackmail. Nevertheless, the incident at Ahmedabad demonstrated the political effectiveness of Gandhi's knack of turning his needs inside out for personal control and power.

It should be noted that Gandhi's principle of satyagraha did not prohibit him from ever supporting violence. He wanted peace, but not at any price, particularly where justice was concerned. In helping to shape the Indian national movement he was later to move "from truth to truth" in political situations and conflicts. Indeed, as late as 1918 he tried unsuccessfully to recruit Indians for the British army, believing that India was more likely to become a dominion within the British Empire, like Canada, if she had the ability to bear arms and to use them. Political shrewdness always tempered Gandhi's religion. His realistic idealism was influenced to a great extent by the social facts of Indian nationalism that he faced upon returning from South Africa. The political movement for home rule had spread greatly during his absence. In shaping his own role of national leadership, Gandhi had to tread carefully between two factions: a group of militant extremists headed by Bal Gangadhar Tilak, a tough, fanatic revolutionary, and a faction for constitutional reform led by Gopal Krishna Gokhale, a moderate intellectual respected in England as well as at home. Gokhale and Gandhi were brought together because of a common interest in rural reform. As always, Gandhi took care to learn from his elders before subtly replacing their authority with his own.

Sovereignty and Nationalism

Rural reform, based on ashrams that would strive for self-sufficiency, became the foundation of Gandhi's plan for India. He envisioned a decentralized Indian state, which based its sovereignty, or claim to legal authority, upon village life in order that local power might evolve into legitimate government. Since he realized that many competing power bases were incompatible with national sovereignty, Gandhi hoped for sovereignty of the people based on pure moral authority. Although he preferred reform growing from self-disciplined individuals, he recognized the need for state regulation in matters of economics, social justice, and law enforcement.

Gandhi's vision of national sovereignty was colored by the British colonial policy in India. Indeed, at first Gandhi pointed out the benefits the Indians had derived from the British empire and worked for moderate reform within that context. However, in 1919 and 1920 three events finally alienated him from the British system: the Punjab massacre, in which 400 Indians were shot down without warning for holding a public meeting; the injustices of the treaty imposed by the victorious allies on Turkey after World War I; and the so-called Rowlatt Act that gave British officials extraordinary powers to deal with lawlessness and disaffection.[16] Gandhi was sufficiently angered to persuade the Indian National Congress to pass a resolution for progressive, nonviolent noncooperation with the government.

In part, the resolution was passed because Gandhi's effective speaking throughout India had aroused the wide-spread support of the masses for his program. Gandhi did not advocate immediate, all-out civil disobedience but a phased program. Young Indians were to drop out of government schools and form new national schools; lawyers were to refuse to work in government law courts and set up national boards of arbitration; alcohol and drugs were not to be used, since the government profited; foreign cloth was to be discarded; soldiers and police were to refuse to serve the government; and everyone was to refuse to pay taxes. Each of the actions was to be phased in slowly. Furthermore, Gandhi advocated the support of certain positive principles: the elimination of communal antagonism between Hindus and Moslems; the destruction of the unjust doctrine of untouchability and the end of forced labor.

Through actions and principles such as these Gandhi rose slowly to become the unquestioned leader of the Indian national movement. Nationalism is the belief that a particular nation-state merits Everyman's absolute loyalty and constitutes the ultimate solution to the tensions of his life. It grows out of common culture, language, and historical experience. By working from the grass roots and fighting continually for the rights of the poor and underprivileged Gandhi shaped Indian nationalism into a positive nonviolent force for self-determination and Indian dignity.

Political leaders use ideologies or collective political beliefs and myths as tools to satisfy their needs and maximize their values. The ultimate ideological tool is nationalism: the belief that a particular nation-state is the ultimate solution to all one's needs and merits absolute loyalty. Nationalism serves to maintain the importance of the state and reduce the significance of individuals. The state is an organization given legal authority to govern over power relationships on a particular territory. The people who make up the sociocultural world controlled by the state are called the nation. Social scientist Kenneth Boulding writes that "the national image is basically a lie, or at least a perspective distortion of the truth. . . . Love of country is perverted into hatred of the foreigner." Nationalism often justifies peace and prosperity at home paid for by violence, injustice, and war abroad.

Gandhi's rise to power was more erratic than predictable and was, in part, due to the weakness of his political opponents. As English scholar Judith Brown has pointed out, a new leader could seize power because the bonds uniting the politicians were weak and because their range of supporters was limited. Gandhi drew support from people who had, up to this time, been outside of the political nation of India. Those officially in the Indian nation were basically Western educated and oriented. Gandhi was very critical of Western political development and values and believed that many classical Indian values and traditions were far superior. Moreover, Gandhi's universal creed and broad appeal moved many people to enter politics for the first time because they had a leader who, at last, represented their interests. As Everyman's leader, Gandhi's power was often underrated, especially when he was thrown in jail by the British, yet without British acquiescence to his activities (often because of their sincere nonviolence) Gandhi would never have succeeded. To do politics, even politics of conflict, the participants must share basic values and rules of the game. If Britain had been a dictatorship rather than a democracy, Gandhi would undoubtedly have been eliminated as soon as he became a threat to British rule. Certainly some British leaders thought he should have been put out of business. Winston Churchill once said, "It is alarming and also nauseating to see Mr. Gandhi, a seditious Middle Temple lawyer, now posing as a fakir of a type well known in the East, striding half-naked up the steps of the Viceregal Palace, while he is still organizing and conducting a defiant campaign of civil disobedience, to parley on equal terms with the

Gandhi working at his spinning. *Wide World photo.*

representative of the King-Emperor."[17] Churchill never did like the idea of presiding over the liquidation of the British Empire, and Gandhi, of course, was one of the causes of its decline. Gandhi had great difficulty unifying the various Indian factions and interests to make a strong Indian nationalist movement possible. Without the civilized attitude of the British government toward his actions, India could never have gained independence as nonviolently as she did.

Gandhi's nonviolent nationalism was based upon embarrassing the colonial power into giving up. Here walked a skinny little man who sacrificed his own needs for those of his community, who spun his own few garments on his own spinning wheel and asked others to do the same, and who exhorted the population to go to jail as he did rather than to cooperate with the British. In 1930 when the British imposed a heavy salt tax, Gandhi even led a march 165 miles to the sea to make his own salt. His was a shrewd, spiritual, nonviolent nationalism based on bringing Hindus and Moslems, rich and poor together. His emphasis upon spiritual rather than physical power helped India to increase her independence or national sovereignty between 1900 and 1947. In 1948 one of the least violent of national world leaders was destroyed by the violence of an assassin's bullet. A fanatic Hindu could not stand the political man who asked him to compromise his beliefs to cooperate with Moslems. The death of ahimsa arose from the birth of a victorious Indian nationalism.

II. Principles of World Politics

Needs, Values, and Social Facts

The case of Gandhi demonstrates that world politics originates with human needs, values, and social facts. Such needs include lower bodily and security needs and higher love, self-esteem, and self-actualization needs. Gandhi often sacrificed his lower needs for the sake of higher ones. He felt that political leaders should be willing to fast unto death for a political principle, which for him was usually the same as an ethical principle. By sacrificing his personal bodily needs for the sake of his own self-esteem and for the self-determination of his countrymen, Gandhi became a living, charismatic symbol of the purest goals of Indian nationalism.

Gandhi was a profoundly political man because of his acute awareness of the tensions between his values and existing social facts. The values Gandhi wanted were independence for his people, achieved nonviolently, and elimination of all racial, religious, and economic discrimination. Those values brought him into tension and conflict with the existing social facts of the Indian caste system, the sharp divisions between Hindus and Moslems, and the repressive presence of the British Empire and its laws.

As we have seen, social facts are existing man-made conditions that frustrate or satisfy human needs. When men act out long-term social relationships, which they have created to satisfy needs, such relationships become routines or institutions and are called social facts. Initially Gandhi perceived the British Empire's administration of India as a social relationship that could help solve Indian needs. However, as soon as the British government became a repressive social fact Gandhi rebelled in order to create new social relationships more advantageous to the Indians.

Political Consciousness and Personality

Awareness of the tension between human needs and existing social facts is political consciousness. When Gandhi arrived in South Africa and was thrown out of the first-class compartment on the train, he was politically conscious of the tension between his need for self-esteem and the social fact of unjust discrimination. Acting out of such consciousness is politics, and whether or not one chooses to make politics out of political consciousness depends upon one's personality. Personality refers to how an individual integrates his needs and values to form an identity. Such integration is based upon his biological, psychological, and sociological circumstances.[18] A person's biological and psychological makeup determines his drives or the selective mobilization of his energies. The facts of his social and cultural world reinforce the reduction of certain of these drives and tensions. For example, young Gandhi had a strong sexual drive growing out of his biological and psychological constitution. However, the religious background of his mother and his cultural world eventually helped him reduce that tension through sexual abstinence and the sublimation of his drive in religious and public service. Recall that man's attempts to restrain his drives to respect the facts and values of his social world lead to civilization. The products of the tension between personal desire and society constitute culture.[19] Political scientist Harold Lasswell has applied Freud's ideas to political leadership, claiming that leaders like Gandhi were motivated to enter politics because of their repression of more basic drives like sex.[20]

The most important political consequence of personality is the conscious will of a person to solve the tension between his needs and social facts. Personal political competence means the ability to determine oneself. Great world leaders usually develop dynamic personality traits and desire self-determination for their people as well as for themselves. Gandhi's strong personality would not allow him to be kicked out of a train compartment in South Africa because he was an Indian without fighting back. So he organized Indians in South Africa to fight for their self-determination as well as his own.

Roles and Power

Personality is colored by the social and political roles in which we live. The role of husband forced upon Gandhi by his family at thirteen marked his personality for life. His role of certified lawyer became the basis for his later role of political reformer and national leader. Roles are specific patterns of social conduct that provide the basis for potential power.

Social and political organizations are usually structured in authority pyramids: the roles of the elite, with greatest potential power, at the top and the roles of the masses at the bottom. In that hierarchical sense role potency, or the potential power of a particular role, is determined in most cases by the number of people affected by decisions made by a person occupying this position.

Elites, or the groups of people in higher roles in the social hierarchy, possess different belief systems than the masses of ordinary people in lower social roles. Political scientist Philip Converse has shown that elitist belief systems are marked by the possession of information, the ability to articulate thoughts, and the interest in abstract values like freedom or stability. On the other hand, the belief systems of ordinary people or mass publics are marked by lack of information, difficulty in articulating thoughts, and interest in simple, concrete values like higher wages and better living conditions.[21] Elites are everyday citizens who share the same world view as ordinary people. When they rise in the social hierarchy, however, they usually come to possess a monopoly of information, as well as power and wealth. Because of this potential power, when divisions occur in the national world-view, the interests of the elites are usually decisive.

Whether or not potential power is turned into actual power depends upon perceived opportunity, personality, and self-determination. To know how and when to jump in and out of social roles is a key to great political leadership. Gandhi's decisions to become involved in the struggle for Indian rights in South Africa and to postpone immediate involvement in national political affairs upon his return to India were perceptive role decisions that contributed to his later political success.

Once men like Gandhi have been politically conscious for a long time, they realize that the ideal condition in which to live is one that is totally governed by one's own intention and that permits complete self-determination. The ideal develops from many personal attempts to will the satisfaction of one's own needs, despite the obstructions of social facts. Most frustrating for political man are people who obstruct him. For power is a social relationship in which some people can satisfy more of their needs than other people.[22] When Everyman becomes politically aware of what power means for his needs, he soon desires to be free to totally determine himself to his own satisfaction. Total self-determination is what freedom means.

A basic difference between Everyman and a great man like Gandhi is that the great man has arrived at an unusual condition of self-determination whereas Everyman has not. In defining self-determination as an unusual amount of competence in achieving personal goals, psychologist M. Brewster Smith notes that "Some people more than others seem to be in charge of their lives—to be Agents or 'Origins' of personal causation rather than Pawns. The unprecedented human situation with its headlong trends toward multiple disaster sets a high premium upon Agency, upon the rearing of people who will not passively take these trends for granted. . . . If, in the realm of the reflexive self, the 'self-fulfilling prophecy' is a causal mechanism, then people's causally rooted conceptions of themselves as Origins or as Pawns may make the crucial difference as to whether they actively *live* their lives or merely suffer them."[23] Great men become self-fulfilling origins or agents rather than self-fulfilling pawns. Like Gandhi, they refuse to take for granted social facts that put them down. They turn social pyramids on their heads, as Gandhi did with civil disobedience, so that their own needs and the needs of their people are satisfied. The needs and nature of Everyman become symbolized in the self-determination of great men who act competently in their social world to strive for national self-determination for their people.

Ideology and Nationalism

Almost all political leaders use ideology as a tool to help them achieve self-determination and other values for themselves and their followers. **Ideology** is simply a reified or frozen set of beliefs used as a basis for political action. Gandhi was a great master in the use of ideology. Indeed, Gandhi's personal behavior became so identified with his ideological creed that one could say he was the personification of political action.

Political scientist David Apter points out that "Ideology is a generic term applied to general ideas potent in specific situations of conduct: for example, not *any* ideals, only political ones; not *any* values, only those specifying a given set of preferences; not *any* beliefs, only those governing particular modes of thought. Because it is the link between action and fundamental belief, ideology helps to make more explicit the moral basis of action."[24] Gandhi demonstrated that ideology is the application of moral prescriptions to collective action. His ideology began with ahimsa, the doctrine of nonviolence and respect for other living beings, combined with satyagraha, the truth force of principled noncooperation, or militant nonviolence. From those politicized moral principles Gandhi arrived eventually at an ideology of Indian socialism called **sarvodaya**, or the welfare of all: a society based on the destruction of class but not on the destruction of the individuals who made up the classes. Although he denied himself the right to hold any private property, which gave him a purer moral basis for political authority or leadership in his culture, he did not envision a world in which there would be no private property. He believed, however, that private property should be restricted to what was necessary to allow an honorable livelihood. Excess property would then be held by capitalists who would regard themselves as trustees for those who allowed them to keep and increase their capital.

Ideology serves to bind the social community together, to organize the various roles that an individual plays into a personal identity and to rigidify perceptions, thus making conflict more likely. Gandhi's case illustrates the positive aspects of ideology: it helped him to organize his beliefs and personality into a powerful tool to make him an agent rather than a pawn, and it provided him with a system of political and ethical beliefs which would serve as a social basis for the Indian national movement. Negatively, Gandhi's ideology of self-help and "home economics," as the basis of the national economy, and his anti-Western bias blinded him to benefits which Western economic techniques could have brought India at the time. The dark side of ideology is the pathology it breeds: the belief in a rigid image of reality that is too simplistic to correspond to actual reality.

The dark, cohesive character of ideology is best illustrated by its most widespread form, nationalism. Nationalism is an ideology enforced by violence that is the greatest plague on world politics in the modern era. Our dominant myth, the myth of the nation-state, socializes citizens to think of nationalism as patriotism—"My Country right or wrong." As a myth nationalism has tremendous symbolic power, which is rooted in the symbols of a common territory, language, heritage, and cultural world. Internationally speaking, nationalism is the ultimate psychological rigidity that a group of people can fall into. It is a pathological belief in belonging to a group no matter what atrocities that group commits in the name of national honor. World war is the *reducto ad absurdum* of nationalism.

If nationalism is such a sick ideology, why do so many of us allow ourselves to believe in it? Why can great leaders like Gandhi use nationalism to mobilize us like robots behind the causes of their choosing, just or unjust? Those questions pose perhaps the greatest enigma of world politics: men join together to create nation-states to gain more collective self-determination only to see the later development of the nation-state restrict their individual self-determination or freedom and stimulate international conflict and world war. Gandhi's life has introduced us to the human motivations behind this enigma. The lives of other great leaders to follow will serve to further deepen our understanding and to reveal the limits of man's power in world politics.

The Nation-State and Limits of Nationalism

To create a state people organize social relationships on a given territory so that cooperative agreements or laws can be authoritatively worked out, reviewed, and executed. Gandhi worked to replace the British state in India with an Indian state by arguing that sovereignty, or the legal right to self-determination, should be given to the Indian people. If the people making up the sociocultural world controlled by the state, the nation, recognize the authority of the state as legitimate, the relationship is called a nation-state. By claiming that British authority in India was illegitimate, Gandhi used nationalism, or loyalty to his vision of the Indian nation-state, as a powerful tool for civil disobedience and nation-making.

In developing nation-states like Gandhi's India, nationalism is a necessary political tool for centralizing social and economic relationships to improve the standard of living and opportunities of the people involved. The possibilities of misusing nationalism to exploit people and to legitimize violence are infinite. Furthermore, the probabilities of international conflict become mind staggering when one realizes that the world is made up of over 130 nationalistic nation-states. Each officially claims total sovereignty or self-determination over its own territory, but each depends unofficially upon other nation-states for its economic welfare, military security, and cultural and technological advancement. Even the most developed nations, the most sovereign superpowers like the United States and the Soviet Union, have come to depend increasingly on each other and on smaller states for their own military security and economic and cultural advancement. In a way the world is like a large madhouse full of groups of people claiming to be independent, or to have the right to be, where, in fact, independence has become an impossible condition to achieve.

The impossibility of any people or nation obtaining total self-determination or freedom in the modern world has led many theorists to suggest that the nation-state has become obsolete and will inevitably be replaced by larger, more international units, based on regional integration or world government. That view applies, at best, only to the more highly developed nation-states, such as those of Western Europe, and even there the dominant reality is still the nation-state, not a "United States of Europe." In less developed countries, such as those in parts of Africa, Asia, and Latin America, the nation-state and the nationalism it implies are still present in early stages of development and will probably remain the dominant, official form of world politics for decades to come.

As we will see in later chapters, **multinational corporations**, international organizations, and superpower military and economic alliances will poke so many holes in the sovereignty of most nation-states that they will be like sieves. Nevertheless, formal groups of people will keep up the tradition of the nation-state, and elites will use nationalism to achieve their goals. Men will continue to cling to the territory on which they were born, convinced that it is the only country that can satisfy their needs. In short, despite its limits and its tendency to lead to conflict and war, nationalism will continue to be a self-fulfilling prophecy for the majority of men for some time to come.

Nonviolence as a Method of Political Change

Gandhi showed that under certain conditions political movements can benefit by restricting themselves to nonviolent forms of nationalism or ideology to obtain social change. The conditions for effective nonviolence on a national scale appear to be rigorous indeed. Nonviolence would never have succeeded unless the colonizing power, Great Britain, was a civilized democracy—not a totalitarian dictatorship—and a declining rather than an expanding empire. Furthermore, the strong religious beliefs, held by many Indians, created a cultural environment in which nonviolence as a political tradition was possible. More secular societies might have tended toward violence and have been less apt to accept nonviolence as a realistic form of ideology. Even in India Gandhi often had to call off nonviolent demonstrations because he believed that the people involved were not yet sufficiently mature and self-disciplined to make satyagraha successful.

Gandhi believed that militant nonviolence was only effective if it used the minimum force necessary to achieve its goal. He was forever bending over backwards to understand his opponents and make sure that they understood him, so that the integrity of both parties could be maintained at all costs. Needless to say, an amateur strategist of nonviolence might not be so cautious or wise and use too much or too little force to be effective. Take the example of fasting as a political tool of satyagraha. As late as 1967 the Indian scholar Pyarelal found it necessary to use the Indian press to reassert the rules Gandhi had laid down for political fasting.

> [Fasting] cannot be resorted to against those who regard us as their enemy, or on whose love we have not established a claim by dint of selfless service; it cannot be resorted to by a person who has not identified himself with, or worked for the cause he is fasting for; it cannot be used for gaining a material selfish end, or to change the honestly held opinion of another or in support of an issue that is not clear, feasible and demonstrably just. . . . To be legitimate, a fast should be capable of response.[25]

In short, Gandhi expected fasting to be used politically only by one who had dutifully served his opponent, who felt no hate toward him, and who had long since identified himself in other ways with a cause, which even the opponent would admit to be just. Clearly such restraint depends upon a long education in self-discipline and perceptive judgment in matters of social justice. In the United States Martin Luther King seemed to achieve this mature stage of restrained nonviolence, and King was not accidentally a minister. However, the culture in which King operated was much more violent than Gandhi's India, and it is not surprising that the assassin's bullet came much sooner to King than to Gandhi. In both cases the effectiveness of nonviolent tactics was in part due to charismatic leadership by a great ethical figure who had devoted his life to a cause. Yet that very unyielding personal sacrifice for an ideology—even though expressed in nonviolent terms—sparked intense emotional reactions against the charismatic figure and his creed and inspired violence on the part of those with different beliefs. Militant nonviolence is only effective as a political tactic in a civilized political relationship in which both parties prefer to use the minimum amount of force, and desire to preserve each other's integrity. Unfortunately, many periods of rebellion and nation-making fail to meet those conditions and militant nonviolence may be the exception, not the rule, in the developing nation-states of the world.

III. Present Implications

Gandhi's Heritage Today

Mohandas Gandhi's life spanned three continents and three quarters of a century. He brought the cultures of Asia, Europe, and Africa together in his thought, action, and simple existence. In India he is seen by many as a saint, in other countries as a model of civilized, nonviolent rebellion. He proved that under the proper conditions an ideology of militant nonviolence can be an effective route to social justice and self-determination for a people. However, his very ideology blinded him to the violent consequences that some of his nonviolent policies would lead to. For example, many Indians believe that the conflicts between India and Pakistan, and now with Bangladesh, are due, in part, to Gandhi's refusal to forcibly unite all the territory under Indian rule. His very respect for different religious beliefs planted the seeds for violent conflicts growing out of such differences. Indeed, in a country like India with fourteen languages and one fifth of the world's population, it is amazing that more violent conflicts have not occurred. Perhaps the education of self-discipline and nonviolence inspired by Gandhi is responsible for India's civilized neutrality. Equally important is the acceptance of poverty as a way of life by many of the people, as well as the positive aspects of British colonial rule, which provide a model for many Indian leaders. Had Gandhi's successful example not existed in the twentieth century, many political leaders undoubtedly would not have been inspired to attempt nonviolent social change, and our age would have been bloodier still.

One of the most penetrating summaries of Gandhi's unique heritage to the world was made by the Indian poet Rabindranath Tagore. "He stopped at the thresholds of the huts of the thousands of the dispossessed, dressed like one of their own. He spoke to them in their own language; here was living truth at last, not quotations from books. . . . In direct contact with truth, the crushed forces of the soul rise again. . . . At Gandhi's call India blossomed forth to new greatness, just as once before in earlier times, when Buddha proclaimed the truth of fellow-feeling and compassion among all living creatures."[26]

Gandhi's friend Tagore may have been his ultimate propaganda agent. Such an idealistic and poetic summary of his life hides the political shrewdness of the man, which may be more easily adaptable by future political leaders in all countries. The incredible extent of that shrewdness only comes in focus when one recalls that the skinny little man began his political movement and nation building with scarcely any material resources! By flaunting his own material needs, he raised the spirits of his countrymen, and he was able to transform spiritual power into effective political ideology. He used his poverty, his spinning wheel, and his protest marches as symbols of self-righteous Indian nationalism. He made himself into "The Good Cause." Although few countries may have the deep religious tradition of India, Gandhi's political strategies can be applied elsewhere with surprising effect. Martin Luther King used them to promote black civil rights in America. The young Indian guru Maharaj Ji has demonstrated amazing political organizational skills in building up his religious following throughout the world, especially in the United States. All of these leaders offered anxious people A Cause and used symbols and ideologies to create large political movements that surprised the entire world. They were spiritual but shrewd.

Notes

1. M. K. Gandhi, *The Story of My Experiments with Truth* (London: Phoenix Press, 1949), Part I, Chap. 4, pp. 10-12. Another source not specifically referred to in the notes is Norman Thomas, *Great Dissenters* (New York: W. W. Norton & Co., 1961), Chap. 6.

2. From an address at the Guild Hall, London, September 27, 1931 in D. G. Tendulkar, *Mahatma: The Life of Mohandas Karamchand Gandhi*, 8 vols (Bombay: Vithalbhai K. Jhaveri and D. G. Tendulkar, Vol. 3, March, 1952), p. 157.

3. M. K. Gandhi, *From Yeravda Mandir* (Ahmedabad, India: Navajivan Publishing Co., 1937), Chap. 6.

4. Gandhi, *Experiments*, Part I, Chap. 11, pp. 30-33.

5. Ibid., Part IV, Chap. 18, p. 250.

6. F. Lowtzky, "Mahatma Gandhi: A Contribution to the Psychoanalytic Understanding of the Causes of War and the Means of Preventing Wars," *International Journal of Psycho-analysis* 33 (1952): 485-488.

7. Gandhi, *Experiments*, p. 94.

8. Erik Erikson, *Gandhi's Truth: On the Origins of Militant Nonviolence* (New York: W. W. Norton & Co., 1969), p. 397.

9. Louis Fischer, *The Essential Gandhi* (New York: Random House, Inc, 1962), p. 42.

10. Ibid., p. 44.

11. Gandhi, *Experiments*, Part II, Chap. 20, p. 129.

12. Paul Powers, *Gandhi on World Affairs* (Washington, D. C.: Public Affairs Press, 1960), p. 29.

13. Erikson, *Gandhi's Truth*, pp. 412-413.

14. Gandhi, *Experiments*, Part III, Chap. 10, p. 179.

15. M. K. Gandhi, *Satyagraha in South Africa* (Madras: S. Ganesane, 1928), p 155.

16. Horace Alexander, *Gandhi Through Western Eyes* (Bombay: Asia Publishing House, 1969), pp. 35-37.

17. Geoffrey Ashe, *Gandhi* (New York: Stein & Day, 1968), p. xi.

18. See Robert W. White, *Lives in Progress* (New York: Holt, Rinehart & Winston, 1966), pp. 1-26.

19. Sigmund Freud, *Civilization and Its Discontents*, Standard ed., trans. James Strachey (New York: W. W. Norton, & Co., 1961).

20. Harold Lasswell, *Psychopathology and Politics* (New York: Viking Press, 1966; originally published in 1930).

21. Philip E. Converse, "The Nature of Belief Systems in Mass Publics," in David E. Apter, ed., *Ideology and Discontent* (New York: Free Press, 1964), pp. 206-261.

22. Although self-determination and ideology are developed here in a new way, the view of politics as the attempt to solve the tension between needs and social facts was first explicated in Robert A. Isaak and Ralph P. Hummel, *Politics for Human Beings* (North Scituate, Mass.: Duxbury Press, 1975).

23. M. Brewster Smith, "On Self-Actualization: A Transambivalent Examination of A Focal Theme in Maslow's Psychology," *Journal of Humanistic Psychology* 13, no. 2 (1973): 17-33.

24. David E. Apter, "Ideology and Discontent," in D. E. Apter, ed., *Ideology and Discontent* (New York: Free Press, 1964), p. 17.

25. As cited in Erikson, *Gandhi's Truth*, p. 417.

26. As cited in Ashe, *Gandhi*, p. ix.

CHAPTER 2

Elites, Imperialism, and Revolution — Lenin

> People always have been and they always will be
> stupid victims of deceit and self-deception in
> politics, until they learn behind every kind of
> moral, religious, political, social phrase, declara-
> tion and promise to seek out the interests of this
> or that class or classes.
>
> NIKOLAI LENIN

In summertime in Moscow after standing in a long line in hot sun, you descend into the cold, red, formal atmosphere of stone where Lenin and his ideology lie frozen and carefully preserved over time. His face is clean shaven and real in its wax-like way. Perhaps he now looks better than he did when alive. Who knows? Guards order people to take their hands out of their pockets for the sake of respect and security. The eery feeling pervades the room that this bald, bearded man is not dead but alive: immortalized by the ideas, actions, and ideology that consumed him and still consume the Russian people.

Like Mohandas Gandhi, Lenin sacrificed lower-level need satisfactions for the sake of his ideological cause, and became the embodiment of the spirit of his nation in the twentieth century. But unlike Gandhi, Lenin did not locate the impetus for revolution in self-transformation as much as in repressive social facts. Gandhi was primarily a moral force who became political in the religious culture of India. Lenin was basically an ideological politician whose ideas became the religion of the post-revolutionary culture of Russia. Both men became revolutionary agents to help solve the tensions between the human needs of their peoples and existing social facts.[1] In terms of personal political style, however, Gandhi worked delicately like a flame whereas Lenin drove incessantly like a jackhammer.

It is difficult to comprehend the nature of world politics today without understanding Lenin's adaptation of the ideas of Karl Marx to execute an unprecedented revolution that followed principles of class consciousness and the dictatorship of an elite vanguard. Lenin demonstrated how intellectuals can totally transform society, how class interest groups can lead to conflict and imperialism, and how socialist ideology can be used to direct the minds and actions of men the world over.

47

Nikolai Lenin (right) with Leon Trotsky. *United Press International photo.*

I. Lenin: A Political Portrait

Intellectuals and Society

The history of Russia is permeated by the courage of intellectuals and their revolutionary tradition. Even today visitors to the Soviet Union can stumble upon intellectual, anti-government meeting places like "Cafe Saigon" in Leningrad, where young and old quietly discuss current forbidden books and where fishermen who want to become philosophers meet poets who wish to smuggle their unpublished poems to the West. In many ways Lenin was merely one outgrowth of the revolutionary tradition of the Russian intelligentsia.

Lenin's mind developed in the tension between the Russian tendencies toward nationalistic isolation on the one hand and dependency upon the West on the other. As the great scholar of communism R.N. Carew Hunt noted, "The history of Russia is characterized by a continual oscillation between the extremes of isolation and dependence upon the west—between a jealous pride in the native genius and tradition of Russia and an equally jealous desire to profit by the achievements of the west and to surpass them."[2] This tension often took the form of an intellectual debate between "the westerners," who demanded in the name of reason and enlightenment that Russia should adopt liberal European ideas, and the **Slavophils**, who argued that Russia should nurture her own, independent tradition and unique civilization, creating an original path of development to match.

Men are like plants: their intellects reflect the soil of their birth, the air which they breathe, and the color of the social world in which they grow up. Intellectuals attempt to transcend the national world-view of their traditional culture to lead their societies beyond themselves to better satisfy the needs of their people. But belief in ethnocentrism or cultural supremacy is an overwhelming social fact that permeates the subconsciousness of even the intellectual leaders. Anthropologist Melville Herskovits notes, "No culture in its totality is a commodity for export. This is why any people who, by any method, whether by conquest or persuasion, assume that they can cause another group to change its entire way of life, are building policy on a psychological unreality. . . . Culture is not a straightjacket."[3]

In 1870 Vladimir Ulianov, who later assumed the name Nikolai Lenin, was born. During that decade the **Populist party** arose in the 1870s and tried to combine the stress that the Westerners placed on science and education with the Slavophil devotion to the genius of Russia. It sponsored a "Go to the People" movement: 2,000 young members of the intelligentsia, dressed in homespun clothes, went out to live among the emancipated peasants to convert them to revolutionary socialism. The peasants, however, did not want revolution but more land. The failure of this movement encouraged the development of a terrorist organization called the "People's Will," which Vladimir's older brother, Alexander, joined as a university student in St. Petersburg. In 1887 Alexander was making bombs and leading a student group that plotted to kill Tsar Alexander III on the sixth anniversary of the assassination of his father, Alexander II. Someone tipped off the Tsar, however, and the plot failed. The secret police arrested Alexander and his group in a tavern.

At his trial Alexander Ulianov confessed to acts he never committed to save his comrades. He ended by saying, "My purpose was to aid in the liberation of the unhappy Russian people. Under a system which permits no freedom of expression and crushes every attempt to work for their welfare and enlightenment by legal means, the only instrument that remains is terror." Alexander was sentenced to die and was hanged on May 8, 1887. Historian David Shub wrote:

> When the St. Petersburg newspaper carrying the news of Alexander's execution reached Vladimir in Simbirsk, he threw the paper on the floor and cried:
> "I'll make them pay for this! I swear it!"
> "You'll make who pay?" asked a neighbor, Maria Savenko.
> "Never mind, I know," Vladimir replied.[4]

When his brother was executed, Vladimir Ulianov had just turned seventeen. His father, who was a teacher, director of primary schools, and a devout member of the Russian Orthodox Church, had just died, leaving the family nothing. His mother was the daughter of Volga-German parents, who had brought her up as a Lutheran in the disciplined German tradition. She was a strong woman who could cope with the deaths of her husband and oldest son and the financial burden of bringing up her five remaining children. Vladimir's own controlled reaction to these traumatic events was, undoubtedly, due in part to the strong moral character of his parents and a family upbringing marked by industry, austerity, and devotion. Later, however, in filling out a party questionnaire, he wrote that he stopped believing in God when he was sixteen.

Political consciousness, or individual awareness of the tensions between human needs and social facts, is a question of historical chance as well as of human choice. Vladimir had been exposed to the repressive nature of existing social facts in Russia and to the possibility of revolutionary response through his older brother, Alexander, whom he greatly admired. Alexander's execution focused and concentrated his brother's political consciousness. The activities of his family were carefully watched by the secret police. Neighbors avoided social contact with them out of fear.

Following Alexander's example Vladimir won the gold medal for being the outstanding student of his class and entered Kazan University where he was quickly drawn into student disorders. Again, repressive social facts caused the trouble. Professors were expelled for mildly liberal opinions and students who were thought to be involved in political activities were exiled. Vladimir and forty other students demonstrated in front of the dean's office to demand certain changes; they were arrested and expelled. At his mother's request, Vladimir was allowed to live under police surveillance at the family's isolated Kokushkino estate. There, at the age of eighteen, he began reading Karl Marx. From this point on, it is not possible to understand the development of Lenin without knowing the meaning of Karl Marx.

The nineteenth-century German scholars and close friends, Karl Marx and Friedrich Engels, developed the theories of communism that became the basis of the communist world-view in the twentieth century. The diplomatic and domestic actions of political leaders in contemporary socialist states cannot be comprehended fully without a knowledge of these theories. Yet many Westerners—Americans in particular—have evaded the relevance of Marxist theories for present world politics. They condemn Marx ideologically without ever having read him or understanding the perceptiveness of some of his insights for the analysis of the social decadence of many capitalist societies.[5] Marx wasn't totally right, but neither was he totally wrong. For Lenin his ideas became a religious dogma used to rationalize all of his political actions. As Hunt has pointed out, "It is impossible to understand communist activity without a knowledge of the system upon which it rests. Every communist who holds any important position has been well instructed in it so that he knows just where he stands, and has an answer to everything, which is far from being the case with the majority of his opponents . . ."[6]

It is impossible to understand Lenin's political thinking without knowing a bit about Hegel and Marx. Hegel viewed history as a continual dialectical process, a constant unfolding of a more perfect and more real "Absolute." Specifically, the dialectic referred to the theory of the union of opposites. For Hegel, the dialectical process consisted of a thesis, or affirmation of a proposition, countered by an antithesis, the denial or negation of the proposition, and the synthesis, or the interaction of the thesis and the antithesis, which brought one closer to reality and perfection. In Hegel's idealistic philosophy, the thesis was "Law" and the antithesis "Morality." The synthesis was "Social Ethics," the whole system of rules, disciplines, and influences that governed social life.[7]

Each society and nation, according to Hegel, not only underwent dialectical development internally, but the resulting domestic synthesis became a thesis internationally. He saw the world stage as a progressive drama of inevitable and noble conflicts between the various representative theses or the national spirits of states. Moreover, he believed that the better and more progressive thesis, or state, would win; that no judge existed who could stand above states; and that war was a noble and heroic event that brought opportunity for further historical perfection. For Hegel "the State" was the closest thing to absolute perfection that men could experience on earth. Individuals were only moral and significant to the extent to which they dutifully performed a role for the state. On the one hand, Hegel's dialectic became the source of proletarian radicalism that resulted in communism, and on the other, his worship of the state became the basis of conservative nationalism from which fascism sprang.[8]

Hegel was an idealist; his basic concern was with the dialectics of ideas and the evolving spirit of history. Marx claimed that he found Hegel upside down—on his head—and that it was necessary to turn him around. In short, Marx transformed Hegel's dialectical idealism into **dialectical materialism**, which viewed the primary reality to be not an interaction of ideas or spirits but the interaction of material, economic forces and social classes.

In his introduction to the first volume of his famous *Capital*, Marx wrote:

> My own dialectic method is not only different from the Hegelian, but is its direct opposite. For Hegel . . . the thinking process is the demiurge (creator) of the real world, and the real world is only the outward manifestation of "the Idea." With me, on the other hand, the ideal is nothing else than the material world reflected by the human mind and translated into terms of thought.

Both Marx and Lenin—and most Marxists today—began with Hegel's three laws of the dialectic out of which they constructed an economic theory of revolutionary action: the law of the transformation of quantity into quality, and vice versa; the law of the unity of opposites; and the law of the negation of the negation. According to the first law, just as the quantitative heating of water to 100 degrees C changed it in quality to steam, so abrupt revolutionary changes in quality occur in human society. The evolution of early capitalism into the **monopoly capitalism** of imperialism was a qualitative change resulting from quantitative growth. The second law, the unity of opposites, asserted that reality consists of contradictions that exist in unity, or that reality is made up of interdependent opposites. For example, in capitalist society interdependence exists between the bourgeoisie (the middle-class property owners) and the proletariat (the working class). Each of these classes depends for its existence upon the other: the middle class exploits the labor of the workers, and the working class sells its labor to the bourgeoisie. The third law of the dialectic, the negation of the negation, claims that a thesis is negated by an antithesis which is, in turn, negated by the synthesis.

In turning Hegel's idealism on its head, Marx's materialism did not equate the dialectic thesis-antithesis-synthesis with Law-Morality-Social Ethics as Hegel did, but with feudalism-capitalism-socialism. That is, internal contradictions in feudalism, where the feudal lord owned most of the society's means of production would lead to its negation by capitalism, where the capitalist owned the means of production. Contradictions within capitalism would lead inevitably to the negation of the negation, or socialism. Here the workers would own the means of production, and in the absence of the internal contradictions of capitalism, production would reach its greatest level of development.

Dialectical materialism applied to human relations within society is called **historical materialism**. Marx based his philosophy of history on two theses: that the most basic causes of social life are economic; and that these causes operate according to the dialectic principle. Hunt noted the latter is accepted only by Marxists, but the former is widely accepted. Marx argued that man has to live before he can think; therefore, causes of social change are not to be found in eternal notions of truth and justice but in changes of the mode of production and exchange.

> The way in which men produce their means of subsistence depends first of all on the nature of the actual means they find in existence and have to reproduce. This mode of production must not be considered simply as being the reproduction of the physical existence of the individuals. Rather, it is a definite form of activity of these individuals, a definite form of expressing their life, a definite mode of life on their part. As individuals express their life, so they are. What they are, therefore, coincides with their production, both with *what* they produce and with *how* they produce. The nature of individuals thus depends on the material conditions determining their production.[9]

Men are how they express themselves. Marx goes further to argue that material conditions and social facts determine the nature of man, of what he produces, and how he produces. Millions of people around the world believe in Marx's economic vision of man as a materially determined being. Yet if Marx is totally right, from where does man's psychic motivation to improve himself and his society come? Why does he become aware of the tension between human needs and social facts? Philosopher Benedetto Croce wrote, "And the sterility of matter will not bring forth and cause to blossom either morals or religion or poetry or philosophy, and not even economics itself, which requires the glow of life, keen intelligence and eagerness."[10]

Take the case of Outer Slabovia, a primitive, agricultural country that produces wheat for its survival. As more and more wheat is produced, large landowners take over and create larger, more efficient farms. Soon the common worker who harvests the wheat finds himself alienated both from the product of his labor, the bread, and from his fellow workers, the millers and the bakers. As the efficiency of production increases, the workers become more like parts of a machine; they lose their individuality and the sense of the collective unity of the work as a whole. Now assume that some lucky Outer Slabovian discovers oil on his wheat field. Soon he becomes richer than all of his fellows, hires farmers for his oil production, and transforms the society from a feudal agrarian economy to an industrialized capitalist economy. Marx argued that such action enables a minority to live off the labor of the majority and that the private ownership of the means of production inclines men to take advantage of one another. The result is two antagonistic classes. Marx declared in his *Communist Manifesto*, "the history of all hitherto existing societies is the history of the class struggle": the struggle between the bourgeoisie and the proletariat. However, he argued that the transition of places like Outer Slabovia from a feudal agrarian society to an industrial capitalist society would not take place without a struggle, since those of the old order would fight to preserve their interests. Furthermore, a more clear-cut struggle or revolution would occur when industrial Outer Slabovia developed into a monopoly-capitalist state. Marx believed that with this transformation workers would become worse and worse off until they took over the state through revolution to initiate a socialist society which would eventually result in communism: a classless society or ideal community in which the state itself withers away. In the historical perspective, however, the lot of workers has improved under monopoly capitalism, in most cases; violent revolution has been the exception, not the rule; and no socialist state has yet withered away.

Put yourself, for a moment, in Lenin's shoes when he was first exposed to the ideas of Hegel and Marx. The decade of the 1880s was a disastrous one for Lenin's family: not only had the father died and the oldest son been executed, but everything the family stood for had been crushed by oppressive social facts. After the murder of Tsar Alexander II, Alexander III withdrew all the policies of reform of his predecessor. He threw out a plan for consultative commissions, designed as a concession to the educated classes, and initiated an efficient program of reaction, strengthening the Orthodox Church, weakening local councils, autocratically controlling peasant communes, repressing Western influence, and forcing his non-Russian subjects to speak Russian. Indeed, on the margin of the paper drawn up by Alexander Ulianov for his group, the Tsar wrote, next to a statement maintaining that the present political regime made it impossible to elevate the people, "This is reassuring."[11]

In such a family and historical situation, if you had just been expelled from a university for mildly participating in a student demonstration and were picked upon by the authorities because of your older brother's political activities, you, too, might have been ripe for the revolutionary ideas of Marx. As a bright, reserved, realistic intellectual, Vladimir Ulianov seemed beset by social facts that conspired to make him a revolutionary. Political consciousness was steamrolled over him by the events of his everyday life. The tensions between the human needs he perceived and existing social facts became increasingly intolerable. Edmund Wilson concisely summarized how Lenin's political consciousness of frustrating social facts led Vladimir to grasp the ideas of Karl Marx:

> In the meantime, since the days of the People's Will, the industrial development of Russia, though still far behind that of the Western countries, had been going ahead at a pace which made it seem as unlikely as Karl Marx had thought it, that the Russians would be able to make a short cut straight from the peasant commune to the socialism of a mechanized society. In the twenty years between 1877 and 1897, the production of textiles doubled and production of metals trebled; in the ten years between 1887 and 1897, the three hundred thousand textile workers doubled and the hundred thousand metal workers inceased to a hundred and fifty thousand. The eighties had been a period of desperate strikes which had been repressed with the utmost brutality, but which had had the result of procuring some rudimentary industrial legislation: factory inspection, the abolition of child labor, certain restrictions on the work of adolescents and women, and the regular payment in cash of wages which had hitherto been dribbled out—sometimes only twice a year—by employers as capricious with their hands as the landlords had been with their servants. In that dim house of the Russian spirit, the Marxist view seemed to Vladimir realistic: it was the only theory in sight that could make sense of the Russian situation and relate it to the rest of the world. And Vladimir's peculiar temperament had fitted him to be its spokesman. His trenchant intellect, his combative nature, his penchant for harsh and caustic criticism, his deep feeling combined with detachment, all made him sympathetic to Marx.[12]

Ironically, by preventing him from continuing his university studies, the Russian authorities gave Vladimir so much free time that he had nothing to do but to study Marx and play chess with his younger brother. His mother soon grew fearful that his political associations would get him into trouble in Kazan and made him move with her to her small country estate near Simbirsk. This move also illustrates the role of chance in history: a few weeks later the other members of the political group to which Vladimir had belonged in Kazan were arrested and given heavy sentences.

As a landlord, Vladimir did not fare very well. He later told his wife that his mother wanted him to go in for farming, but he saw that it wasn't working out. He thought his relations with the peasants became abnormal. By abnormal he probably meant any master-servant relationship. Indeed, the next landlord to take over was murdered by the peasants in the 1905 revolution. Although he was not too successful, Vladimir was able to use his landlord experience to cultivate his father's gift for talking with all sorts of people on their own terms. He discovered by collecting agricultural statistics that far from being a homogeneous group, the peasants had recently broken into roughly two categories: one somewhat like the bourgeoisie, the other similar to the proletariat. Such observations became important in his later revolutionary theory.

In 1889, Vladimir applied to take his final examination as an outside student at the university. His request was denied. The next year Vladimir's mother went to the minister of education to appeal her son's case herself and received permission for him to take his final exams at a law school of one of the universities. Vladimir prepared for a four-year course of study in less than a year and a half and came out first among 124 students taking the examination. At the same time the family was struck with another tragedy: Olga, Vladimir's sister, came down with typhoid fever and died on the anniversary of Alexander's execution.

Vladimir returned to his mother's Samara estate and began an unsuccessful legal practice, which recalls Gandhi's similar failure. He spent most of his time working for a clandestine Marxist club he had started. His first disciples were his remaining two sisters and brother.

In 1892 the province of Samara was hit by a famine. When a committee of citizens was formed to help the poor most affected by the tragedy, Lenin took a surprising but characteristic stand. He argued that:

> The famine is the direct consequence of a particular social order. So long as that order exists, famines are inevitable. They can be abolished only by the abolition of that order of society. Being in this sense inevitable, famine today performs a progressive function. . .
>
> . . . It is easy to understand the desire of so-called "society" to come to the assistance of the starving, to ameliorate their lot. . . .The famine threatens to create serious disturbances and possibly the destruction of the entire bourgeois order. Hence the efforts of the well-to-do to mitigate the effect of the famine are quite natural. . . . *Psychologically this talk of feeding the starving is nothing but an expression of the saccharine sweet sentimentality so characteristic of our intelligentsia.*[13]

The statement illustrates Lenin's acceptance of Hegel's inevitable dialectic of historical process and of Marx's historical determinism and class consciousness. Lenin wraps these theories around him to create an ironclad,

unsentimental, ideological mask which becomes his means and his rationalization for all future events and political action. Notice, furthermore, how
ideological rigidities can separate one from specific individuals, who are
suffering here and now, for the sake of more universal and significant
principles to be initiated in the future. The starving peasants be damned;
full steam ahead towards the inevitable revolution and socialist utopia!
Ideological thinking sacrifices the present to the altar of the future for
leftists, and freezes the present for the sake of the past for rightists. Either
way, the message for the common man is clear: sacrifice your present needs
for the sake of the ideological cause; you believe therefore you are.

*Ideology is a love affair between a human being and a set of ideas which he
feels to be his solution. Just as love is blind, so is ideological thinking. It
tends to go one way only—left or right. To be "to the left" is to be in love
with man as an end in himself. To be "to the right" is to be in love with a
standard outside man for which man must discipline himself. In writing
about this universal ideological polarity, psychologist Silvan Tomkins said,
"Man is an end in himself versus man is not an end in himself: the valuable
exists independent of man. . . . On the left he conceives himself to be an end
in himself, to be of ultimate value; he wishes to be himself and to realize the
potentialities which are inherent in him. On the right man is at best neutral,
without value. There exists a norm, an objective value, independent of him,
and he may become valuable by participation in, conformity to, or
achievement of this norm."[14]*

In 1893, Lenin went to St. Petersburg and joined an underground social
democratic organization called the Elders of which he soon became the
leader. Indeed, by the time he was twenty-four he became known as the
"old man." From this time onward, Lenin was totally self-confident, never
doubting his eventual success and viewing the apathy and ineptitude of his
followers merely as temporary obstacles to be overcome. Wilson wrote:

> He evidently owed to his German blood that solidity and
> efficiency and diligence that were so untypical of the Russian
> intelligentsia. The moral consistency of Vladimir seems to
> belong to a different system from that uncontrollable fluctua-
> tion between emotional and moral extremes—good for drama but
> bad for real action—which makes even so great a Russian as
> Tolstoy seem a little ridiculous to the West. Vladimir knew no
> truancies into skepticism, no drops into self-indulgence or
> indifference . . . Vladimir, released, becomes Lenin. The son of
> the Councillor of State divests himself of his social identity,
> assumes the anti-social character of a conspirator; and, in

graduating into the world-view of Marxism, he even partly loses his identity as a Russian and is occupied with lines of force that make of national boundaries conventions and extend through the whole human world.[15]

Although initially Lenin's confidence and enthusiasm got in the way of effective conspiratorial activity, he aged fast, both intellectually and physically. He became almost totally bald in his twenties, and often his health suffered greatly from overwork. In St. Petersburg he was soon arrested by the secret police for his activities, caught with the proofs for the first issue of a clandestine newspaper. Ironically, it is the anti-Marxist Leninists who undergo this fate today in Russia. While in prison Lenin became recognized as the head of the "League for the Liberation of Labor," a combination of the various social democratic groups. In 1896 he wrote a pamphlet on strikes—effective propaganda for the walkout of 35,000 textile workers. At this time he also started his first major work, *The Development of Capitalism in Russia*, which was to establish him as an important Marxist theorist when he published in 1899. While he was in prison he read every book on economics and finance that he could get a hold of to substantiate his arguments. After fourteen months he was released but was banished for three years to the village of Shushenskoe in eastern Siberia.

In Siberia Lenin spent his time hunting, fishing, swimming, studying, and writing. In May 1898 Nadezhda Krupskaya, a close friend from St. Petersburg, arrived in his village. She had been granted permission to join Lenin by describing him as her fiance. Both of them despised the legal convention of marriage but went through the ceremony soon after she arrived. She became his ideal secretary and comrade for life, subordinating herself entirely to his work. They spent their honeymoon translating Sidney and Beatrice Webb's *Theory and Practice of Trade Unionism* and copying the text of the *Development of Capitalism in Russia*.

Interest Groups and Party Organization

While Lenin was in Siberia, nine social democratic leagues held a congress at Minsk in 1898 and founded the Russian Social Democratic Labor Party, RSDLP. In 1900 Lenin returned from Siberia. The police were trailing the Social Democrats so Lenin decided that convening another congress was too risky. The alternative he chose was to go abroad to publish a newspaper. In Munich he founded *Iskra*, The Spark, followed two years later with the publication of a pamphlet in Stuttgart called *What Is to Be Done?* in which he sketched a program for the creation of a revolutionary party.

What Is to Be Done? sets out Lenin's theory of the revolutionary party and bitterly attacks bread-and-butter unionism, on the one hand, and most forms of **Marxist revisionism**, on the other. Its basic thesis became the organizing principle of Lenin's party. "A small, compact core, consisting of reliable, experienced and hardened workers, with responsible agents in the principal districts and connected by all the rules of strict secrecy with the organizations of revolutionists, can, with the wide support of the masses and without an elaborate set of rules, perform *all* the functions of a trade-union organization, and perform them, moreover, in the manner the Social Democrats desire."[16] Almost all of Lenin's writing is functional, aimed towards a tactical task at hand. It is impersonal, austere, hard-hitting. The great Russian writer Gorky once wrote that Lenin's speeches gave him the impression of "the cold glitter of steel shavings," from which "there rose, with amazing simplicity, the perfectly fashioned figure of truth."[17]

However, Lenin's view of Marxist truth differed from that of his colleagues in many cases. In 1903 at the second Congress of the RSDLP, two distinct ideological factions emerged among the Social Democrats, the **Bolsheviks** and the **Mensheviks**. Lenin's view of party organization became the basis of the Bolshevik or majority faction, which believed that the center of the movement should be an inner group or vanguard of professional revolutionaries working through secret, extralegal activities. The Bolsheviks represented an outgrowth of the Slavophil revolutionary tradition in Russia, which argued that the elite should not lower itself to the level of "primitive handicraftsmen" but rather "*elevate* the primitive craftsmen to the level of revolutionists."* Lenin argued that under a despotism like Russia's it is impossible to have democracy in a revolutionary party; a highly centralized, dedicated elite working in secret with absolute loyalty among the rank and file is necessary. He wrote, "Think it over a little and you will realize that 'broad democracy' in party organization, amidst the darkness of the autocracy and the domination of the gendarmes, is nothing more than a *useless and harmful toy.*"[18]

The Menshevik or minority faction, on the other hand, looked to the Marxist developments in Western Europe or to the Westerners for their model of party development. They advocated an open party for working men, organized somewhat in the democratic tradition of labor union politics, and opposed extralegal actions. The Bolsheviks were not, by far, the majority in this debate all the time, but Lenin kept the label for tactical reasons.

Lenin's theory of party organization grew out of the existing social fact in Russia of the great distance between the intelligentsia and elites on the one hand and the masses of the population on the other. He argued that the masses of people were not in a position to judge who the best, dedicated revolutionary party workers were, and he held that trade unionism was "the ideological enslavement of the workers to the bourgeoisie" and would lead to ineffectual reforms, as it had in Western Europe. The proper role of the

---

*Lenin was abandoned at this point by his old master Plekhanov, who attacked him in a treatise significantly called *What is not to be done? A New Attempt to bring to their Senses the Frogs who asked for a King.*

unions was to use practical economic issues to raise the political consciousness of the workers.[19] Many who initially supported Lenin in the 1903 debate eventually went over to the Menshevist camp, which tended to take Marx literally. Lenin, on the other hand, argued that the principles of Marx must be subordinated to the primary task of carrying out the revolution. For Lenin theory always merged with realistic practice in the existing world of social facts.

"Those who get the most are elite: the rest are mass," said political scientist Harold Lasswell.[20] The social world is divided into economic classes based upon how much one has got of what there is to get, how one got it, and how one uses it. From classes emerge interest groups: political organizations designed to satisfy the needs and maximize the values of their members before all others. Interest groups, in turn, provide support for political parties led by elites. The belief systems of mass publics are marked by difficulties in articulation, lack of information, and interest in simple, concrete values like wages. As Hegel noted, "The Few assume to be the deputies, but they are often only the despoilers of the Many."

Despite their differences, the Bolsheviks and Mensheviks worked side by side until they officially split in 1912. Leon Trotsky represented a third interest group in the party. He favored the seizure of power by the working class; opposed collaboration with the bourgeoisie; rejected Lenin's proposed alliance between the proletariat and the peasants, whom he distrusted; and argued that a Russian revolution would only succeed if it sparked other revolutions in more economically advanced countries. In short, Trotsky was arguing on the basis of his famous theory of "permanent revolution."

Marxist-Leninism

In his lifetime Lenin derived five basic political solutions to the tensions he perceived between human needs and the social facts of his everyday world. Each of these political notions was based on a pragmatic adaption of Marxist principles to Lenin's own needs. Westerners have come to know them as the basis for Marxist-Leninism or Russian communism:

1. A practical theory of revolution based on "a revolutionary-democratic dictatorship of the proletariat and the peasantry."
2. The theory of the dictatorship of the proletariat.
3. The theory of the party as "the vanguard of the proletariat" to lead the masses before and after the revolution.
4. The theory that imperialism as "the final stage of capitalism" creates revolutionary situations.[21]

5. The communist party strategy of world revolution.

Lenin's ideas on revolution grew as much out of the actual revolutions of 1905 and 1917 as out of abstract theory. As Stalin put it, "Leninism is marxism of the era of imperialism and of the proletarian revolution." The abortive revolution of 1905 resulted from the disastrous effects of the Russo-Japanese War. The event began with the Bloody Sunday massacre: a peaceful demonstration before the Tsar's palace that became a target for police fire. Strikes erupted in response. Mutiny raged on the battleship *Potemkin*. To calm things down Tsar Nicholas II promised to create a so-called parliament, the **Duma**, and to grant a constitution. Yet within two months the first workers' soviet was set up in St. Petersburg and another followed in Moscow—not to seize power but to prepare for a constituent assembly with the widest possible support. Lenin did not return to Russia until a month later, too late to influence what occurred. In 1906 the Duma was granted only limited powers in part because of worker rebellions in the streets of Moscow, and in 1907 it was dissolved. The next December Lenin was obliged to go into exile, and he didn't return to Russia until 1917.

The failure of the spontaneous mass uprising of 1905 did not deter Lenin from his Marxist view of history. He had captured the party machinery and gained control of the Central Committee. Lenin spent a good deal of time raising funds to keep the Bolshevik movement alive.

Lenin raised money any way he could by fair means or foul. He secured large donations so that the Bolshevik movement could subsidize the Bolshevik-controlled St. Petersburg committee of the Social Democratic party as well as the Moscow Committee. Writers such as Maxim Gorky and Garin-Mikhailovsky gave Lenin thousands of rubles. However, a much greater contribution came from the armed holdups of the Bolshevik *boyeviki* gang—the largest being the Tiflis heist of 1907 for at least 250,000 rubles. In this period of Lenin's "Lower Depths," to use Gorky's phrase, the Caucasus strong-arm squad, consisting of Joseph Stalin among others, came in handy. Although the London Party Congress of 1910 had officially repudiated strong-arm tactics, Lenin did not hesitate to use them discreetly when he thought they were needed.

Just before the Tiflis robbery, Prussian police discovered a Berlin storehouse full of watermarked paper to be used for counterfeiting three-ruble notes. Some Bolsheviks were arrested. When "more bourgeois" factions of the German Social Deomocrats voiced outrage that the address of the party paper *Vorwaerts* had been used in the counterfeit operation, Lenin responded, "When I see Social Democrats announcing with pride and self-satisfaction that 'we are no anarchists, no thieves, no brigands, we are above that, we reject the partisan struggle,' then I ask myself—do these people understand what they are saying?"[22]

Since many Bolsheviks demanded an investigation of the counterfeit plot, the party's Foreign Bureau appointed George Chicherin to look into things. Lenin was sure that all the evidence had been destroyed. But Chicherin found the German manufacturer of the watermarked paper who could identify through their photographs the Bolsheviks who had ordered it. Lenin was greatly upset and wanted a cover-up. At his suggestion the investigation was delegated back to the Foreign Bureau of the party, where the Bolshevik majority buried the evidence. At the same time Lenin's influence caused the Bolshevik majority to restore the good standing of the Caucasion strong-arm men, including Stalin. From Lenin's struggle to the Watergate Affair, political men have often been willing to use any means available to solve the tension between their momentary needs and existing social facts. The Bolsheviks had other means for getting money. For example, a man named Victor was one of several Bolsheviks directed to marry into rich families for the sake of the party coffers. When Victor's money never quite reached the party, Lenin shrugged off reproaches of the Central Committee in London arguing: "A Central Committee to be effective must be made up of gifted writers, able organizers, and a few intelligent scoundrels. I recommended Comrade X [Victor] as an intelligent scoundrel."[23]

Like all such leaders, Lenin quickly made enemies in his own party. Some deserted the Bolshevik movement, indicting Lenin for ignoring the majority opinion of his own faction and for illegally using party funds and the party press to suppress the independent views of others. Lenin remained firm, however, and refused to seek reconciliation with his opponents (although he held no grudges and welcomed apostates back into the true faith). When someone asked one of these dissidents how one man could really ruin the whole party, he observed that there was no other man who thought and dreamed of nothing but revolution—twenty-four hours a day.

Both the Mensheviks and the Bolsheviks believed that the 1905 revolution could not be socialist but had to be bourgeois-democratic to bring about the industrial development, which was the precondition for the proletarian revolution. The Mensheviks further believed that it was much too early for a proletarian dictatorship and that the bourgeoisie should be allowed to take power with the socialists forming an opposition party on the Western model. Although Lenin agreed that, given the present stage of capitalist development, only a bourgeois-democratic revolution was possible, he argued that such a revolution required that the bourgeoisie be liberal, which in Russia it was not. Therefore, he claimed that the proletariat must lead the revolution and establish "a revolutionary dictatorship of the proletariat and the peasantry." Although this regime would initially conform to the democratic pattern, it would seek as soon as possible to convert the revolution from the bourgeois-democratic to the final proletarian phase. The effect of the Menshevist approach was to postpone revolution indefinitely. Lenin argued that the 1905 revolution was a useful dress rehearsal for the revolution to come—a mass revolution to destroy tsarism, led by the proletariat with the active cooperation of the peasantry.

Capitalism, Imperialism, and War

Just as the Russo-Japanese War had set the stage for the 1905 revolution, Lenin anticipated that another war would help to create the occasion for the next revolution. Lenin wrote Gorky in 1913, "War between Austria and Russia would be very useful to the cause of the revolution in Western Europe. But it is hard to believe that Franz Josef and Nicholas will grant us this pleasure."[24] In 1914 they did exactly that. Lenin viewed the First World War as the inevitable outgrowth of the conflicts of class interest among capitalist nations. He considered the view that war could be abolished under capitalism to be pernicious, arguing that imperialism gives rise to fierce rivalry among the capitalist states for the division and redivision of the world and that, consequently, under capitalism, wars are inevitable.

The great ideological debate today is of capitalism versus socialism, of private ownership, individual investment, and the profit motive versus public ownership, state investment, and the welfare motive. Imperialism is the practice of using such ideologies to extend the control of a nation or an empire. Underlying the capitalist or socialist creed of elites is a subtle nationalism—a desire to satisfy one's own needs and those of one's people before all others in the world. In a world in which the rich are getting richer, the poor poorer, and the resources scarcer, conflicts between such elites leading to social revolutions are inevitable. The rich, industrial nations of the Northern Hemisphere dominate the poor, rural nations of the Southern Hemisphere. As tensions between increasing human needs and unjust social facts build up, violence and world war increasingly mark our age.

In 1916 Lenin wrote *Imperialism, The Highest Stage of Capitalism* in Switzerland. He argued that World War I was imperialist on both sides and that imperialism is a direct continuation of the basic characteristics of capitalism. The basic cause of imperialism, according to Lenin, was the emergence of **finance capital**—a dubious proposition since the phenomenon of imperialism existed long before the new factor of finance capital was created by Western industrial societies. Nevertheless, Lenin wrote that "imperialism is capitalism in that stage of development in which the domination of monopoly and finance capital has taken shape; in which the export of capital has acquired pronounced importance; in which the division of the world by international trusts has begun; and in which the partition of all the territory of the earth by the greatest capitalist countries has been completed."[25] Lenin believed that the first, flourishing stage of capitalism was transformed by internal contradictions into a stagnant, monopoly-capitalist stage in which large monopolies and **cartels** would divide the world among themselves and expand imperialistically in search of new resourcces and markets. This phase, too, would break down and lead dialectically to socialism. Compared to agricultural feudalism, capitalism seemed to Lenin to be a progressive and necessary phase, one which extended democratic institutions, liberated nationalities, and created the proletariat. However, in the First World War the capitalist phase had reached its peak, and the bourgeoisie was no longer progressive but decadent and reactionary, interested primarily in consumption rather than production. Thus, an alliance between the proletariat and the bourgeoisie no longer made sense, and the goal of the working class had to be to overthrow the existing social structure of international finance capitalism.

In March, 1917 rioting broke out in the streets of Petrograd—the new name of St. Petersburg, later changed again to Leningrad. The workers wanted bread and peace. Police fired on the many looters, and were, in turn, roasted in flames as rioters set fire to police stations. The government of Tsar Nicholas II collapsed; the Tsar abdicated; and a provisional government was soon established through the Duma, headed by Alexander Kerensky. Lenin was still in Switzerland and began a period of nervous waiting, of grasping for any shred of news he could find, and of longing to get back to the revolutionary situation as soon as possible. Finally he was able to negotiate a deal with the Germans who wanted him back in Russia to further social unrest and divert Russian attention from the war. He and his wife with thirty revolutionaries were put in a sealed train headed for Russia via the Finland Station. On the way Lenin worked feverishly writing propaganda articles and plans for the coming revolution. He half expected to be arrested, but when he arrived in Russia he was greeted enthusiastically, except by the few who thought he had sold out to the Germans. In Petrograd he found things in a state of great confusion. The Provisional Government was competing for power with the soviets. Lenin was greeted by a large reception on Easter Monday night. The next morning he jotted down on a small piece of paper some basic points he wanted to make that day. That small piece of paper became an historical document comparable in importance to the American Declaration of Independence. The pithy statement came to be known as The April Theses and was made up of ten topics calling for the destruction of the parliament, the republic, the army, the bureaucracy, the police, the banks, and the landed estates. It even advocated the destruction of socialism itself momentarily, in favor of the immediate seizure of power by the Soviets of Workers' Deputies. The April Theses abolished the Social Democratic party and the state itself to establish the **Communist International**.

When Lenin gave his speech many thought he was crazy. Bolsheviks thought it was too early to speak of a new revolution and of distributing land to the peasants, and the Mensheviks were totally upset, realizing that if they accepted Lenin's theses the only form of government that would result would be the dictatorship of Lenin. There were great splits in Lenin's own party, and some even accused him of being in the pay of the German General Staff. Overnight Lenin was transformed from a conquering hero to a foreign spy. He never gave up, however, and slowly persuaded many Bolsheviks that his theses were, indeed, a sane plan for seizing power. Great leaders in world politics are marked by tenacious self-determination and willpower even in the face of overwhelming opposition.

The State and Revolution

An unsuccessful coup was attempted in July, 1917. Neither Lenin nor Leon Trotsky would admit having had a hand in that undisciplined uprising, though the evidence does not seem to support their story. Kerensky ordered Lenin's arrest. Lenin shaved his beard, disguised himself as a middle-aged workman, and went into hiding until he could flee to Finland.

While in exile, Lenin continued to make plans for the maturing revolution and wrote *The State and Revolution*, which made him one of the few revolutionaries to commit his intentions to paper before committing his revolution. Here Lenin argued that the revolution would destroy the bourgeois state and replace it with the **dictatorship of the proletariat**: a new form of government modeled after the Paris Commune—a bold insurrection in 1848 that lasted for two and a half months—and following the revolutionary pattern set forth by Marx and Engels. Lenin further distinguished two different stages in Engels' theory of the destruction of the state: in the first the proletariat assumed power and put "an end to the State . . . as a State;" in the second the state would "wither away." The abolition of the State meant the destruction of the bourgeois economic and political order immediately after the revolution; the withering away of the state would occur at a much later stage of historical development.

Lenin grew increasingly restless in exile since he believed the time was fully ripe for the revolution. However, the Central Committee in Petrograd disagreed with his interpretation of events. Finally on October 14 he wrote the committee an urgent message demanding an immediate uprising and arguing that to delay would be a crime. He suggested the slogan: "Power to the Soviets, Peace to All Peoples, Bread to the Starving." Although the committee was still not ready to start an uprising they agreed to let Lenin come back to Petrograd and helped to make the arrangements. Upon his arrival Lenin called a secret meeting of the majority of the Central Committee where the final decision was made to launch the revolution. Lenin's will overwhelmed all opposition and six days later the Military Revolutionary Committee of the party led by Trotsky decided to strike.

The preparations for the revolution were made at the Smolny Institute, a former school for the daughters of the nobility. On November 5 Kerensky received word of the coming Bolshevik uprising. He ordered the cutting of the telephone lines to Smolny and surrounded the Bolshevik newspaper headquarters with a military guard, after first sealing the doors and burning the papers inside. The revolution had begun.

Trotsky responded to Kerensky's move by ordering a company of his men to surround the party press offices, cut the seals on the doors, and stand guard to assure the printing of the paper. This was the first of many Bolshevik revolutionary decrees. Soon the Smolny became a heavily armed military fortress from which patrols, passwords, and orders poured. The uprising was partly directed by radio from the cruiser *Aurora*. Soon the government of Petrograd was in the hands of the revolutionaries.

Lenin, unbearably impatient to join the action, left his hiding place to go to the Smolny without party permission and at considerable risk. His wits and disguise proved effective, and he was soon at the headquarters going over all the details of the revolutionary campaign. When asked about shooting looters on sight, Lenin brushed away his initial hesitations and said, "Yes, of course!" Lenin used any means, including terror, to gain his ends efficiently, for the situation was precarious, and he lacked reliable support. However, Kerensky soon fled, and the Bolsheviks seized all the government buildings except the Winter Palace. Up to that point, the revolution had been amazingly free of noticeable mobs, bullets, and violence. Even after the palace had been taken only nine guards and six sailors were dead, although thousands of rounds of ammunition had been exploded.

That evening Lenin read his "Decree of Peace," proposing a just, democratic peace without annexations or indemnities to the Congress of Soviets. It was followed by his "Decree on Land," which abolished landlord property without compensation and transferred it "to the whole people." The Bolshevik victory was complete. Lenin had only to consolidate his power by undermining all opposition, including the Constituent Assembly, the "democratic body" of the Bolshevik regime. To aid him in maintaining complete control he created "Cheka," the "Extraordinary Commission for Combatting Counterrevolution." Lenin had gone a long way to prove to the world that the meaning of political theory is its embodiment in party organization and action at the proper historical moment. He believed that the world communist revolution would inevitably follow.

II. Principles of World Politics

Class, Interests, and Elites

Lenin was a great analyst of the social facts that provide potential power. As a Marxist, Lenin believed that class determined the other aspects of an individual's place in society. He viewed class in economic terms: what one gets of what there is to get, how one gets it, and who one must serve to get it. To predict how human beings will behave politically, one must determine to which class they belong and where their economic interests lie. People who have the same economic interests form parties. The group in the most advantageous position within the party is the elite.

Revolutionary leaders like Lenin specialize in raising the political consciousness or awareness of those whose needs are frustrated by existing social facts. Lenin believed that his own human needs and those of the majority of the Russian people were frustrated and repressed by the tsarist regime. Specifically, he believed that the conservative bourgeoisie exploited the proletariat or working class. His mission became to make the workers and peasants aware of that exploitation, and of the need for a revolution and for a new socialist party led by a vanguard of the proletarian elite. Marxism became a powerful tool of analysis and propaganda for Lenin who argued that political theory is meaningless unless it is translated into action at one's own moment in history.

Imperialism and International Economics

Imperialism is the policy of seeking to extend the control of a nation or an empire. As we have seen, according to Lenin, imperialism results from finance capitalism. After a period of normal capitalist industrialization, developed countries enter a stage of finance or monopoly capitalism in which large industries or corporations dominate a nation's political and economic structure. Contradictions in monopoly capitalism, however, lead economic leaders in such countries to go abroad for cheaper resources and more markets for their goods. Thus Great Britain occupied colonies, investing about £1,700 million overseas and earning an annual income of at least £100 million. Political control by the colonizer was the natural result of such economic investment.

Lenin's famous theory of imperialism had several important implications. First, imperialism could explain the accumulation of capital, since imperialist countries could buy natural resources at low prices and then sell their products back to the lesser developed countries. Indeed, contrary to Marx's prediction of worsening conditions at this stage of capitalism, the lot of workers in large metropolitan areas improved. Furthermore, the exploitation of backward countries had created a new proletariat which Lenin called the "labor aristocracy": a class that had sold out to the bourgeoisie for higher wages paid for by the wind-fall profits of imperialism. Secondly, Lenin claimed that imperialism had its own contradictions that would speed the downfall of capitalism, since conflict would increase in intensity as the world became more sharply divided into the exploiters and exploited. All exploited and oppressed countries became potential centers for revolutions, although perhaps not proletarian revolutions. Finally, imperialism would intensify conflict until war became inevitable. Imperialist rivalries would decrease international stability. Hence, as Hunt pointed out, "Marxists contend, contrary to all evidence, that both the world wars were due to imperialism in their sense of the struggle for colonial outlets, in accordance with their central thesis that every conflict must have an economic cause."[26] On the other hand, of course, democratic idealists have persistently underestimated the economic causes of war, preferring to cite psychological and ideological causes.

In trying to explain war or peace, it is important to avoid weighing any one single factor too heavily. The reliance of Marxist-Leninism upon **economic determinism** as its basic assumption makes the ideological viewpoint particularly vulnerable to **the fallacy of single factor analysis**. Indeed, almost all ideological viewpoints are open to that criticism, since the very nature of ideology demands that it freeze, or reify, certain aspects of social facts to the point of excluding other aspects. The tendency of ideological thinking to make certain things more real or concrete than they actually are is called **the fallacy of reification**.[27] Whereas the ideological rigidity of communism tends to blind Russians to idealistic and psychological aspects of political reality, the ideological reifications of anti-Marxist, capitalist democracy tend to lead Americans to neglect important economic aspects.[28] All too often we are what we have been carefully taught not to see.

Revolutionary Consciousness and Party Organization

Ideology is a love affair of feelings and ideas, focused by political consciousness and turned into dogma by the political party it brings into being. The initial humanistic focus of political consciousness for Marx was the **alienation** of the common worker from both the product and process of his labor, and therefore from his fellow man. The need of the worker to identify himself with the products he created and to receive the fruits of his labor came into tension with existing exploitative management structures of industrial capitalism, according to Marx. Only to the extent that the worker could be made aware of this tension would he be politically conscious and ripe for revolutionary action. In his later life Marx moved more and more away from analyzing the psychology of alienation and the humanistic basis of community, and focused increasingly upon the material, economic structures he believed to be the basic cause of this frustrated condition. Lenin seized this materialistic spirit of Marxism and rigidified it into a dogmatic program of political action that became the basis for the Bolshevik faction fo the Social Democratic party and later the Communist party.

Although Lenin's entire ideological approach to politics focused upon the economic basis of social facts in the historical context of his time, he was also acutely aware of the basic human needs perceived by the average Russian worker and peasant. His communication with the masses always began with the promise of peace and bread. We can apply Professor John Kenneth Galbraith's description of President Nixon to Lenin: he had both ears to the ground. Unlike Marx, Lenin did not believe that the emancipa-

Lenin addressing a rally in Red Square on May Day, 1918. *Culver Pictures, Inc.*

tion of the working class was merely the job of the working class itself. Lenin saw the need for an enlightened elite, a professional vanguard, to lead the revolution and become the basis of a trustworthy dictatorship of the proletariat. Political theory was of no use to him unless it provided a guide to action, and he was convinced that theory so transformed into an ideological tool was of little use without strong party organization and dedicated leadership to back it up. Lenin despised amateurism in political activities in much the same way that he felt contempt for the factionalism and the turtle-like progress of parliamentarianism. He advocated initial democratization on tactical grounds only, believing this was a necessary historical phase before he could subvert parliamentarianism with his own dictatorship of the elite.

In the course of his life Lenin came to identify himself with history as an objective historical force. It is in that sense that he might be considered one of the most selfless of great men. Soon he believed himself to be as inevitable as dialectical materialism in historical development and, there-fore, demanded absolute loyalty from his followers both to his creed and his own leadership. He would break totally with opponents, compromising as little as possible, and identifying those as enemies who did not go along with his views. His success indicates that in certain historical situations such rigid, ideological, either-or thinking is indeed effective for political action, no matter how it distorts intellectually. In the twentieth century of mass politics, effective political organization seems to cry out for oversimplified sloganeering that appeals to the people's short-term interests and fears rather than to their long-term welfare. Lenin, of course, did greatly lament human suffering of all kinds in the world, as Gorky pointed out. However as his political consciousness became hardened into party ideology and the consolidation of his power, he became increasingly willing to accept individual suffering and terrorism as legitimate means to bring about the goal of a new communist social structure. After all, he had sacrificed many of his own personal needs for the cause of a better ordering of social facts. Why shouldn't others do so as well? Perhaps the single most important principle of Leninism, which operates just as effectively today, is that political consciousness alone is of little immediate use in mass societies unless it is carefully focused by party organization, has solid materialistic support, and is led by a small, professional vanguard of elite.

Soviet Communism

All potential political leaders can learn from Lenin the art of accurately perceiving the dominant social facts of one's own historical period and the need to adapt one's ideology to new conditions as political organization progresses through the historical cycle of creation, maintenance, and decay.[29] When creating Soviet communism, Lenin was most concerned with adapting the theories of Marx to his own day-to-day political needs in a way that would not be too incongruent with the needs of the majority of the

Russian people, who counted on his obtaining and holding power. However, when he actually came into power, the initial revolutionary idealism and flexibility became rigidified into bureaucracy, dogma, and control mechanisms, indicating that Soviet communism left its creative phase and entered its period of maintenance. The civil war that broke out after the Russian Revolution demanded that Lenin do everything he could politically to keep himself and his party in power.

Furthermore, just before his death in 1924, Lenin began to realize that history was not yet ripe for a worldwide communist revolution and emphasized the need to have a strong bastion of successful communism in one country first. That perception led to the great power struggle after Lenin's death between the idealistic Leon Trotsky, who advocated immediate worldwide communist revolution, and the realist Joseph Stalin, who argued strongly for socialism in one country as a necessary precondition for any revolutionary foreign policy. Stalin's realism won the day, largely due to his skillful use of party organization and force. The result, in the first half of the twentieth century, was the continual subversion of the international communist movement, organized by national Soviet interests. Stalin argued that it was the duty of all communists in the world to build up the only successful communist state as the basis for the spread of worldwide communism later. Often this development has led to a two-front Soviet foreign policy: the official front advocating peaceful coexistence with Western democracies in order to gain material advantages and military security; and the unofficial front advocating an undercover policy of revolutionary, communist subversion wherever it is most effective and helpful to Soviet interests throughout the world. Given such a tradition, it is easy to understand why Soviet leaders often fear communist Chinese activities more than Western diplomacy. The Soviets want to remain the one ideal model of revolutionary communism for all countries everywhere and are not happy to have a successful competitor.

III. Present Implications

Marxist-Leninism in Russia Today

The history and doctrine of Marxist-Leninism permeates the Soviet Union today and is the basis for domestic education and foreign propaganda. Lenin's creation of the Soviet "**party-state**," that is, a state made up of only one party, has been regimented and formalized so that a few thousand appointed members of the party elite manage the party-state. At the very top of this hierarchy is the **politburo** made up of twenty or so party members or candidate members. *Pravda*, "truth," the official party newspaper has called the police and propaganda the pillars of the Soviet State. The whole structure is held together by the ideology of communism. Those who are loyal to this ideology, as it is represented by the party, are rewarded; those who are not are harassed or punished. For example, the English publication in 1974 of dissident writer Aleksandr Solzhenitsyn's *The Gulag Archipelago, 1918-1956* outside the Soviet Union has been called a "blanket of slander of the Soviet people" by *Pravda*. The Soviet political leaders have good reason to be concerned since the book is, for the most part, a nonfictional description of life in Soviet prisons and of secret police methods during the Stalin era, prefaced by the author's warning that "if freedom does not come to my country for a long time" the very reading of this work "will be very dangerous."[30]

Dissident intellectuals are not the only problem of Soviet officials. Widespread economic problems, demands for liberalism from the satellite states of Eastern Europe, especially Rumania, and the communist Chinese ideological and military threat all cause the Soviet elite many headaches. Ideologically, Soviet Marxism may have met its match in Marxist human- ism, advocated by many leaders in other socialist countries and relying heavily upon Marx's early humanisitic manuscripts stressing alienation rather than the later stress on economic determinism.

Archduke Otto von Hapsburg has recently claimed that the Soviet Union is not a superpower as much as it is a paper tiger because of the internal weaknesses that undermine the strong, aggressive image it has so successfully maintained in the West. Von Hapsburg noted that for a rich country, Soviet productivity has been amazingly low especially in agricul- ture. For example, in the United States in 1972 one man working in agriculture fed 142 people otherwise employed as compared to 38 in Western Europe and just 3.5 in the Soviet Union. Furthermore, in 1913 one agricultural worker could feed 2.8 people in tsarist Russia meaning that progress has not been very impressive in this area in the last six decades.[31]

The Multinational Corporation and Economic Imperialism

Despite problems at home and threats from abroad, Soviet leaders have continued to be extremely effective in using propaganda to spread Lenin's political principles particularly on the issue of economic imperial- ism. Not only is Lenin the best selling author within the Soviet Union, but the state publishing committee claims that worldwide, Lenin's works outsell even the Bible. According to the committee, the works of Lenin have been printed 11,000 times in 102 languages and in 400 million copies, not counting another 200 million copies of books about Lenin. The Soviet and Eastern European communist governments have developed more subtle propaganda techniques as well, such as sponsoring communist scholars to give papers at Western academic conventions, which illustrate or extend basic Marxist-Leninist theses. For example, at the 1973 Convention of the International Studies Association in New York, Gyorgy Adam of the Karl Marx University of Economic Sciences in Budapest gave a paper on "Multinational Corporations and the Outlines of a Global Economy." Adam argued that the late 1960s and early 1970s have introduced the era of the "global corporation," and that multinational corporations are establishing business empires with widespread logistic networks and strategies that do not necessarily coincide with the interests of their home country. His basic concern was the impact of such large corporations upon less developed countries and the gap in world economic development, in which the rich get richer and the poor poorer. His solution was regulation of such corporations and the transfer of their technology to less developed socialist countries to close that gap.[32]

In terms of the future impact of the multinational corporation upon world economic relations, Adam is undoubtedly correct. In late 1973, business created by multinational enterprises outside their home countries amounted to $350 billion worth of goods and services a year (three-fifths of it by U.S. companies) or one-eighth of the gross product of the non-communist world. Furthermore, the volume of such multinational corporation business is increasing rapidly and can be expected to be responsible for at least one-fourth of the production of the non-communist world by the early 1980s.[33] However, although Adam is accurate on the increasing influence of multinational corporations, the tone of his argument and the nature of his solution point to undermining "imperialist" industries in rich, capitalist countries like the United States in order to strengthen poorer socialist countries. Whereas economically such a socialist redistribution of the world's wealth might indeed move the world closer to a more peaceful and equitable existence for the majority of men, the political implications of Adam's socialist solution are carefully avoided in his argument. For if Adam's policy were adopted overnight by all countries and multinational corporations in the world, the Soviet ideology and material power of Marxist-Leninism would serve to gain most for itself and its allies, whereas the "capitalist-democratic" ideology of Western governments and multinational corporations would be in a position to lose most, at least materially in the immediate future.

The point is that Lenin's principles of economic imperialism do help to explain international economic imperialism in the late twentieth century, though they give only a partial explanation. However, Marxist-Leninist solutions to such international economic injustices are not apt to be easily accepted by the rich and powerful multinational corporations of the West, which thrive on the capitalist profit motive and which are the main source of economic growth in their home countries. National interest in economic growth can be expected to prevail over the international interest in reducing the gap between the rich and poor peoples of the world in the foreseeable future.

Soviet Foreign Policy and the Future

In projecting present Soviet foreign policy into the future, the history and meaning of Marxist-Leninism is critical for understanding the basic motivations behind Soviet policy. Soviet leaders can be expected to do everything diplomatically possible to improve the material economic condition of the Soviet Union, as the great American wheat sale fiasco of 1973 demonstrated in no uncertain terms. Equally important as a motivation is the traditional Russian concern for military security. Like past regimes the Soviets are faced with large threats on two fronts—Europe and Asia—and they must maintain a relationship of totally peaceful coexistence on one front in order to be aggressive and effective on the other. Clearly since the Sino-Soviet split in the 1960s, the Soviet elite has perceived the greatest threat both ideologically and militarily to be from communist China. Hence, about half of the Soviet forces are stationed on the Chinese border, and Soviet leaders have been pressing hard for international security guarantees on the Western European front.

The Soviet elite has found a way to combine its needs for economic improvement and military security: the policy of **detente** with the United States. Detente is a loose, unofficial agreement on the part of the elites of two or more nation-states to bring their nations into warmer relations by cooperating in certain limited areas such as trade, the exchange of technological information, and military security consultations. Because of the clear-cut American economic superiority over the Soviet Union, the American-Soviet detente has more advantages for the Soviets than for Americans.

In fact, Professor Raymond Vernon has argued that the United States could easily lose a great deal both economically and politically from detente, if American decision makers attempt to use the same cooperative approach toward the Soviets that they would use toward Western democracies like Canada, Italy, or Taiwan.[34] The danger is due to the critical difference in the rules of the game according to which Soviets and American play international politics. The American rule of transaction with the rest of the world is that anything is allowed unless it has been restricted by the state. The Soviet rule, on the other hand, is the opposite. Nothing is permitted unless it has been initiated by the state. Thus Vernon points out that if American policymakers use concepts like tariff protection, anti-dumping laws, most-favored nation treatment, currency convertibility, and patent licensing, originally designed for the American rules in bargaining with the Soviet Union, they may find themselves further upsetting America's trade and monetary position, as well as undermining agreements with her normal allies in Europe.

In short, to enforce the Soviet-American detente, American foreign policymakers may be tempted to undermine the American rules of the game by centralizing all American economic policy and putting controls on American trade, which make sense in terms of the detente but which are absurd in terms of economic relationships with other countries. Furthermore, both the United States and the Soviet Union stand to lose international prestige because the elites of less developed countries accurately perceive that an American-Soviet condominium has been created to preserve the position of the two superpowers in the economic, military, and political status quo, and to keep other countries down. Such perceptions open the opportunity for great gains by communist Chinese leaders who can accuse both the United States and the Soviet Union of being fat, imperialist nations, which support reactionary rather than revolutionary forces in the world. In this way the powerful revolutionary principles of Lenin can come full circle to undermine any communist state in which revolutionary doctrines have hardened into ideological dogma, enforced by reactionary bureaucrats.

In anticipating the future of Soviet foreign policy, it is vital to keep in mind that the Soviets have rejected the traditional Western system of nation-states and the traditional rules of the game, and have provided a constant, disruptive influence in world politics in the twentieth century. If Western diplomats expect the Soviets to behave as Westerners would, in terms of respecting agreements and treaties, they will be constantly deceived. Moreover, the psychological dogma and arrogance of the belief that Lenin imparted to Soviet elites—that they possess the truth and key to history—will continue to have a profound impact on future Soviet actions. Such a self-righteous and rigid ideology reinforces and justifies the Soviet Union in the age-old Russian practice of insulating the Russian people from Western ideas and currents and maintaining a garrison state at home. Lenin, most of all, represented the need of impoverished people for a comprehensive faith that justified the elites in controlling the masses. This powerful belief will continue to exist in many underdeveloped and overpopulated countries, as the People's Republic of China so clearly illustrates. Without a meaningful principle of international justice and effective efforts to redistribute the wealth of the world to benefit economically desperate societies, the leaders of have-not nations, feeling a need to control and comfort their people, will create movements that attack the existing world system of nation-states as unjust and illegitimate. Such movements will keep global politics in a constant state of unrest, and we can expect many future leaders like Lenin to perpetuate that unrest.

Notes

1. B. N. Ganguli, "Lenin and Gandhi," *India Quarterly* 27, no. 1 (1971): 325. Basically I agree with Ganguli who argues that understanding means stressing the similarities rather than the differences between great men like Lenin and Gandhi.

2. R. N. Carew Hunt, *The Theory and Practice of Communism* (Baltimore: Penguin Books, 1966), p. 159. Hunt's is an excellent introduction to Lenin's thought and its Marxist heritage. Other basic sources for the portrait of Lenin, but which are not referred to in specific notes, include: Louis Fischer, *The Life of Lenin* (New York: Harper & Row, 1964); Leon Trotsky, *The Young Lenin*, trans. Max Eastman (New York: Doubleday & Co., 1972); James Connor, ed., *Lenin on Politics and Revolution* (New York: Pegasus, 1968); and E. Victor Wolfenstein, *The Revolutionary Personality—Lenin, Trotsky, Gandhi* (Princeton, N. J.: Princeton University Press, 1971).

3. Melville J. Herskovits, *Cultural Relativism* (New York: Random House, Vintage Books, 1973), p. 71.

4. David Shub, *Lenin: A Biography* (New York: New American Library, 1948), p. 11.

5. See William A. Williams, *The Great Evasion—An Essay on the Contemporary Relevance of Karl Marx and on the Wisdom of Admitting the Heretic into the Dialogue about America's Future.* (Chicago: Quadrangle Books, 1964). This is a brilliant and much evaded book.

6. Hunt, *Theory and Practice*, p. 30.

7. Ernest Barker, *Principles of Social and Political Theory* (London: Oxford University Press, 1965). Here is an excellent short summary of Hegel's thought and its link to Marxist-Leninism.

8. George H. Sabine, *A History of Political Theory* (New York: Holt, Rinehart & Winston, 1961), Chap. 30.

9. Friedrich Engels and Karl Marx, *German Ideology*, ed. R. Pascal (New York: International Publishers Co., 1939), p. 7.

10. Benedetto Croce, *History of Europe in the Nineteenth Century*, trans., Henry Furst (New York: Harcourt, Brace & World, 1933), p. 37.

11. Edmund Wilson, *To the Finland Station* (Garden City, N. Y.: Doubleday & Co., Anchor Press, 1953), p. 360.

12. Ibid., pp. 362-363.

13. As cited in Shub, *Lenin*, p. 22.

14. Silvan Tomkins, "Left and Right: A Basic Dimension of Ideology and Personality," in *The Study of Lives* (Chicago: Aldine-Atherton, 1971), p. 400.

15. Wilson, *Finland Station*, pp. 372-373.

16. V. I. Lenin, *Collected Works* (New York: International Publishers Co.), Vol. 4, Bk. 2, p. 194.

17. Wilson, *Finland Station*, p. 383.

18. Ibid., p. 396.

19. V. I. Lenin, *What is to be Done?* in *Selected Works* (Moscow: Lenin Institute, 1963-69), Vol. 1, p. 175.

20. Harold Lasswell, *Politics: Who Gets What, When, How* (New York: World Publishing Co.-Meridian Books, 1958), p. 13.

21. Hunt, *Theory and Practice*, Chap. 15.

22. Shub, *Lenin*, p. 62.

23. Ibid., p. 64.

24. Ibid., p. 76.

25. Lenin, *Selected Works*, Vol 2, p. 709.

26. Ibid., p. 209.

27. For the role of reification in international politics see Robert A. Isaak, "The Individual in International Politics: Solving the Level-of-Analysis Problem," *Polity* 7, no. 2 (1974).

28. See Williams, *The Great Evasion* and Louis Hartz, *The Liberal Tradition in America* (New York: Harcourt, Brace & World, 1955).

29. See Robert A. Isaak and Ralph P. Hummel, *Politics for Human Beings* (North Scituate, Mass.: Duxbury Press, 1975). The theory of creation, maintenance and decay is not new. Oswald Spengler, Arnold Toynbee, and Pitirim Sorokin all had similar theories.

30. Thomas Butson and John Van Doorn, "A Bad Review for Solzhenitsyn," *New York Times*, 6 January, 1974.

31. Otto von Hapsburg, "U.S.S.R.: Superpower or Paper Tiger?" *Saturday Evening Post*, July-August, 1973, p. 10.

32. Gyorgy Adam, "Multinational Corporations and the Outlines of a Global Economy," (Paper given at the fourteenth Annual Convention of the International Studies Association, New York, March 14-17, 1973).

33. These statistics are from John Diebold, "Multinational Corporations . . . Why be Scared of Them?" *Foreign Policy* no. 12 (1973): 80.

34. Raymond Vernon, "Apparatchiks and Entrepreneurs: U.S.-Soviet Economic Relations," *Foreign Affairs* 52, no. 2 (January 1974): 249-262.

CHAPTER 3

Charisma, Limited Warfare, and Modernization — Mao

> Political power grows out of the barrel of a gun.
> Our principle is that the Party commands the
> gun, and the gun must never be allowed to
> command the Party. Yet, having guns, we can
> create schools, create cultures, create mass move-
> ments. . . . All things grow out of the barrel of a
> gun.
>
> MAO TSE-TUNG

Mao Tse-tung is a revolutionary hero, a poet of the possible, and the greatest political figure of the second half of the twentieth century. His skill and theories enabled him to recreate China into a great world power from the grass roots up with very limited means. Mao's poems have sold more copies than all English poets put together, and his theories of warfare and modernization have become models for less developed countries throughout the world.

Gandhi symbolized how the careful control of personal needs can be transformed into political power in a nonviolent, religious culture like that of India. Lenin, in contrast, was more concerned with manipulating social facts than with satisfying needs and used dialectical materialism to transform Russia into the world's first communist superpower. Mao mastered the principles of Lenin and adapted them brilliantly to the Chinese situation, demonstrating how effectively the Chinese tradition of concrete pragmatism can be applied to political modernization and strategies of world politics.

I. Mao: A Political Portrait

Origins of Charismatic Leadership

Relating man to world politics raises a fascinating question which Mao Tse-tung helps to answer. How do charismatic leaders emerge in world politics? What combination of human needs and social facts causes one individual to be able to sweep masses of people off their feet?

Mao Tse-tung with his wife Chiang Ch'ing in Yenan, about 1945.
Eastfoto.

a social relationship in which a large number of people attribute great spiritual power to one person whom they come to regard as the solution to their social problems. Political scientist Ralph Hummel has pointed out that charismatic situations usually develop in times of great social crisis and that the trauma of change in social facts perceived by the masses is probably more significant in creating charisma than any particular personality characteristics the leader might possess.[1] Mao did, indeed, grow up in a time of tremendous social crisis in China.

Mao was born in 1893 in the village of Changsha in Hunan province, which is located in the southern half of mainland China. He was the eldest of four children. Although his father had once been a soldier, at the time of Mao's birth he was a peasant rapidly becoming well-to-do as a successful grain merchant. He was a harsh, driving man, putting his eldest son to work at the age of five or six, and their relationship was significant in the development of Mao's rebellious personality. In an interview with journalist Edgar Snow, Mao told the following story about his relationship with his father:

> One incident I especially remember. When I was about thirteen my father invited many guests to his home, and while they were present a dispute arose between the two of us. My father denounced me before the whole group, calling me lazy and useless. This infuriated me. I cursed him and left the house. My mother ran after me and tried to persuade me to return. My father also pursued me, cursing at the same time that he commanded me to come back. I reached the edge of a pond and threatened to jump in if he came nearer.
>
> In this situation demands and counterdemands were presented for cessation of the civil war. My father insisted that I apologize and k'ou-t'ou as a sign of submission. I agreed to give a one-knee k'ou-t'ou if he would promise not to beat me. Thus the war ended, and from it I learned that when I defended my rights by open rebellion my father relented, but when I remained meek and submissive he only cursed and beat me the more.
>
> Reflecting on this, I think that in the end the strictness of my father defeated him. I learned to hate him, and we created a real united front against him.[2]

Mao, like Gandhi and Lenin, began to develop a revolutionary personality as he became increasingly conscious of the tension between his needs and the social facts of his everyday life. Reactionary social facts, represented by one of his teachers and his father, led him to run away from school when he was ten and to openly rebel against his father at thirteen. Significantly, he used military language to describe the tension with his father and demonstrated a knowledge of threats, counterdemands, compromise, the need for open rebellion, and a united front. In the social facts of his family, the political situation was clear-cut. There were two parties: the ruling power, his father, and the opposition, Mao, his mother, a brother, and at times an employee of his father. While his mother always advocated a policy of indirect attacks, the traditional Chinese way, Mao's political successes always depended upon displaying emotions and open rebellion. Indeed Mao's greatest failures later on resulted largely from compliant Chinese people who preferred to give in and follow the traditional Chinese way.[3]

At fifteen, Mao won another battle with his father by deciding to go back to school. He went to the Tungshand Higher Primary School fifteen miles from home. It was an institution full of well-dressed sons of landlords. In contrast, Mao was six years older than most of the students, was roughly dressed, and behaved like the son of a peasant. He was ridiculed for being different, and it is likely that his later antagonism toward the landlord class and his ambivalence toward middle and upper-class intellectuals originated in this experience.[4]

Another reason for tension between father and son was Mao's dislike for farm work. When he came home his father would often send him out to collect manure in a basket. Mao would leave accordingly but find a spot to hide in order to read history and novels, which further disturbed his father who believed that if one read at all, one should read the classics.

As in the case of Gandhi, Mao's mother was extremely religious and refused to kill any living thing. She believed that salvation depended upon charitable deeds like rice offerings to the poor. When he was young, she took Mao regularly to Buddhist ceremonies where he sang Buddhist hymns. Significantly, one of the traditions of Buddhism which undoubtedly influenced Mao's way of thinking was the belief in the need to locate oneself selflessly in the natural situation of the moment, acting spontaneously and concretely for the benefit of the whole community. Contrary to Western opinion, Buddhism is not passive but encourages one to fit naturally into the flow of historical change, not confronting or fighting social facts but listening to them in order to use their movement for one's own needs. To cling to a rigid thought or image is to be in constant conflict with existing reality and must be avoided. In the words of the Zen Buddhist master Yunmen, "In walking, just walk. In sitting, just sit. Above all, don't wobble."[5] While a Westerner might call Mao's later adaptations of Marxist-Leninist ideology opportunism, an Oriental might call it natural wisdom or following the Way. Mao's conscious rejection of Buddhism does not mean that it did not continue subconsciously to color his way of thinking.

Both of Mao's parents supported the Manchu monarchy of the Empress Dowager. However, the traditional regime sat on shaky ground. In the late nineteenth and early twentieth centuries China was weak and open to the exploitation of her resources and markets by Western colonial powers, which could back up their representatives with guns and large navies. In addition to these social facts that frustrated Chinese needs, natural events like famine made social problems even more acute. In 1906 Mao's village of Changsha was struck by a severe famine. Poor, hungry peasants rose in insurrection demanding that the rice granaries be opened. The authorities executed the peasant leaders and punished the rest. "Everything in which Mao believed was now put to the test. His Buddhism, his belief in the monarchical system, his family's comparative wealth based on rice, even his growing delight in learning—all these were assailed by the fact that innocent peasants were executed in broad daylight, officially, with all the sanctions of the monarchy. What could he believe in?"[6] Mao discussed the murders a great deal in the schoolhouse with fellow students. His political consciousness moved from the family arena to society at large.

At that time Mao's reading led him to admire tales of heroes, rebellions, and banditry. He had great respect for Shih Huang-ti, the revolutionary emperor of the Ch'in dynasty who united China, subjugated feudal lords, took land away from the aristocracy, replaced the powerful scholar-officials with military officers, ordered the burning of their books, and built the Great Wall at the cost of thousands of lives. He liked romantic tales of intricate warfare and admired the revolutionary leadership of George Washington and Napoleon.[7] Mao's reading and experience both pointed to the need and desirability for heroic leadership in China.

While at the middle school, Mao's diligence soon brought him to the top of his class. There he met a younger student, Hsiao Chu-chang, who became his close friend, bodyguard, nurse, and constant companion for the next ten years. He was aristocratic, complementing Mao's peasant rough-ness and teaching him something of European culture. Mao was able to read twice or three times as fast as most people and devoured books in order to get at the basic principles of civilization. He was heavily influenced by the views of Lian Ch'i-ch'ao, who advocated the Social-Darwinist, evolution-ary theories of Herbert Spencer. Mao read Spencer's theories in the *Hsin Min Chung Pao, The New Peoples' Journal*, secretly printed in China, which demanded that the new people take the future of China into their own hands and restore strength to their country by upholding the virile spirit of nationalism and dominating other races. Indeed, it was through the ideas of Herbert Spencer and his interpreters, rather than through Karl Marx, that Mao came to believe that the individual must be sacrificed to the state.[8] But at that time he supported constitutional reform on the English model and only later turned to violent revolutionary ideas.

In his reading, Mao constantly wondered why the peasants and their heroes had been so neglected in historical and literary writing. He came to evaluate everything in terms of its energy, liking only those things that demonstrated great energy. His theory was that all such energy came from the sun, and he and a friend were almost arrested for walking around half naked in order to absorb its rays. The Manchu police feared that the two students might start a dangerous cult.

In 1911 Mao and his friend Hsiao San entered a teacher training institute in Changsha. Soon thereafter the revolutionary Hwang Hsing led 130 followers in the fourth *Kuomintang*, or Nationalist party, uprising against the governing Manchu headquarters of Canton. They failed, and many revolutionaries were killed or captured. The general excitement stimulated Mao to begin to write political articles which he posted on the wall under a pseudonym. At that time he also occupied himself in "queue-chopping expeditions," the revolutionary act of cutting off Chinese pigtails, and he claimed to have chopped ten. Mao believed in the importance of willpower and self-discipline, although he maintained slovenly personal habits and complained, "In the educational system of our country, required courses are as thick as the hairs of a cow."[9] He took cold baths and engaged in hard exercise to strengthen his will. "Exercise should be savage and rude. To be able to leap on horseback and to shoot at the same time; to go from battle to battle; to shake the mountain by one's cries, and the colors of the sky by one's roars of anger; to have the strength to uproot mountains like Hsiang Yu and to pierce the mark like Yu Chi—all this is savage and rude and has nothing to do with delicacy."[10]

"The term 'charisma' will be applied to a certain quality of an individual personality by virtue of which he is set apart from ordinary men and treated as endowed with supernatural, superhuman, or at least specifically exceptional powers or qualities. These are...not accessible to the ordinary person, but are regarded as of divine origin or as exemplary, and on the basis of them the individual concerned is treated as a leader," wrote sociologist Max Weber.[11] But to become a charismatic leader it is not enough merely to cultivate exceptional or heroic personal traits. A social crisis is required as well: a breakdown of social facts that stirs a profound need in the masses for a person who represents the cure for their emotional crisis. Social crises are thus transformed into crises in meaning and lead individuals, who fear the ambivalence of such a situation, to project superhuman powers onto a leader who becomes their certainty and their solution.

In 1918 Mao graduated from normal school and was given a job at the library of the Peking University through the introduction of his former professor Yang Ch'ang-chi. The job paid only eight dollars a month, and Mao slept in a room with seven other men. But the parks and palace grounds in Peking were beautiful, and soon Mao met and fell in love with Professor Yang's daughter, Yang K'ai-hui, who later became his first wife. While in Peking Mao also met two professors (Li Ta-chao and Ch'en Tu-hsiu) whose social criticism attracted him strongly and who later were the principal founders of the Chinese Communist party.

In 1919 Mao returned to Changsha. At that time diplomats at the World War I peace negotiations in Versailles were discussing territorial settlements, including the Kiaochow Bay area of the Shantung Province, which the Japanese wanted. When the Council of Ministers at Versailles announced the decision in favor of Japan, thousands of students demonstrated in Peking, beating the Chinese minister to Tokyo, organizing strikes, and boycotting Japanese goods. The government tried to control the situation with arrests, but the May Fourth Movement was too widespread. Some pro-Japanese officials were ousted, and the Chinese refused to sign the Versailles treaty. However, the Japanese still maintained the rights to Shantung. Mao participated in the movement. The experience revealed to him the potential power of students and teachers, as well as the close relationship of foreign affairs and domestic politics. He later used students in a similar fashion in his 1966 Cultural Revolution.

Having signed a separate peace with Germany, Soviet Russia had no hand in the Versailles settlement and became an attractive revolutionary model for frustrated Chinese intellectuals. Moreover, in July 1918, Soviet Foreign Affairs Commissar Chicherin had officially reversed the tsarist policy toward China and claimed no Soviet interest there. During that period the Soviet Union escaped the intense hatred of foreigners which exploitation by the Japanese and European powers had engendered in many Chinese including Mao.

Civil War and Guerrilla Organization

Although the Soviets officially claimed no interests in China, this was just half of a two-fronted policy, as we discussed in the chapter on Lenin. In the early 1920s the Soviet Union was a defeated power, which had just experienced a civil war and was run by an insecure revolutionary regime with many enemies and few friends. Moreover, a chronic headache for all Soviet leaders is the protection of the longest border in the world between Russia and China. Because of their extreme vulnerability and the folly of having enemies on both the European and Asian borders, Soviet leaders were determined to maintain good relations with China. The Soviet elite began its traditional two-pronged policy. Its official diplomatic representatives established good relations with the government in Peking while at the same time its **Comintern** agents promoted a revolution to overthrow that government.

The Chinese Communist party was founded in 1921. Although the Soviets worked to strengthen it, the Comintern was equally interested in the much larger opposition party, the Kuomintang, led by Sun Yat-sen, a well-known, Western-oriented, democratic revolutionary. However, the Soviets were also aware of the weaknesses of the Kuomintang because of its amorphous organization and lack of a strong, efficient military force. Sun Yat-sen was unwilling to listen when the Soviets advised him to establish a military academy, although he did eventually agree that the Communist party and the Kuomintang could cooperate profitably.

In 1919 Mao was back in Hunan and taught school for a short while before dedicating himself totally to Marxism and the life of a professional revolutionary. He became the leader of the Chinese Communist party in Hunan and spent his time launching a trade union movement. His success in such a local political organization helped earn him a place in the national party leadership in 1923, and he went to Shanghai and later to Canton to serve in the largest party headquarters. He often grew restless in the party bureaucracy and city atmosphere and seized any opportunity he had to return to Hunan and to work among the peasants. In Shanghai he worked as a laundryman, but when he returned to Changsha he accepted a position as principal of an elementary school, which enabled him to marry Yang K'ai-hui who bore him the first two of his many children. At that time Mao wrote a report on the tremendous, latent political power among the peasants.

> In a very short time, several hundred million peasants in China's central, southern, and northern provinces will rise like a tornado or tempest—a force so extraordinarily swift and violent that no power, however great, will be able to suppress it. . . . With the fall of the authority of the landlords, the peasant association becomes the sole organ of authority. Whatever nonsense the people from the association talk in the meetings is considered sacred. . . . Supreme in authority, the peasant association allows the landlord no say and sweeps away his prestige. . . . At the slightest provocation they make arrests, crown the arrested with tall paper hats, and parade them through the villages, saying, "You dirty landlords, now you know who we are!" Doing whatever they like and turning everything upside down, they have created a kind of terror in the countryside. . . . A revolution is an insurrection, an act of violence by which one class overthrows another. . . . The rural areas need a mighty revolutionary upsurge, for it alone can rouse the people in their millions to become a powerful force.[12]

In the mid-1920s, China was in the throes of civil war between the government forces of Chiang Kai-shek and the United Front of the Kuomintang and the Communists.* The alliance of the United Front lasted until 1927, and Mao received various posts in it including chief propagandist. Instead of waiting, however, for the inevitable collapse of the alliance, Mao returned to Hunan and staged his first peasant uprisings. The Kuomintang troops repressed the rebellions until Mao was finally forced to flee to the hills in 1927.

In the next three years in the hills, roaming, gathering men, and joining bandits, Mao began to formulate his principles of guerrilla warfare. To gain

*Chiang Kai-shek succeeded Sun Yat-sen as leader of the Kuomintang, or Nationalist party, after Sun's death in 1925. Chiang's party soon came to dominate the republiic.

morale in the rough conditions, the soldiers invented the slogan, "Down with capitalism, eat squash." Chiang's troops attacked and were then lured into ambushes on Mao's home ground. He soon succeeded in establishing Red enclaves within the encirclement of "White" (Nationalist) political power, and he claimed his success was due to two factors: factionalism and wars within Chiang's regime, and a localized peasant economy rather than a unified capitalist economy. In short, the peasants could meet almost all their needs in the countryside, if they were cut off from the city markets, whereas the cities were heavily dependent upon the agriculture of the countryside. Furthermore, the official government resided in the cities leaving a power vacuum to be exploited by the Communists in the countryside. Mao's guerrilla strategy was to mobilize peasants in the countryside against the landlords, to seize and redistribute the land to the peasants, who then had to arm and defend their gains, and to use the armed peasants to expand Communist control by surrounding and attacking cities from the countryside.

Although such a strategy was eventually to allow Mao to conquer all of mainland China, the road was long and full of frustration and failures. For example, Mao proclaimed a soviet republic in 1931 in Kiangsi and became chairman. Actually he shared power with a Soviet-trained group of leaders who believed that his Marxism was weak and his motivation was opportunistic. Many of them disapproved of his strategy of allowing the enemy to infiltrate home territory and then ambushing him at the right moment. They argued that their knowledge of Chiang Kai-shek's secret military plans made it possible for them to attack more conventionally and defend their home ground without infiltration. Furthermore, they believed Mao's inborn peasant mentality encouraged him to be content with filling party positions with backward peasants who would weaken the organization. The Soviet-oriented leaders came to distrust Mao's guerrilla tactics so much that they finally influenced the red elite to change to conventional, positional warfare. However, this new kind of defense failed to withstand the next attack by larger Kuomintang forces; the soviet republic was abandoned; and Mao's strategy was vindicated.

War is not merely a political act, but also a political instrument, a continuation of political relations, carried out by other means, military strategist Karl Von Clausewitz noted in 1832. War is the use of potential or actual force to help resolve the tensions between human needs and social facts. To view war in merely military terms and not in terms of political aims is to mistake means for ends. Military specialist Seymour Deitchman put wars in three basic classes: "(1) Conventional wars: organized, conventional military forces are overtly involved on both sides; (2) Unconventional wars: unconventional military forces in the form of paramilitary,

irregular, or guerrilla forces are involved on one side, and conventional military forces as well as police and civil guards are used on the other side in the attempt to suppress or defeat the former; and (3) Deterred wars: conventional or unconventional military forces face each other in a threat of war, but there is no active armed conflict between the two sides."[13] But hear well the poet John Davidson:

> *"And blood in torrents pour*
> *In vain—always in vain,*
> *For war breeds war again."*

〜〜〜〜〜〜〜〜〜

Like other charismatic leaders in world history, Mao lived totally for his political cause regardless of the costs in his personal life. His wife and sister had already been executed by the Kuomintang governor of Changsha when the Communists had been forced to withdraw, and Mao lost track of his two sons for years thereafter. However, he did not hesitate to satisfy his basic needs in a life of rapid change and was somewhat revolutionary in his relations with women. Two years before his wife was killed he had begun living with a second wife, a pretty comrade named Ho Shih-chen who helped him with his work.

Indeed, in a situation of constant, violent struggle and warfare, Mao did not hesitate to use whatever means were necessary to further his military ends. For example in 1930 some of his followers deserted him, and when he caught up with them he had them liquidated, probably costing the lives of 2,000 to 3,000 men. Moreover, in order to assure the loyalty of his former opponent Ch'en Yi, Mao assigned him the job of executioner, since such a role would make any future collaboration by Ch'en Yi with Mao's enemies impossible. The maneuver demonstrated Mao's characteristic Chinese ability to create one simple strategy that served more than one purpose.

The Long March to Power

After defeat at the hands of the Nationalist Army in October, 1934, Mao led some 90,000 Red Army troops out of the Kiangsi soviet republic westward with women, children, and wounded in tow. This was the beginning of the heroic Long March that finally ended at Yenan. In 368 days the Red Army fought fifteen battles and daily skirmishes, covered 6,000 to 8,000 miles over mountains, through deserts, snow, and swamps. Planes bombarded them almost daily. Of the hundreds of women who began the march thirty survived. Mao had to abandon three of his children to peasants; his brother was killed in the fighting, and his pregnant wife was badly wounded. Mao celebrated the march in a poem.

THE LONG MARCH
October 1935

The Red Army does not fear
the Long March toughness.
Thousands of rivers, hundreds of mountains, easy.
The Five Ridges
merely little ripples.
Immense Wu Meng Mountain—
merely a mound of earth.
Warm are the cloudy cliffs
beaten by Gold Sand River.
Cold are the iron chains
bridging Tatu River.
Joy over Min Mountain,
thousand miles of snow:
when the army crossed,
every face smiled.[14]

Mao and his party have carefully used the Long March and the poem for propaganda purposes. Mao wrote, "Speaking of the Long March, one may ask, 'What is its significance?' We answer that the Long March is the first of its kind in the annals of history, that it is a manifesto, a propaganda force, a seeding-machine." Mao has always been a great propaganda artist; art, for him, always has a political purpose. To the extent that most of his poems are explicitly ideological, they reify abstractions, like Red Army versus White reactionaries, and suffocate individualism, making worse poems for being better propaganda. The contrast between individualism and abstractions was also noted by Macaulay. "In proportion as men know more, they look less at individuals and more at classes. They therefore make better theories and worse poems."

The Long March enabled Mao to gain control of the Communist party, and by 1938 he was determining its policies and translating them into political dogma. In following Lenin's belief that political power grows out of military power, Mao made the army into not merely an effective military force, but a political, economic, cultural, and propaganda force as well. The many functions of the army were designed to promote democracy within the military and in military-civilian relations, unity between officers and men and unity between the army and the people. Mao was very perceptive in noting how the concepts of democracy and equality could be used to obtain internal party cohesion and absolute control. When equality is reified or frozen into an absolute ideological dogma enforced by a small elite, it can become the basis for authoritarian dictatorship.

Values of the Chinese Revolution

In 1933 the Japanese invaded Mongolia. Chiang Kai-shek made concessions to get peace. Many Chinese became increasingly discontent since each act of appeasement seemed to lead to new Japanese aggression, each Kuomintang policy into a temporary armistice, causing Mao to moderate his policies and winning him liberal support. When Japan surrendered, the civil war resumed. During the war, Mao had solidified his position in the party and matured in political tactics. For example, he learned that physically liquidating opponents, as he had done in Kiangsi, was often not the best way of eliminating them and created other problems. "Furthermore," he commented, "the head of a man does not grow like the leek, and once it is cut, another will not come out. If a head is wrongly cut, there would be no way to correct the mistake."[15]

Mao also used the war years at the Communist headquarters in Yenan to do much of his writing and develop social ideas for the future of China. Each person in Yenan was expected not merely to fulfill his major job, but to spend his extra time satisfying other community needs such as raising food, knitting, or running a workshop. To refuse such extra tasks was considered selfish and against the egalitarian creed and moral code. To set an example, Mao cultivated a garden in his spare time.

Experience taught Mao to view all of life as an unremitting struggle toward high, heroic ideals. He came to distrust specialists, preferring the jack-of-all trades. Mao also freed himself from the gentle Ho Shih-chen, who had borne him three children, and took a third wife, a gutsy actress named Li Yün-ho or, professionally, Chiang Ch'ing, who also had a living spouse. Mao's behavior caused a scandal in Yenan, which was viewed as a sacrosanct, religious commune by many idealistic Chinese.

The values of the Chinese communist revolutionary movement—and the Chinese state today—were those of Mao's social theory. For Mao, man had the central role in historical development, but the importance of man lay in his service to his people, the masses, his class, and his peer group. Mao's thought began from a point exactly opposite to that of democratic Western thought or American ideology. Society did not exist to serve the individual; the individual existed to serve society. Mao wrote, "The people, and the people alone, are the motive force in the making of world history."[16] "In class society everyone lives as a member of a particular class."[17] In contrast to Western tradition, man was not seen primarily as an individual, a word Mao usually used in a pejorative sense. The individual had duties but no natural rights. Chinese communist ideology produces what Professor Benjamin Schwartz called "the emphasis on the individual's total self-abnegation and total immersion in the collectivities as ultimate goods."[18] Although the individual did not have the freedom or rights that were given him in Western political thought, society did have total responsibility for the individual and had to merit his respect and service. By transforming himself, the individual also transformed society. The meaning of man in history depended upon the morality of both.[19]

Mao's collective view of man grew naturally out of Eastern tradition, the collectivism of military base camps, and guerrilla warfare. Skillful Communist leadership enabled the Red Army to maintain high collective morale with the use of Maoist ideology and to win the civil war in 1949, proclaiming the establishment of the People's Republic of China. Although impressed, the rest of the world was only beginning to sense the emergence of a new superpower based on the glories of a peasant hero.

Stalin's Model and Chinese Modernization

When a revolution occurs in a traditional society, the first priorities of the ruling elite become security and modernization. Once it comes into power the revolutionary regime is transformed from a creative to a maintenance force. Yet to maintain its legitimacy and integrity, leaders of the revolutionary movement must sustain an image of revolutionary creativity, and modernize traditional institutions to satisfy the needs of the people and strengthen national security. Modernization, in short, is the transformation of a traditional society into a more efficient and productive organization of economic, political, and social institutions. When Mao came into power he wanted to secure his position and simultaneously make China into a model communist society for the world. The immediate goal of modernization is to increase the range of options or choices of the governing elite.

Modernization is often perceived as Westernization because it is a process in which existing social facts are rationalized and bureaucratized to control and order national energies toward more efficient production and the development of modern, technological forms of organization.[20] The thrust of Western thought and development in our era has been toward man's control and manipulation of nature for his material ends. Traditional Eastern thought has accented man's acceptance of his place in nature and the universe in order to become a part of the whole rather than to try to steer it. The East-West tension reveals itself explicitly in the later stages of modernization in traditional Eastern cultures and explains, to a great extent, the particular character of Mao's modernization policies in China.

Modernization is the attempt to increase the range of choice and the standard of living of a people by making a traditional society more productive through reorganization of its economic, political and social institutions. To do so, elites often use Western and Northern concepts of technological efficiency and self-determination to replace Eastern and Southern aesthetic and philosophical values. For example, nature is to be manipulated and controlled not loved and accepted; citizens are urged to

live to work, not to work to live. Traditional social relationships created to satisfy human needs are rationalized, institutionalized, and bureaucratized to maintain a modern image of technological society. Sidewalk cafés are out; red tape and production targets are in. As political sociologist Kalman Silvert noted: "The essential measure of political modernization is the degree to which ritualistic decisions cede to rational determinations in political choice-making."[21]

Initially, Mao was concerned with gaining increased control over his new revolutionary state, and between 1949 and 1956 he relied heavily upon Western methods, particularly Joseph Stalin's adaptation of Marxist-Leninism to a nationalistic model for modernization in Russia. Indeed, the entire policy process in China to this day has largely revolved around Mao's attempts to enlarge his range of options and enforce his commands, while his subordinates have often attempted to narrow his options and directives in a manner more favorable to them.[22] The more Mao succeeded in controlling and modernizing Chinese economic and military organization by Western methods, the more concerned he became that Chinese development maintain a distinctive Eastern and Chinese character to distinguish it clearly from Western societies, including the Soviet Union.

The Soviet method of modernization emerged in 1925 after Lenin's death when Stalin announced his policy of socialism in one country. Marx had believed that communist revolutions must occur almost simultaneously in several industrial countries, which would then form an allied socialist league to prevent the restoration of capitalism. Stalin revised the theory. He argued that the Soviet Union had to build up its economic and military power so it could stand alone and become the fortress for future world revolution. He used all authoritarian means in his possession to brutally crush his opponents like Leon Trotsky, who believed in the doctrine of simultaneous world revolution. Furthermore, Stalin argued that in this period of rapid national modernization, the Soviet Union must live in peaceful coexistence with Western countries, avoiding war and seeking trade until the Soviet Union had the time to become a great military-industrial power. Initially, Mao adopted both of Stalin's policies as the basis for Chinese modernization.

However, the full Stalinist model involved not only the nationalization of the means of production and the collectivization of agriculture but the total subordination of the agricultural sector of the economy to the rapid development of heavy industry. The Chinese were unwilling to go this far. They were aware that in heavily populated, rural China, agricultural production must be increased and not allowed to stagnate as it had in the Soviet Union. Furthermore, Mao believed that his close relationship with the peasants would allow him to modernize Chinese agriculture through **collectivism** more effectively than the Soviets had been able to.

When he first read literature on Soviet development at Yenan in the 1940s, Mao was convinced that Stalin's model was universally applicable, although he was more impressed with his economic than his military or political policies. It is not surprising, therefore, that during the Soviet oriented period in China following the revolution a campaign was launched for all cadres to study Stalin's *Short Course* as a guide to economic development. Mao was particularly impressed by the Soviet politicization of the economy. However, tensions between the Chinese and Soviet working styles began to surface in the early 1950s. The tensions came to a head in the 1956 Hundred Flowers Campaign when Mao began seriously to question the applicability of the Soviet model to China's vast, rural population, threatened by famine. At that time Mao reemphasized the importance of agriculture and light industry without abandoning the policy of heavy industry as the core of Chinese modernization. When it became apparent that collectivization alone would not solve the problems of Chinese agriculture, Mao initiated the Great Leap Forward. The Great Leap Forward "in many ways marks the triumph of the Maoist approach over Soviet modes."[23] Mao realized that the Yenan maxims, which worked when applied to tasks of revolution, would also work for the tasks of modernization. He did not break entirely with the Stalinist emphasis on investing in the heavy-industrial sector of the economy, but rather concentrated on organizing human energy for the agricultural and light-industrial sectors without diverting material capital from heavy industry. Mao's faith was based on men more than machines.

According to Mao's new policy industry must emphasize agriculture until the agricultural foundation of the Chinese economy became steady policy. More attention was paid to producing fertilizer, improving seeds, developing irrigation and farm equipment. The Chinese became used to slower growth in heavy industry with the exception of development vital for national security.

One significant policy conflict that emerged among the Chinese elite was Mao's strong opposition to the tendency toward capitalism that developed among some of the small producers as agriculture became the focus. His opponents argued that material incentives were necessary, and such arguments probably resulted in the initiation of the recent stress on private plots and free markets. Mao has consistently urged that the primary element of Chinese modernization be an emphasis on the internalization of communist values through socialist education and moral injections of public spirit. He even sacrificed economic progress and used students politically to spread his educational and moral creed in the Cultural Revolution of 1966.

The most distinctive contrast between Mao's model of Chinese modernization and that of the Soviet Union beginning with Stalin is the Chinese focus on the rural village as opposed to the Soviet concentration on urban areas. Mao's cultural indoctrination began by breaking down family

Mao (right), Lin Piao, Chou En-lai, and Chiang Ch'ing, wearing Red
Guard armbands, address a Peking rally in 1966. *Eastfoto.*

ties and transferring loyalties to the village community and Maoist
ideology, relying heavily upon the peasants and students as a basis for his
reforms. The Soviets, on the other hand, have focused upon the urban
proletariat as the traditional basis for revolutionary change and reform,
accepting the Western image of modernization through large cities. Idealists
have argued that the Chinese model is more attractive because it is less
technological, centralized, and dehumanizing. However, Mao and other
Chinese leaders have far from rejected technology as a tool, and stress the
human element and rural life as much out of the necessity of social
facts—China's large population concentrated in rural areas—as out of
philosophical belief. Indeed, if modernization is defined to mean opening
more options for the masses of the population, it could be argued that the
Chinese model is less modern because it restricts people to the countryside
where they are more easily controlled by the state and where their individual
options may well be more limited. Nevertheless, for developing countries
with large rural populations, the Chinese model is apt to be much more
applicable and influential than the heavy-industrial thrust of the Soviet
pattern, even though industrialization is perhaps the key indicator of the
modernization process.

Mao's Strategy of World Politics

Mao's strategy of world politics is based upon the traditional Chinese cultural image of the world, Marxist-Leninist ideology and methods, his own notions of guerrilla warfare, and his belief in Chinese modernization as a universal model. The traditional view of old Chinese culture places China and its emperor or leader at the center of the universe. All other states surrounding it are subordinate in its hierarchy of values and must pay tribute to the superior Chinese empire. Even as late as the nineteenth century, Western diplomats were forced to kowtow to be admitted to the Chinese courts, and all people from the West were viewed as barbarians by many cultivated Chinese. Therefore, it is not surprising to find that Mao has been able to create his own "empire" in China with himself worshipped at its center, autocratically controlling the people. It is a cultural ideology that implies China's continued superiority over all other existing nation-states. Mao is the sun in a dark political world.

From the West, Mao not only derived a respect for democracy and science, but has relied very heavily upon his adaptation of the ideas of Marx and Lenin to the unique Chinese situation. His fascination with the power of individual men and heroes to change the world through political and military action led him naturally to the Marxist-Leninist notion that theory which does not lead to concrete social change is empty air. Moreover, Lenin's idea of nationalism as a political tool and his theories of imperialism and capitalist exploitation became key elements in Chinese Communist explanations of the great exploitation of China by the West in the nineteenth and twentieth centuries. The corrupt international system dominated by decadent Western powers would now be forced to grant the new China her due.

As Mao began to perceive the differences in the Chinese and Soviet situations, however, he took the ideas of Marx, Lenin, and Stalin only as far as they helped him to accomplish his political objectives. From that point he created revolutionary and modernization strategies of his own. Politically, such thinking led to the official Sino-Soviet split and to the remarkably subversive Chinese Communist doctrine, which claimed that the decisions of any national party, including their own, were binding only within the area of that party's jurisdiction. Mao has effectively used this doctrine to undermine the Soviet Union's heavy-handed relationship with its satellite subordinates in Eastern Europe. No wonder the Soviet leaders are so worried about Chinese foreign policy and the replacement of the Soviet model for world communism by Mao's vision! Mao believes that the center of communist authority has clearly shifted from Moscow to Peking. Mao's Way would become the Way.

Mao's revolutionary strategy in domestic politics flows naturally into his international revolutionary strategy. Indeed, to Mao the analytic categories relevant to domestic and international politics are identical.[24]

Accordingly, the Chinese overthrow of the Kuomintang government by revolution was also seen by Communist Chinese leaders as a fight against the lackeys of Western imperialism, particularly American imperialism late in the struggle.

In 1946 Mao proclaimed four theses on international situations which still guide communist Chinese world strategy to a great extent. The first predicts that in the near future all-out war between the United States and the Soviet Union is unlikely. The second is the concept of the intermediate zone, which says that the struggles of the immediate future between socialists and imperialists will take place in the vast zone separating the Soviet Union and the United States. The third describes the atomic bomb as a paper tiger since "the outcome of a war is decided by the people, not by one or two new types of weapons," and the fourth says that all reactionaries, including American reactionaries, are paper tigers. "In appearance, the reactionaries are terrifying, but in reality they are not so powerful from the long-term point of view."[25] Since these theses imply that military confrontations are apt to be conventional rather than nuclear, Mao's revolutionary guerrilla tactics become almost universally applicable. Thus, in defeating General MacArthur in the Korean War, the Chinese forces followed Mao's strategy of retreating into one's own base area, waiting for the enemy to make mistakes, and then fighting a surprise battle of quick decision as a prelude to a general counteroffensive. The Viet Minh applied similar Maoist guerrilla tactics to win surprising victories in Vietnam, despite overwhelming enemy superiority in materiel. Yet few Americans understand to what extent the disastrous American defeat in the Vietnam War was due to the subtle, international revolutionary ideas of Mao. Moreover, documents emerging from the Sino-Soviet dispute demonstrate that Mao's long-term, global strategy against the West is to encircle the developed areas from the underdeveloped areas. That strategy is an extension abroad of the domestic strategy of surrounding the cities from the countryside, which he used so effectively in the long Chinese civil war.[26]

II. Principles of World Politics

The Cycle of Social Development

Social relationships are created initially to satisfy human needs. As the relationships become daily routines, they are maintained as existing social facts and are rationalized, institutionalized, and bureaucratized. As social relationships age into social facts and institutions become increasingly unresponsive to the original needs they were created to satisfy, decay sets in. Old social facts break apart, revolutions throw them over, and new relationships are created in their stead. All phases of social development go through recurring cycles of creation, maintenance and decay from the simplest love and business relationships to the complex relations of governments, nations, and empires.[27]

Ancient Chinese society was originally created to solve human needs. With time those social bonds became institutionalized. They were maintained with the forms and rituals of an empire. Finally in the eighteenth and nineteenth centuries, the empire decayed, lost its legitimacy, and was infiltrated and exploited by foreigners. The result was the Chinese Revolution of 1949, where Mao's movement turned over the old social facts—existing values, personalities, social and political institutions, and rules of the game—and replaced them with new social relationships designed to solve the needs of all the people. The cycle began again.

Modernization and Charisma

In the creation, maintenance, and decay cycles of social development, at least three distinct phases of **modernization** can be identified: the traditional, the legal-rational, and the technological. Modernization aims to increase the range of choice and standard of living of a people by transforming a traditional society into a more efficient and productive organization of economic, political, and social institutions.

The routines and traditions that grow up around an institutionalized society after its initial period of creation characterize its traditional phase. **Traditional societies** tend to be based on affective or pre-rational community relationships, diffuse role structures, and ascriptive notions of social and political authority. In other words, in a traditional society I will be acutely aware of my emotional ties to my family and community; I am likely to perform a great number of roles without specializing very much in any one; and my authority or prestige is more apt to depend upon whether I come from the royal family than whether I am competent at particular tasks. Traditional societies are most useful for satisfying my lower-level physiological, security, and love needs. They are unlikely to satisfy my self-actualization needs unless I happen to be one of the royal family. However, should a foreign visitor from a more highly developed society drop in on mine, I may become aware of things I don't have. Knowledge from outsiders makes one politically conscious of needs that one's own culture fails to satisfy.

If enough people in a traditional society become aware that their needs are being unnecessarily frustrated by existing social facts, a social crisis is likely to result. Such crises can lead to a flow of political authority away from traditional roles, such as a witch doctor or a king, toward a charismatic leader like Mao. The leader must be a strong figure with personal characteristics that make him seem to be an ideal solution or alternative to the social crisis of the time. As we saw earlier in the chapter the need for charisma arises when external events of social crisis are seen to undermine the basic existing values of individual world-views in the society. Social crises are thus transformed into crises in meaning leading individuals who fear the ambivalence of such situations to project superhuman powers onto a leader who symbolizes certainty and a solution to their problems.[28] Just so did Mao's Way replace the traditional Chinese way and become *the way* in China. In historical periods of crisis and change in a traditional society a charismatic leader can bring about the transitional phase to a more modern, legal-rational society, given the right domestic and international conditions. Mao seized the theories of Marx and Lenin and Stalin's model of modernization and applied them flexibly to Chinese conditions when the time was ripe.

In moving from a period of creation to a period of maintenance, traditional societies can retain the traditional mode of authority by maintaining the old social facts, or they can change into a **legal-rational society**. A legal-rational society is characterized by contractual community relations with specific role structures and achievement-oriented modes of social and political authority. In human terms, in a legal-rational type of society I could expect to be prepared for a specialized role or profession, to be less emotional about social relationships, seeing them as convenient legal contracts, and to be recognized as a man of social prestige or political authority based on proven skills or achievements rather than mere royal blood ties. Naturally, such legal-rational societies often retain some of their traditional aspects, since there are no pure traditional, legal-rational or technological societies in the world. Each is what sociologist Max Weber called an ideal type, or abstract theoretical construct, that represents or typifies a certain kind of social reality. Nevertheless, in legal-rational societies I can expect authority and leadership to be based upon achievement and skill.

A fuller range of opportunities for the average citizen to satisfy his basic needs is more likely to exist in a legal-rational than in a traditional society, since social mobility is based more on competent achievement than the ascriptive authority of blood relationships. My specialized role is apt to provide me with opportunity for self-esteem, and achievement in this role and in society can open the door of opportunity to more self-fulfilling roles, where personal self-actualization in a general sense becomes possible.

Civilized traditional societies have three traits that distinguish them from even more primitive social forms: (1) a centralized ruling power or state organization; (2) the division of society by classes rather than by kinship status; and (3) the prevalence of a central world-view to legitimate political power thereby converting power into authority. Civilizations are established on the basis of a relatively developed technology and of division of labor, which make possible a surplus product, or a quantity of goods exceeding that needed for the satisfaction of immediate and elementary needs.[29] Civilized traditional societies maintain those traits as long as they contain the development of **subsystems** of **purposive-rational** action. That is, such traditional societies become modern societies when their cultural norms of legitimacy are undermined and overwhelmed by the forces of rationalization. Such forces are represented by new bureaucratic reorganizations in legal-rational societies and by the dominance of applied scientific technology in the **technological societies**. As traditional societies become more rationalized they become legal-rational societies; as legal-rational societies become more technologized they become technological societies. The critical difference between traditional and modern societies is that in modern societies the amount of technologically exploitable knowledge becomes so great that traditional cultural norms of social cooperation are undermined. Traditions are overthrown by scientific techniques used for purposive-rational action. Monarchs are replaced by technological maintenance men. Personalities become roles. Socialization becomes conditioning. Man as a traditionally cultured being becomes overwhelmed and dominated by the so-called apolitics of scientific technique and expertise. Indeed, the most modern ideology becomes apolitics itself, or the belief that all social problems should be handed over to technological experts rather than left up to commonsense solutions of everyday people who seek to satisfy their own needs.

Ultimately, then, the modern society is an ideological society based on the ideology of rational, scientific technique. In such a society, I can expect to have few deep friendships but many detached comradeships based upon levels of skill or technological consciousness. Modern technological societies consume the individual's whole psychic being and demand that his personal self-determination or freedom be consistent with the technological elite's social vision and priorities. In such societies man is taught to believe he is free but finds himself everywhere in technological chains. The transition from traditional to modern legal-rational or technological societies occurs when the norms of the old society begin to break down. At such times of social crisis, charismatic leaders often symbolize the way to a new social order using a new ideology as a political tool.

Mao's personality, interests, and experiences as a youth all served as preconditions for his charismatic appeal and call for a modern, ideological society. He loved romantic tales of heroic leaders and bandits; he became totally dedicated to a Marxist-Leninist vision of China; he developed revolutionary theories of military force that enabled him to seize power in the civil war, and he used Stalin's model of modernization, mixed with his own Yenan principles, to create a solution to China's social problems. Mao's way of modernization has become a model for less developed countries the world over.

National Power and Ecological Limits

Just as the particular social facts of Mao's personal background provided the basis and limits for his potential political power in the future, the potential power of all nation-states depends upon existing social facts and ecological limits. All national plans for modernization, military strategy, and foreign policy depend upon the following ecological conditions:

1. *Geography* (location, size, and nature of land mass).
2. *Untapped Resources* (material resources plus the existence or absence of outstanding mental and cultural qualities in the population).
3. *Population* (present size, growth rate, ethnic homogeneity, or heterogeneity).
4. *Tapped Resources* (degree of industrialization and agricultural modernization, size of gross national product).
5. *Actual Military Power* (number and quality of existing armies, navies, weapons, quality of weapons, research, and technology, etc.).
6. *Potential Military Power* (realistic estimate of future possibilities, such as developing nuclear weapons and delivery systems—determined by conditions 1-5).
7. *Domestic Stability and National Morale* (presence or absence of polarization, alienation, will to fight, civil war, value consensus, etc.).
8. *Literacy and Educational Level of Population.*
9. *Degree of Government Organization and Efficiency* (organizational structure, mobilization ability, socialization and elite recruitment patterns, bureaucratic tradition, institutional flexibility, etc.).
10. *Quality of Political and Military Leadership* (presence or absence of charismatic or outstanding leaders and diplomats plus average leadership education and ability in both political and military hierarchies).
11. *Equal or Great Power Support, Neutrality or Animosity* (allies, potential enemies, great power allegiances and commitments of any power equal to or greater than the nation in question—especially those next door).

These eleven ecological conditions determine the potential national power and decision making of the elite of any nation-state. Take the example of China at the time of the 1949 Communist Revolution. Mao was confronted with an incredibly large Asian land mass (geography) that was basically agricultural and not industrialized (untapped resources). China had the largest single group of people in the world (population), who survived off the food of the land as peasants in rural areas (tapped resources). The unstable situation of civil war (domestic stability) had split the population and its existing military forces (actual military power), making it advantageous for a charismatic leader (political and military leadership) to use an attractive ideology to call for a new national movement (national morale). Through highly efficient party organization (government organization and efficiency) he appealed to the masses (literacy and educational level of the population). Furthermore, Mao was able to focus guerrilla warfare (potential military power) upon domestic enemies, since the great power next door, the Soviet Union, was preoccupied with problems at home and with her European border (great power support and neutrality). By perceptively exploiting these national ecological conditions, Mao took brilliant risks and made unbelieveable gains on the basis of relatively little material support.

Strategies of Conflict and Limited Warfare

While political strategy refers to the exploitation of potential power, military strategy is concerned with the exploitation of potential force. Both play with theories based on existing ecological conditions and social facts. For many strategists, such as Mao Tse-tung, the proof of a military strategy is in the resulting political pudding. Mao viewed the army, the party, and the united front as the three essential elements of the Chinese Revolution. Military strategies for him were only justifiable in terms of their political consequences.

Mao's military strategies and his principles of limited, protracted war derived largely from the ecological and political conditions of pre-revolutionary China. Mao identified the following conditions that distinguished China from other countries. As a colonial, semicolonial and semifeudal country, China was oppressed domestically by feudal forces and externally by imperialist countries. China's territory was vast with a huge, largely peasant, population and great potential military power. Domestic and foreign reactionaries were identified with counterrevolutionary military strategies. As a developing country, China was weaker than her potential foreign opponents due to uneven political, economic, and military development. Yet China was now beginning a progressive phase, represented by the Communist party and Red Army. From these conditions Mao concluded that the Chinese revolution would involve a long, protracted military struggle; that the revolutionary party and army would have to retreat to the countryside and form bases there, depending on rural populations and food supplies; and that peasant guerrilla warfare would be the basic form of armed struggle. As a revolutionary force with limited material resources in a vastly populated area, Mao perceptively relied upon people in the countryside as his main source of strength, always referring to the heroic human element as being more important than mere weapons or machines. Mao's focus on the countryside was due to China's concentration of population there and his observation that the reactionary power of imperialism and feudalism was centered in the cities. To win this protracted war Mao was convinced it was necessary to begin with bases in the countryside and to consolidate and expand the Red regime until it surrounded the cities from the rural areas and choked the enemy to death.

According to Mao, a protracted war that is limited by revolutionary political aims goes through three phases: strategic defensive, strategic stalemate, and strategic counteroffensive. Since the revolutionaries are weak in the beginning, they must often retreat to protect themselves. In the second phase stalemate occurs as the revolutionaries become stronger and the enemy weaker. In the last phase, the revolutionaries finally become militarily superior to the reactionaries and initiate the decisive offensive. Mao summed up his theory of limited war in his famous formula: "The enemy advances, we retreat; the enemy tires, we attack; the enemy camps, we harass; the enemy tires, we attack; the enemy retreats, we pursue."[30]

In a colonial and semicolonial country where the revolutionary forces are weak, guerrilla warfare is the most appropriate kind of armed force. Such warfare considers time to be more important than space, and the preservation and slow increase of one's own force to be more vital than capturing and holding cities. The object is more to harass the enemy and wear it down slowly than to destroy it immediately. Guerrilla warfare breaks up the enemy's lines of communication, disperses its forces and undermines it morale. As the enemy weakens the revolutionary force slowly replaces its guerrilla strategies with more conventional warfare, which is appropriate when one's own force is equal to, or stronger than, the enemy force. Mao put it in a nutshell: "A Single Spark Can Start a Prairie Fire."

III. Present Implications

Conflict: From East-West to North-South

Perhaps the most important shift of political tensions that has occurred in the late twentieth century is the movement of the lines of conflict from East-West to North-South. After World War II world politics was dominated by the cold war between the "Eastern" communist countries, such as the Soviet Union, the People's Republic of China, and Eastern Europe, and the "Western" capitalist countries like the United States, Western Europe, and Japan. The strategies of Mao Tse-tung were influential in shifting this East-West axis of conflict to a North-South axis: the rich, industrialized nations of the northern hemisphere versus the poor, less developed, rural nations of the southern hemisphere.

During China's period of Stalinist modernization in the 1950s, both China and the Soviet Union were lumped together by Western strategists on the same side of world communist conspiracy. However, Mao's modernization plans began to go beyond the Soviet model and to become more distinctively Chinese and Maoist. The Soviet elite perceived the threat of another, non-Soviet model for national communist development. The long Chinese-Soviet geographical border compounded the ideological threat with a military threat, as China developed a more efficient military force and nuclear weapons. The result was the profoundly important Sino-Soviet split.

In moving away from the Soviet Union politically, the Chinese Communist elite extended Mao's theory of protracted war to the whole world as a way of encircling the rich, capitalist, urban-oriented countries of the northern hemisphere with the poor, socialist, rural-oriented countries of the southern hemisphere. The Chinese strategic doctrine was proclaimed in Mao's name by Defense Minister Lin Piao in 1965 on the occasion of the twentieth anniversary of the defeat of Japan.

> Taking the entire globe, if North America and Western Europe can be called "the cities of the world," then Asia, Africa and Latin America constitute "the rural areas of the world." Since World War II, the proletarian revolutionary movement has for various reasons been temporarily held back in the North America and West European capitalist countries, while the people's revolutionary movement in Asia, Africa and Latin America has been growing vigorously. In a sense, the contemporary world revolution also presents a picture of the encirclement of cities by the rural areas. In the final analysis, the whole cause of world revolution hinges on the revolutionary struggles of the Asian, African and Latin American peoples who make up the overwhelming majority of the world's population.[31]

Mao's perceptive strategy of North-South conflict, with China as the leader of southern revolution, allowed China to develop toward becoming a superpower while simultaneously gaining political support from fellow, less developed, rural states, who were caught in a tragic world situation in which the rich get richer and the poor poorer. In short, Mao's strategy enabled China to maintain a revolutionary, underdeveloped image while becoming a dominant, successful great power in the status quo. Mao brilliantly manipulated social facts to satisfy the needs of Chinese modernization.

China's Choices

However, all strategies of modernization eventually become caught in the inevitable creation, maintenance, and decay cycle of social development. Mao's creative, revolutionary state has now entered a period of maintenance, in which revolutionary political ideas come in conflict with technocratic and bureaucratic economic and military elites. In the late 1960s and early 1970s Mao has come into constant conflict with budding maintenance men, especially those who would like to replace him when he is gone. The Cultural Revolution in the sixties was largely an attempt by Mao to revitalize China's revolutionary political culture regardless of temporary losses in economic growth and military power. In the early seventies the decline and fall of Mao's intended successor, Lin Piao, can be explained by

Mao's fear of increasing military power and the need to soften the "Mao deification" propaganda, which Lin Piao represented, in order to preserve China's revolutionary essence after Mao's death.[32] Mao believes that China must represent permanent revolution and that economic or military bureaucracies, or undue worship of one charismatic figure, will suffocate that revolutionary aim. How long after Mao's death the Chinese elite will follow Mao's policy of permanent revolution and the simultaneous attempt to maintain Chinese Communist party power at home and abroad remains to be seen.

Another fact that has pushed China further toward being a normal maintenance society and superpower with stakes in the status quo is the Kissinger era of American foreign policy. The successful Nixon-Kissinger policy of opening American ties with China in order to bring her into the family of nations with a stake in the preservation of the existing status quo has given the Chinese great political gains in world status, in the short run, but raised many foreign policy problems for them in the long run. For how can a revolutionary, less developed ally of the poor Third World countries of the south keep a credible image of southern revolutionary leadership while simultaneously making secret and public deals with the most powerful, reactionary nation of the industrial, capitalistic north? In short, the diplomatic moves of Secretary of State Henry Kissinger have put Mao and his colleagues in an uncomfortable position. Should they officially join the other two superpowers and as a member of the world elite run the world and share in its spoils, or should they withdraw and become the unquestioned leaders of the Third World countries of the south? Although Chinese leaders will undoubtedly try to have their cake and eat it too, their strategy is clear. The Chinese will not hesitate to sacrifice their original, creative, revolutionary ideology and allies in order to further their maintenance and modernization aims at home in economic, military and technological areas. Although he still has incredible, revolutionary vigor, Mao may indeed have become an institution: a monument to an ideology and to a former member country of "the old South."

Mao's ideological rhetoric of revolution from the countryside as opposed to revolution from the city should be seen more as a direction in foreign policy than a fixed blueprint of future action. More pertinent for Third World countries seeking a revolutionary principle is Mao's demonstration that a determined, popular movement and guerrilla force can defeat the best equipped Western armies. His idea that the "mass line," or putting the right idea in the minds of the people, is more effective than atomic bombs contributes an important political thought that is likely to affect future world relations for years. It could be especially meaningful for leaders of economically backward states, who now see a way of becoming powerful without sophisticated weapons or technology. Despite economic weaknesses, Mao's system has enabled his country to become a potential superpower by using the political effectiveness of united masses to make up for economic deficiencies both at home and abroad. Moreover, at such a stage of development, Mao is conscious of the need to avoid an all-out Western style of modernization, which might well lead to foreign dependence and domination. Maoism has, in short, become a model for economically and militarily backward nations who see in this ideology and example a way to make people as important as material in building up national power both domestically and internationally.

Notes

1. See Ralph P. Hummel, *Charisma in Politics: Psycho-Social Causes of Revolutions as Pre-Conditions of Charismatic Outbreaks within the Framework of Weber's Epistemology;* Ph.D. dissertation (Ann Arbor, Mich.: University Microfilms, 1973); Robet A. Isaak and Ralph P. Hummel, *Politics for Human Beings* (North Scituate, Mass.: Duxbury Press, 1975).

2. Edgar Snow, *Red Star Over China* (New York: Random House, 1944), p. 125. This interview took place in 1936. Other major sources for the portrait of Mao, but which are not referred to in specific notes, include: Edgar Snow, *Red China Today,* 1971 edition (New York: Random House, 1971); and Mostafa Rejai, ed., *Mao Tse-tung on Revolution and War* (Garden City, N. Y.: Doubleday & Co., Anchor Press, 1970).

3. Edward Rice, *Mao's Way* (Berkeley & Los Angeles, Calif.: University of California Press, 1972), pp. 4-5.

4. Siao-Yu, *Mao Tse-tung and I were Beggers* (Syracuse, N.Y.: Syracuse University Press, 1959), pp. 6-8.

5. For a lucid introduction to the history and principles of Zen Buddhism see Alan Watts, *The Way of Zen* (New York: Random House, Vintage Books, 1965).

6. Robert Payne, *Mao Tse-tung,* 3rd ed. rev. (New York: Weybright & Talley, 1969), p. 30.

7. Mao was particularly impressed by a book called *Great Heroes of the World,* which describes the lives of Peter the Great, Wellington, Washington, Lincoln, Rousseau, Montesquieu, Catherine the Great, Gladstone, and Napoleon. See Payne, *Mao Tse-tung,* p. 36.

8. Payne, *Mao Tse-tung,* p. 40.

9. Siao-Yu, *Mao Tse-tung and I,* pp. 68-69; Stuart Schram, *Political Thought of Mao Tse-tung* (New York: Praeger Publishers, 1967), p. 154.

10. Schram, *Political Thought,* p. 160.

11. Max Weber, *Economy and Society,* 4th ed., eds. Guenther Roth and Claus Wittich (New York, Bedminster Press, 1968), Vol. 1, p. 241.

12. Mao Tse-tung, *Selected Works of Mao Tse-tung* (Peking: Foreign Language Press, 1961-1965), Vol. 1, pp. 23-24.

13. Seymour Deitchman, *Limited War and American Defense Policy: Building and Using Military Power in a World at War* (Cambridge, Mass.: M.I.T. Press, 1969), p. 18.

14. Mao Tse-tung, *Poems of Mao Tse-tung,* trans. Hua-Ling Nieh Engle and Paul Engle (New York: Dell Publishing Co., 1972), p. 70.

15. Rice, *Mao's Way,* p. 100.

16. Mao, *Selected Works,* Vol. 3, p. 257.

17. Ibid., Vol. 1, p. 296.

18. Benjamin Schwartz, "Modernization and the Maoist Vision," *China Quarterly* no. 21 (1965): 11.

19. Tang Tsou, "The Values of the Chinese Revolution," in Michel Oksenberg, ed., *China's Developmental Experience* (New York: Praeger Publishers, 1973), pp. 27-41.

20. The concepts of "rationalization" and "bureaucratization," as well as the "traditional," "legal-rational," and "charismatic" types of authority referred to later, are those of Max Weber. See Weber, *Economy and Society*.

21. Kalman H. Silvert, *Man's Power* (New York: Viking Press, 1970), p. xxiv.

22. Michel Oksenberg, "Policy Making under Mao Tse-tung, 1949-1968," *Comparative Politics* 3, no. 3 (April 1971): 323-360.

23. Benjamin Schwartz, "China's Developmental Experience 1949-72," in Michel Oksenberg, ed., *China's Developmental Experience* (New York: Praeger Publishers, 1973), p. 22.

24. See Andrew C. Janos, "The Communist Theory of the State and Revolution," in Cyril E. Black and Thomas P. Thornton, eds., *Communism and Revolution* (Princeton, N. J.: Princeton University Press, 1964), pp. 32-36.

25. Mao Tse-tung, "Talk with American Correspondent Anna Louise Strong," in *Selected Works*, Vol. 4, pp. 97-101. Also see Mortin Halperin and Tang Tsou, "Mao Tse-tung's Revolutionary Strategy and Peking's International Behavior," mimeographed (Cambridge, Mass.: East Asian Research Center, Harvard University, 1967).

26. Tang Tsou, "Mao Tse-tung and Peaceful Coexistence," *Orbis*, Spring (1964): 36-51.

27. For a detailed description of this cycle of social relationships at all levels of community see Robert A. Isaak and Ralph P. Hummel, *Politics for Human Beings* (North Scituate, Mass.: Duxbury Press, 1975).

28. Ralph P. Hummel, "Freud's Totem Theory as Complement to Max Weber's Theory of Charisma," *Psychological Reports* 35 (October 1974): 683-686.

29. Gerhard E. Lenski, *Power and Privilege: A Theory of Social Stratification* (New York: McGraw-Hill, 1966).

30. Mao Tse-tung, "A Single Spark Can Start a Prairie Fire," in *Selected Works*, Vol. 1, p. 124.

31. Lin Piao, *Long Live the Victory in People's War* (Peking: Foreign Language Press, 1965), pp. 47-49.

32. Joseph Lelyveld, "The Ghost of Lin Piao," *New York Times Magazine*, 17 January 1974.

PART THREE

Total Peace
and Total War

One day when I went out to my wood-pile, or rather my pile of stumps, I observed two large ants, the one red, the other much larger, nearly half an inch long, and black, fiercely contending with one another. . . . Looking farther, I was surprised to find that the chips were covered with such combatants, that it was not a *duellum*, but a *bellum*, a war between two races of ants, the red always pitted against the black, and frequently two red ones to one black . . . the red republicans on the one hand, and the black imperialists on the other. . . . I should not have wondered by this time to find that they had their respective musical bands stationed on some eminent chip, and playing their national airs the while, to excite the slow and cheer the dying combatants. I was myself excited somewhat even as if they had been men. . . .

HENRY DAVID THOREAU
Walden

After observing how human needs and personality formation contribute to the creation of ideologies, revolutionary movements, nation building and strategies of modernization (Part Two), the study of world politics naturally progresses to questions of peace and conflict between nation-states once formed. Part Three examines the history and nature of the nation-state system and the effects of World War I and World War II upon that system in terms of the experiences of Woodrow Wilson and Adolf Hitler. The focus is upon the theoretical extremes of total peace and total war, which these men symbolize respectively.

Once again, we begin with individuals who create world-views and ideologies out of the tension between their own needs and values and the social conditions in which they find themselves. This time, however, because of curious upbringings, odd personalities, and extreme world conditions the two individuals in question develop such rigid images of the world that they no longer fit reality. Their world-views become entirely self-justified and self-evident, so rigid, in fact, that these men become incapable of learning. Their states of mind become pathological.

Woodrow Wilson and Adolf Hitler represent the pathological extremes of the classic debate in world politics between Idealism and Realism. Wilson's pathological idealism became so obsessed with man's potential goodness and the ideal of world peace that he failed to see the social facts as they really were and was unable to learn to operate effectively to gain political support for his ideas. Hitler's pathological realism became power mad rather than idea mad, and his bent toward aggressive action and imperial expansion made him forget all sense of limits as he tried to eliminate physically people who opposed his ideas and overextended himself militarily. Wilson broke down while trying to move the world toward total peace while Hitler fell apart after leading the world into total war.

It is impossible to understand world politics in the late twentieth century without being aware of the nature and consequences of the two world wars that shaped our world and the ideas of total peace and total war that emerged from these experiences. The Wilson study goes further to illustrate how the American tradition of ideological liberalism and economic conservatism affected American attitudes toward war and peace issues in general. Hitler demonstrated how the German tradition of nationalism and hero worship led the German people to support a neurotic, authoritarian leader who manipulated the masses brilliantly to create a totalitarian system from which the world has not yet fully recovered.

CHAPTER 4

The Nation-State System and International Organization — Wilson

> It must be a peace without victory.... Victory
> would mean peace forced upon the loser, a
> victor's terms imposed upon the vanquished. It
> would be accepted in humiliation, under duress,
> at an intolerable sacrifice, and would leave a
> sting, a resentment, a bitter memory upon which
> terms of peace would rest, not permanently, but
> only as upon quicksand. Only a peace between
> equals can last.
>
> WOODROW WILSON

Woodrow Wilson's moral fervor inspired the world to create an international organization for total peace based on equality between democratic nation-states. Such an idealistic vision also blinded Wilson and other world leaders to the aggressive plans of nondemocratic forces in the world. Wilson's personal tragic flaw became an international tragic flaw among peace-seeking statesmen and helped to bring about the most catastrophic war the world has ever known. Wilson's liberal vision simultaneously planted seeds for the United Nations and for the appeasement policies that encouraged Hitler to start World War II. Paradoxically, too much belief in total peace may help to bring about total war.

A world without winners, a world without losers, a world without conflict: a utopian dream? Exactly. For the overwhelming evidence of world history points toward the inevitability of tension and conflict in human affairs. Yet without such utopian dreams, man would be an ignoble beast. To mistake such dreams for reality makes man into a tragic figure, or a fool. The essence of human wisdom is to strive for high ideals, knowing all the while that they will never be attained and that the majority of men cannot be counted on to go along with such endless, idealistic struggle.

Wilson reminds one of Sisyphus who was punished for excessive pride by the Greek gods and fated to roll a stone toward the top of a hill forever, only to see it fall back upon him as he neared the summit. Albert Camus suggested that "the struggle towards the heights is enough to fill a man's heart. One must imagine Sisyphus happy."[1] Wilson's tragedy was greater, however; his heart was never full. He thought that God was on his side, and

111

Woodrow Wilson (left) at Princeton University. *Brown Brothers photo.*

he believed that all men could be eventually persuaded to accept his vision of the duty of Sisyphus: to push the nation-states of the world toward an Eden II of world peace.

I. Wilson: A Political Portrait

The Origins of an Academic Idealist

Thomas Woodrow Wilson, born in Staunton, Virginia in 1856, was raised to become a great man. His mother, who came from a learned, religious Scottish family, known for its scholars and Presbyterian ministers, was simple, reserved, and devoted to her family. His father, whom Wilson called "that incomparable man," was an impressive, Presbyterian minister of Scotch-Irish extraction. Both sides of the family were deeply religious and believed in the Calvinist doctrine that man is an innately corrupt sinner whose only chance for salvation lies in being elected by God to a state of grace and eternal life. Woodrow Wilson was born into an impossible state of tension, which forced him to believe that he was either eternally damned or that he was capable of saving himself and receiving the grace of God by a life of unbending, moral service. This unremitting tension both raised him to the heights of greatness and dashed him to the depths of self-inflicted failure and despair.

Wilson once noted that a boy never gets over his boyhood; he never can change the subtle influences which have become a part of him and were bred into him when he was a child. The heavy influence of his father upon his own development proved his point. Dr. Joseph Ruggles Wilson was a learned, witty man of great presence who was intensely ambitious for his eldest son and was almost unbearably active in his education. He often applied his caustic wit and perfectionist standards to the young Wilson who, unlike Mao, never smarted nor rebelled but did all he could to meet his father's standards, believing himself to be inadequate and inferior to this stern taskmaster.

The boy was not enrolled in school until he was ten. He dropped immediately to the bottom of his class. Moreover, he had been ignorant of the written alphabet until he was nine and could not read readily until eleven. Social scientists Alexander George and Juliette George suggest that perhaps Wilson's failure to learn was the one way the boy dared to express resentment against his father and his repressive perfectionism. They argue that it is perhaps a central feeling of inadequacy and fundamental worthlessness, engendered by his father, that led to Wilson's tremendous need for affection, power, and achievement and his compulsive striving for perfection. "For one of the ways in which human beings troubled with low estimates of themselves seek to obliterate their inner pain is through high achievement and the acquisition of power. The trouble is that no matter how dazzling, their accomplishments are likely to prove only momentarily satisfying because the deep-seated low estimates persist and in short order begin to clamor anew for assuagement."[2]

Upon hearing about his difficulties at school Wilson's family intervened quickly, and the boy soon achieved literacy. At that point his father would ask him questions and then have him write compositions to be sure he understood the matter at hand, directing him often to rewrite his essays four or five times to clear up ambiguous language. In fact, his father even required him to examine the classics, sentence by sentence, and rewrite parts of them in a better style! Such rigorous attention to language no doubt helped Wilson to achieve his later lucidity in writing and speaking. Language can be a powerful tool in national and international politics.[3]

Wilson's potential political power, like other human beings', depended heavily upon the social facts of his childhood: his values, his social class and family upbringing, his institutional socialization in terms of religion, education, and social roles, and his personality and its roots in the American ethos. From his family, he adopted stern Christian, Presbyterian values colored by an American emphasis on rugged individualism and salvation through hard work. In terms of class, his family was not rich and had no desire to be, preferring a genteel poverty and the value of moral achievement above all else.

In his youth Wilson's social world was colored by the traditional family preoccupation with the Presbyterian ministry and individual scholarship. When he was a teenager he became wrapped up with thoughts about religion and his future. At seventeen he joined the First Presbyterian Church of Columbia, and he began to study the lives of great men (as did Mao, Hitler, de Gaulle and Kissinger). A year earlier Wilson's young cousin had come to his desk where he was practicing shorthand and asked about a picture of an austere looking man hanging above. "That is Gladstone, the greatest statesman that ever lived," Wilson replied solemnly. "I intend to be a statesman, too."[4] At some point great world leaders intend to become great, and unlike most of us, their personalities and willpower drive them to fulfill this intention despite the odds against them. Wilson "spent his childhood and youth industriously preparing to be a great man."

While his schoolmates perceived him to be different, they did not think Wilson was queer, and they liked and respected him. When he was still sixteen, he entered Davidson College, a Presbyterian school in North Carolina, where he spent much time with the debating society. However, he had to drop out as the school year came to an end because of ill health. He stayed home for fifteen months reading on his own, discussing ideas and books with a friend, and dropping in now and then on local girls.

He entered Princeton University in 1875 and immediately joined the Whig Society, a debating group which helped to improve his oratory. Never satisfied with mediocrity, he did library research on the great orators of history and wrote an article on the aims of oratory, published in the

Princetonian. He argued, "Its object is persuasion and conviction—the control of other minds by a strange personal influence and power."[5] He saw oratory as a means to statecraft, not as an end in itself.

The end of all individual and national action for Wilson was "the fixed and eternal standard" of judgment expressed in the Bible. In every daily choice a man makes, he risks the integrity of his own soul and he should conduct himself in such a way that the world could see that there was "one immovable thing in it, a moral principle embodied in a particular man."[6] Such individual responsibility before God was the basis for liberty in the modern world and the test of greatness in a man, according to Wilson.

✸✹✺✹✺✹✺✹✺✹✺✹

Those who put ideas and moral principles first are idealists; those who put action and reality first are realists. Historian E. H. Carr writes: "The antithesis of utopia and reality also coincides with the antithesis of theory and practice. The utopian makes political theory a norm to which political practice ought to conform. The realist regards political theory as a sort of codification of political practice. . . . The radical is necessarily utopian, and the conservative realist. The intellectual, the man of theory, will gravitate towards the Left just as naturally as the bureaucrat, the man of practice, will gravitate towards the Right. Hence the Right is weak in theory, and suffers through its inaccessibility to ideas. The characteristic weakness of the Left is failure to translate its theory into practice. . . ."[7] Pathological realists are so in love with action they are forever blind to ideas, whereas pathological idealists are so in love with ideas they cannot see reality.

✸✹✺✹✺✹✺✹✺✹✺✹

While at Princeton, Wilson researched the lives of great English statesmen and began to compare the British and American systems of government. He devoured all books he could find on the themes of political theory, history, and politics. Perhaps the writers who influenced him most were Walter Bagehot and Edmund Burke. The essays of Bagehot became the model later on for his *Congressional Government.* As an undergraduate, Wilson decided he would like to become a senator and even wrote out a number of cards with his name followed by "Senator from Virginia." Although far from being a brilliant undergraduate in all fields, when something caught his interest, he went at it with tenacity and in depth. His great admiration for the British House of Commons, where floor discussion and debate were more significant than in the American Congress, led him to write "Cabinet Government in the United States." This article was published in the *International Review,* a prominent journal at the time. He even organized a "Liberal Debating Club" based on a British type of constitution and was soon installed as its prime minister.

When Wilson graduated at twenty-two, he enrolled in the law school of the University of Virginia. Memorizing the endless cases bored him, but he was convinced that the training would be important for his later career. He continued his debating activities in the Jefferson Society where he was elected president. He wrote for the student magazine and was busy with a courtship as well. In December, 1880 he collapsed in illness and returned home to continue his studies on his own. Thereafter, he decided to set up a law practice in Atlanta, Georgia. He wrote Ellen Axson in 1883, "The profession I chose was politics; the profession I entered was the law. I entered the one because I thought it would lead to the other."[8]

Wilson's law practice failed like Ghandi's and Lenin's. His romance with Ellen Axson succeeded. He decided to become an academic to earn a living to support a wife. In 1883 he became engaged and entered a graduate program in political science and history at Johns Hopkins University. Wilson viewed the required courses as necessary evils and put most of his energy into writing two books: one on American economic thought, which was never published, and the other *Congressional Government*, an evaluation of the American governmental system in terms of the day-to-day operation of the constitutional framework. After many self-imposed revisions, Wison finished the latter and sent it off to Houghton Mifflin and Company, who agreed to publish it.

When the book was published the next year it was an impressive success that brought Wilson much respect in the academic community. Gamaliel Bradford's review in the *Nation* called it "one of the most important books, dealing with political subjects, which have ever issued from the American press."[9] Wilson's reputation spread and he was offered teaching posts. He accepted a position at Bryn Mawr. There he was able to marry Ellen, a tender and devoted woman, who could feel and work out his moods. Wilson taught European history, but was not enthralled with teaching women or serving under a woman dean. Six months later he tried unsuccessfully to get a post in the State Department.

During the next three years, Ellen became pregnant and Wilson taught and wrote on *The State*, which surveyed the governments of all nations in the world. He then accepted a teaching post at Wesleyan, which pleased him since he would be teaching men. There he organized a "House of Commons" debating society for the students. As Wilson's reputation grew with the publication of *The State* he worked to fulfill his academic dream, to teach political science at Princeton. With the help of a friend he was offered a position, and in 1890 he began his twenty-year career there, twelve years teaching and eight as president of the university. Professionally speaking, Wilson had arrived.

Wilson's lectures at Princeton on American constitutional law, international law, English common law, and administration were superior performances. The students at times even broke into applause. His prolific writing of books and articles brought him national fame. He was soon offered many teaching posts and the presidencies of many universities but was persuaded to become president of Princeton.

In order to strengthen his national reputation Wilson continued to write articles on political topics of the day and tried to create an image of himself as a practical thinker to whom politicians in the government might turn for advice, much as Henry Kissinger has done more recently. Yet he continually longed for political action, for he could not be satisfied with the role of a mere adviser or the trade of words. He had a passion to lead just as he had a passion for friendship. In both leadership and friendship relations, he demanded uncritical acceptance of his opinions, at least on major issues. He always associated disagreement with him with dislike for him: a tragic flaw in a political leader who must be able to slip into the shoes of others in order to bring them around to his own position.

Wilson's political leadership at Princeton illustrated in a microcosm the strengths and weaknesses he would later reveal as president of the United States. He began with great enthusiasm and idealism to reform undergraduate intellectual life according to the Oxford model of tutorials and preceptors. All went well until the board of trustees appointed Andrew West as the new dean to lead the new graduate school. West soon came into conflict with Wilson over graduate and undergraduate priorities. Wilson had already made some enemies among senior faculty by demanding control over the hiring and firing of all faculty and by initiating his reforms without much faculty consultation. The conflict came into the open when Wilson quietly received the approval of the board of trustees for an expensive plan for residential quadrangles where groups of undergraduates and graduates could live and eat together and hold informal discussions. Dean West and others were angry since Wilson's plan would put plans for the graduate school on the back burner again. A major controversy developed and Wilson's plan was defeated. Moreover, Wilson's closest friend had not supported his plan, so he completely broke off the relationship. Later Harvard and Yale both adopted the essence of Wilson's proposed quadrangle plan and the principles of his preceptorial plan found general approval in American colleges.

However, Wilson's conflict with Dean West was not over. The latter received the offer of a half-million dollar gift to Princeton from a friend, if West approved of the location for the site of new buildings for the graduate school. West wanted the buildings in a new area away from the original campus to allow for expansion. Wilson opposed his position, arguing that the undergraduates and graduates should mingle together democratically on the same, old campus. Soon Wilson made a moral crusade out of the issue, calling for the dean's resignation and speaking to alumni throughout the country about the dangers of wealth corrupting the ideal democratic principles that should govern educational policy. Overwhelming opposition built up against Wilson, but he refused to back down or compromise in the slightest. The issue was only settled when fate intervened mysteriously on West's side. Princeton was willed several million dollars for the construction of a graduate school, and West was named as one of the executors of the will. Wilson knew the game was up and accepted West's site for the school and West as dean.

Pathological idealism and pathological realism are neurotic styles of thinking marked by extreme rigidity and dogmatism. Such thinking makes it impossible for an individual either to understand his opponent's viewpoint or to successfully counter it. The result is inevitable tension and personal conflict that can spell political disaster. In analyzing personal rigidity, psychoanalyst David Shapiro wrote: "It may refer to a stiff body posture, a stilted social manner, or a general tendency to persist in a course of action that has become irrelevant or even absurd. . . . Consider as a commonplace example the sort of thinking one encounters in a discussion with a compulsive, rigid person, the kind of person we also call "dogmatic" or "opinionated." Even casual conversation with such a person is often very frustrating, and it is so for a particular reason. It is not simply that one meets with unexpected opposition. On the contrary, such discussion is typically frustrating just because one experiences neither real disagreement nor agreement. Instead, there is no meeting of minds at all, and the impression is simply of not being heard, of not receiving any but perfunctory attention."[10]

At just the time when things at Princeton looked their worst, political opportunities arose for Wilson, which he had nurtured for the past couple of years. The conservative element of the Democratic party in New Jersey was looking for a candidate to help wrest control from the liberals, who were out to restrict the power of the industrial trusts, tycoons, and old-machine politicians. At that point Wilson was over fifty years old. He had to play his cards carefully in order to exploit the opportunity offered by the conservatives without damaging his larger, presidential ambitions by unnecessarily alienating the liberals. In 1910 he became the Democratic candidate for governor, and, at the same time the trustees asked him to resign as president of Princeton. He resigned and ran a fearless campaign, gaining progressive support throughout New Jersey, and was elected by a plurality of 49,000 votes.

As governor, Wilson soon made it clear that he was going to carry out the liberal promises he made in the campaign regardless of the consequences for the conservatives who had supported him. His energetic leadership in the legislature led to the passage of many reform bills: a direct primaries act and a corrupt practices act, which together cleaned up the political atmosphere in New Jersey, an employers' liability act, the creation of a public utilities commission, and municipal government reforms. Wilson even provided the impetus for the Seven Sisters Bills, which aimed to protect the public from exploitation by trusts. It was a significant triumph

at a time when the campaign for presidential nomination was appproach-
ing.

His clear leadership and successful reforms in New Jersey brought
Wilson into the national political arena, and he soon organized an active
campaign. Although the odds were against him, he was nominated as the
Democratic candidate for president on the forty-sixth ballot at the Baltimore Convention in 1912. Wilson's New Freedom domestic program was
effective in the presidential campaign against Theodore Roosevelt's New
Nationalism. He argued that federal authority must be expanded not so
much to regulate industry, but to free the people from the control of
privileged groups. Wilson won, and the Democrats gained control of both
houses of Congress, which meant that he could expect progressive support
for his reform proposals.

America's Liberal Ethos and Isolation

When Wilson took over the presidency, he became the voice of the
United States. He acted immediately to initiate and carry through the major
legislative reforms he had promised in his campaign: the Underwood Tariff
Act to levy a federal income tax to counterbalance the downward revision of
tariff rates; the Federal Reserve Act to supplant with a public board the so-
called dictatorship of private banks; the creation of the Federal Trade
Commission to allow the federal government to keep conditions in trade
competitive; and the far-reaching Clayton Anti-Trust Act, which prohibit-
ed injunctions in labor disputes, unless needed to stave off irreparable
damage, and declared that labor strikes and boycotts were not violations of
the law. In short, Wilson tried to translate the American traditional liberal
creed into an economic liberalism adapted to the social facts of the modern,
industrial world.

The seeds for Wilson's economic and foreign policies lie deep within
the American ethos. American revolutionary ideology, her virgin lands, and
her rich material opportunities on the frontier all combined to encourage a
creed of rugged individualism, grass roots democracy, and competitive
capitalism. As the nineteenth-century French observer, Alexis de Tocque-
ville, pointed out in *Democracy in America*: "The great advantage of the
Americans is, that they have arrived at a state of democracy without having
to endure a democratic revolution; and that they are born equal instead of
becoming so." Wilson grew up in this unique American ethos and became a
manifestation of its dogmatic liberalism.

American liberalism became dogmatic largely because of American
isolation from the rest of the world. Historian Louis Hartz has argued that
since Americans have experienced neither feudalism nor the socialist
reaction to feudalism, they can never really understand the meaning of such
experiences nor the reactionary and revolutionary extremes which they
imply. Hartz notes "that America's very liberal joy lay in the escape from a

decadent Old World that could only infect it with its own diseases."[11] Such thinking led George Washington to proclaim in his inaugural address that the United States would isolate herself from the messy intrigues of European politics. Yet, Hartz continued:

> In the twentieth century, "Americanism" has also crusaded abroad in a Wilsonian way, projecting itself headlong over the strange and ancient societies of Europe and Asia. . . . Embodying an absolute moral ethos, "Americanism," once it is driven on to the world stage by events, is inspired willy-nilly to reconstruct the very alien things it tries to avoid. Its messianism is the polar counterpart of its isolationism, which is why Harding and Wilson are both "Americanist" thinkers, and why, as Mr. George Kennan has recently noted, Americans seem to oscillate between fleeing from the rest of the world and embracing it with too ardent a passion. An absolute national morality is inspired either to withdraw from "alien" things or to transform them: it cannot live in comfort constantly by their side."[12]

However, the American ethos is not only marked by an unreconcilable tension between "neutral" isolationism and messianic interventionism in foreign affairs. A greater tension lies beneath, and that is the agonizing conflict between bourgeois and Protestant beliefs within American liberalism. Political scientist H. Mark Roelofs described the agony of America's liberal spirit:

> Liberalism, especially in the form in which it came to America, is itself an anxious faith. The European middle class was both Protestant and bourgeois, anxious both to save souls through personal acts of faith and to create material wealth through systems of private capitalism. To some degree, the two aims complemented each other, at least in practice. The Protestant churches ennobled the private entrepreneur for his virtues of industry and plain living and gave a religious sanction to his thrift. He, in turn, gave generous financial support to their institutions. At the same time, the alliance between Protestant and bourgeois was not easy. Protestantism preached piety, asceticism, otherworldliness. The bourgeois capitalist was, as bourgeois, mostly interested in the competitive race for financial success and industrial power. The result was a tension, a spiritual agony that became a standard motif of novels and plays throughout the liberal world.[13]

Wilson's severely Protestant family heritage made that tension particularly acute when his moral creed came up against the social facts of bourgeois industrial interests and materialistic politicians at home and abroad.

When people "do" international relations—when they have to relate to others from other nations with other cultures and world-views—their own nationalism and ideological mental rigidity reveal themselves. Gestures, language, ideas and actions all unmask one's national origins and expose his limitations. "The Americans are dogmatic and simplistic about their creed. . . . If the Americans have been purely and merely liberal from the beginning, then liberalism is all they know. All other doctrines, whether of fascism or communism or even just new variations on the original liberalism, become for the American people, therefore, not only anathema but also simply incomprehensible. . . . Contemporary Americans tend . . . not to develop and experiment with their liberalism but rather to hang on to it in rigid fear that some part of it, by this or that chqnge, might be lost"[14] Likewise, the French hang on to their aestheticism, the Germans to their order and the British to their propriety.

As Wilson's foreign policy developed, the conflict between bourgeois and Protestant beliefs within American liberalism became translated into the agony between the American "manifest economic destiny," or the right to monopolize foreign markets, and American messianism, or the right to make the world safe for democracy. In the Wilson period, the tension in the American ethos between spiritual and material elements shifted from a policy of ascetic isolationism at the beginning of World War I to a policy of violent interventionism to save the world for democracy.

Dollar Diplomacy, Neutrality, and World War I

Wilson's foreign policy emerged not merely from the raw material of the American ethos, but from the influence of American intellectuals who extracted a unique, expansionistic role for the United States from their interpretations of her historical development. At the turn of the century, when Wilson was perhaps the leading political scientist in the United States, the influence of historian Frederick Jackson Turner's frontier thesis became particularly strong in the academic community. Following Turner's thesis Wilson's description of American development expressed a national consensus: "This great pressure of a people moving always to new frontiers, in search of new lands, new power, the full freedom of a virgin world, has ruled our course and formed our policies like a fate."[15] By conquering virgin land, Americans would express a unique kind of idealism and achieve manhood:

Nature was much bigger and stronger than man. She would suffer no sudden highways to be thrown across her spaces; she abated not an inch of her mountains, compromised not a foot of her forests. Still, she did not daunt the designs of the new nation born on the sea-edge of her wilds. Here is the secret. . . . The history of the country and the ambitions of its people have been deemed both sordid and mean, inspired by nothing better than a desire for the gross comforts of material abundance, and it has been pronounced grotesque that mere bigness and wealth should be put forward as the most prominent grounds for the boast of greatness. The obvious fact is that for the creation of the nation the conquest of her proper territory from Nature was first necessary. . . . A bold race has derived inspiration from the size, the difficulty, the danger of the task.[16]"

This passage embodies the tension between the Protestant and bourgeois ethics and reveals the most characteristic symptom of that American tension, unavoidable guilt. Rather than seeking the sources of the guilt in order to smother the agony at the roots, Americans like Wilson often project the guilt outside themselves into projects of action or onto alien ideologies and people. Wilson did both, encouraging American economic expansion as the basis of an international, liberal, capitalist system, and projecting frustration and guilt on an enemy ideology and state that represented the opposite of Wilsonian liberalism, namely Lenin's communism in the Soviet Union. Wilson's ideal, liberal vision stimulated American economic imperialism and the cold war of the 1950s.[17]

In specific terms, Wilson's ideology emerged harmlessly enough. He began by asserting the principle that the material power of the United States would not be exerted against weaker nations, and he repudiated the so-called "dollar diplomacy" of the previous administration. Thus, he took steps to prepare the Filipinos for self-government and discouraged American bankers from taking part in international Chinese loans. However, Wilson had inherited policies of expansionism in Latin America and the Far East, and those policies were reinforced by his belief that the United States needed new economic frontiers and that her "manifest destiny" would guide the world toward democracy and prosperity. Although Wilson denounced dollar diplomacy, he pursued the same objectives.[18] When confronted with the Nicaraguan and Mexican Revolutions, he used economic and diplomatic coercion to open up and consolidate a sphere for the United States. He thus further transformed the Monroe Doctrine of 1823, which proclaimed that the United States had the right to protect Latin America from European powers, into "the Monroe Manifesto," which declared that Americans had the right and duty to go down and help out our Latin brothers for their own good.[19] Neither the resort to force nor its justification in terms of Wilson's belief in Anglo-Saxon political superiority and Calvinist moral superiority pacified Latin American hostility. The Mexican Revolution, in particular, frustrated Wilson's Latin ambitions throughout his presidency.

Wilson was troubled with the growing factionalism and instability in American society, and he believed that they resulted from the influx of non-Anglo-Saxon influences and a decline in economic opportunity, due to the closing of the frontier. The solution, he thought, was strong, centralized leadership at home and the expansion of American economic opportunity abroad. Opposing the necessity of a mechanistic view of government, the checks and balances of forces along the lines of Newtonian mechanics, Wilson believed in an organic theory of the nation-state, or a whole being greater than the sum of its parts, which would bring the United States together again under strong leadership and moral purpose.

> Government is not a machine but a living thing. . . . No living thing can have its organs offset against each other as checks, and live. . . . Government is not a body of blind forces; it is a body of men. . . . There can be no successful government without leadership or without the intimate, almost instinctive, coordination of the organs of life and action. . . . Living political constitutions must be Darwinian in structure and practice.[20]

Later Wilson was to stretch that organic theory of the state to become an organic theory of world government symbolized by the League of Nations. In doing so, he was looking more for democratic and moral similarities than for material or national differences. Such blurry farsighted vision often led him to try so hard to see the forest that he could not make out the trees.

At the start of World War I in 1914, Wilson proclaimed that the United States would remain neutral and encouraged the people to remain impartial in word and deed. Such a policy was a natural outgrowth of the tradition of American isolationism in world affairs and American fears of becoming involved in Old World intrigues of power politics. However, the neutrality soon began to break down as Americans increasingly supported Britain and France economically, encouraged by effective British propaganda, and as shock set in regarding the vigorous successes of the German submarine warfare, which often paid little attention to the Anglo-Saxon notion of the etiquette of belligerent states toward neutral countries.

Neutrality represents one kind of international law that has developed among individuals from different nations to keep conflicts and war at a minimum when possible. In international law the only individuals that really matter are the elites who officially represent the governments involved. Only they can declare a nation to be neutral. According to

international lawyer William Bishop the chief duties of neutral states toward belligerent states are (1) strict impartiality, (2) abstention from assistance by the neutral governments to either belligerent, (3) prevention of the use of neutral territory as a base for belligerent operations, and (4) acquiescence in such belligerent interference with neutral commerce as is permissible under international law. . . . The primary duties of belligerent states toward neutrals may be grouped under the notions of (1) no violation of neutral territory or neutral territorial waters or air, (2) respect for the neutral's impartiality, and (3) refraining from interference with neutral commerce with other neutrals or with the enemy except in so far as international law permits such interference.''[21] But what international law permits often ends up depending upon a nation's ability and willingness to enforce it.

~♈~♈~♈~♈~♈~♈~♈~♈

American neutrality provided Wilson with the time and resources to work on his domestic reforms and conceive of ways in which the United States could benefit economically from the circumstances. His moral beliefs, ambition, and ego drove him to attempt to initiate peace negotiations now and again. He failed. Neutrality became increasingly difficult to maintain as the British tried to blockade German ports by using their naval power, extending the doctrine of continuous voyage, enlarging the lists of what counted as illegal or contraband, bringing neutral ships into harbor, and detaining neutral cargoes. Americans were outraged at the violation of those traditional rules of international law. The German reaction was more severe. In 1915, the government in Berlin declared the waters around Britain to be a war zone, threatening to sink all belligerent ships there and warning neutral countries that their ships might be sunk too.

Wilson responded immediately that he would hold the German government strictly accountable for any lawless acts by submarine commanders. Any destruction of an American ship or loss of American lives, he said, would be viewed as an "indefensible violation of neutral rights." However, the Germans maintained their policy, and a few months later they sank the British liner *Lusitania*, drowning 1,000 people, of whom 128 were American. From this point on, Wilson sided against Germany psychologically although he was determined to avoid war, saying: "There is such a thing as a nation being too proud to fight."

Although Wilson wanted to avoid war, he pushed hard against the German policy on the diplomatic front. He was determined to make them abide by the established rules of cruiser warfare. The wording of his protest to Germany was so strong that isolationist Secretary of State William Jennings Bryan resigned rather than sign it. When the *Arabic* was sunk in August, 1915, the Germans promised not to attack liners without warning. However, in 1916, the channel steamer *Sussex* was torpedoed, and Wilson's protest amounted to an ultimatum: stop the savage submarine warfare or the United States will become involved in the war. Things subsided for seven months.

Wilson's momentary diplomatic victory not only delayed American intervention in the war but proved to be politically useful in the 1916 presidential campaign. Wilson barely squeaked through to win the election, a victory generally ascribed to the support of the pacifists. In response, he again attempted to initiate peace negotiations, even suggesting that, if the French and British allies accepted the proposal and the Germans did not, the United States would probably enter the war against Germany. However, the British and French made no move to support Wilson's efforts, even though the German chancellor wanted to open peace negotiations rather than risk American entrance into the war. After the Germans published a notification that they were ready for peace negotiations, Wilson published his own note asking their terms. Although the German response was not encouraging, it gave Wilson the opportunity to outline his own principles of a lasting peace settlement in an address to the Senate on January 22, 1917.

In his famous address Wilson claimed that "no covenant of cooperative peace that does not include the peoples of the New World can suffice to keep the future safe against war." He also noted that no one should get together to guarantee anything but a just peace, "a peace without victory." The United States would refrain from supporting anything but "a peace among equals," for "only a peace among equals can last." Wilson said that "there must be not a balance of power, but a community of power," backed by "the organized major force of mankind."[22] In suggesting a shift from the existing **balance of power** rules of the international game to **collective security** rules, Wilson's proposals were revolutionary.

The Balance of Power, Collective Security, and Self-Determination

A balance of power system is an equilibrium made up of approximately equal powers or nations set against each other so that no one power can predominate. World War I resulted largely from the breakdown of the classical European balance of power system. That breakdown occurred when Germany rose to a position of great strength in Europe in the late nineteenth century, threatening the cozy domination of that continent by Britain and France. German leaders wanted colonies and overseas markets like the British and French and were determined to build a world empire. The British and French, on the other hand, wanted to keep their position in the world and maintain their superiority by exploiting the remaining attractive territories available. Such Anglo-French domination allowed the United States to maintain a policy of isolation from world affairs by keeping behind the protection of the strong British Navy. Then came the aggressive German submarines. Clearly Wilson's moral shock over the German violation of neutral rights on the sea gave support to Britain's attempt to maintain the status quo in the balance of power. Although his antipathy toward the Germans grew, allied superiority in the war allowed Wilson to postpone any decision on American involvement for a while.

"The balance of power is a chimera! It is not a fallacy, a mistake, an imposture—it is an undescribed, indescribable, incomprehensible nothing; mere words, conveying to the mind not ideas, but sound," said Richard Cobden in 1867.[23] *As a theory the idea of the balance of power has often dominated the rules of world politics. There are two main rules in the balance of power system. First, membership in the system is limited to five to seven dominant nation-states in a region or in the world, which are relatively equal militarily and economically and which have a similar cultural heritage. If there are more than seven states, there are too many to juggle at once; but if there are fewer than five, there are too few for flexibility. Second, any leader of one of the member states must work to prevent any other leader, or coalition of leaders, from becoming strong enough to overwhelm any state or coalition of states.*

As a moral idealist of the Protestant mold, Wilson was not about to play the game of cynical balance of power politics forever. He wanted more than that. He wanted a new organization with new rules that could establish a permanent peace for mankind: "I shall never myself consent to an entangling alliance, but I would gladly assent to a disentangling alliance—an alliance which would disentangle the peoples of the world from those combinations in which they seek their own separate and private interests and unite the people of the world to preserve the peace of the world upon a basis of common right and justice."[24] Collective security implies a universal alliance, that eliminates the competitive alignments which characterize the balance system. Such a universal arrangement would avoid entanglement in organized rivalries which Wilson claimed were conducive to war. Collective security calls for an alliance which unites nations in defense of community order, rather than one which divides them into antagonistic groups. Wilson did not want a balance of power system that treated conflict as a norm and cooperation as an exception; he wanted a collective security system with cooperation as the normal, general condition and conflict as the exception.

The proposal for a League of Nations that would protect a just and permanent peace through collective security was overwhelmed by events. The Germans renewed their unrestricted submarine campaign effectively blockading cargoes in American ports. The provocative publication of the Zimmerman telegram suggested a German-Mexican-Japanese alliance and the Mexican reconquest of Texas, New Mexico, and Arizona. Finally the loss of American lives in the sinking of the *Laconia* shocked the American public. Unable to resist the mounting pressures, Wilson asked and received a declaration of war against Germany from the United States Congress.

Wilson's rigid idealism and determination to keep the United States out of the war had so preoccupied him that when war came the United States was ill prepared for it. His close friend and adviser, Colonel Edward House, had tried unsuccessfully to push Wilson towards building a "war machine" and mobilizing the nation for military action. On January 17, 1918, House wrote in his diary: "He [Wilson] knows that I do not believe that he has an effective war organization, and I have been content to let it go at that. The fact that he does not consult me about these matters indicates that he knows we disagree, but he has believed he could work it out along the lines which he has pursued."[25] Typically, Wilson avoided confronting facts and opinions that undermined his idea of how things should be. When world leaders put on such blinders, the people of their nations suffer accordingly.

Once in the war, Wilson tried to focus all his oratorical gifts to create a national consciousness of common effort to fight a war to end all wars. He saw the war as a crusade. It was "a war for freedom and justice and self-government amongst all the nations of the world . . . the German people themselves included." The principles of democratic freedom and **self-determination** became the themes of his many wartime speeches, particularly his speech of January 8, 1918 when he presented his famous "Fourteen Points" as a basis for a just and lasting peace.* He believed that the war was also an opportunity for the world to affirm its belief in Christian principles and to establish that nations as well as men must conform to moral laws. Such a belief complemented his creed of self-determination: the belief in the capacity and the right of people to rule themselves. The final element of Wilson's foreign policy was his belief that the United States was destined to perform a unique mission in history: to lead the world spiritually and politically to create a just and lasting peace protected by an international organization that would embody the ultimate moral authority.

The Peace Treaty of Versailles and the League of Nations

When World War I ended in November, 1918 with the complete defeat of the central powers, Germany, Austria-Hungary, Bulgaria, and Turkey, not all of the victorious twenty-four allied and associated powers were equally enthusiastic about Wilson's peace plan. The Germans had initially requested an armistice and peace based on Wilson's Fourteen Points and other principles. The European allies accepted the Fourteen Points as a beginning, but the French and British expressed important reservations concerning Wilson's views on freedom of the seas and reparations. It was said at the peace conference at Paris that every delegate wanted to apply the Fourteen Points to every country but his own.

Wilson did achieve an early triumph at the peace conference when the other powers accepted, in principle, his fourteenth point, that a League of

*For the text of Wilson's Fourteen Points, see Appendix I.

Nations should become an integral part of the treaties. A draft of the covenant for the League was unanimously adopted.* The covenant did not represent a new idea in the world, but was inspired by many historical sources: dreams of permanent peace by churchmen and philosophers; the growing body of international law calling for mediation and arbitration between nations in conflict; and the tradition of international cooperation emerging from nineteenth-century international organizations regulating international waterway rights, postal and other communications, the Red Cross, and philanthropic services. Although the creation of the League of Nations was one of Wilson's crowning personal achievements, he was more its spokesman than its creator, more its diplomatic instrument than its origin. His upbringing had prepared him for a higher law and order of international morality, but his political skills and personal initiatives brought him the historical opportunity to actualize his potential.

Following Wilson's vision of a world made safe for democracy, the League was structured on a democratic pattern with an assembly of representatives from all member nations, a council composed of the principal allied and associated powers and four nonpermanent representatives chosen on a rotating basis by the assembly, and a secretariat made up of a secretary general and his staff.

However, Wilson's success in the founding of the League was overshadowed by concessions he was forced to make in return to particular national governments at the bargaining table. The French wanted part of the Rhineland to protect themselves from the Germans in the future. The Italians wanted the Adriatic port of Fiume to compensate for Dalmatia, which had been promised to them earlier by the British but was now to be incorporated into Yugoslavia. Most serious of all, the Japanese wanted Shantung, which clearly belonged to China according to Wilson's principles. The French gave in to a compromise that was never realized; the Italians walked out for a while. The Japanese did, however, get temporary possession of Shantung when Wilson compromised, for he was too tired from the other nationalistic disputes to fight. In short, he would do almost anything, including a public appeal to the Italians over their heads of state, to bring about his dream of the League. The unbearable tension between his need for a world organization for freedom, peace, and democracy and the frustrating social facts of the nation-state system literally tore Wilson apart psychologically and physically. In his dream was his greatness, in his situation, his tragedy; and his tragedy was a prelude to a larger catastrophe in the future.

The darkest shades of the treaties settling World War I surrounded the fate of Germany. The unilateral disarmament and "blank check" reparations agreement imposed on Germany made a mockery of Wilson's principle of a peace with equality and without victors or humiliation. Not only did the Germans have to cede territory and rights, but the war guilt

*For the text of the Covenant of The League of Nations, see Appendix II.

clauses of the treaty virtually forced them to take full responsibility for the war and war crimes of the past, against Denmark in 1864 and against France in 1871. They were even forced to return trophies and works of art captured from France by the Prussian Army in the 1870-71 war. Since many of the German people believed the government propaganda that painted a picture of German victory, the detailed humiliations following decisive defeat were almost unbearable. The Treaty of Versailles, which resulted from the Paris conferences, later became a symbol of all the injustices imposed upon the German people and was used by nationalistic politicians like Hitler. The seeds of World War II were planted in the settlement of World War I.

Wilson's moral idealism and optimism blinded him to the negative implications of the treaty for the future. Compare his reaction to the settlement to those of the other diplomats:

> "I should have preferred a different peace," said Colonel House.

> "I think it will be found that the compromises, which were accepted as inevitable, nowhere cut at the heart of any principle; the work of the Conference squares, as a whole, with the principles agreed upon as the basis of peace as well as with the practical possibilities," said President Wilson.

> "It is a stern but just treaty," said Lloyd George.

> "This is not peace; it is an armistice for twenty years," said Marshal Foch.

> "The promise of the new life, the victory of the great human ideals are not written in this treaty. . . . The real peace of the peoples ought to follow, complete, and amend the peace of the statesmen," said General Smuts.

> "What hand would not wither that signed such a peace?" said Scheidemann.

> "Do not expect us to be our own executioners," said Erzberger.[26]

Wilson was happy with the treaty in so far as it recognized the claims of the smaller nationalities to a degree never before approached in history and gave them the promise of peace through the establishment of the League of Nations. He signed and sailed for the United States. When he arrived he was totally drained psychologically and physically. The strains of the negotiations had taken their toll and he was in no shape to confront his Republican opponents in the Senate who would have to ratify the treaty. Moreover, Wilson refused to compromise at all with the chairman of the

The Big Four at Versailles (Wilson at right). *Brown Brothers photo.*

powerful Senate Foreign Relations Committee, Senator Henry Cabot Lodge. Lodge once confessed that he hated Wilson more than he expected to hate anyone in politics, and he stayed up nights conceiving of ways to undermine the President's prestige both in Paris and at home. Of course he also had eyes on the next presidential election and was determined to gain political influence any way he could. He spread propaganda throughout Congress arguing that Wilson's League was fraught with extreme dangers for American interests in the world and that the Senate must change the Covenant to make it safe, or reject it.

Wilson was in no condition physically or mentally to cope with Lodge's pragmatic, caustic criticisms. He felt that he was morally right and Lodge wrong and that was that. Under other circumstances he might have been detached enough from the issue to stand back and rally support politically in the Senate for his viewpoint. He had just fought with his whole heart and soul for his dream of the League, and his pride was too married to it to perceive the common sense of political compromise. Instead he looked for popular support with which to overwhelm the Senate. He traveled across the country on a crusade on behalf of the treaty and the League. After thirty-four major speeches, many parades, and minor talks Wilson returned to Washington in a state of physical collapse. A week later he suffered from a thrombus, which affected his brain, and he lost control of the left side of his body.

Wilson was isolated, and no one else possessed the authority or ability to create a compromise. Rather than compromise with Lodge, who wanted to amend the collective security aspect of the League, Wilson chose to have his followers vote against the resolution, keeping the United States out of the League of Nations entirely. Historian Thomas A. Bailey wrote, "In the final analysis the treaty was slain in the house of its friends rather than in the house of its enemies. In the final analysis it was not the two-thirds rule, or the 'irreconcilables,' or Lodge, or the 'strong' and 'mild reservationists,' but Wilson and his docile following who delivered the fatal stab. . . . With his own sickly hands Wilson slew his own brain child. . . ."[27]

Rather than becoming a popular referendum on the issues involved in his wrangle with Lodge, as Wilson hoped, the 1920 presidential election became instead a great victory for Republican Warren Harding. Wilson's spirits were somewhat lifted when he was awarded the Noble Peace Prize in late 1920. Thereafter, a broken man in health and spirit, he retired from public life to die in his sleep in 1924. Thomas F. Woodlock wrote:

> "The nemesis that Woodrow Wilson vainly fought was within himself, but it was as unchangeable, as inexorable as the Greek fates. In the last few years of his life there was something Promethean about him. The eagle's beak and claws were in his vitals as he lay bound and helpless on his rock of sickness, but he was grimly enduring and coldly defiant to the last. In the lonely citadel of his soul, proud in the conviction that his cause was wholly just, utterly intolerant of criticism, utterly ruthless to opposition, he could not compromise his daemon. Tragedy if it be not noble is not tragedy, and no one will deny to Woodrow Wilson the elements of nobility. Yet it must be said that the world suffers when Prometheus suffers, and that the very essence of statesmanship lies not in the grim endurance of foreordained defeat, but rather in the wisdom to know when to take occasion by the hand and by yielding the shadow to gain the substance. To deny to Woodrow Wilson the quality of supreme statesmanship is only to say that he followed his daemon to the last. And his is a tragedy that Sophocles might well have imagined."[28]

II. Principles of World Politics

Idealism Versus Realism

The story of Woodrow Wilson is the tale of a rigid idealist who tried to defy convention but was defeated by social facts he failed to understand. Philosopher George Santayana suggested that mankind is divided into two classes: Sancho Panzas who have a sense of reality but no ideals, and Don Quixotes who have ideals but are mad. The form of madness or neurosis from which Wilson suffered was pathological idealism, and that kind of neurosis helped to bring about its polar opposite, the pathological realism of Hitler and World War II.

Social scientist Kenneth Boulding has defined a pathological belief as a rigid image of the world that does not fit reality. He noted that

> what we ordinarily think of as mental disease is the inability to perform reality-testing—the progressive elimination of error—on the folk-learning level. If a person's image of the world is entirely self-justified and self-evident, he will soon get into serious trouble. Suppose, for instance, that he is a paranoid and thinks that everybody hates him. All his experience will confirm this image no matter what the experience is. Experience that fails to confirm the image will be dismissed as due to either false inferences or mistaken images of the past. His fundamental image of the world is unshakable by any event that seems to contradict it. Such a person is incapable of learning, and it is this incapacity that really constitutes mental disease.[29]

Wilson's mental rigidity was revealed in his Princeton dispute with Dean West and in his conflict with Senator Lodge over the ratification of the Covenant of the League of Nations. In each of these cases, the acute tension between the need or desire for his ideal and the hostile social facts of the real world led him to overreact with disastrous consequences. He hung on to his ideal, to his rigid image of the world, refusing to compromise. As a result, he was dismissed from his job as president of Princeton University. Later for the same reasons the United States did not become a member of the League of Nations, and Wilson died a broken man.

In politics there are two dominant kinds of pathology: pathological idealism, which comes from the fixation on ideas, and pathological realism, which results from a fixation on action. Pathological idealists are so enchanted with their ideas or ideals that they are blind to the practical considerations that are necessary in order to bring them about in the real world. Pathological realists, on the other hand, are so immersed in action that their pursuit of power is never ending, for they lack ideas to put into practice. The outcome of pathological realism is corruption from power whereas the outcome of pathological idealism is corruption from lack of power. The motivations that drive men to become great world leaders often make them go mad with power or ideas. In both cases they mistake their own image of how things are or must be for the real world and overextend themselves for the sake of power or an ideal.

Not surprisingly, those pathological mental states are the extremes in the classic debate among theorists of world politics: the realists versus the idealists. The realist school maintains that world politics can only be explained in terms of power and potential power. In his classic *Politics Among Nations*, Hans Morgenthau claims that the realist theory is based upon the belief that human nature seeks to live, to propagate, and to dominate others and assumes that human nature is unchangeable. Therefore, objective, natural laws can be discovered through reason and experience which are based upon interest and defined in terms of power and power balances that can be calculated to form rational foreign policies. The opposite viewpoint, that of the idealists, stresses values other than power, such as international organization, law, or morality. Put another way, realists tend to spend their time studying conditions that lead to conflict and total war whereas idealists focus upon cooperation and total peace. The realists' belief that man is evil and aggressive blinds them to his potentially good and cooperative qualities; whereas the idealists' notion that man is basically good sets them up for deception and destruction.

Liberalism and Isolationalism

Wilson's pathological idealism derived in part from the obsessive-compulsive mentality of the culture in which he grew up. He was a product of America's dogmatic liberalism and stubborn, rugged individualism combined with the Protestant work ethic. Moreover, the high and firm religious and scholastic standards of his father intensified the obsessive-compulsive neurotic style in Wilson's case. Psychologist Wilhelm Reich called compulsive characters "living machines," which recalls Wilson's unceasing efforts to prepare to become a great man. More precisely, psychiatrist David Shapiro has empirically identified three characteristics of the obsessive-compulsive style: (1) rigidity, (2) the mode of activity and the distortion of the experience of autonomy, and (3) the loss of reality.[30] Wilson's rigidity showed in his dogmatism, his sharp focus of attention upon only what he wanted to hear, and his rejection of those with different opinions. His nervous, tense activity led him to look for facts more than to weigh them, and he distorted his experience of autonomy by avoiding introspection whenever he could. Finally, he continually sensed a loss of reality by living in continual doubt and uncertainty that was reinforced by the Calvinist risk of damnation and led to overreaction and dogmatism in ambiguous situations. Such uncertainty and doubt made him give up close friendships because of minor disputes.

Although any attempt by an amateur to psychoanalyze a national culture should be taken with a grain of salt, hypotheses can at least be suggested. In a land of rich resources and great opportunity the spirit of the American people was heavily influenced by the Protestant ethic and bourgeois capitalism. With the coming of the industrial revolution those qualities were intensified, and the American character became dominated by an obsessive-compulsive mentality. Its neurotic reactions to unbearable ambiguity have taken the form of pendular swings between dogmatic isolationism and dogmatic interventionism in foreign policy. According to that thesis, Wilson's policy of neutrality at the outset of the war was an expression of deep-seated American isolationism from foreign affairs dating back to George Washington's inaugural address. When Wilson decided it was time for the United States to intervene, he made it an intervention for all time. The United States was destined to save the world for democracy and create permanent peace through a League of Nations. Such alternation between the hermit and the messiah may be a unique American mode of obsessive-compulsive neurosis.

The United States is only an example of larger patterns of development that affect democratic industrial states throughout the world. In *The Protestant Ethic and the Spirit of Capitalism*, sociologist Max Weber showed that the Protestant conscience and liberal freedom created the iron cage of bureaucratic capitalism and the technical and economic conditions of machine production, which now determine the lives of all individuals born into it. Moreover, he believed that the ascetic spirit which created the cage had fled from it, particularly in the United States, where capitalism had achieved its highest development. Moreover, when a democratic industrial-ized country runs out of new frontiers at home, it profits from intervening abroad in search of new resources and markets and can do so under the ideological banners of free world trade everywhere and save the world for democracy. Wilson's liberal idealism thus later became the tool for the bourgeois realism of economic self-interest which called for more exports in order to increase production and wealth at home. Inevitably the countries which the Americans freed for democracy became American markets and were vulnerable to the establishment of extensions of American corpo-rations there. Of course the countries often benefited from such American investment, but few would debate that Americans benefited the most. The United States demonstrated in the twentieth century what Britain had in the nineteenth—that rich and powerful capitalist, democratic states gain the most from advocating a liberal world economy.[31]

The History of the Nation-State System

To fully understand how Wilsonian internationalism benefited the United States economically and politically, it is necessary to know a bit about the history of the nation-state system which Wilson wanted so badly to reform. Indeed, familiarity with that history is vital to an understanding of how any great leader emerges to change the world in our times.

For an individual to affect world history or international politics, the most important source of political power is his nation-state. If he is born in "Lilliput," a tiny dependent state, and stays there, it is unlikely he will ever affect world politics as much as he might were he a native of the great power "Megoslavia." In past world history, Lilliputians have always been forced to kowtow to Megoslavians. In the twentieth-century international system, all significant political power begins and ends at the nation-state level. How did the nation-state system develop, and what makes it such an important factor in world politics?

Although roots of the nation-state can be traced back to ancient China, India, classical Greece and early European history, our modern nation-state system has basically emerged since the thirteenth century, and particularly in the sixteenth and seventeenth centuries in Europe. Following the breakdown of the unity of medieval Christendom, the European multistate system was first officially recognized with the Peace of Westphalia in 1648 and the Treaty of Utrecht in 1713. The European conception of the modern type of sovereign state was one with a great concentration of political power within it, which possessed a monopoly of the use of force within its borders. Such consolidation of political power normally corresponded with growing economic power after the industrial revolution.

The modern theory of state sovereignty was formulated explicitly by Jean Bodin in his *De Republica* of 1576. According to Bodin, a power exists somewhere in every state called sovereignty, which is the sole source of laws but is not itself bound by them. During the sixteenth and seventeenth centuries, that power was usually manifested in an individual monarch, and was not officially invested in the people through democratic constitutionalism until the nineteenth and twentieth centuries. Bodin thought that although the sovereign power was free from all domestic law, it remained bound by the divine law, the law of nature, and the law of nations.

The legal notion of sovereignty led to a paradoxical development. It provided a common principle upon which all nation-states could agree, thus forming a foundation for the law of nations or international law. Yet, that very principle limited the effectiveness which international law could have, since it maintained that political leaders could do whatever they chose within their own state boundaries. As long as the principle of sovereignty was considered to be primary, no principle of higher law could legally exist that allowed an international organization or any other foreign force to intervene in the domestic affairs of any country, regardless of how inhumane or immoral those affairs might be. That paradox manifested itself in Wilson's thought in the contradiction between his belief in self-determination, or the right of every nation to choose its own form of government through democratic principles, and his belief in the higher law and moral order of the Covenant of the League of Nations, according to which nations would willingly give up some of their rights and sovereignty to an international organization for the sake of world peace.

Not only does the concept of sovereignty limit the potency of international law, it freezes the peculiarities and vested interests of the nation-states in the world, insuring the predominance of parochial, selfish nationalism over cooperative universal internationalism. State leaders in that kind of system are encouraged to put their own vital national interests above the interests of the whole international community and in some cases even above the interests of humanity itself.

Hegel represented the *reducto ad absurdum* of the development of nationalism in the nineteenth century by arguing that the state was everything, and the individual nothing. The individual owed everything to the state, his physical as well as his spiritual existence. Hegel viewed international conflict and war to be not only inevitable, but noble. Only through such conflicts, he argued, do the noble, cultural spirits of individual nation-states express themselves, the strong justly over-whelming the weak in the dynamic, spiritual progress of history. Hegel transformed nationalism into the highest virtue, particularly in his native Prussia under Frederick William III, and he viewed international law as sentimental nonsense. Indeed, World Wars I and II seemed to put flesh on Hegel's theoretical bones. Foreign policies focused on the nobility of national interests, and state leaders called upon subjects to sacrifice their lives and humanity in international violence to preserve the modern secular religion and territory of the nation-state. In the twentieth century, the nation-state has come to be viewed as a collective survival enterprise that allows a limited group of people to satisfy their needs and to organize politically, economically, and militarily to get more of what there is to get.

However, the nation-state can become all-consuming and eradicate the very freedom it was designed to protect. For, whereas sovereign state is a legal and rational concept that implies limits, the concepts of nation and nationalism are spiritual and emotional, admitting no limits. As philosopher Benedetto Croce wrote:

> "Nation" is a spiritual and historical concept and therefore in the act of becoming, not a naturalistic and fixed concept, like that of race. The very hegemony or primacy claimed for this or that people—by Fichte and others for the Germanic peoples, by Guizot and others for the French, by Mazzini and Gioberti for the Italians, and by still others for the Poles and the Slavs in general—was theorized as the right and duty of that people to take its place at the head of all the nations in order to act as their leader in the movement towards civilization, towards human perfection, towards spiritual greatness.[32]

Wilson's vision of American destiny was to lead the world into a new civilized era, crowned by the League of Nations. However, underlying such self-selecting leadership is national glory and self-interest, a parochial self-righteous nationalism that breeds international conflict and world war.

The Balance of Power Principle

If man is not to be trusted, as Thomas Hobbes, Jonathan Swift, Lord Acton, and other realists claim, then how does one power-hungry prince prevent another, who is even more power hungry, from upsetting the status quo? Is there not some surefire plan to contain potentially aggressive princes within the international system so that those rulers with the most powerful nation-states can sleep at night without worrying about their political security? Many diplomatic chess players believe that the balance of power game is the only solution to this nagging dilemma.

The balance of power concept dates back at least to 1648, when the Treaty of Westphalia marked the end of the epoch of religious wars which had been sparked by the Reformation. The society of sovereign states that then developed was personified by their princes, each with a set of limited interests which he tried to maximize in the international game. By the eighteenth century, the rationalistic era of the Enlightenment, the rules and tactics of the game had become clear-cut. The methods of a typical prince, for example, would include bargaining, forming coalitions, marriage alliances in which princes added territory with dowries and legitimacy with more royal blood and war of a limited variety. The diplomacy and battles of that period remind one of a traditional chess game or minuet. As though he were at a grand ball, a prince would form loose bilateral alliances for a spell but quickly break them if they did not suit his well-being. Hard-fought battles were avoided, for they were too costly because the unreliable mercenary soldiers who made up the armies would often switch sides if the fighting began to go against them or if they saw a better way to further their ambitions, like American business executives today. The goal was to get one's armies in a position of strategic advantage, whereupon it was not dishonorable for the other side to capitulate, just as a good chess player gives up when he sees that he has been outmaneuvered.

Historian Edward Gulick described the assumptions and aims of this pre-Napoleonic diplomatic game: first, the existence of a system of independent states with, more or less, equal potential power; second, a framework or recognized size of the system with a limited number of entities to be balanced; third, relative homogeneity among members of the state system; and fourth, a rational system of estimating power.[33] The mechanistic philosophy of Newton and the rationalism of the thinkers of the Enlightenment underlay these assumptions. The conflict of individual bodies or interests could only be kept in equilibrium if those interacting units were more or less equal and set against each other, so that no one unit would predominate. In order to maintain such an equilibrium, however, it was vital to limit the maximum number of interacting units within the system to make a rational calculation of interest and an appropriate balance possible. Otherwise, just as an expert juggler used to handling a half dozen eggs might be driven crazy if he was given a dozen, balance of power diplomats required that the number of variables they needed to manipulate be limited.

One way to limit the system was by the criterion of **relative homogeneity**. If a prospective member did not fit in a cultural or political sense, he must be excluded to make equilibrium within the system possible. The eighteenth-century philosopher Immanuel Kant claimed in *Perpetual Peace* that it was necessary that European governments possess a rough similarity, namely a republican form of government or, a separation of the executive and legislative functions. Edmund Burke also argued that similar cultural traditions and institutions were indispensable for the European balance of power, and opposed a strong British relationship with the Turkish Empire, which he said was Asiatic and did not fit culturally into the European system. In the twentieth century, Charles de Gaulle and others have used similar arguments to limit the membership of the European Common Market. Such thinking reveals an implicit tendency in the balance of power system to move towards increasing integration: from anarchy to loose alliances, to coalition equilibrium, to confederation, and finally to federation. In sum, the eighteenth-century balance of power idea advocated a balanced, limited integration, based upon a limited membership and the exclusion of those who did not fit.

As Gulick has noted, the aims of the balance of power system were to preserve the survival of its member states and the system itself, to see that no state predominated in the system, and to preserve a peace based on the maintenance of the status quo through the equilibrium principle. Taking the assumptions and aims of the theory together, one finds that the balance of power game is a kind of systems thinking, relying heavily upon Western concepts of rationality and calculable, concrete, national interests, and grounded on a conservative ideology. The Enlightenment assumptions of mechanistic rationality fail to take account of human emotions, ambiguity, and the desire for revolutionary change. Such difficulties undermined the classical European balance of power system and gave Napoleon his chance to change the rules of the game of world politics at the beginning of the nineteenth century.

Napoleon did not merely upset the balance of power apple cart with his leadership in the French Revolution; he introduced an entirely new conception of warfare as well, one in which the individual was to play a much more important role in world politics. As we have seen, in the old classical balancing system, the princes would play at war like chess, buying off each other's mercenary soldiers, but leaving the peasants to cultivate their fields, and striving only for limited victories. Napoleon, on the other hand, smashed the Enlightenment chess board in two with a romantic, heroic creed; took most of his soldiers from untrained French citizenry;

made all the peasants into citizens, thereby qualifying them for the draft; and aimed for absolute military victory. The mass emotions aroused by Napoleon's new tactics shattered the eighteenth-century rationalistic notion of diplomacy and war and caught the advocates of the balance of power system totally off guard. The high-pitched patriotism of the French soldier overwhelmed the dusty old mercenaries who were not looking out for their country as much as for their rational self-interests. Napoleon exploited the contrast brilliantly, raising the emotions of his troops in speeches that dramatically appealed to nationalism and encouraged murderous artillery fire in order to obliterate the enemy regardless of cost. He made a shambles of the old rules of world politics as well as the old rules of war. By universalizing politics for the sake of power, he taught the world that the potential power of physical destruction could be used to overwhelm all other notions of politics. Reason appeared to be reduced to its last gasp and romantic emotion, in the guise of French nationalism and ideology, seemed to be in absolute control.

Like Hitler later on, Napoleon overstepped his potentiality, emotion became exhausted, and reaction settled in. When Napoleon was defeated, what did the victors do? They fell back on habit and tried to reconstruct the only kind of solution they knew, the balance of power system. For a while it worked. There were no major wars for an entire century after the settlement of 1815.

In that settlement at the Congress of Vienna, Metternich of Austria personified the ideology of the balance of power. Indeed, he was so successful that he, alone, was able to dominate much of European politics for the next thirty years. The diplomats of England, Prussia, Russia, and France went along with Metternich's plan to return to the old scheme of things, making the Congress a nearly perfect example of the balance of power game. Tsar Alexander of Russia wanted all of Poland, but was only given the major part of it, lest excessive French power merely be replaced by Russian dominance. And so it went. Each of the four major victors received part of the pie, but not all they wanted for fear that one state would become too powerful and upset the equilibrium in the future. France was readmitted into the European system as an essential, legitimate member, although territory was allotted to the other four members with an eye to preventing French expansion in the future.

As an individual, Talleyrand, the French representative, exploited his situation amazingly well in pursuing France's national interests, even though France was technically the loser. For example, in January, 1815 a treaty of alliance was made between France, Britain, and Austria to oppose, by force of arms if necessary, the Russo-Prussian coalition. Talleyrand used this alliance and the difficult Polish-Saxon issue to wedge France back into the councils of the major powers. If an individual is aware of the rules of the game being played in world politics and has the position and personal perception necessary to exploit his situation, he can often influence events to a surprising degree. Both Metternich and Talleyrand are examples, par exellence, of such effective political action.

The Collective Security Principle

Napoleon's all-or-nothing tactics and the intense national movements of the nineteenth century revealed the weaknesses of the balance of power system, which experienced its demise in the elitist strategy of nationalism in World War I. Although the old-fashioned outer garments of the minuet wars of the Enlightenment fell by the wayside, some of the basic elements of the balancing game were resurrected in the new system that replaced it. The system was collective security. Indeed, one can view the collective security notion as a refined extension of the balance of power game, as a more integrated, centralized, and idealistic balancing act.

The basic premise of the collective security concept is simple. The leaders of all member states of the system are to view an attack upon any one of them as an attack upon all of them and respond accordingly. Striking similarities exist between the collective security and the balance of power ideas. Both assume the existence of a system of independent nation-states which are presumably deterred from attacking one another by a combination of force potentially at least as strong as that of the would-be attacker. Effective deterrence presupposes a rational calculation of self-interest on the part of the party to be deterred. Since the elites of the major nation-states had not learned the limits of such a presumption from Napoleon, they were forced to take another lesson from Hitler.

Although the basic similarities in the logic and limits of balance of power and collective security are clear, the differences between the two concepts are more subtle. Although in both there is a mistrust of the member states in the system, the balance of power system focuses that mistrust upon each state's potential or capacity for aggression. On the other hand, the collective security system concentrates on actual aggression in the form of policy or action. Whereas the balance of power game depends upon competitive alliances or coalitions to keep the equilibrium, the collective security notion is rooted in one cooperative alliance of all against any potential dissenter or group of dissenters. The former divides to balance, while the latter unites to prevent imbalance.

The nuances of the notion of collective security can be traced back at least as far as the seventeenth-century Treaty of Osnbrück, which provided that "all and each of the contracting parties . . . shall be held to defend and maintain all and each of the dispositions of this peace, against whomsoever it may be."[34] Later both William Penn and William Pitt suggested collective security schemes for Europe. The ultimate sign of the arrival of the collective security concept as an official international political strategy was undoubtedly Woodrow Wilson's proposal in the Fourteen Points for the

League of Nations. Wilson tried to sell his new program by deliberately overdrawing the contrasts between it and the old balance of power concept. "The center and characteristic of the old order was that unstable thing which we used to call the 'balance of power'—a thing in which the balance was determined by the sword which was thrown in [on] the one side or the other; a balance which was determined by the unstable equilibrium or competitive interests; a balance which was maintained by jealous watchfulness and an antagonism of interests which, though it was generally latent, was always deep-seated."[35] In contrast, Wilson described the collective security idea in his proposal for the League of Nations as "a new and more wholesome diplomacy," replacing the cynical competitive alliances of the past with a new system of cooperation in which states would strive for their common security and justice.

In sum, collective security was a more integrated and centralized concept than the balance of power, relying more upon one large cooperative alliance than upon a balance between antagonistic groups. Collective security strives to maintain total peace, whereas the balance of power tries to balance the status quo to prevent total war. Clearly the unity and idealism of collective security makes it an ideal much more difficult to achieve than the more realistic game of the balance of power, as World War II made clear.

III. Present Implications

The League and its Lessons

Wilson used the concept of collective security to father the League of Nations and to demonstrate that the voice of the United States was the voice of world peace. He elevated his organic theory of the state to an organic theory of international organization, arguing that all men must look beyond the conflict of interest to the common good, beyond the particular to the universal, and beyond the national to the supranational. The League covenant went a long way toward formally establishing the collective security principle as Wilson envisioned it. Every state that joined the League was under the obligation to preserve the territorial integrity and political independence of all the members against external aggression. Any war or threat of war was a matter of concern to the whole League. Why did not this noble, ground-breaking organization succeed?

The League failed for the same reason that Wilson failed. Both suffered from pathological idealism. They were the embodiment of extreme idealism, and were too rigid to adapt to existing social facts in order to effect their ideas.

Article 16 of the covenant provided for economic boycotts against states disobeying the agreements of the covenant and allowed for the possibility of collective military sanctions. However, because of the obstructive power of universal veto, which could be used by obstinate states, the economic sanctions were never followed consistently enough to be effective, and military sanctions never came into being at all. Wilsonian idealism had created a young, utopian animal without any teeth.

In short, the League lacked the legal authority and practical competence to make the international political decisions necessary to manage a collective security system. Potential aggressors were not discouraged sufficiently by law, and member states were not stringently required to enforce the League's principles when they were disregarded. For instance, even though members of the League banded together long enough in 1935 to initiate economic boycotts against Italy because of the Italian attack on Ethiopia, national interest soon outweighed the need for unity; the boycott withered, and Mussolini triumphed in his contempt for the League. Of course, Wilson's failure to get the United States to join the League left a critical void in the organization from which it never recovered. Founded to prevent another World War I, the League was ill equipped to handle the more calculated and organized initiation of World War II by Hitler. Without Wilsonian idealism, the noble principle of the covenant would never have been fleshed out into an organization. But powerlessness corrupts pathological idealism, and the League's lack of realism became its blindness and tragic flaw.

The Future of American Liberalism and Self-Determination

In a nutshell, Wilson's idealistic vision was of a world composed of little liberal nations. Each ethnic group would use its own self-determination at the ballot box to create perfect democratic regimes that would respect each other's rights and coexist in perfect harmony with the help of the League of Nations. However, behind that democratic idealism lay deep-seated psychological drives that had been conditioned by the American ethos and the ideological and economic advantages to be gained in the upcoming American-Soviet ideological struggle. Wilson's administration symbolized the American tension between the moral self-righteousness of the Protestant ethic and the capitalistic drive towards bourgeois success and economic profit. As a country rich in natural resources and opportunity within her own borders, the United States served to benefit more than many other countries from a policy of self-determination for all. In expanding her markets to save the world for democratic-capitalistic systems, American international idealism could easily appear self-serving in the eyes of foreigners. Moreover, the policy of liberal self-determination gave American officials an ideological basis for alternating between international interventionism and isolationism.

The Protestant-bourgeois tension and guilt that characterizes American liberalism and democratic ideology has only recently surfaced in the political consciousness of many Americans. As Americans perceive their country to become richer and richer while others become poorer and poorer, the preconditioned guilt spills out. That guilt is absorbed by greater devotion to work or the consumption of unneeded material goods and pleasures. So as Americans become increasingly aware of the dogmatic aspect of their liberal heritage and the conservative implications of their wealth and power, some new ideology must be created to keep their psyches together, one which retains the myths of the American ethos but goes beyond them. The most likely trend is a new wave of American, aristocratic individualism with a liberal face and conservative fingers. Caught in the larger global tension between the rich, industrial countries and the poor, rural countries, Americans may look toward their own self-interests first, while traveling about the world as representatives of liberal self-determination for those who can afford it and empathy and token contributions for those who cannot.

The possibility of such a conservative future has been supported recently by the representatives of the American people, their congressmen, who have developed into an art the trimming, if not the slashing, of foreign aid bills. As a nation Americans give a smaller percentage of their Gross National Product annually in foreign aid than do more than ten other countries in the world, some of whom are less able to afford it. As the economic situation worsens worldwide, Americans may become even tighter with their foreign aid purse strings than they have been in the recent past. For Americans may be naive, but they are not innocent. When they experience the slow decline of the military and economic power of the American empire, as it becomes more isolationist in the post-Vietnam War period, their remaining naiveté may be transformed into an individualistic conservatism, which looks toward values that will maintain the stability of their threatened prosperity and security while there is still time.

Yet the possibility of a more liberal future remains open for American foreign policy. The international oil, money, and food crises of the 1970s have made it clearer than ever that no nation-state in the world, including the richest nuclear superpower, can be truly independent and self-determining. Americans need foreign oil and goods, cooperative weapons reductions with the Soviet Union, and other things, which only inter-dependent interactions with other nations can provide. The old theory of the totally independent, sovereign nation-state is breaking apart in the world crises of the late twentieth century. Americans can go back to their more liberal, Jeffersonian tradition of humanism rather than the conservative, Hamiltonian tradition of bourgeois self-interest for a basis for future foreign policymaking. They can try to help create future democracies that will be oriented toward satisfying basic human needs by initiating the cooperative policies and financial incentives necessary to create a more equitable world economic system, energy pool, and international food market. To summon the courage to meet these tremendous challenges head on, a little Wilsonian idealism might not hurt at all.

Notes

1. Albert Camus, *The Myth of Sisyphus* (New York: Random House, Vintage Books, 1955), p. 91.

2. Alexander L. George and Juliette L. George, *Woodrow Wilson and Colonel House—A Personality Study*, 1964 edition (New York: Dover Publications, 1964), p. 8. The Georges' interpretation here rests heavily upon the theories of political psychologist Harold Lasswell, who in turn owes much to Sigmund Freud. See Harold Lasswell, *Psychopathology and Politics* (Chicago: University of Chicago Press, 1930). See also, William C. Bullitt and Sigmund Freud, *Thomas Woodrow Wilson* (Boston: Houghton Mifflin Co., 1967), although the reader should be warned that this psychoanalysis of a dead man is of dubious value, especially as it is based more on a fanatic devotion to Freud's belief in the Oedipus complex than on the historical facts of Wilson's life. Finally, see the brilliant critique by Arthur S. Link, "The Case for Woodrow Wilson," in A. S. Link, *The Higher Realism of Woodrow Wilson and Other Essays* (Nashville, Tenn.: Vanderbilt University Press, 1971), pp. 140-154.

3. On the importance of language as a diplomatic tool, see Thomas M. Franck and Edward Weisband, *Word Politics: Verbal Strategy among the Superpowers* (New York: Oxford University Press, 1972).

4. George and George, *Wilson and House*, p. 9. See also Stannard Baker, *Woodrow Wilson: Life and Letters*, 8 vols. (Garden City, N.Y.: Doubleday, Page & Co., 1927, 1931, 1935, 1937, 1939); and The Ray Stannard Baker Papers, (Library of Congress).

5. Baker, *Wilson: Life and Letters*, Vol. 1, pp. 92-93.

6. Harley Notter, *The Origins of the Foreign Policy of Woodrow Wilson* (Baltimore, Md.: Johns Hopkins Press, 1937), p. 8.

7. Edward Hallett Carr, *The Twenty Years' Crisis: 1919-1939* (New York: Harper & Row, 1964), pp. 12-19.

8. Baker, *Wilson: Life and Letters*, Vol. 1, p. 109.

9. George and George, *Wilson and House*, p. 23.

10. David Shapiro, *Neurotic Styles* (New York: Basic Books, 1965), Chap. 2.

11. Louis Hartz, *The Liberal Tradition in America* (New York: Harcourt, Brace & World, 1955), p. 285.

12. Ibid., p. 286.

13. H. Mark Roelofs, *The Language of Modern Politics* (Homewood, Ill.: Dorsey Press, 1967), p. 255. See also H. Mark Roelofs, *Ideology and Myth: A Critique of the American Political System* (Boston: Little, Brown & Co., forthcoming)

14. Roelofs, *Language*, pp. 224-225.

15. Woodrow Wilson, "The Ideals of America," *Atlantic Monthly* 90 (December 1902): 726.

16. Woodrow Wilson, *Division and Reunion, 1829-1889*, 11th ed. (New York: P. F. Collier & Son, 1962), p. 22.

17. See N. Gordon Levin, Jr., *Woodrow Wilson and World Politics* (New York: Oxford University Press, 1968).

18. Sidney Bell, *Woodrow Wilson and the Evolution of the New Diplomacy* (Ann Arbor, Mich.: University Microfilms, 1969).

19. Richard W. Van Alstyne, *The American Empire* (Berkeley and Los Angeles,

Calif.: University of California Press, 1960).

20. Woodrow Wilson, *Constitutional Government in the United States* (New York: Columbia University Press, 1908), pp. 56-57.

21. William W. Bishop, *International Law: Cases and Materials* (Boston: Little, Brown & Co., 1962), p. 861.

22. Ray Stannard Baker and William E. Dodd, eds., *The Public Papers of Woodrow Wilson*, 2 vols. (New York: Harper & Bros., 1925-56), Vol. 2, pp. 407-414.

23. As cited by Edward V. Gulick, *Europe's Classical Balance of Power* (New York: W.W. Norton & Co., 1965), p. 42.

24. Inis L. Claude, *Power and International Relations* (New York: Random House, 1962), p. 144.

25. As cited in George and George, *Wilson and House*, p. 189.

26. As cited in Frank P. Chambers, *This Age of Conflict—The Western World—1914 to the Present* (New York: Harcourt, Brace & World, 1962), pp. 109-110.

27. Thomas Andrew Bailey, *Woodrow Wilson and the Great Betrayal* (New York: Macmillan, Co., 1945), p. 277.

28. As cited in George and George, *Wilson and House*, p. xx.

29. Kenneth E. Boulding, "Learning and Reality-Testing Process in the International System," in John Farrell and Asa Smith, eds., *Image and Reality in World Politics* (New York: Columbia University Press, 1968), p. 3.

30. Shapiro, *Neurotic Styles*, pp. 23-53.

31. See David Calleo and Benjamin Rowland, *America and the World Political Economy* (Bloomington, Ind.: Indiana University Press, 1973); Robert A. Isaak, "American Policy and the World Economic Crisis," *Journal of International Affairs* 28, no. 1 (1974).

32. Benedetto Croce, *History of Europe in the Nineteenth Century*, trans., Henry Furst (New York: Harcourt, Brace & World, 1933), pp. 13-14.

33. Gulick, *Europe's Classical Balance of Power*, Chap. 1.

34. Article 17 as cited in George A. Finch, *The Sources of Modern International Law* (Washington, D.C.: Carnegie Endowment for International Peace, 1937), p. 67.

35. Baker and Dodd, *Public Papers of Wilson*, Vol. 1, p. 342.

Power, Racism and Total War — Hitler

A bird must sing because it is a bird.
A man who is born to be a dictator
has a right to step forward.

ADOLF HITLER

Adolf Hitler went mad with a vision for his nation and brought the world down with him. His very existence and incredible accomplishments proved his genius for political power, oratory and propaganda. Indeed, had he not attacked the Soviet Union he might have become the greatest world conqueror since Alexander the Great. However, his rigidity, cruelty, and mass slaughter of the Jewish people revealed his madness and his perversion of what it means to be human. Political genius and personal madness are often two sides of the same coin, as the twentieth century may teach us yet. Until then, the story of Hitler may serve as a warning of things to come.

In many ways the pathological idealism of individuals like Woodrow Wilson set the stage for the pathological realism of a leader like Adolf Hitler. Naive idealists open the way for brutish realists. Still many people refuse to learn what Hitler had to teach. They see him as an exception, a pervert, a racist too abominable to mention, much less to study. Yet if we cannot take time to slip into the shoes of such pathological realists to see how they think and why they are so effective, we are much more apt to become their victims in the future. Understanding peace and war is not a pleasant undertaking, and the bitter must be swallowed more often than the sweet. Moreover, those who express emotional and moral repugnance at the mention of Hitler and the term Nazi often reveal an unhealthy self-righteousness. There are many racists, nationalists, and power mongers among us. They are individuals who often find it politically useful to make scapegoats of other races, religions, and nationalities and, like Hitler, to commit historical atrocities. Hitler can never be excused and undoubtedly represents the ultimate perversion of humanity. He must be understood, however, insofar as that is possible, for who is to say that we are totally pure ourselves of all racist, nationalistic and militaristic tendencies? Who is to say that we are not capable of hating and fighting? By understanding the psychosocial and political principles that moved Hitler and the overwhelming majority of the

147

Adolf Hitler addresses the Hitler Youth Association in Nuremberg in 1934. *Wide World* photo.

German people into Nazism and world war, we may come to understand the uglier parts of ourselves and be better able to control collective human tendencies toward racism, nationalism, and war.

I. Hitler: A Political Portrait

Origins of Authoritarian Personality

Like any other human being's, Adolf Hitler's world-view was shaped by the tensions between his needs and social facts and by his effort to solve these tensions. In Hitler's case, however, a neurotic personality and perverted values, combined with the chaotic social facts of the historical period following World War I, distorted normal psychological tensions in violent ways.

Hitler was born on April 20, 1889 in the small Austrian village of Braunau on the German border. He was the third child of his father's third unhappy marriage. His father was an ill-tempered, crusty customs official of fifty-two; his mother, a peasant woman in her twenties. Both sides of the family were of peasant stock. Hitler's grandfather, Johann Georg Hiedler, was a wandering peasant who seduced a peasant girl, Maria Anna Schicklgruber. Hitler's father was born five years before his parents were married and he went by his mother's name until he was forty, when he changed his name to Hitler. As historian Louis Snyder put it, "What a stroke of fortune for the future dictator! Imagine mobs of obedient Germans shouting *Heil* Schicklgruber!"[1]

In *Mein Kampf* (My Struggle) written in 1924 Hitler tried to present himself as a child of poverty and privation, but his father had an adequate pension and gave him the opportunity for a normal education. The boy had an unhappy childhood during which he lived in constant conflict with his father and used his mother to get what he wanted. The tension came to a head when he decided he would become an artist, rather than a civil servant, as his father wished:

> I did not want to become a civil servant, no, and again no. All attempt on my father's part to inspire me with love or pleasure in this profession by stories from his own life accomplished the exact opposite. . . . One day it became clear to me that I would become a painter, an artist. . . . My father was struck speechless. . . . "Artist! No! Never as long as I live!. . . ." My father would never depart from his "Never!" And I intensified my "Nevertheless!"[2]

Hitler was a poor student and had to switch schools in 1904 because of his unsatisfactory performance. He left school at sixteen without receiving the customary Leaving Certificate. During that period he made all kinds of excuses: illness, his father's tyranny, his frustrated artistic ambitions, and political prejudice. Significantly, he did receive occasional "Excellents" in history, freehand drawing, and gymnastics—all subjects he would later tap to help create the powerful psychological symbols of the Third Reich.

After leaving school the young Hitler spent two years dreaming of becoming an artist. He did nothing to support himself, instead living off his overindulgent mother. Finally, he went to Vienna where he applied to the Academy of Fine Arts to study painting. He was rejected. Bitter but not defeated, he stayed on in Vienna as an art student even though his mother was dying of cancer at home. He went home only for her funeral and then returned to Vienna to live on an orphan's pension. There he led a solitary life and had few friends. Women were more interested in him than he in them. He was moody and often broke out in excited bursts of talk, revealing the emotional temperament of an artist without the requisite talent or training. Applying again to the Academy of Fine Arts, he was again rejected and advised to apply to the School of Architecture where he was refused for not having his School Leaving Certificate. To Hitler social facts seemed to conspire to prevent him from fulfilling his needs for self-esteem and self-actualization, and those needs drove him to seek other outlets. In that respect he was not far different from any ambitious, lower-class individual who continually perceives his needs and wants to be frustrated by a social world that rejects him.

Racism and Pathological Realism

Hitler spent the next five years in obscurity in Vienna. Many scholars believe that it was during this period of his life, as a drifter, casual laborer, and seller of second-rate picture postcards, that he picked up the anti-Semitism and ideological extremism that permeated the city. Although the frustrations of Hitler's own personality and family upbringing were acute, many of his attitudes and prejudices were typical products of his times. In 1909 Vienna was an imperial and prosperous city for the bourgeois aristocracy and the middle class, but it was an unfriendly and callous city to the growing working class and the poor. Moreover, many immigrants, including many Jews, flowed into Vienna in great numbers from Eastern Europe. Resentment quickly arose against these immigrants, since they took jobs away from the native Viennese, and that resentment was focused particularly on the successful Jews. Although Hitler received the only overcoat he owned as a gift from a Hungarian Jew, he later described his perceptions of Jews in Vienna as follows:

> Once, as I was strolling through the Inner City, I suddenly encountered an apparition in a black caftan and black hair locks. Is this a Jew? was my first thought. . . . the longer I stared at this

foreign face, scrutinizing feature for feature, the more my first question assumed a new form: Is this a German? . . . Wherever I went, I began to see Jews, and the more I saw, the more sharply they became distinguished in my eyes from the rest of humanity. Particularly the Inner City and the districts north of the Danube Canal swarmed with a people which even outwardly had lost all resemblance to Germans . . . By their very exterior you could tell that these were no lovers of water, and, to your distress, you often knew it with your eyes closed . . . Was there any form of filth or profligacy, particularly in cultural life, without at least one Jew involved in it?

If you cut even cautiously into such an abscess, you found, like a maggot in a rotting body, often dazzled by the sudden light—a kike![3]

In The Authoritarian Personality, *a study published by a group of social scientists in 1950, significant relationships were found to exist between personal attitudes of ideological extremism, racism, and authoritarianism. The research group noted the following tendencies of the authoritarian of the Right:*

(a) extreme hostility toward "outgroups";

(b) extreme submissiveness toward "ingroups";

(c) the establishment of sharp boundaries between the group of which one is a member and all others;

(d) the tendency to categorize persons with respect to certain particular qualities and to make sweeping judgments;

(e) a vision of the world as a realm of conflict;

(f) the belief that an individual and his group are the objects of manipulative designs and that survival is possible only by the manipulation of others; and so on.

Sociologist Edward Shils noted that those attitudes are true not only of Fascists on the authoritarian Right but also of Bolsheviks on the authoritarian Left. Whether "Left" or "Right;" such personalities are pathological realists whose mental rigidity uses racism and ideology as tools to gain power through constant threats and violent conflict.[4]

Pretend, for a moment, to be in Hitler's shoes. You are born at a time when the Austrian Empire is decaying; the old aristocracy and the old values are being undermined as bourgeois industrialists and merchants take over; the lower class of which you are a member is increasingly left out in the cold. Your childhood has been unhappy and your personal ambitions frustrated. You have become lazy, bitter, and hysterical at times. Jews always seem to get the jobs you want. You learn to hate, and you seek some means of revenge against the hostile social world that continually puts you down. What would be more natural than to seek some group that feels as you do about the social injustices you are experiencing and where you can lose your loneliness and find some self-esteem at long last?

Hitler found two groups that satisfied his needs, hardened his personality and political abilities, and set the stage for the Nazi movement: the German Army and the German Workers' party. Hitler had been examined for military service by the Austrian Army, which he wanted badly to join, and was declared unfit. When World War I broke out, he volunteered for the German Army and served throughout the war, being wounded in 1916 and gassed two years later. He spent most of his time as a headquarters runner on the front line. Here he finally felt significant. His bravery in action was rewarded with the Iron Cross second class and the Iron Cross first class, a rare decoration for a corporal. Years later Hitler referred to "the stupendous impression produced upon me by the war—the greatest of all experiences. For, that individual interest—the interest of one's own ego—could be subordinated to the common interest—that the great, heroic struggle of our people demonstrated in overwhelming fashion."[5] Like many of his comrades he found the war experience much more exciting and romantic than the dreary life of peacetime. Indeed, it was one of the high points of his life. The crushing German defeat and the disappointment of all the soldiers, who were thrown back into comparatively meaningless civilian roles, were two of the critical social conditions that later facilitated the rise of Hitler and the Nazi party.

To understand Hitler's later appeal to the masses of German people, it must be kept in mind that Germany's defeat in 1918 came as a profound blow to the population. They knew only of striking German victories in early 1918, for the government had kept the sudden reversal from them until the last minute. Many did not think it was possible that they had been defeated. They believed there had been some trick, some subversion or treason that had brought about the catastrophe. To have the German government request a peace settlement was even more humiliating. The final outrage was the Treaty of Versailles, which forced the Germans to sign a war guilt clause and imposed heavy territorial and financial sanctions upon them. Indeed, the reparations were impossible to pay, making the treaty a symbol of heartless injustice and humiliation. Much later, in December, 1941 Hitler announced to his troops, "After fifteen years of work I have achieved, as a common German soldier and merely with my fanatical will power, the unity of the German nation, and have freed it from the death sentence of Versailles." A treaty that stems from a vindictive spirit of pathological realism stimulates extreme reactions in the future by other pathological realists. A war that is badly settled leads inevitably to another war.

After World War I, Hitler was determined to enter politics in order to destroy the Treaty of Versailles. He went to Munich where he was soon appointed as an instruction officer with the job of innoculating the men against the contagious diseases of socialism, pacifism, and democracy. That was the first time Hitler recognized that he had any political ability. Soon thereafter, the Political Department of the German Army appointed him to investigate a small group of extremists meeting in Munich called the German Workers' party. It was an investigation that proved to have shattering consequences for the entire world.

The German Workers' party had been started by a locksmith in 1918 to combine working-class and nationalist ideals. When Hitler investigated it and then joined it, there were little more than forty members. They met in beer halls in Munich, and Hitler later admitted that he was attracted by their obscurity. He soon became the seventh member of the party's committee and began giving speeches in the Hofbrauhaus. In 1920 the committee put him in charge of propaganda, a function he performed brilliantly, drawing nearly two thousand people to the party's first mass meeting. He soon became the leader of the party and lost no chance to test his oratory on a group of people wherever he could find one.

Propaganda and Neurotic Styles of Leadership

The party's name was changed to the National Socialist German Workers' party, Nazi for short. In 1920 Hitler announced the party's twenty-five point program, which was designed to please almost everybody. Among other things, this program demanded: the end of the Treaty of Versailles; the union of all Germans in a great Germany; colonies for surplus population; a requirement permitting only those of German blood to be German citizens, thereby excluding Jews; the nationalization of all large businesses; a healthy middle class and land reform; the formation of a national army; and a strong central authority in the *Reich* to carry out this program. Hitler channeled his artistic longings into propaganda, giving the party a flag of its own and organizing a newspaper, the *Völkischer Beobachter*, the *People's Observer*.

The psychosocial tensions between needs and social facts worked out in propaganda and political organization were not Hitler's alone. These tensions were widespread among the German people, who were suffering from the failure of the Weimar democracy and the resultant political and economic chaos. Leadership, after all, is not possible without followership, and political power is a psychosocial relationship between leaders and followers to satisfy mutual needs and maximize compatible values. As a political artist who could listen to the social tremors and fears of his time, Hitler created power for himself by becoming one of the great propagandists of all time. Propaganda is the calculated spreading of political principles and doctrines. In a media-conscious age, Hitler's astute use of propaganda and political organization to rally the masses of German people behind him is vital political knowledge, for both those who might use such tools and those who want to defend themselves from such manipulation. Clearly propaganda can be used for both humane and inhumane purposes and must be taken seriously in an age of mass politics.

Psychologist William Langer identified the following principles pertaining to group psychology that Hitler used as the basis for his effective propaganda and political organization: (1) appreciation for the importance of the masses in any political movement, particularly the lower classes; (2) realization that the support of young people, who can be conditioned by early training and indoctrination, gives a social movement great momentum; (3) perception of the growing importance of the role of women in social movements and of the fact that the reactions of the masses as a whole have many feminine characteristics. For example, in 1923 Hitler said:

> Do you know the audience at a circus is just like a woman. Someone who does not understand the intrinsically feminine character of the masses will never be an effective speaker. Ask yourself: "What does a woman expect from a man?" Clearness, decision, power, and action. What we want is to get the masses to act. Like a woman, the masses fluctuate between extremes. . . . The crowd is not only like a woman, but women constitute the most important element in an audience. The women usually lead, then follow the children, and at last, when I have already won over the whole family—follow the fathers.[6]

Langer noted further psychosocial principles that Hitler used to maximize his own values and power by identifying his needs and tensions with those of the German population: (4) "The ability to feel, identify with, and express in passionate language the deepest needs and sentiments of the average German and to present opportunities or possibilities for their gratification;" (5) "Capacity to appeal to the most primitive, as well as the most ideal inclinations in man, to arouse the basest instincts and yet cloak them with nobility, justifying all actions as means to the attainment of an ideal goal;" (6) "Appreciation of the fact that the masses are as hungry for a sustaining ideology in political action as they are for daily bread. Any movement that does not satisfy this spiritual hunger in the masses will not mobilize their wholehearted support and is destined to fail;" (7) "The ability to portray conflicting human forces in vivid concrete imagery that is understandable and moving to the ordinary man;" (8) "The faculty of drawing on the traditions of the people and by reference to the great classical mythological themes evoking the deepest unconscious emotions of the audience;" (9) "Realization of the importance of artistry and dramatic intensity in conducting large meetings, rallies and festivals;" (10) "A keen appreciation of the values of slogans, catchwords, dramatic phrases, and happy epigrams in penetrating the deeper levels of the psyche;" and so on.[7] Can one doubt that Hitler was one of the most effective propaganda artists of all time and that all human beings had better pay attention to these principles which proved to be so devastatingly effective? By demonstrating that he was "every German" writ large and in almost every conceivable symbolic way, Hitler became one of history's most powerful psychic leaders of the masses and showed how easily the neuroses of authoritarian leadership can complement the crowd neuroses of submissive fellowership.

⌇⌇⌇⌇⌇⌇⌇

Neurotic authoritarianism in leadership cannot exist without neurotic submission in followership. Psychologist Erich Fromm analyzed the history of the German people through their experience of inflation, material suffering, the Lutheran religion, the resentments over the Versailles treaty and claimed that these collective social facts preconditioned many Germans to develop a sadomasochistic character. That sadomasochism predisposed them to accept a hierarchic system in which the individual owed allegiance to those higher up in the scale of authority while demanding strict obedience from those below. Such psychosocial factors explain why the German people desired an escape from freedom, longing for Hitler and the Nazi party to make difficult decisions for them in order to avoid the pain of such decision making themselves.[8]

⌇⌇⌇⌇⌇⌇⌇

German Social Facts and the Weltanschauung of the Elite

To be a German in the 1920's was no easy thing. Every day the German people suffered economically, politically, and socially the humiliation of defeat in World War I. The democratic government of the Weimar Republic was tainted from the start for having signed the repugnant Versailles treaty. On the eve of the great world depression of 1929 people suffered economic and social dislocations everywhere. The old aristocrats saw their status slipping with the rise of large industrial cartels and middle-class elites. Officers and soldiers, who had found real meaning in life in the war, now found themselves without a cause, without status, and often without a job. Germans at that time longed for leadership and a meaningful alternative to the economic and social crises. When Hitler rose to power no other viable alternative for strong political leadership seemed to exist.

Political sociologist Seymour Martin Lipset has argued that German Fascism was basically a lower middle-class movement representing a protest against both capitalism and socialism, big business and big unions.[9] Political psychologist Harold Lasswell supported that view in his study of the psychology of Hitlerism:

Insofar as Hitlerism is a desperation reaction of the lower middle classes, it continues a movement which began during the closing years of the nineteenth century. Materially speaking, it is not necessary to assume that the small shopkeepers, teachers, preachers, lawyers, doctors, farmers and craftsmen were worse off at the end than they had been in the middle of the century. Psychologically speaking, however, the lower middle class was increasingly overshadowed by the workers and the upper bourgeoisie, whose unions, cartels and parties took the center of the stage. The psychological impoverishment of the lower middle class precipitated emotional insecurities within the personalities of its members, thus fertilizing the ground for the various movements of mass protest through which the middle classes might revenge themselves.[10]

Like other lower middle-class Germans', Hitler's world-view was shaped by the tensions between his psychological needs and the depressing social facts of his environment. His father had humiliated him, the school system had deflated his artistic ambitions, and the existing social order kept him down. To the extent that he could identify those tensions and aspects of his own past with the German people, he could use such similarities to communicate with them, to create a powerful political ideology, and to make himself into a charismatic leader with a solution to their social problems. As we noted earlier in the chapter on Mao, such leaders emerge in times of social crisis because they hold out an alternative or possible solution, a dream or vision to replace the crumbling social status quo around them. Oddly enough, although no one would deny that Hitler had a world-view like any other human being, scholars following World War II have often tried to deny that he had anything that approached a vision or **Weltanschauung**, an almost untranslatable German term for a world-view with "overtones of ideology, of a tendency towards, but not necessarily a fulfillment of, a systematic, comprehensive view of the world."[11] In short, a *Weltanschauung* is a comprehensive and carefully articulated world-view that has the potential to become a philosophy of life or ideology for action.

Everyman is assumed to have a world-view, or a way of looking at the world growing out of the tensions between his peculiar needs and wants and the facts of his social environment and upbringing. Special individuals try to make their world-views into Weltanschauungen and turn them into coherent thought, ideology, or action. However, the illusion that only philosophers of high moral integrity are able to articulate workable Weltanschauungen persists despite the pathological realists, like Hitler, who have used them with devastating effectiveness. Hitler's slaughter of the Jews, Stalin's elimination of the peasant class of Kulaks, and the

American use of the atomic bomb on Japan are all examples of morally questionable world-views.

Historian Eberhard Jäckel has demonstrated that Hitler did, indeed, have a *Weltanschauung* that became the Nazi party's blueprint for the seizure of power.[12] Motivated in large part by personal needs and those of the German people, particularly their need for self-esteem, Hitler drew on his fragmentary reading in history, philosophy, and racist journalism to create a vision of a new German empire based on a master race of blond, blue-eyed, Aryan Germans, who would purify themselves of all inferior non-German elements, beginning with the Jews. Of course, Hitler himself did not have blond hair or blue eyes and may even have had Jewish blood in his background, but that did not stop his wild vision. Nor did it stop the masses of German people to whom he sold his vision as the way to satisfy their needs and desires. Linking hero worship and *Volk* worship, or worship of the German people, with state worship, Hitler and the propaganda artists he engaged created a powerful psychopolitical ideology that became the basis for violent political action.

Hitler's foreign policy designs grew naturally out of his *Weltanschauung*. He decided to play states against each other to further his vision of a German empire, the Third Reich. As early as 1920 he planned to exploit Italian-French antagonisms to win an alliance with Italy. He then hoped for a further alliance with either the Soviet Union or Great Britain, preferably the latter, so that he could isolate France, his primary enemy. After France had been conquered Hitler planned to launch an offensive against Eastern Europe and the Soviet Union, allowing Germany to fulfill her revisionist demands of 1918 and to create living space for future Germans. Such strategies that make geography the basis for power in international politics are called **geopolitics**.

The greatest ideological enemy for Hitler was not liberal democracy but the other rival *Weltanschauung*, Marxism, behind which he saw the Jew whom he identified as a mythical incarnation of evil. Thus, his later decision to attack the Soviet Union was already deeply embedded in his ideological outlook.

The social and economic instability created by the 1929 world depression and the inability of the Weimar Republic to deal with the growing problems in Germany greatly facilitated the growth of the Nazi party and Hitler's rise to power. As social facts became unstable and uncertainty mounted, the masses of the population longed for strong leadership to put things right again and to create stability. At that point, Hitler revealed his skills as a shrewd political tactician. He cooperated with the Nationalist party to use its organization and newspapers for his purposes. That enabled him, in turn, to appeal as a gifted agitator to leaders of large business and industrial concerns who desired to support a strong right-wing, antiworking-class government with their funds. Such funding made Hitler's mass agitation and constant propaganda much more effective. The Nazi party became the second largest party in the country in 1930 with more than 6,000,000 votes. Moreover, Hitler always had his private army, the SA or **Sturmabteilungen**, handy to threaten politicians with local street violence if they did not go along with him or at least compromise. Such clever political manipulations finally resulted in his appointment in 1933 as chancellor of Germany by President von Hindenburg.

Pathological Realism and Total War

Once chancellor, Hitler soon persuaded the president to call another election following the **Reichstag** fire, which was supposedly set by a Communist. The Nazis polled 43 percent of the votes, and soon thereafter, the Reichstag passed an enabling bill giving Hitler full power to settle the social violence that he himself had helped to instigate. Hitler's was a rightist revolution of hatred based on pathological realism—the seizure of power by any means regardless of other values or long-term consequences. In 1934 when the leaders of his own SA refused to agree with him, Hitler had them executed without trial. Not accidentally, those executions won the support of the German Army, which feared the SA. The recovery of the world economy helped to better economic and employment conditions in Germany, for which Hitler took credit, and made the Nazi regime more acceptable. Indeed, 90 percent of the voters supported Hitler in a plebiscite.*

Hitler's use of terror and the execution of all political enemies, not to mention his use of Jews, Slavs, Communists, and dissidents as scapegoats, both intimidated the population and inspired their respect. Here at last was a strong leader in times of great economic and social disorder. After consolidating his dictatorship at home, Hitler began immediately to initiate his Pan-German foreign policy, based on the reunion of all German people in Europe under one political authority. He hated the Slavs, especially the Bolsheviks, and planned to subordinate the Poles and the Slavic people of the Soviet Union to the Teutonic master race and the new German Reich that was to last for 1,000 years. *Mein Kampf* spelled out his objectives in detail, and yet at the time it was totally ignored by the world. Indeed *Mein Kampf* was one of the least read best-sellers in history.

To make his plans for expansion possible, Hitler used all of his propaganda techniques to allay the suspicions of the other powers and to eliminate the restrictions placed on Germany by the Versailles treaty. Posing as the champion of Europe against the threat of communist Russia, Hitler claimed to be a man of peace, interested only in righting the injustices forced upon Germany following World War I. However, he withdrew from

---

*This official percentage is somewhat misleading since resistance was not expressed in the form of the plebiscite as much as in other ways (destroying one's ballot totally, and other non-electoral ways).

the Disarmament Conference and the League of Nations in 1933, although he quickly signed a nonaggression pact with Poland. National Socialist sympathizers created small Nazi parties in Austria and Czechoslovakia which Hitler used. An attempt at a coup d'etat in Austria by Austrian Nazis failed after the murder of the Austrian chancellor. Hitler disclaimed all involvement and eliminated those responsible, even though they had, in fact, acted with his sanction. A 1935 plebiscite returned the Saarland to Germany, and Hitler officially proclaimed he had no further interest in French territory. As the ultimate pathological realist, Hitler believed that big lies worked much more effectively than small ones.

In 1936 he used a French-Soviet pact as an excuse to remilitarize the Rhineland, ignoring the Treaty of Versailles and the advice of his own military staff. Soon he established German alliances with both Italy and Japan and began the total mobilization of the German population and resources for war. Hitler demonstrated how a pathological realist functions diplomatically when he invited the Austrian Chancellor, Kurt von Schuschnigg, to his headquarters for a visit and then forced him to sign an agreement freeing the Austrian Nazis from jail to do what they wanted. Returning home, Schuschnigg tried to repudiate the agreement and announced a plebiscite on the question of **Anschluss** or union with Germany. Hitler ordered his troops to occupy Austria, and his enthusiastic reception there encouraged him to annex Austria outright. As Hitler returned in triumph to the Vienna that had treated him so badly in his youth, the French and the British stood by and did nothing. Only another realist can stop a pathological realist on the march and neither the French nor the British leaders were at all realistic. Typically, their view of realism and self-interest was not to become involved, a selfish, shortsighted policy that was to cost them dearly.

Announcing that the Anschluss would not affect German relations with Czechoslovakia, Hitler immediately made his plans against that country. He ordered the leader of the German minority in Czechoslovakia to press for impossible demands to justify German annexation. The British and French were willing to compel the Czech government to give in to those demands and cede the Sudetenland to Germany. Such counselling was part of the notorious French-English policy of appeasement during that period, which, in effect, argued that when a sheep donates one of his legs to a wolf, the wolf will be satisfied and will let him alone. Mussolini of Italy also intervened, so Hitler settled reluctantly for a nonmilitary conquest of Czechoslovakia and signed the Munich agreement.

However, Hitler fostered Slovak discontent to justify his occupation of the whole of Czechoslovakia in 1939. He was now ready for his main objective, **Lebensraum**, or German living space in the East. Ignoring the British and French guarantee to defend Poland, Hitler prepared to attack that country by strengthening his alliance with Italy and signing a nonaggression pact with the Soviet Union. The day after the Hitler-Stalin pact was signed in Moscow, Hitler said to his generals:

> I shall give a propagandist cause for starting the war. Never
> mind whether it is plausible or not. The victor will not be asked,
> later on, whether we told the truth or not. In starting and waging
> war, it is not Right that matters, but Victory. Have no pity.
> Adopt a brutal attitude. . . . Complete destruction of Poland is
> the military aim. To be fast is the main thing. Pursue until
> complete annihilation.[13]

*The ultimate outcome of pathological realism is total war. A total war is an
unlimited war in which all human and material resources of the aggressors
are mobilized and used against every aspect of the national life of the
enemy. Only the weapons technology of the twentieth century has made
total war possible. In previous centuries, men had had to settle for
"unlimited wars" in which all means were used to obtain unlimited
objectives, but the military means themselves prevented the aggressors
from totally destroying the enemy, as in the war between Rome and
Carthage. Political scientist Raymond Aron writes, "The essential difference between the thermonuclear age and the pre-Atomic Age . . . is the
difference in the cost of a total war, that is a war with all available weapons
until absolute victory. Henceforth a state can be destroyed, a population
exterminated in the very course of hostilities without having been previously disarmed. . . . A state which has no retaliatory capacity must accept
any ultimatum presented by a state possessing a thermonuclear system."[14]*

On September 1, 1939 Hitler invaded Poland. Two days later the
French and British declared war on Germany, and World War II began. The
French and English were ill prepared for war. Appeasement politics did not
prepare them for total conflict. Hitler had been mobilizing and planning for
war for literally years. Throughout the thirties he showed great astuteness
in analyzing and exploiting the weaknesses of democracies and indecisive
politicians. He quickly succeeded in Poland, further reinforcing his belief in
his infallibility. Although he immediately ordered his army to prepare for
an attack on the West, bad weather postponed his plans. Instead, the Nazis
launched an attack on Denmark and Norway and another through the
Ardennes, which were both brilliant successes and for which Hitler could
claim much credit for the overall planning. In June, 1940 Mussolini led Italy
into the war on the German side, and Hitler revenged the Treaty of
Versailles by forcing the French to sign an armistice on the same spot where
the 1918 armistice was signed.

Next Hitler initiated the aerial bombardment of Britain. Expecting the

British to be quickly defeated, he went ahead with plans for his major campaign, Operation Barbarossa against the hated Slavic Communists in the Soviet Union. Political scientist John Stoessinger has written:

> What he really yearned to do with all the passion of his demonic nature was to destroy Russia altogether, to crush her government, to pulverize her economy, to enslave her people, and to eliminate her as a political entity. . . . It was this childlike single-mindedness that made Hitler's attack on Russia so utterly destructive and so difficult to comprehend. Stalin was indeed afraid that Hitler might attack some day, but he believed that the Führer would first present him with an ultimatum to which a rational response might be possible. It did not occur to the Soviet leader that Hitler would attack no matter what, and he was not alone in this belief. [15]

Hitler's *Weltanschauung*, the determination to restructure world order according to his own imperial view and the transference of his own intense personal and social frustrations to the Russians and the Jews, led to such an extreme ideological hatred that it blinded him to the strategic realities of 1940 and 1941. His desire to attack the Soviet Union was so strong that he underestimated the ability of the British to resist, and he thought that a swift victory in the Soviet Union would totally undermine British morale. Furthermore, his belief in German infallibility led him to divert German troops to Greece to help Mussolini and to Yugoslavia to stamp out a coup. Those two diversions postponed Operation Barbarossa four weeks, a critical time period as the German soldiers bitterly discovered during the brutal winter of 1941 on harsh Russian terrain. Indeed, Hitler realized his great error shortly before his death and, while Russians surrounded him in the bunker of the Reich chancellery he was supposed to have screamed at a painting of Frederick the Great, "Give me back my four weeks!" [16]

So confident was Hitler of success when he launched his attack upon the Soviet Union in June, 1941 that he failed to provide winter clothing and equipment for his troops, which proved to be a cruel mistake. As the Russian campaign began to go badly, Hitler grew increasingly dogmatic and insisted on directing military policy himself. When Japan attacked Pearl Harbor, Hitler immediately declared war on the United States, for his rigid Central European vision blinded him to the force the United States could bring to bear on Europe. In short, when Hitler's neurotic mental rigidity set in, he became so intensely emotional and dogmatic that his will froze and he lost all sense of perspective. In 1942 such obsessive-compulsive rigidity caused him to pay insufficient attention to the Atlantic and Mediterranean arenas, where a little extra effort might have turned the tide toward Germany. His mental state even prevented him from concentrating totally on his main objective, the defeat of the Soviet Union, and he lost the opportunity to capture Stalingrad while it was lightly defended.

Moreover, many of Hitler's military advisers were also pathological realists who desired total power and victory above all other human values. The **Führer** directed Heinrich Himmler to set the stage for a "new order" in Europe. Concentration camps were established in 1933 and between 4,500,000 and 6,000,000 Jews of Germany, Poland and the Soviet Union were murdered. The Nazis achieved ultimate dehumanization of human technology as millions of human beings were efficiently gassed and their bodies used for soap, wigs, and lampshades. Later the American military elite exhibited similar extreme dehumanization when it ordered the atomic bombing of Japan. In total war, pathological realism becomes normal, and there is no limit, except for that built into technology, to man's inhuman torture of man.

Even when defeat became inevitable, Hitler did not step back and try to save what he could but condemned his troops to senseless death by refusing to surrender. In the final hours of the war, Hitler married his mistress, Eva Braun, and then shot himself while she took poison. The world has yet to recover from the amazingly effective, perverted willpower of this one man.

II. Principles of World Politics

Psychopathology and Authoritarian Leadership

Hitler epitomized the psychopathology of realism just as Wilson represented the psychopathology of idealism. The Führer's image of the world, or his *Weltanschauung*, became so rigid that it did not fit reality and led him to emotional bursts of senseless activity rather than to the reconsideration of new ideas and evidence. Oddly enough, at critical moments the masses of men perceived both Wilson and Hitler to be strong, highly respectable leaders exactly because of their uncompromising mental rigidity. The psychopathology of leadership is only matched by the psychopathology of followership.

As political psychologist Harold Lasswell wrote in his classic, *Psychopathology and Politics:*

> The pathological mind, if one may indulge in a lame analogy, is like an automobile with its control lever stuck in one gear: the normal mind can shift. One has a queer feeling as one passes around the wards of a hospital for the custody of the more seriously disordered patients that if one could assemble the scattered parts of the mind that one could create at least a single supermind.[17]

Pathological world leaders are like single-minded control levers stuck in one gear, while their pathological followers jump on board because they feel that here is a driver who knows exactly where he is going. Both have in common the repugnance for uncertainty and the intolerance of ambiguity that mark authoritarian personality types.

Psychologist Abraham Maslow noted that in Western civilization strong cultural forces foster both authoritarian and democratic characters, that is, capitalism, nationalism, militarism, authoritarian education, the patriarchal family versus the Christian ideal, humanitarianism, socialism, cooperative movements.[18] In a world of unusually chaotic social facts many scholars believe that, because of their predisposition toward authoritarian social relationships and political structure, the German people perceived an acute need for authoritarian leadership in the 1920s and 1930s. For example, some believe that this need for authoritarian leadership resulted from the typical authoritarian structure of the German family, where the father's word was absolute law.[19] Opportunities for authoritarian leadership are particularly great in an age of mass politics marked by continual socioeconomic crises and political upheaval. In short, Hitler came to represent the solution to the extreme tensions between the frustrated personal, social, and political needs of the German people, on the one hand, and the social facts of German humiliation, economic chaos, and political uncertainty following World War I, on the other. The German people longed for order, and Hitler gave it to them. *Authoritarianism* is a longing for absolute authority and order to the point of blindness to all other values. And it takes two to tango: the elite and the mass. The authoritarian leader must be able to put himself psychologically into his followers' shoes to feel and epitomize their needs in his propaganda and actions.

The Socio-Psychology of Nationalism

To fall in love with a leader is one thing. To fall in love with a state is quite another. If a person falls in love with an authoritarian leader, there is a chance that he will break off the affair, if he is deceived, or that the leader will fall out of power. People who fall in love with their nation-state are much more hopeless cases, for nation-states are far more permanent than leaders.

Recall that nation-states are groups of people on specific territories who have similar world-views and who are organized and directed around by elites. Harold Guetzkow, psychologist, sociologist, and political scientist, has shown that "groups in general are organized to meet human needs: their structures and processes are in part molded by these needs."[20] He has further suggested that national groups fulfill economic, sociocultural, and political needs, including security, group loyalty, and prestige. In terms of these needs, the German people felt acute deprivation after World War I, and therefore their longing for strong, nationalistic leadership became extremely great.

The study *The Authoritarian Personality* demonstrated a strong relationship between extreme nationalism and racism. Patriotism did not indicate "love of country" as much as "blind attachment to certain national cultural values, uncritical conformity with the prevailing group ways, and the rejection of other nations as outgroups."[21] The study focused mainly on the social and psychological roots of fascism and anti-Semitism in Hitler's Germany. The implication is clear, however: extreme nationalists everywhere tend to suffer from racism and ethnocentrism. To the extent that we are all brought up on our own brand of nationalism at home and in school, we are all apt to reveal the mental rigidity underlying nationalism and racism at certain points in our lives.

The difficulty, of course, in falling in love with one's own race or nation-state is that cooperative interracial and international relations become almost impossible. Delusions of racial and national superiority are among the basic causes of violence and war.

Propaganda and Mass Behavior

Racism, nationalism, authoritarianism—in fact, any ism imaginable—can be made into an ideology for a mass political movement through propaganda. Recall that propaganda is the calculated propagation of political principles and doctrines. Doubts concerning Hitler's intelligence vanish quickly when one turns to his ability as a propaganda artist. He knew that propaganda must be addressed only to the masses, and he wrote in *Mein Kampf*:

> The function of propaganda does not lie in the scientific training of the individual, but in calling the masses' attention to certain facts, processes, necessities, etc., whose significance is thus for the first time placed within their field of vision.
>
> The whole art consists in doing this so skillfully that everyone will be convinced that the fact is real, the process necessary, the necessity correct, etc. But since propaganda is not and cannot be the necessity in itself, since its function, like the poster, consists in attracting the attention of the crowd, and not in educating those who are already educated or who are striving after education and knowledge, its effect for the most part must be aimed at the emotions and only to a very limited degree at the so-called intellect.
>
> All propaganda must be popular and its intellectual level must be adjusted to the most limited intelligence among those it is addressed to. Consequently, the greater the mass it is intended to reach, the lower its purely intellectual level will have to be. . . .
>
> It is a mistake to make propaganda many-sided, like scientific instruction, for instance.

Hitler delivers a war tirade to the Reichstag on the morning of the invasion of Poland. *Wide World photo.*

The receptivity of the great masses is very limited, their intelligence is small, but their power of forgetting is enormous. In consequence of these facts, all effective propaganda must be limited to a very few points and must harp on these in slogans until the last member of the public understands what you want him to understand by your slogan. . . .

The function of propaganda is, for example, not to weigh and ponder the rights of different people, but exclusively to emphasize the one right which it has set out to argue for. Its task is not to make an objective study of the truth, in so far as it favors the enemy, and then set it before the masses with academic fairness; its task is to serve our own right, always and unflinchingly."[22]

Hitler realized that propaganda appeals to the subconscious emotions of the masses. Like Madison Avenue advertisers he knew that a simple slogan often repeated is most effective and that big lies are more persuasive than small ones. Moreover, he used propaganda in every phase of political life—in the symbols of the swastika, the flag, the Hitler salute, and the goose step. There were Hitler youth groups, Nazi sports events, and national baby production. Women did not have to be married to have babies, and even fourteen-year-old girls could have "the Führer's children."

In short, Hitler was a master of shaping powerful propaganda symbols that would raise the emotions and represent the needs of masses of German people. As philosopher and psychologist Herbert Spencer has noted, symbolic expression does not dissipate emotions but concentrates them. Although symbolic activity allows us to direct our emotions and frustrations outside of ourselves, our feelings are intensified and brought to a climax in the process. Symbols play upon our irrational impulses and needs and allow us to identify with other people. Hitler used all kinds of symbols and dramatic procedures at mass political rallies to excite his audience before he even appeared. Then, in a speech often bordering on hysteria he offered them a solution that appealed to them both rationally and irrationally. The ultimate expression of propaganda is the charismatic leader himself who embodies the solution to the many problems of people caught in crisis situations.

Totalitarianism

Hitler's *Weltanschauung* was based on pushing his political logic to its extreme conclusion, to make it total, encompassing everything. The desire to control all forms of social and cultural life by the state and the governing elite is totalitarianism. Indeed, much of Western political thought can be characterized by the extent to which society is separate from or consumed by the state. It is not accidental that totalitarian regimes are often headed by authoritarian, charismatic figures who symbolize the epitome of the official and the only permissible ideology. Indeed, as we have seen in the stories of Lenin, Mao, and Hitler, totalitarian states are often merely the concretization of a total vision or *Weltanschauung* of strong political leaders and their chosen associates. The division of power, or checks and balances, between executive, legislative, and judicial branches of government in Western democracies is one of the few safeguards against totalitarianism that man has devised. Yet even here, quasi-totalitarian or authoritarian regimes can emerge, as we will note in the tale of de Gaulle's France in the next chapter.

Paranoia and the Zero-Sum Game

The all-or-nothing mental rigidity characteristic of authoritarian personalities and totalitarian regimes is often reflected in uncompromising diplomatic strategies as well. Hitler's belief in total war and the total elimination of Slavic and Soviet power, not to mention the Jews, is a case in point. That kind of thinking is a type of pathological realism that manifests itself in everyday life as paranoia. Paranoia is a mental disorder marked by systematic delusions of persecution and of one's own greatness. Because of the egomania required to become a strong national leader and because others are actually out to get you, legally or illegally, paranoia is a mental illness almost as widespread as the common cold among politicians.

Logically speaking, paranoid people view all situations as potential pure-conflict situations and consequently do not fully trust anyone. Such logical situations are often symbolized by conflict theorists by the **zero-sum game**—a game like chess or checkers in which whatever one side gains the other side loses exactly. To see all political situations as zero-sum games is paranoid since you assume that cooperation is never in your rational interest and that your opponent will get the goods if you don't get them first. To see everything as a zero-sum game is to live psychologically in a constant state of war. Hitler saw all of political life as constant struggle and war in which all the spoils would go to the victor and humiliation and death to the loser.

Madness and Total War

If one national elite is planning total war against another nation or its allies and the leaders of the latter ignore evidence of such intentions, they are pathological idealists, since they are unable to think in zero-sum terms when the situation calls for it. The British and French elites, not to mention the Soviet and American, ignored the many warnings Hitler gave them of his intentions of total war: his renunciation of the Treaty of Versailles; his withdrawal from the League of Nations and the Disarmament talks; his rearmament and mobilization of troops; his occupation of the Rhineland; his *Anschluss* with Austria; his seizure of the Sudetenland in Czechoslovakia; and his string of broken promises. If madness consists of frozen mental images that do not fit or communicate effectively with the actual events of the world, one could argue that in the 1930s all the national elites who advocated appeasement or nonintervention were stark raving mad and did much to encourage Hitler to start World War II. Their pathological idealism stimulated his greater pathological realism to the point of total war.

Although political uses of madness have long been described in literature (e.g. Hamlet, who feigned mental disorder to bring about the Danish king's downfall and restore justice to his country), political scientists have been oddly reluctant to study such phenomena. Perhaps it is the obsession with rationality and optimistic scientism in Western thought that deters Western social scientists from probing the emotional and subconscious sides of political behavior, the aspects Hitler manipulated brilliantly. It should be noted that the controversial Daniel Ellsberg, who released "The Pentagon Papers" on the Vietnam War, much to the horror of the United States government, gave a series of lectures on "The Art of Coercion," at the Lowell Institute at Boston in 1959, including lectures on "The Political Uses of Madness," and "The Theory and Practice of Blackmail." But, alas, such people are so effective they do not stay long in academia, and political science is still without theories of political madness and blackmail.

Indeed, in many ways, the world of nation-states today is a madhouse. Diplomats lie and mislead; elites ignore larger global realities to cultivate their own nationalistic fantasy worlds; the poor starve in one room while the rich live luxuriously in the next; and international status is determined in accordance with a nation-state's ability to fight total nuclear war. To be a superpower is to be capable of being the maddest of the mad. We can perhaps measure our own mental health on the worldwide scale by determining how closely we see the world as it really is, as an emotional, violent insane asylum. As psychiatrist Ronald Laing noted in 1967, normal men have killed perhaps 100,000,000 of their fellow men in the last fifty years.[23] Such killing has been most efficiently executed based on ideologies of nationalistic folk learning like Nazism, which even Hitler himself carefully distinguished from scientific world-views when he wrote on propaganda. Social scientist Kenneth Boulding wrote in 1967:

> Between the world of folk learning and the folk images derived from it, and the world of scientific learning and the scientific images derived from it, there lies another world of images that I have elsewhere described, perhaps unkindly, as the world of literary images. It is in this world, however, that we find the images of the international system by which its decision-makers are largely governed, and it is for this reason that the international system is by far the most pathological and costly

segment of the total social system, or sociosphere, as it is sometimes called. If we look at the various elements that are ordinarily regarded as pathological, such as crime, mental and physical disease, and economic stagnation, the international system probably costs about as much as all these put together, with the possible exception of economic stagnation, which is itself in part a function of the nature of the international system.

The direct cost of the international system must now amount to something like 150 billion dollars a year. This would include the total spent by all the nations on their military establishments, information systems, foreign offices, diplomatic corps, and so on. In addition, some estimate of the present value of possible future destruction should be included. . . . To be pessimistic, let us suppose that the destruction of a third world war would amount to half the present physical capital of the world, or about two thousand billion dollars, and that the chance of this happening is about five per cent in any one year; in this case we should add a kind of depreciation or discounting factor to existing world wealth of about 100 billion dollars a year.[24]

Here Boulding is describing the costs of another total war that are built into the the present international system and that make it pathological. Recall that a total war is an unlimited war in which all human and material resources of the aggressors are mobilized and used against every aspect of the national life of the enemy. It is a sad world in which the status of a nation-state and its elite are dependent upon its ability to wage total war.

III. Present Implications

Neurotic Styles in Diplomatic Bargaining

In a mad world where nationalistic leaders build up their status by authorizing nuclear arms buildups that have the potential to eliminate their worst enemy several times over, it should not be surprising that neurotic styles often prove to be effective in diplomatic bargaining, particularly in crisis situations. For example, Hitler's hatred, racism, and general mental rigidity aided him in intimidating his opponents over the bargaining table where he would often go into a rage to obtain the desired results. Indeed, in an interview with Dr. Emil Hácha, the president of Czechoslovakia, just before German troops entered that country, Hitler's rage and hatred for the Slavs were so great that Hácha's later political capitulation was undoubtedly due to the effectiveness of Hitler's neurotic diplomatic style, as well as his threat to bomb Prague.

Another notorious example of an effective neurotic diplomatic move was Premier Nikita Khrushchev's apparent display of temper in 1960 at the United Nations, where he banged his shoe on the rostrum and smiled all the while. Such behavior was probably meant to confuse the opponents of Soviet policy and create a fear of Soviet unpredictability in order to achieve psychological power. Strategic experts have noted that "we might compare the alternations between Khrushchev's avowals of peaceful intentions and threats of nuclear destruction with the alternate ringing of high and low frequency bells which, in the Pavlovian experiment with dogs and rabbits, were gradually brought closer together until the animal became paralyzed by terror or went berserk."[25]

Similarly, political scientist John Stoessinger has observed, "Another Soviet device in its relations with the West has been the employment of zigzag tactics. It seems that the rationale of such tactics is to cause the opponent to build up a defense against zig, and shortly before it becomes effective, to 'annul' this defense by performing a zag."[26] Hitler likewise threw his enemies off guard by proclaiming peace one day and then initiating quick, massive, surprise attacks soon thereafter. Stalin was so shocked when Hitler attacked that he suffered a nervous breakdown. The essence of neurotic bargaining is to persuade your opponent that you will do one thing and then surprise him by doing the opposite. The method is effective precisely because the reversal seems so risky and inconsistent that your opponent cannot believe any sane person would do it. Shakespeare said: "Though this be madness, yet there is method in't".

Nationalism, Racism, and Ethonocentrism

Hitler's power came in large part from his ability to identify with the needs and values of his people, neurotic or normal. Indeed, all the leaders considered in this book have created power for themselves at one time or another in their careers by appealing directly or indirectly to the nationalistic and cultural feelings of their people. Such values are existing social facts, which, however perverted, serve as the basis for powerful leadership of mass publics in our age. As long as people are divided up into antagonistic nation-states many will think "my country, race, and culture, right or wrong" and nationalism, racism, and ethnocentrism will continue to plague the world. When will people learn to think "my humanity right or wrong" and try to live up to that? Until then, elites will continue to manipulate the masses by playing upon their instinctive psychological fears and their delusions of ethnic superiority. Moreover, in periods of international tension and crisis, such as those which seem probable in the future, the primitive emotions of nationalism, racism, and ethnocentrism can be expected to dominate world politics. Under such conditions neurotic and pathological modes of adapting to a mad world will seem to be the most rational response to many insecure human beings.

Future Totalitarianism and Technological Repression

As less developed societies strive for rapid modernization, the temptation to use totalitarian solutions and authoritarian leaders will be great indeed, if not irresistible. Moreover, in advanced industrial and post-industrial societies, technology gives rise to its own kinds of authoritarianism and repression which are as powerful as those of avowedly totalitarian states. In *One-Dimensional Man*, radical philosopher Herbert Marcuse argued that Americans are being psychosocially reduced to a single dimension, and he warned that technology has the potential power to repress human freedom. Technology has refined the role of torture in order to transform it into an administrative means to govern in both the physical and psychological realms. The Nazi concentration camps were examples of the ultimate abuse of modern technology if it is not carefully related to humanistic values. The technological coercion of consumerism through the media is a less harmful variety of repression, but is repression and mind control nevertheless. Such consumerism for its own sake does have human implications in a world where millions are suffering from hunger and real needs while a fortunate minority is persuaded to seek continually to satisfy needs that are artificially created by the media. Furthermore, the excessive stimulation toward violence on television is another example of the dehumanizing and repressive powers of technology that are not guided by humanistic moral standards.

Swiss novelist Max Frisch once said that technology is "the knack of so arranging the world that we don't have to experience it." And social scientist Jürgen Habermas incisively observed that as a nation-state becomes modernized through technology, its amount of technologically exploitable knowledge increases without a similar advancement in the creation of democratic controls of such technology.[27] In short, the purposive reason behind the scientism of technological knowledge is the desire of the technocratic elites to manipulate the masses for their own ends. Technological reason is not objectively detached from human affairs but is based on the maximization of certain human interests as opposed to others. The technology of world war has thus advanced more more rapidly than the technology of world food production, since elites of well-to-do countries continually favor their interest in their own security over their interest in solving the world food crisis. The technological repression of authoritarian societies involves an elite imposing its own dehumanized arrangements upon masses of people and forcing them to suffer in ways that the elites themselves never have.

From Hitler we should learn what can result if we give up individual responsibility and willpower to technological experts and supermen, if we give up critical thinking for the sake of simplistic solutions that appeal to our prejudices and material comfort, and if we go along with the easy conformity of national mass movements rather than picking our way slowly through the social world to fight for our individual freedom choice by choice. As Nietzsche said, "It is annihilators who set traps for the many and call them 'state': they hang a sword and a hundred appetites over them. . . . Only where the state ends, there begins the human being who is not superfluous: there begins the song of necessity, the unique and inimitable tune."[28]

Notes

1. Louis L. Snyder, *Hitler and Nazism* (New York: Bantam Books, 1971), p. 2.

2. Adolf Hitler, *Mein Kampf*, trans., James Murphy (London: Hurst and Blackett, 1939), p. 22. Other sources for the portrait of Hitler, but which are not referred to in specific notes, include: Werner Maser, *Hitler's Mein Kampf: An Analysis*, trans., R. H. Barry (London: Faber & Faber, 1970); Adolf Hitler, *Hitler's Secret Conversations 1941-1944*, trans. N. Cameron and R. Stevens (New York: Octagon Books, 1972); Joachim Fest, *The Face of the Third Reich: Portraits of the Nazi Leadership*, trans. M. Bullock (New York: Ace Books, 1970); Adolf Hitler, *Hitler's Secret Book*, trans. S. Attanasio (New York: Grove Press, 1961); and Adolf Hitler, *My New Order*. ed. Raoul Deroussey De Sales (New York: Reynal & Hitchcock, 1941).

3. Written in 1924 when Hitler served his prison term in the fortress of Landsberg am Lech, from Adolf Hitler, *Mein Kampf*, trans. Ralph Manheim (Boston: Houghton Mifflin Co., 1943), pp. 56-57.

4. See T. Adorno et al., *The Authoritarian Personality* (New York: Harper & Row, 1950); E. A. Shils, "Authoritarianism: 'Right' and 'Left'," in R. Christie and M. Jahoda, eds., *Studies in the Scope and Method of the Authoritarian Personality* (New York: Macmillan, Free Press, 1954), pp. 27-49.

5. Alan Bullock, *Hitler, A Study in Tyranny* (New York: Harper & Row, 1962), p. 53.

6. Walter Langer, *The Mind of Adolf Hitler* (New York: Basic Books, 1972), pp. 63-64.

7. Ibid., pp. 64-68.

8. Erich Fromm, *Escape From Freedom* (New York: Holt, Rinehart & Winston, 1941).

9. Seymour Martin Lipset, *Political Man: The Social Basis of Politics* (New York: Doubleday Co., Anchor Press 1963), p. 131.

10. Harold Lasswell, "The Psychology of Hitlerism," *Political Quarterly* 4 (1933): 374.

11. This is Herbert Arnold's definition, which he presents in his "translator's Forward" to Eberhard Jäckel, *Hitler's Weltanschauung: A Blueprint for Power*, trans. Herbert Arnold (Middletown, Conn.: Wesleyan University Press, 1972), p. 8. Jäckel demonstrates that Hitler did have a *Weltanschauung* despite the claims of others to the contrary.

12. Ibid.

13. Robert Payne, *The Life and Death of Adolf Hitler* (New York: Praeger Publishers, 1973), p. 361.

14. Raymond Aron, *Peace and War: A Theory of International Relations* (New York: Praeger Publishers, 1967), p. 435.

15. John Stoessinger, *Why Nations Go to War* (New York: St. Martin's Press, 1974), pp. 33-34.

16. Ibid., p. 45.

17. Harold Lasswell, *Psychopathology and Politics* (New York: Viking Press, 1966), p. 16.

18. Abraham Maslow as cited in Fred Krinsky and June Tapp, *Ambivalent America: A Psycho-political Dialogue* (Beverly Hills, Calif.: Glencoe Press, 1971), p. 2.

19. See Erik Erikson, *Childhood and Society* (New York: W. W. Norton, & Co., 1950), pp. 289-300; Stoessinger, *Why Nations Go to War*, pp. 60-63.

20. Harold Guetzkow, "Isolation and Collaboration: A Practical Theory of International Relations," *Journal of Conflict Resolution* 1 (1957): 49-68.

21. Adorno et al., *Authoritarian Personality*, p. 107.

22. Hitler, *Mein Kampf*, trans. Ralph Manheim, pp. 179-182.

23. R. D. Laing, *The Politics of Experience* (New York: Ballantine Books, 1967), p. 28.

24. Kenneth E. Boulding, "Learning and Reality-Testing Process in the International System," in John C. Farrell and Asa P. Smith, eds., *Image and Reality in World Politics* (New York: Columbia University Press, 1968), p. 5.

25. Robert Strausz-Hupé et al., *Protracted Conflict* (New York: Harper & Bros., 1959), pp. 23-24.

26. John Stoessinger, *The Might of Nations* (New York: Random House, 1965), p. 63.

27. Jürgen Habermas, *Toward A Rational Society* (Boston: Beacon Press, 1970).

28. Friedrich Nietzsche, *Thus Spoke Zarathustra* in *The Portable Nietzsche*, trans. Walter Kaufmann (New York: Viking Press, 1972), pp. 161-163.

PART FOUR

International Integration, Organization, and Diplomacy

At the very moment when mankind has the power to destroy the earth, men also have begun to perceive the planet as a whole.

JOHN STOESSINGER
Why Nations Go to War

From the theoretical extremes of total peace and total war there is a natural progression of thought to less ambitious processes of interaction between nations and their leaders: international integration, international organization, international law and foreign policy decision making. How do national leaders satisfy the needs of their people in regional arrangements and world organizations that do not achieve the ideal of total peace? And what strategies and tactics of threat and conflict can such leaders use to attain their goals without risking total war? These are the questions explored by Part Four.

Once again we will use the world-views of successful individuals to illuminate international processes in a human way. The method begins with the events themselves as experienced by national leaders. Theories and abstractions grow naturally out of concrete, flesh and blood relationships in recent times. De Gaulle demonstrates how his background, talents, and historical opportunities combined to allow him to use cultural nationalism in France to reunite that country after World War II; to persuade others to redefine France as a great power; and to bargain effectively to get the most for France in the Common Market. His case highlights the differences between national and supranational loyalties in the process of international integration and regional cooperation, and it raises the question, How much must a nation-state give up individually in order to create a better future for all nation-states in the region? The process of transferring national to supranational loyalty in international integration is extended even further with the story of Dag Hammarskjöld who lived for international law through the United Nations and the international civil service and whose activities involved a global loyalty and interest more than a regional one. Finally, the greatest secretary of state the United States has had, Henry Kissinger, brings us back to earth and very much up to the present day by epitomizing effective foreign policy and decision making in a nuclear age of violence and scarcity of basic resources. Behind Kissinger's colorful style and his belief in indeterminacy emerges a subtle pattern that indicates he may be creating a superbalance of power in world politics that preserves American interests but often conflicts with the needs of poorer, developing nations in the world. He may, indeed, become the last of the West's great maintenance men.

CHAPTER

National Bargaining and
Regional Integration — de Gaulle

> What are the pillars on which [Europe] can be
> built? In truth, they are the States, States that are,
> certainly, very different from one another, each
> having its soul, its history and its language, its
> glories and its ambitions, but States that are the
> only entities with the right to give orders and the
> power to be obeyed. To fancy one can build
> something effective in action, and acceptable to
> the peoples, outside or above the States, is a
> chimera.
>
> CHARLES DE GAULLE

Charles de Gaulle was the master of the self-fulfilling prophecy. He made himself as inevitable as he thought the nation-state to be. De Gaulle fell passionately in love with France, and to that extent, he fell in love with himself, for in his case the two were inseparable. His story epitomizes one of the most significant world conflicts in our time: the need to fight for the selfish interests of one's own nation-state versus the need to cooperate with other nation-states in one's own region for the short- and long-term benefit of the whole community. The tension between nationalism and regionalism affects all individuals everywhere, and the political solutions to that tension can mean peace or war, life or death.

A classic question in international politics is whether the nation-state as a form of human organization is obsolete, inevitable, or capable of modification to make a structure better suited to satisfy human needs. By taking an extreme stand on the inevitability of the nation-state at a time when politicians are striving toward integration and a regional cooperative organization that could become a United Europe, de Gaulle is a dramatic example of the political arguments that are bound to emerge in all regional politics in the future. The question is whether to be for or against the nation-state as the ultimate political solution to human problems. The creation of the European Common Market as a possible alternative to the nation-state in the future provides a model of international integration that fascinates political leaders in the developed and less developed worlds alike.

On French soil for the first time since the German occupation, General
Charles de Gaulle walks through Bayeux, Normandy, eight days after
the D-Day landings. *Camera Press photo.*

I. De Gaulle: A Political Portrait

The Development of a Refined Nationalist

Charles André Joseph Marie de Gaulle was born in 1890 in Lille, France, a gray, industrial city north of Paris. His father taught philosophy and literature at a Jesuit college, and was a devout Catholic and royalist who would not take a post in a state school. That conservative teacher had always wanted to be a soldier and served as a lieutenant in the Franco-Prussian war. Since he had no money, he was forced to leave the army after the French defeat. He continually impressed upon his son his deep feeling for France and the need to avenge French humiliation in the future. De Gaulle's mother had "an uncompromising passion for her country equal to her religious loyalty."[1] De Gaulle, in short, was born and bred to become a French nationalist determined to right the wrongs recently suffered by his country.

Moreover, his father loved history and traced the family line back to the hero Sieur Jehan de Gaulle who was part of the last great charge of feudal knights against the British archers at the Battle of Agincourt. None of the children was ever allowed to learn English, and as a boy de Gaulle even forced the other children to learn to speak French backward. In the military games they played, he always took the role of France for himself. Ethnocentrism was a family tradition, and it is little wonder that de Gaulle later came to identify his own personal needs with the needs and honor of the French nation. In seeking to solve the tensions between his human needs and social facts, he always tried to reconstruct social facts to make himself one with France.

De Gaulle's personality "was often so cold and forbidding that his family used to say that he must have been born in an ice house."[2] Such aloofness often accompanies great political leadership, as though by making the psychic distance between oneself and others greater one appears to raise one's status and uniqueness. Deference is directly related to psychosocial distance.

De Gaulle went to school at the Jesuit school where his father taught until 1907 when the Jesuits were expelled from France. He became good at classical scholarship and, like Hammarskjöld and Kissinger after him, he liked philosophy. He once wanted to be a monk and to serve as a missionary overseas. When he was ten, his father took him to see Edmond Rostand's play *Cyrano de Bergerac*. He was so impressed with Cyrano, a seventeenth-century soldier and poet, that he decided to become a soldier and never changed his mind for a moment. He learned from his parents of the sad defeats of the French in political history and longed to avenge this humiliation.

After graduating first in his class he went to the Military College of Saint-Cyr in 1909 when he was nineteeen. There he revealed his strong and somewhat strange character. He was taller than most men, had not yet developed an interest in girls, and enjoyed going on long walks with a carefully chosen friend. Although he was not as religious as his parents, he attended mass quite regularly. Already he showed a tendency to state what he believed in an uncompromising way and was self-assertive in proclaiming what was right and wrong. Spending vacations with conservative relatives, he lived a relatively cloistered life.

Upon graduating with distinction from the military school, he joined the Thirty-third Infantry Regiment commanded by Colonel Philippe Pétain in 1913. He fought in World War I until the Battle of Verdun in 1916 when he was wounded and taken prisoner.

After the armistice, de Gaulle rejoined his old regiment and then went to lecture at Saint-Cyr. Upon graduating from another military school, de Gaulle was asked to join Marshal Pétain's war consulate staff. De Gaulle had been humiliated earlier in military life for being an undisciplined, stubborn cadet who was often critical of the French Army. His unusual relationship with Pétain inspired him to rejoin the same group that had humiliated him. Later when Pétain capitulated to Hitler in the name of France de Gaulle fled to England to raise the standard of the French resistance. The tragic end of that profoundly influential friendship recalls the dramas of classical Greece.

As a second lieutenant, de Gaulle exhibited uncompromising self-confidence, as though he knew he was destined to become the spirit of the great books he had read. He served in Trier in the army occupying the Rhineland and moved to Lebanon two years later. In 1931 he returned to Paris.

Possessing unusual intellectual and literary qualities, de Gaulle was forever coming into conflict with orthodox military opinion. He did not believe his needs or those of France could be met by the existing hierarchy of social facts, or the dominant values, strategies, personalities, institutions, and rules of the game. He published three books that offered criticism and alternatives, *Edge of the Sword* (1931), *Army of the Future* (1934), *France and Her Army* (1938).

Humiliation and the Recovery of Status

In *Army of the Future*, de Gaulle argued for a highly trained, highly specialized, mechanized army of six divisions (100,000 men), an army "moving entirely on caterpillar tractors." Opposing the immobility of fixed fortifications, de Gaulle wanted an army of great mobility and striking power that could attack by surprise under a curtain of aircraft, independent of a particular base and capable of going deep into enemy territory to disrupt communication centers. As historian Frank P. Chambers noted, "De Gaulle, in a word, predicted with astonishing accuracy the blitzkrieg of the Second World War."[3]

However, de Gaulle wrote not only of military strategy but of leadership as well. Leadership for de Gaulle was the extension of character and character was destiny. Nietzsche, it should be noted, called character neurosis. Political scientists Stanley and Inge Hoffmann summarized de Gaulle's view of leadership: "The way to tame history and to leave a mark (for this is the name of the game) is to be and to have *un caractère*—the *caractère* of the leader. Without such a character, no set of ideas will help; indeed, they will harm, for they will interpose a screen between reality and the leader. . . . The right *caractère* will, by definition, have the craft and strength to dominate events. The leader is the man who owes his power to no one but himself, who is propelled by what is in him, not by other people's doctrines."[4]

Self-determination is the desire for complete autonomy and freedom of individual action on the part of individuals and nations. To be totally self-determined is the meaning of freedom. Man as a political animal is determined to act to solve the tensions between his needs and social facts. Nations as groups of political animals see self-determination as the means to national liberation from oppressive social facts. Psychologist Sigmund Freud has shown that the tension between man's drives on the one hand and the norms of his social world on the other is the source of culture. The control of those drives by giving in to social norms and laws is civilization. Political leaders, in turn, use cultural products and forms of civilization as tools to further their own ideologies and national power. They make their own self-determination appear to be national self-determination.

De Gaulle knew that a great leader must put himself above the moment, cast himself in an historical role, and submit with messianic zeal to a cause. He would become destiny's instrument for the cause of the French nation. Nay, he would become the epitome of France herself: proud, nationalistic, the embodiment of French culture and civilization. French novelist Francois Mauriac wrote, "What I found, in that first meeting with General de Gaulle, was not the disdain of all other men that his enemies attribute to him, but the narrow, unbridgeable gulf between them and himself, created not by the pride of self-conscious greatness, but by the calm certainty that he is the State and, it is not too much to say, France herself."[5]

De Gaulle was a colonel commanding a brigade of tanks when World War II began. He was appointed brigadier general by General Henri Giraud to lead the Fourth Armored Division under desperate conditions in May, 1940. The division fought effectively, and de Gaulle's reputation increased. A month later when German troops resumed their attack, General Weygand appointed de Gaulle to be under secretary of defense. In that role he met Winston Churchill twice in London. Most of de Gaulle's criticisms of the existing French military structure became a self-fulfilling prophecy as the French were overrun by the speedy, mobile German forces of the type de Gaulle had proposed for France much earlier. Pètain became premier and sought an armistice while de Gaulle fled to London.

On June 18, 1940 de Gaulle gave his famous broadcast to the French people from London appealing to them to fight on and to make him the head of the new Free French movement. " 'London here! General de Gaulle speaking . . .' That was at Malagar, in the dead of the blackest winter of all our lives. In our cellar, we listened to the boots of the German officer pounding overhead," wrote Mauriac.[6]

Organizing the Free French Committee in London, de Gaulle soon controlled important military resources and territory in French Equatorial Africa and in the Pacific. His ability to organize and seize authority was amazing. He soon became president of the Free French Committee of National Liberation in Algiers, and he became the symbol of French resistance to occupation and a stubborn ally of the West. In the meantime, Pétain had been court-martialed by the French and sentenced to death.

The French resistance in World War II was one of the most romantic political struggles of our era. Great French literary figures were involved, and the philosophy of existentialism emerged largely out of the experience. After the war, novelist and existentialist Albert Camus told a reporter, "You ask me why I took the side of the Resistance. This is a question which has no meaning for a certain number of men, of whom I am one. It seemed to me, and it still seems to me, that you cannot be on the side of concentration camps. I understood then that I hated violence less than the institutions of violence. . . ."[7] Camus not only joined the underground and edited the underground newspaper, *Combat*, but his famous works *The Rebel* and *The Plague* emerged from that period. The Nazi invasion of France was like a hopeless plague spreading over a city. To be truly human one had to rebel against dehumanizing social facts, and physical and spiritual disease, even if it was a losing battle. To rebel to improve the human condition is to prove that as an individual one is a member of humanity: "I rebel therefore we exist."[8]

De Gaulle's principle became "I rebel therefore France exists." After the liberation of Paris, he formed a provisional government on September 10, 1944. Two constituent assemblies were elected, and a new constitution was written, against which de Gaulle later campaigned because he thought it was likely to produce a weak and unstable government. Mauriac described the reaction of the French elite to de Gaulle:

> As for those whose profession was politics, who constituted the fauna of committees and congresses, they discovered what was to be their tragedy. This meteoric general, the product of Saint-Cyr and the Ecole de Guerre, seemed to them the incarnation of

all that was most hateful: the absolute preponderance of the State, the cult of the nation, the indifference to ideologies, the mistrust of political parties, plus an antagonism to them personally and a determination to dominate, to defy and, if possible, to destroy them. The professional politicians understood on that day [of the liberation of Paris] that this man would be their tragedy. This staff of iron would not bend. They would have to take him or leave him, as we say, but the history that began that day, and that is still being made, would come down to this: each time they rejected him, they would be obliged to take him back, on pain of death. This insupportable man was an inevitable man.[9]

Like Lenin and Mao before him and Kissinger after him, de Gaulle knew that the secret to becoming a great world leader was to so identify one's own needs with the needs and interests of one's nation-state in the existing world of social facts that one would be perceived to be inevitable. The myth of inevitability is one of the most permanent forms of power that a population can grant any individual in world politics. However, such a myth must be cultivated to some extent by the leader himself. As an artist of statesmanship, de Gaulle was one of the great masters of all time. His personal outrage and humiliation was soon translated into the outrage and humiliation of France. All through the war de Gaulle had been snubbed by the leaders of the great Western powers. Indeed, he had even been excluded from the Yalta Conference, which arranged the peace agreements. He, in turn, carefully snubbed Western leaders for years afterward as a part of a general strategy to force them to recognize France as a great power in the world and himself as the great, legitimate leader of France. Calculated diplomatic snubbing is one effective way a leader increases his own importance and respect for his country in the eyes of other leaders.

When de Gaulle took power, the physical and moral chaos of France was widespread. Since the war began, 500,000 Frenchmen had lost their lives, and railroads, roads, bridges, seaports, canals, and river shipping had been destroyed. There were psychological as well as physical scars from German servitude. Historian Frank Chambers noted, "Young people who had grown up in a time of war in an atmosphere of fake identity cards, fake ration cards, black marketing, lying propaganda, betrayal and terror could hardly be converted overnight into a citizenry fit for a newly redeemed democracy in time of peace."[10] It was no accident that General de Gaulle took over in a period of decay when the people longed for law and order and strong leadership.

In 1946, de Gaulle resigned as prime minister, and the next year he formed the Rassemblement du Peuple Francais (RPF), a party which expressed discontent with the weak parliamentary system and exploited fears of communism. We recall that Hitler's Nazi party appealed to some of those same sentiments, as do many rightist parties. However, the party became weaker and was finally disbanded in 1953. Retiring into private life, de Gaulle then wrote three volumes of his war memoirs.

Weak, factional governments attempted unsuccessfully to govern France. Then in May, 1958 French Army leaders in Algeria openly defied the government in Paris. France was faced with a possible civil war. With some self-help, de Gaulle emerged as the only figure who could unite the country once again in a time of crisis. At a press conference he said, "I am a man who belongs to no one and therefore who belongs to everybody... Can anyone believe that at age sixty-seven I am going to begin the career of a dictator?"[11] But as the French people were to learn, seeing is believing!

Nationalism and Regionalism:
The Value of Sovereignty

An astute political bargainer, de Gaulle set conditions before he would assume power. He must have absolute powers for two years and be free to send parliament into recess while he himself drafted a constitution and brought France's affairs back into order. Refusing to compromise on those conditions, he was able to take power with almost full sovereignty, or supreme legal authority. Such stubbornness later became an extremely effective bargaining tactic in maximizing French national interests in European Common Market negotiations.

In September, 1958 the people approved de Gaulle's constitution which gave the president wide powers. In December he was elected president of the Fifth Republic. He soon saw to it that elections were held in all French overseas possessions, and he put down a brief revolt by Europeans in Algeria in 1960 without bloodshed. Also he strengthened ties with West Germany to institutionalize Franco-German reconciliation and to make it the basis of European integration.

International integration is a process of transferring loyalty from national to supranational organizations and of increasing interdependence and cooperation between nation-states in a given region. Supranational loyalty refers to a loyalty to symbols or organizations "beyond the nation-state," such as devotion to the European Common Market or to the United Nations. Integration means a movement away from nationalism toward regionalism or internationalism, a movement away from the fragmentation of the world into states and toward supranational unification. Political scientist Stanley Hoffmann's words still hold true: "The critical issue for every student of world order is the fate of the nation-state. In the nuclear age, the fragmentation of the world into countless units, each of which has a claim to independence, is obviously dangerous for peace and illogical for welfare."[12]

De Gaulle's strategy in regard to European integration was simple. If European integration was, indeed, inevitable as an historical process, why should not he, "France," influence its shape as much as possible to further French national interest? Advocating a loose concept of European integration that would be based upon the member states as distinctive, independent units, de Gaulle opposed a supranationalist concept of a united Europe in which states would have to sacrifice their sovereignty. Moreover, he opposed the admission of Britain to the European Common Market (EEC), which was made up of France, West Germany, Italy, Belgium, the Netherlands, and Luxembourg, largely out of fear that Britain would become a strong economic and political rival there and would make it more difficult for the French to shape the market's destiny. In order to maintain the benefits of good relations with France, Chancellor Konrad Adenauer of West Germany reluctantly went along with de Gaulle's view of Europe, which caused divisions within both countries and fears on the part of European integrationists that the Franco-German position would undermine the movement toward Western European unity.

Economic and Military Bargaining

Perhaps the most brilliant principle that de Gaulle used in international politics was his consistent reliance upon a coherent philosophical and cultural world-view, which enabled him to maximize French interests at the bargaining table. His opponents knew that on certain principles, such as French sovereignty and the vision of a Europe of separate states, de Gaulle would not bend, and there was no point in pushing him for concessions. Recall that Gandhi used his political ideology of militant nonviolence in the same way. Likewise it is not possible to understand de Gaulle's success in economic and military bargaining without understanding his cause, the noble vision of French grandeur and cultural superiority.

De Gaulle's view accented the unique cultural contributions of each nation-state as a source of strength. Sovereign nation-states would be the pillars on which Europe would be built. In a press conference on May 15, 1962 he said, "Europe can never be a living reality if it does not include France with its Frenchmen, Germany with its Germans, Italy with its Italians, etc. Dante, Goethe, Chateaubriand, belong to all Europe to the very extent that they are, respectively and eminently, Italian, German and French. They would not have served Europe if they had been countryless, or if they had thought and written in some integrated 'esperanto' or 'volapük.' "[13] Moreover, de Gaulle criticized the effectiveness of European regional organizations, claiming that they work well only in noncrisis situations. For in crisis situations national, not supranational, policies are dominant.

Opposing the Gaullist, nationalist viewpoint was the perspective of the "Europeanists," or the supranationalists. They were men like French

Foreign Minister Robert Schuman and businessman Jean Monnet who helped to bring the European Common Market into being by planning the European Coal and Steel Community, which was the economic basis for Franco-German reconciliation after World War II. Such organizations were based on **variable-sum** or general game cooperation. Recall that zero-sum or pure conflict games or situations are those assuming that whatever one party gains, the other party necessarily loses and that cooperation is, therefore, irrational. The variable-sum game, on the other hand, assumes that two or more parties can gain more individually by cooperating, especially in the long run. Rather than always arguing over the existing economic pie it is more satisfying to cooperate and create more pie for everyone by using means that individual parties would not have available if they merely worked on their own.* In short, de Gaulle was basically concerned with getting all of the existing pie he could for France, whereas the Europeanists wanted everyone to make national sacrifices in order ultimately to produce a bigger pie for everyone to share. Jean Monnet's Action Committee for the United States of Europe is perhaps the best known exponent of the Europeanists' integrative vision.

To further his own vision, de Gaulle proposed the formation of a permanent political secretariat of the six EEC members and of coordinating commissions to harmonize policy in various ministries. The Europeanist response was to ask, Was this to become a French Europe or a European France? Many Socialists and Christian Democrats in West Germany, for example, feared that de Gaulle's proposed council of government heads would undermine the Monnet view of political integration, for which they had been campaigning for ten years.

Although de Gaulle was able to persuade Chancellor Adenauer of West Germany to continually support his European policy proposals, he was not so successful with the Belgians and the Dutch, who finally blocked his proposals under the leadership of the well-known Europeanist, Paul-Henri Spaak. Although angered by the check to his plans, de Gaulle did not change them. He revealed his determination when he vetoed British membership in the Common Market in 1963.

The Action Committee for the United States of Europe enthusiastically supported Britain's application for Common Market membership, believing that such an addition would reinforce the unity of Europe and increase Europe's political impact in world politics. The Benelux countries, Belgium, the Netherlands, and Luxembourg, favored British membership, since they expected Britain would protect the smaller nations against the growing weight of the Franco-German axis. West Germany supported British entry since German leaders thought it might end the division of Europe into

---

*The concepts of zero-sum and variable-sum games originated in one of the classic works of economics in the 20th century: John Von Neumann and Oscar Morgenstern, *Theory of Games and Economic Behavior* (Princeton, New Jersey: Princeton University Press, 1947). There is evidence that indicates that some of the basic principles of "game theory" were worked out at the poker tables at Princeton University.

competing trade blocs and since Germany would stand to gain greatly from trade with Britain and the Commonwealth. Significantly, at that time West German trade with the seven members of the European Free Trade Association (EFTA),* Britain's counterorganization to the EEC, totaled over three times the sum of French trade with those countries. French imports from EFTA were little more than one-quarter of Germany's.[14] Therefore, British membership in the EEC would pay much more to West Germany than to France. De Gaulle's veto of British membership in his January 1963 press conference left little doubt that acute differences existed between French and German policy that would obstruct the movement toward European integration.

Typically, de Gaulle's main reason for vetoing British EEC membership was that Britain's cultural, economic, and political traditions and viewpoints were too dissimilar from those of "the Six" to be successfully integrated into the Common Market. He said that the Treaty of Rome creating the Common Market was concluded between six countries whose similar modes of industrial and agricultural production, foreign trade, and commerce made them a natural economic unit. Britain, however, was different in those aspects because she was "insular, maritime and linked by trade—by both markets and suppliers—to the most diverse and faraway countries." In short, the British had habits and traditions that made their national image distinct from the continental image or world-view. For example, Britain imported cheap foodstuffs from the Americas and the foreign Dominions, granting subsidies to her own farmers. The subsidies would have to be radically changed if the country were to accept a common tariff and the abandonment of all preference to the countries in the Commonwealth, both agricultural protectionism and special links with the EFTA.[15] The principle behind de Gaulle's view was that Britain's lack of geographic proximity to the rest of the region of integration, Continental Europe, made her so different economically, culturally, and politically that she could not be easily assimilated.

ᘛᘚᘛᘚᘛᘚᘛᘚᘛᘚ

International integration is stimulated by similarities in the cultural, economic, and political images or world-views held by the nations in the region. Likewise, cultural, economic, and political differences in national viewpoints make disintegration and conflict more probable. Nationalists argue the realist position and stress national differences, potential conflict, and the limits of integration. They tend to see the world as a zero-sum game of conflict in which each nation should struggle to get as much of the existing pie as it can before someone else does. Regionalists or integrationists, such as Europeanists, on the other hand, take the idealist position that national similarities and common needs are more important than national differences and power conflict. They tend to see regional

*EFTA was created in response to the EEC threat in 1959 by the commerce ministers of Britain, Denmark, Sweden, Norway, Switzerland, Austria and Portugal.

politics in terms of the variable-sum or general cooperative game that provides options allowing all nations to create more pie in the future than nations working individually could create in the present.

❀✿❀✿❀✿❀✿❀

Just as de Gaulle wanted the maximum economic and political benefits of European integration at the least cost to France, so he also wanted military protection from the North Atlantic Treaty Organization (NATO) at the least cost and with as little dependence upon the United States as possible. Again de Gaulle's stubborn, nationalistic world-view became an amazingly effective basis of bargaining for his objectives. In 1966 he announced that although France would remain a member of the Atlantic Alliance, it would gradually withdraw from the military branches of NATO within the next three years. He wrote a letter to President Lyndon Johnson stating his terms: foreign military forces would have to be withdrawn from French territory, and the French would withdraw from the integrated NATO commands and pull out their troops from NATO.[16] Later he wrote to his European allies that he was willing to keep French troops in Germany under the 1954 Paris Agreements. In short, de Gaulle asked himself, What do I have to lose if my nation pulls out of NATO physically although not officially? The Russians won't attack and the other NATO allies will do what they can to keep me in the alliance on any basis. Moreover, France will thereby become much more independent and will have to be reckoned with on her own grounds.

As if to make sure American policymakers got the message after his NATO bombshell, de Gaulle visited the Soviet Union and then went to other countries, especially those where French culture was significantly present: French Somaliland, Ethiopia, Cambodia, New Caledonia, New Hebrides, Tahiti and Canada. In Canada he displayed his proud view of French cultural grandeur with flourish. The Canadian government cut short his visit after his sensational support of French Canadian separatism, ending a speech at Montreal with "Vive le Québec libre!" "Long live free Quebec!" Such a speech epitomized both the decline of France as a major power in the world and de Gaulle's stubborn attempts to maintain the image and color, if not the substance, of a great power for his country. His creation of France's meager nuclear force to bring France the prestige of being in "the nuclear club" was another symbol of grandeur he erected to cover French decay. For de Gaulle was, in essence, a great political artist who knew how to use France's prestigious cultural tradition for political effects in economic and military bargaining.

The Politics of Culture and Language

De Gaulle can perhaps be best understood as a frustrated novelist or playwright who was forced by upbringing and destiny to pervert his notable literary and acting talents into the field of politics. His tremendous personal needs for self-esteem and self-actualization could only be satisfied by cultural forms of self-expression. Since socialization and social facts steered him into a military and political career, he had to manage as best he could by fashioning the materials of these fields like a sculptor's clay into a cultural product of which he and all France could be proud. His rebellion proved that art and politics are deeply interconnected. As the literary critic Richard Poirier wrote in *The Performing Self*, "Any effort to find accommodation for human shapes or sounds is an act that partakes of political meaning. It involves negotiation, struggle, and compromise with the stubborn material of existence, be it language or stone."[17]

Fully aware that culture and language are, themselves, political solutions to the tensions between human needs and social facts, de Gaulle nourished famous literary figures in his circle, and they nourished him. Each respected the other's ability to use language and culture to satisfy his own personal needs in a restrictive world of social facts and decay. The first thing de Gaulle did when he entered Paris after the liberation in World War II was to call together the famous writers of France. In 1958 when he came back to power he appointed novelist and war hero André Malraux to his cabinet as the minister of culture. (A brilliant stroke! Does your country have a minister of culture of such a prestigious sort?) Malraux later celebrated de Gaulle in books such as his *Antimémoires*. Note how the cultural spirit of French rebellion even invades the title! And novelist Francois Mauriac wrote his own version of *De Gaulle*.

For example, take the following excerpt from a conversation between de Gaulle and Malraux, summarized by Malraux (with de Gaulle's words in italics):

> "*The great French writers of the eighteenth century were prophets,*" he went on, "*but what began as tragedy is ending once again in comedy. A pity! First because intellectuals, even when they delight in honors and puerilities, are, like me, serving something more important than themselves.*"
>
> Camus, at the time of the crossing of the desert, asked as he left de Gaulle in what way he felt a writer could serve France. "*Every man who writes*" (a hesitation), "*and writes well, serves France.*"
>
> "All the same, there are some Gaullist artists," said I. "Braque and Le Corbusier yesterday, Chagall and Balthus today. And they are not alone."
>
> "*What is a Gaullist artist?*"
>
> "An artist who defends you."
>
> "*All right. You are as familiar as anyone with the complaint: we set France too high. As if they weren't aware how much cowardice there is in modesty!*"

> *"However, our intellectuals and our artists still count for*
> *something in the world. I saw on television the funeral ceremo-*
> *nies you organized for Le Corbusier: the Cour Carrée of the*
> *Louvre, white again, lit up by floodlights, the ambassadors of*
> *Greece and India with their offerings.*
> *. . . The telegram the Indian government sent me: 'India,*
> *where stands the capital laid out by Le Corbusier, will come to*
> *pour on his ashes the water of the Ganges, in supreme hom-*
> *age.'"* [18]

This passage illustrates de Gaulle's use of culture and aesthetic form to increase national grandeur. Each great writer becomes a symbol of the state; his death means that the nation dies a little; his burial becomes part of the national pageant of the passing of a great nation-state.

And de Gaulle too became a part of the pageant of his nation's cultural past. His own conservative, nationalistic rebellion was undone by a fresh rebellion of youth, the student riots of May, 1968. At first he tried to pass over the disturbances as unimportant, but the spring fever rose and he was soon obliged to announce a referendum, particularly since workers had joined the students in the strikes. At the end of the month, de Gaulle dissolved the National Assembly, paving the way for the formation of a new government without him. With the waning of his political power, his physical power also declined, and he died on November 9, 1970. In his lifetime, however, he proved consistently and heroically the truth of the words of Albert Camus: "Every man has at his disposal a certain zone of influence, which he owes as much to his defects as to his qualities. But whichever is the case, this zone is there and can be immediately used. . . . And when you have done what you can in your own zone, in your own field, then you can call a halt and despair as much as you like. Understand this: we can despair of the meaning of life in general, but not of the particular forms that it takes; we can despair of existence, for we have no power over it, but not of history, where the individual can do everything." [19]

II. Principles of World Politics

Self-Determination Through Cultural Symbols

The tale of de Gaulle is a classic story of the nation-state system and how to use it to satisfy your needs and maximize your values. Beginning with the case of Gandhi, we have observed that great world leaders are marked by their desire for freedom, for complete self-determination. They want to be origins rather than pawns. Historically the development of the greatest amount of self-determination in the nation-state system has meant that the individual must usually identify his own self-determination or interest with national self-determination or interest. If the individual goes against the idea of his own nation-state, he is often left without the basis for potential power in world politics. Recently, other opportunities for individual self-determination and autonomy have emerged: multinational corporations and regional and international bureaucracies. However, even in those organizations individuals must constantly take the policies of their own nation-state and their own national citizenship into account.

De Gaulle's gambit was that the nation-state was the ultimate form of human organization and that self-determination was only viable within a national cultural tradition. All of his symbolic gestures—words, snubbings, policies, appointments, and other actions—represented France and her cultural traditions and interests as he saw them. Prestige gained for de Gaulle, in his view, was prestige gained for France. Symbolically speaking, he was France. If he were alive today, for example, he would be extremely proud to know that French is still the official language of the European Common Market in Brussels, although English is often used unofficially.

Political scientist Murray Edelman has shown that in situations characterized by ambiguity and crisis, large mass publics find emotional satisfaction in symbols that encourage them to be politically quiescent or obedient. He noted three significant experimental findings:

> (1) People read their own meaning into situations that are unclear or provocative of emotion. As phrased by Fensterheim, "The less well defined the stimulus situation, or the more emotionally laden, the greater will be the contribution of the perceiver." (2) It is characteristic of large numbers of people in our society that they see and think in terms of stereotypes, personalization, and oversimplifications; that they cannot recognize or tolerate ambiguous and complex situations; and that they accordingly respond chiefly to symbols that over-simplify and distort. . . . (3) Emotional commitment to a symbol is associated with contentment and quiescence regarding problems that would otherwise arouse concern.[20]

Just as Gandhi used his spinning wheel and fasts, Mao his poems, and Hitler the swastika and goose step, so de Gaulle used the French language, culture, and writers as political symbols to satisfy deep subconscious needs of the masses and make them proud to submit to his authority. He even tried to shape himself into the ultimate meaning of what it was to be French, the symbol of symbols.

Sovereignty and the Nation-State's Future

Sovereignty is the legitimate authority of a nation-state. As weak governments came and went in France, the people longed for a legitimate authority that would last a while. De Gaulle served that function twice. In fact, he almost became the sovereign, and he demonstrated that any realistic policy of regional integration must begin with separate nation-states and work slowly towards common policy. De Gaulle proved that, far from being a dead form of political organization, the nation-state still dominates the political process at the bargaining table. His blind spot as a realist was his failure to understand the greater benefits for all European nation-states from cooperative integration.

De Gaulle illustrated how effectively the process of integration could be used by a nation-state to maximize its own interests and gain international prestige. He revealed that the most potent individual, political role in the international system was that of the national leader when he made foreign policy decisions. The nation-state provided a stage and opportunity for individual effectiveness at the global level. Furthermore, those who have predicted the inevitable decline of the nation-state have forgotten or underrated "the Second Coming." New nations have just been born in Africa and Asia, stirred with the nationalistic fervor and idealism which European states felt only centuries ago, and they are not about to give up that organized national glory before they have experienced it fully.

Often the argument is made that the nation-state system is irrational, that it fragments the globe, making international cooperation impossible and international conflict inevitable. However, although the nation-state system is certainly imperfect, it may be better than the simplistic alternative that is often suggested to replace it, the world state. Long ago, philosopher Immanuel Kant maintained in his *Perpetual Peace* that a world state could easily mean a world despotism. International efficiency and order might be gained at the expense of individual freedom and regional diversity. Thus, to do away with the nation-state system, without having a feasible alternative other than world government, might well lead to world government by default and to world despotism by accident. Regional integration, of course, has been suggested as an alternative, a halfway house between the present nation-state system and world government.

Perhaps the most powerful argument made against the viability of the present nation-state system is the military one. The revolution in nuclear weapons technology makes a multistate system untenable, for the more states there are, the more nuclear weapons are likely to spread; the more they spread, the more arms races will be stimulated; and the more arms races are stimulated, the greater the probability of thermonuclear war and global destruction. Moreover, technological innovations have made **the theory of unilateral defense**, one independent state becoming totally capable of defending its own territory all by itself, untenable. Only the nuclear superpowers even approach such self-sufficient defenses, and even they cannot, with any certainty, prevent an enemy from penetrating their territory with missiles, much less with terrorist sabotage. But the myth of unilateral defense goes on.

As conflict theorist Kenneth Boulding has noted:

Wearing a protective overall, de Gaulle visits an atomic laboratory at Donzere in 1963. *Wide World photo.*

The concept of defense has always been somewhat naive in the sense that it has rested on an egocentric and ethnocentric view of the universe that takes the defended person or institution as given, known and valued and the outside enemy as also given but unknown and negatively valued and regards the problem of virtue as that of the preservation of a little island of defended goodness in the middle of the howling chaos of the hostile world. . . . Unilateral national defense has created an enormous amount of human misery through history, but, up to the present century, it has been a workable system, in the sense that it has provided occasional protected heartlands of peace in which civilization and the arts could flourish even though surrounded by a periphery of war. Now it is no longer workable . . . unilateral national defense seems to me to be sheer lunacy; it can only persist as an ideology because of the smallness of men's imaginations and their refusal to let go of an outworn concept that has served them in good stead in the past. The abandonment of the ideology of unilateral national defense is particularly hard for Americans, who for 200 years have been served well by it, because of the accident of geography and history. Unless we abandon it, however, I believe we are doomed.[21]

In short, technological achievements in missiles and communications systems have made all nation-states hopelessly vulnerable and to a great extent dependent for their security upon their most likely enemy. The whole logic of the unilateral defense concept is based on deterring the enemy from using his force upon one's country and involves constant, careful communication with him. As a self-sufficient means of protecting a nation-state's independence and sovereignty, deterrence is a contradiction in terms. In the twentieth century, national security has become dependent in a terribly total sense upon international security.

International Integration and the Spillover Thesis

If the nation-state has become unworkable in our era, some kind of integration process seems to be inevitable. Integration, recall, refers to the process of transferring loyalty from national to supranational organizations and of increasing interdependence and cooperation between nation-states. De Gaulle's clever strategy was based upon getting the most possible for France out of the integration process if it were inevitable, and making himself simultaneously more self-sufficient in case integration was not going to occur. His was the game plan of the conservative, realistic nationalist who believes that one must get what there is to gain now or one's opponent will get it, like a zero-sum chess or checker game where the stakes are fixed.

The opposing viewpoint of the regionalists, integrationists, or Europeanists is that integration is inevitable and that by cooperating sooner the payoffs for everyone will be greater. In short, they see the world not as a fixed pie to be totally divided up now, but as a growing pie, which can increase to everyone's benefit if all are willing to sacrifice short-term for long-term gains. That vision is often compared to the variable-sum, general cooperative game where the stakes are not fixed but determined by what each party does to help or hinder the others.

European idealists see the ideal of the Common Market as a perfect example of the variable-sum game. Everyone will benefit more economically in the long run, they argue, if everyone gives up the short-term gains of selfish, nationalistic policies. The extreme form of that idea is the **spillover thesis**, which claims that economic cooperation between nation-states will inevitably spill over into political cooperation and that, therefore, economic integration will become political integration. The difficulty with such a thesis is that political and economic factors are not easily separable (indeed, the political may precede the economic in integrative decision making) and evidence exists that the transfer from economic to political spheres of cooperation is far from automatic or inevitable. In 1974, for example, the European Common Market went through one of its greatest crises since its formation because of the tendency of its member nations to spill back to selfish, nationalistic policies in hard economic times. Without consulting the other members, Italian leaders suddenly decided to impose import restrictions on goods coming in from abroad. The British economic crisis and change in government prompted her leaders to ask for a renegotiation of her membership arrangement in the Common Market. The death of Georges Pompidou in France made that country's role in the EEC unpredictable and virtually halted most major agreements at the EEC headquarters in Brussels. In short, cooperation and integration may spill over in good times and spill back in bad, as de Gaulle sensed long ago.[22]

III. Present Implications

The Pathology of the Nation-State System

As we have seen, a pathological belief is a rigid image of the world that does not fit reality. In other words, a human being's perception of reality is pathological if he cannot adjust his world-view to take new information into account and if he stubbornly maintains a rigid outlook that becomes increasingly distant from what is actually going on.[23] A pathological condition is one that prevents a human being from using social facts to satisfy his needs. The more basic the need that goes unsatisfied the more extreme the pathology. Kenneth Boulding has come to the logical conclusion that since the nation-state system breeds narrow-minded nationalism and can no longer satisfy the basic human need of physical security, it is pathological.[24]

Boulding is probably correct that the nation-state system is pathological in terms of satisfying basic human needs. After all, two-thirds of the
people in the world are starving or suffering from malnutrition and all
sovereign unilateral defense systems become less and less credible as
nuclear proliferation spreads. Yet de Gaulle poses an intriguing and ironic
paradox. Although the nation-state system may become increasingly less
satisfactory, those who cling to it with nationalistic bargaining policies may
get more of what there is to get in the short run, even though they
undermine the chances for everyone's survival and welfare, including their
own, in the long run. This situation can be compared to the decision to get
inoculated against serious diseases. If no one went through the personal
inconvenience and pain of getting the shot, epidemics would spread quickly
and decrease everyone's chances for health and survival. Yet what is
obvious for physical disease appears to be less obvious for political disease,
and pathological realists like Hitler capitalize on the pathological realism
and nationalism of the masses to make incredible short-term gains and to
destroy thousands of lives and human chances for ultimate need-satisfac-
tion.

As we have noted, the contrast in game theory between zero-sum
realist games and variable-sum idealist games symbolizes the logic behind
the contrast between the nationalists on the one hand and the integrationists
or internationalists on the other. The rational strategy in the real world is a
mixed strategy, sometimes maximizing one's own immediate gain and
sometimes taking a temporary loss to insure the greatest gain for the most
people. However, such mixed strategies are difficult for most people to
understand in our complex age, and rather than struggling toward political
sophistication in order to prepare oneself for the difficulties of the future,
the temptation is to grasp for simplistic solutions, popular ideologies,
charismatic leaders, and one-sided slogans. So although the pathology of
the nation-state system can be expected to be with us for some time to come,
the human responsibility of the educated person in our era is to encourage
the use of variable-sum, cooperative, international thinking to balance the
easy, instinctual, nationalistic tendencies. Otherwise, there may be no
future for any of us.

The Meaning of International Integration

The meaning of international integration now becomes clear. The
process of transferring one's loyalty from national symbols and institutions
to international or supranational symbols and institutions has become not
merely desirable but necessary for the survival of mankind. The ethical
standard has rarely been so obvious. We must all give up our petty
nationalism and ethnocentrism to become internationalists and learn to be
more concerned with the preservation of the world as a whole than with the
preservation of a minority culture, race, or people. The political problem is
more difficult, however. Where, for example, can a politician win a national

election by advocating that the citizens of his country fly the United Nations flag above their own national flag? In what developed countries will the citizens become more concerned with starving children in lesser developed countries than with increasing their own wages or security benefits? With few exceptions, human nature is not very encouraging in these respects.

Idealists have tried to overcome such difficulties with what is called the **functionalist argument** . The functionalists argue that by focusing on the pragmatic solution of present everyday needs, people will be persuaded to cooperate on other issues later on. They believe that cooperation on immediate concrete, functional problems will spill over into cooperation on future political and economic problems.[25] Indeed, such a carrot and stick approach of appealing to concrete interests is one of the few tools we have that sometimes works. But experience has shown that we cannot count on spillover incentives alone. Governments will eventually have to create laws to force people to be free in terms of supporting international, long-range priorities, just as they have had to force people to go to school and become educated in the past. Unfortunately, those things that are necessary for the survival of the human race do not always seem to further each individual's immediate interest. In a world of starvation and war, people in the well-to-do countries must learn to give more and take less. And without strong government intervention such giving on the scale needed seems unlikely to occur.

The Future of Regionalism in World Politics

Regionalism, or loyalty to one's region over loyalty to one's own nation-state, is midway on the integrative continuum between the nation-state and global political organizations. Perhaps the greatest hope for internationalizing large populations is to encourage regional interests and loyalties, Europeanism for example, rather than French or German nationalism. Of course, one can never totally forget one's national origins or overcome them. Nor should one totally. However, most problems in world politics emerge not from too little loyalty to one's nation-state, but from too much.

The Greek poet and novelist Nikos Kazantzakis has suggested that each individual should go on a pilgrimage of four stages: an examination of his own ego or self until he finds a deeper, higher spiritual longing for liberation; a going beyond his ego to his racial and national origins to seek out those forefathers most capable of refining his spirit; a plunging beyond his race and nation to the races of all of mankind to suffer their collective suffering and to struggle to liberate the human spirit as a whole; and a final surge to go beyond mankind, to identify himself with the animate and inanimate, with the environment and the vital spirit of creation in all phenomena.[26] As usual, the poet with a few brief strokes has captured the whole of man's life and of his ideal political progression from self to nation to region to world. Regionalism is an incentive to continue that pilgrimage, to get beyond the limited horizons of our own nationalism and to feel the whole world as if we were really a part of of it. As we rebel against nationalism, we represent the entire human race.

Political scientists have joined artists in supporting relevant human visions beyond nationalism that might begin to solve the needs of the whole of humanity. For example, in contending that the ideology and institutions of the state system are incapable of coping with the problems of the nuclear age and ecological crisis, regionalists Richard Falk and Saul Mendlowitz claim that nation-state loyalties are being broken down by the following developments:

1. The growth of nonstate actors in the economic sphere, especially multinational corporations;

2. The use of global functionalist agencies to cope with many technological developments that occur on a global scale;

3. The rise of transnational sentiments and movements in the professions and among ethnic, ideological, and age reference groups (for example, blacks, the third world, the young) and the decline in advanced countries of national patriotism;

4. The rise of subnational militancy that seeks to disperse authority of national governments;

5. The rise of regional movements and the growth of regional loyalties.[27]

The study and politics of regional integration may well be the appropriate path for realistic idealists to take who wish to move the world beyond the nation-state system but who are skeptical about the possibility or desirability of strong global organizations. The other path away from such an integration process, is, of course, the one that leads to international disintegration and world war.

Notes

1. Aidan Crawley, *De Gaulle* (New York: Bobbs-Merrill Co., 1969), p. 15.

2. Ibid. Other sources for the portrait of de Gaulle, but which are not referred to in specific notes, include: Jacques de Launay, *De Gaulle and His France—A Psychopolitical and Historical Portrait* (New York: Julian Press, 1968); Edward L. Morse, *Foreign Policy and Interdependence in Gaullist France* (Princeton, N. J.: Princeton University Press, 1973); Roy Macridis, *De Gaulle—Implacable Ally* (New York: Harper & Row, 1966); and W. W. Kulski, *De Gaulle and the World—The Foreign Policy of the Fifth French Republic* (Syracuse, N. Y.: Syracuse University Press, 1966).

3. Frank P. Chambers, *This Age of Conflict* (New York: Harcourt, Brace & World, 1962), p. 261.

4. Stanley and Inge Hoffmann, "The Will to Grandeur: De Gaulle as Political Artist," in Dankwart Rustow, ed., *Philosophers and Kings—Studies in Leadership* (New York: George Braziller, 1970), p. 265.

5. Francois Mauriac, *De Gaulle* (New York: Doubleday & Co., 1966), p. 7.

6. Ibid., p. 4.

7. As cited in Conor Cruise O'Brien, *Albert Camus of Europe and Africa* (New York: Viking Press, 1970), p. 35.

8. Albert Camus, *The Rebel* (New York: Random House, Vintage Books, 1956), p. 22.

9. Mauriac, *De Gaulle*, p. 10.

10. Chambers, *This Age of Conflict*, p. 691.

11. As cited in David Schoenbrun, *The Three Lives of Charles De Gaulle* (New York: Atheneum Publishers, 1966), p. 207.

12. Stanley Hoffmann, "Obstinate or Obsolete? The Fate of the Nation-State and the Case of Western Europe," *Daedalus* (Summer 1966), p. 862.

13. As cited in F. Roy Willis, *France, Germany and the New Europe 1945-1967* (New York: Oxford University Press, 1968), p. 298.

14. European Communities, Statistical Office, *Basic Statistics for Fifteen European Countries: Comparison with the United States of America and with the Union of the Socialist Soviet Republics* (Brussels, 1961), pp. 95-98.

15. Willis, *France, Germany and the New Europe*, p. 302.

16. Ibid., p. 354.

17. Richard Poirier, *The Performing Self—Compositions and Decompositions in the Languages of Contemporary Life* (New York: Oxford University Press, 1971), p. viii.

18. André Malraux, *Felled Oaks—Conversations with De Gaulle* (New York: Holt, Rinehart & Winston, 1972), pp. 94-95.

19. Albert Camus, *Notebook III, April 1939-February 1942*, trans. Philip Thrody (New York: Random House, Modern Library, 1965), pp. 151-152.

20. See Murray Edelman, "Symbols and Political Quiescence," *American Political Science Review* 54 (September 1960): 695-704; see also Murray Edelman, *The Symbolic Uses of Politics* (Urbana, Ill.: University of Illinois Press, 1967).

21. Kenneth E. Boulding, *Conflict and Defense: A General Theory* (New York: Harper & Row, 1962), pp. 331-333.

22. On the relationship between integration theory and foreign policy decision making in the context of the European community, see Robert A. Isaak, *International Integration and Foreign Policy Decision-Making*, Ph.D. dissertation for New York University (Ann Arbor, Mich.: University Microfilms, 1971).

23. Kenneth E. Boulding, "Learning and Reality-Testing Process in the International System," in John C. Farrell and Asa P. Smith, *Image and Reality in World Politics* (New York: Columbia University Press, 1968), pp. 1-15.

24. Ibid.

25. For a classic summary of the functionalist argument, see Ernst B. Haas, *Beyond the Nation-State: Functionalism and International Organization* (Stanford, Calif.: Stanford University Press, 1964).

26. See Kimon Friar's "Introduction" to Nikos Kazantzakis, *The Odyssey, A Modern Sequel* (New York: Simon & Schuster, 1958), p. xiii.

27. Richard A. Falk and Saul H. Mendlowitz, *Regional Politics and World Order* (San Francisco: W. H. Freeman & Co., 1973) p. 4.

International Law and the
United Nations—Hammarskjöld

> The road of Beethoven in his Ninth Symphony is
> also the road followed by the authors of the
> Preamble of the [United Nations] Charter. It
> begins with the recognition of the threat under
> which we all live, speaking as it does of the need
> to save succeeding generations from the scourge
> of war which has brought untold sorrow to
> mankind. It moves on to a reaffirmation of faith
> in the dignity and worth of the human person,
> and it ends with the promise to practice tolerance
> and live together in peace with one another as
> good neighbours and to unite our strength to
> maintain peace.
>
> DAG HAMMARSKJÖLD

Dag Hammarskjöld was a secret hero. The wars he prevented were never announced for the history books. He hid himself from everyone but himself to shape world peace with the sensitivity of a poet. Like anonymous hands manipulating marionettes, he influenced events from above, casting his philosophy and spell of integrity over the world and becoming, for a moment, its hope, its symbol, and its tragedy. Only his shadow remains.

One senses this shadow in walking through dehumanized skyscrapers and dirt in Manhattan to come upon the United Nations Building at Hammarskjöld Plaza. The feeling deepens when one goes inside, walking past the painting by Chagall, and finally entering the meditation room that Hammarskjöld had built with a simple block in the center and a nondenominational symbol of all the world's religions on the far wall: an oasis of silence.

Standing in that room, one knows that the man who had it built was the kind of person who meant what he said, and what he didn't say. One wonders: How did such a man ever enter politics? How did he begin that journey? How did he become secretary general of the United Nations? How did he become a myth? What principles did he represent, and how was he able to give them flesh to make international organization and world peace possible? Finally, now that he is dead, what can be expected to happen to the United Nations and world peace in the future?

Dag Hammarskjöld (left) with his predecessor as U.N. Secretary General, Trygve Lie, in 1953. *Wide World photo.*

I. Hammarskjöld: A Political Portrait

The Education of a Renaissance Diplomat

Dag Hammarskjöld's upbringing appeared to make his choice of becoming a devoted, selfless civil servant inevitable. The inner needs of his personality and his drives toward precise knowledge, culture, and spiritual integrity pushed him beyond his background. He never found himself until he became the secretary general of the United Nations and became the embodiment of international law, world organization, and universal morality. Such a confluence of historical forces and individual talents, drives, and opportunity is a rare phenomenon. His principles of political action, selfless anonymity, and personal integrity provide a model for all international civil servants in the future, not to mention for everyday people like you and me.

Dag Hjalmar Agne Carl Hammarskjöld was born on July 29, 1905, in Jönköping, Sweden, the youngest of four sons. His family had a long, aristocratic heritage and prided itself on its selfless service to the kingdom. Literary inclinations were also part of the family background. Hjalmar Hammarskjöld, his father, was a formidable, highly self-disciplined personality who dominated the family and brought his sons up sternly. Dag Hammarskjöld described his father as "one of those who are firm in their roots and firm in their faith, those whose changing fates may well deepen the convictions and directions of their early years, but not change them. . . . What gave an inner unity to his life was that in the period of revolutionary development through which he lived, he remained faithful to his past, faithful also to *the past*."[1]

Hammarskjöld's mother gave him a great deal of attention throughout his life, introducing him to music, poetry, art, literature, and history. Of her he wrote: "Agnes Almquist was different from him [Hjalmar] in many respects. Her characteristics, which appear to me to reflect her family origin, had once emerged with particular clarity and with the somewhat frightening overtones of genius in the poet Carl Jonas Love Almquist, a stepbrother of her father: a radically democratic view of fellow-humans, 'evangelic' if you like, a childlike openness toward life, an anti-rationalism with warm undercurrents of feeling."[2]

Hammarskjöld wove the self-discipline and respect for tradition of his father together with the poetic sensitivity and democratic humanism of his mother into a dynamic but quiet personality. As a child he discussed politics and culture with adults at the dinner table, where his most important education undoubtedly took place. For Hammarskjöld's father was an expert on international law and served as prime minister of Sweden during World War I. Famous political and cultural figures frequently visited the house. It was, in short, a family of great expectations as far as the sons were concerned. Later Hammarskjöld's eldest brother led a highly successful public career, and another brother became registrar of the Permanent Court of International Justice at the Hague when he was twenty-nine, and a judge at forty-three. Selfless public service was deeply embedded in the family tradition, and that ideal colored the way Hammarskjöld perceived tensions between his own personal needs and the social facts around him.

Hammarskjöld did brilliantly in school and amazed everyone with his almost photographic memory of the details of a book he had just glanced through. At eighteen he went to the prestigious University of Uppsala where he majored in French, the history of literature, and practical philosophy. He avoided social activities and preferred being alone to becoming involved with women. Shyness and iron self-discipline caused some of his friends to think he was unfriendly and aloof. He wrote in *Markings*, his poetic diary published after his death; "Every deed and every relationship is surrounded by an atmosphere of silence. Friendship needs no words—it is solitude delivered from the anguish of loneliness."[3] Most of his friendships developed from his passion for skiing and mountain climbing. The serenity of those sports was complemented by his devotion to the music of Johann Sebastian Bach and Antonio Vivaldi, which gave him a sense of order and peace.

Hammarskjöld became fluent in French, German, and English and taught himself classical Greek. Throughout his life he was seen lugging books to and from bookstores and libraries, for he was an unflagging student of philosophy and history. One of his favorite figures was Thomas Becket, the twelfth-century "God-intoxicated" man who served the Church and Henry II simultaneously. Becket, of course, was finally assassinated. What fascinated Hammarskjöld was Becket's philosophical dilemma, the conflict of loyalty which Becket tried to resolve by living a life of great austerity and giving himself to the interests of one nation-state. That model of simplicity and self-sacifice was relived by Hammarskjöld who wrote; "We are not permitted to choose the frame of our destiny. But what we put into it is ours. He who wills adventure will experience it—according to the measure of his courage. He who wills sacrifice will be sacrificed—according to the measure of his purity of heart."[4]

Effective diplomats and international civil servants need to be well versed in the world's languages, literatures, philosophies, and music, as well as in economics and politics. Sacrificing yourself for a nation-state, regional organization, or global organization may be noble if your self is worthy of sacrifice. As Hammarskjöld put it: "Not to encumber the earth—No pathetic Excelsior, but just this: not to encumber the earth."[5] By becoming competent we are able to get beyond ourselves to help others. Budding diplomats must be able to put themselves in other people's situations in order to gain a proper perspective on their own.

After completing his B.A. in two years, Hammarskjöld studied economics. He wrote a brilliant doctoral thesis on the "Expansion of Market Trends" which resulted in his being appointed assistant professor of political economy at the University of Stockholm. At the same time he served as secretary of the Royal Commission on Unemployment. His reputation spread rapidly, and at the unusually young age of thirty he became under secretary of the Swedish Ministry of Finance and served as well as chairman of the governors of the Bank of Sweden.

Hammarskjöld occupied his key post in the center of Sweden's state administration for ten years, including the World War II period. While there he developed his legendary self-discipline that later enabled him to operate so effectively in the United Nations. Sture Petren, a friend, summarized his personal traits during this period:

> For long periods, Hammarskjöld was able to manage with very little sleep, he was able to absorb at breakneck speed the content of documents and books and possessed the gift of retaining the overall view of the principal lines in a large complex of problems while seizing on isolated details of it. He was, however, also able to screen off what occupied him at a given moment, so that at that time this emerged for him as of paramount importance. Taken together, these traits endowed Hammarskjöld with a crushing efficiency, a concomitant of which, however, was a certain disinclination to delegate work to others. The mode of life Hammarskjöld had developed also required, apart from unfailing health, the absence of family life. On the other hand, he became the natural center in the circle of his closest collaborators, whose society he sought also for his scant leisure time and to whom he became, by the radiation of his personality and the multiplicity of his interests, a superior and friend of rare inspiration and stimulus. Also in his relations to staff in general, he was an esteemed and even loved boss by virtue of his natural kindness and personal interest.[6]

Perhaps most significant, during this period of civil service Hammarskjöld regarded himself as nonpolitical and refused to join a political party. Later that nonpartisanship helped him to become secretary general of the United Nations, for he had cultivated the reputation of integrity and neutrality.

Anonymity and Self-Sacrifice

Not only did Hammarskjöld struggle to maintain political neutrality, but he developed a passion for anonymity. When reporters called, Hammarskjöld turned down requests for personal interviews politely but firmly. He believed that the responsibility for our mistakes is ours, but not the credit for our achievements. His view of goodness was helping others, not seeking one's own interest, and keeping oneself in the background. In that sense he was a Christian mystic, trying to live not "I" but "God in myself," a difficult creed that prepares one for self-sacrifice. Shortly after becoming secretary general, Hammarskjöld wrote for the radio program of Edward Murrow:

> From generations of soldiers and government officials on my father's side I inherited a belief that no life was more satisfactory than one of selfless service to your country—or humanity. This service required a sacrifice of all personal interests, but likewise the courage to stand up unflinchingly for your convictions.
>
> From scholars and clergymen on my mother's side I inherited a belief that, in the very radical sense of the Gospels, all men were equals as children of God, and should be met and treated by us as our masters.
>
> . . . I found in the writings of those great medieval mystics for whom "self-surrender" had been the way to self-realization, and who in "singleness of mind" and "inwardness" had found strength to say Yes to every demand which the needs of their neighbors made them face, and to say Yes also to every fate life had in store for them. . . Love—that much misused and misinterpreted word—for them meant simply an overflowing of the strength with which they felt themselves filled when living in true self-oblivion. And this love found natural expression in an unhesitant fulfillment of duty and an unreserved acceptance of life, whatever it brought them personally of toil, suffering—or happiness.[7]

Hammarskjöld's sensitivity was far from being merely philosophical and spiritual. As an early exponent of the theories of economist John Maynard Keynes, he was asked to explain those theories to more traditional economists. Like Kissinger's expertise in theories of nuclear strategy and national security later on, Hammarskjöld's economic expertise brought him prestige and power. In a complicated technological era like ours, class and status are often based on the distribution of knowledge in the higher echelons of political decision making.

As Hammarskjöld's status increased, a series of appointments followed. From under secretary of finance and chairman of the board of governors of the Swedish National Bank, he became financial adviser to the Swedish cabinet, then secretary general of the Foreign Office, and finally secretary general of the United Nations in 1953, the most prestigious diplomatic post in the world.

When Hammarskjöld was chosen secretary general of the United Nations, the cold war between the United States and the Soviet Union was warm indeed. The founding and effectiveness of the United Nations depended entirely on the cooperation of the great powers, who, by the use of the veto in the Security Council, were able to make it helpless to act in critical world situations. Thus the neutrality and integrity of a third party or potential arbiter were critical considerations in the selection of a secretary general. Indeed, the departing secretary general, Trygve Lie of Norway, had been forced to resign largely because the Soviet Union refused to recognize him, and the United States constantly criticized and harassed him.

None of the early candidates for Lie's position could gain enough Eastern and Western support. Finally, four names were submitted to the Soviet Union, which were already acceptable to the United States, Hammarskjöld among them. As a largely unknown, neutral Swede with a reputation for neutrality and anonymity, Hammarskjöld was soon selected. The superpowers probably thought they were getting a faceless, uncontroversial administrator. They were in for a big surprise. When Hammarskjöld was informed by an Associated Press correspondent, he did not believe it and said that his watch must be fast and that it was not yet April Fool's Day. He even had to be persuaded to rewrite his acceptance speech to eliminate undue humility.

Diplomats can increase their status and power through anonymity. As a selfless civil servant who discreetly allows others to become aware of his good works, he will become increasingly trusted and called upon for more important responsibilities by those in power. Such anonymity often flows from a deep, spiritual inner life full of integrity and unaffected by outside show or material gain. As Thomas Carlyle wrote in The Hero As Man Of Letters, *"The suffering man ought really to consume his own smoke; there is no good in emitting smoke till you have made it into fire."*

Becoming Secretary General of the United Nations

In coming to the United Nations, Hammarskjöld transferred his spirit of devotion and self-sacrifice from the Swedish state to the world organization, world law, and the needs of all of mankind. He became a supranationalist almost overnight, as if it had been predestined. His life had been a strenuous search for an object and cause worthy of the sacrifice of his whole being. The United Nations provided him with the ultimate opportunity. As we have seen, Sigmund Freud claimed that man must use his rational ego to contain the instinctual drives of the id, or the subconsciousness, and to submit constantly to the superego, or the social norms and laws, in order to make civilization possible. As W. H. Auden noted,

Hammarskjöld had an exceptionally aggressive superego, probably derived from his father and his spiritual beliefs.[8] In the United Nations he became the world's superego in the flesh, the ultimate civilized man.

Unlike most men, Hammarskjöld was extremely well equipped with tools, training, temperament, life-style, and values for that most impossible of jobs. His abilities in administration and economics at a time of confusion and economic difficulty at the United Nations had undoubtedly been noted by those seeking a new secretary general. His wide philosophical background, knowledge of languages and cultures, and exposure to the principles of neutrality and international law in action through his father gave him a unique combination of traits conducive to becoming the world's superego. Moreover, his self-discipline and long successful career as a civil servant gave others confidence in his integrity, steadfastness, and trustworthiness. His word could be taken as law for he had developed a reputation for not breaking it. Finally, as a confirmed bachelor who was used to bearing grave responsibility alone without any noticeable weaknesses in mental or physical health, he seemed to be ideally suited in temperament for the most lonely and most responsible job in the world. He, of all people, possessed the tools to cope.

Uses of International Law and Morality

From his father, Hammarskjöld had learned that small countries like Sweden depended heavily upon international law for the preservation of their vital interests and, therefore, that it was compelling for such countries to sacrifice short-term egotistical gains for the long-term strengthening of international organization and law. The policy of unreserved neutrality to which Prime Minister Hjalmar Hammarskjöld unflinchingly adhered during World War I was not a popular policy, and he was forced to resign over it in 1917 rather than to enter trade negotiations with Britain, a belligerent power, which would have violated the international laws of behavior appropriate to neutral states. His son, too, would follow the United Nations Charter and international law to the letter regardless of how great the political opposition became. He, too, would probably have been forced to resign eventually had he not given an even greater sacrifice, his life.

International law is the legal embodiment of the superego of the world of states. It consists of treaties, conventions, and customs agreed to by the governments of the nation-states of the world. The Statute of the International Court of Justice cites four sources of international law: "(a) international conventions, whether general or particular, establishing rules expressly recognized by the contesting states; (b) international custom, as evidence of a general practice accepted as law; (c) the general principles of

law recognized by civilized nations; (d) judicial decisions and the teachings of the most highly qualified publicists of the various nations, as subsidiary means for the determination of rules of law."[9]

Hammarskjöld consistently interpreted the United Nations Charter as binding international law and attempted to use the potential powers of the role of secretary general to enforce it. The charter was created as World War II came to a close and was officially signed, opening the United Nations for business, in 1945 in San Francisco.* Unlike the Covenant of the League of Nations, the United Nations Charter attempted to establish a realistic world peace organization based on a number of loosely connected functional bodies, for health, education, welfare, etc. Moreover, the political decision-making structure was designed to reflect the power situation existing between the most important nations in the world after World War II. The three most important political bodies of the United Nations are the Security Council, the General Assembly and the Secretariat, headed by the secretary general. The five major powers in 1945—the United States, the Soviet Union, England, France, and China—were given permanent seats on the Security Council with the right to veto any political action proposed by the United Nations which they felt was opposed to their vital interests. In that sense, the United Nations was founded on the basis of preserving the status quo in the balance of power as the framework for world peace. The General Assembly is to the Security Council what the mass is to the elite. It represents the interests of all member nations on an equal basis, large or small. The Secretariat was conceived as the executive branch of the United Nations and most of the founders viewed it as merely a necessary adminstrative bureaucracy, not associated with great power. However, Hammarskjöld demonstrated that the charter does, in fact, give the secretary general a great deal of potential power, which he can exploit if the conditions are ripe.

The founders of the United Nations were aware that the secretary general more than anyone else would stand for the United Nations as a whole and that he should embody the ideals and principles of the charter and represent loyalty to the world interest or supranationalism rather than loyalty to any particular nation-state or nationalism. That ideal led to the inclusion of Articles 97, 98, and 99 in the charter. Article 97 legitimates the secretary general as the chief administrative officer of the organization; Article 98 extends that capacity to meetings of the General Assembly, Security Council, and Economic and Social Council, and empowers those organs to give him additional functions; Article 99 says, "The Secretary General may bring to the attention of the Security Council any matter which in his opinion may threaten the maintenance of international peace and security." Secretary General Trygve Lie used his political powers

*The text of the United Nations Charter appears as Appendix III at the back of this book.

abundantly. For example, he advocated the seating of the Chinese Communist delegation in the United Nations, provoking animosity from the United States, and strongly supported the American initiative of police action to repel North Korean aggression in the 1950s, causing extreme hostility from the Soviet Union. The cold war clearly made Lie's position untenable. Indeed, it made the very notion of a strong secretary general extremely difficult to realize in practice. Hammarskjöld was chosen out of the belief that he would probably be a passive but efficient bureaucrat, unlike the controversial Lie, and that he would act as a neutral buffer between hostile superpowers.

Indeed, during his tenure as secretary general, Hammarskjöld did all he could to cultivate the image of neutrality, integrity, and strict adherence to the limits placed on his role by the United Nations Charter. However, his interpretation of the charter's provisions was often broader than his critics liked when he became politically active in ways that might not further their short-term interests. Yet, shunning a public diplomacy, Hammarskjöld always tried to use quiet diplomacy and gain authority for all his actions from the Security Council or General Assembly. His diplomatic manipulations occurred behind the scenes, avoiding the spotlight of publicity. His approach gave the superpowers confidence in him and permitted them to compromise without losing face.

Hammarskjöld first demonstrated his brilliant skill at creating social relationships for peace in 1955 when he flew to Peking to negotiate the release of eleven American fliers who had been shot down by Communist China during the Korean conflict. He succeeded against incredible odds, for Communist China had repeatedly been denied membership in the United Nations. The Chinese diplomats were so impressed with his quiet integrity and philosophical ability to match them at their own subtle form of the diplomatic game that they announced the release of the fliers on his birthday. Not only did such a gesture stress the Chinese respect for Hammarskjöld, but it implied that the Chinese were not releasing the fliers as any kind of concession to the West.

Preventive Diplomacy and United Nations Peacekeeping

Just as Woodrow Wilson's name is unquestionably linked to the concept of collective security, Dag Hammarskjöld's is connected with the notion of "preventive diplomacy." Political scientist Inis Claude wrote, "If the United Nations has contributed anything new to the list of direct approaches to the problem of peace, it is in the development of the theory and practice of preventive diplomacy."[10] Preventive diplomacy was Hammarskjöld's approach to United Nations peacekeeping during the era of the cold war between the East and the West. He defined preventive diplomacy as United Nations intervention in areas outside of, or marginal to, the sphere plagued by cold war struggles in order to prevent the rival power blocs from intruding into the area.[11] The idea was an international policy of containment that would create a buffer zone composed of United Nations troops to prevent the spread of the cold war. The theory of preventive diplomacy was applied most notably in the Suez crisis of 1956 and in the Congo crisis of 1960, although the use of its troops almost bankrupted the United Nations and criticism by superpowers politically undermined it. However, important precedents were established for use of United Nations forces directed by the secretary general.

The efforts of Hammarskjöld to prevent the direct intervention of the great powers in the Middle East and the Congo were successful, except for the landing of British and French troops at the Suez Canal in 1956 and American troops in Lebanon in 1958. The Suez crisis erupted when President Gamal Abdel Nasser of Egypt nationalized the Suez Canal, violating the French and British view of the international waterway, not to mention their colonial interests in the Middle East, and upsetting the Israelis whose relationship with the Egyptians was already tense. Israeli troops invaded Egypt in October, 1956, and when the Egyptians rejected an Anglo-French ultimatum, the British and the French bombed Cairo two days later. American and Soviet proposals to stop the fighting were vetoed in the Security Council by the French and British. Creative thinking by the Yugoslav delegation led to a "Uniting for Peace" resolution in the General Assembly, supported by both the United States and Soviet Union. Soon a cease-fire resolution was passed, demanding a withdrawal of all forces behind armistice lines and calling for the creation of an international peace and police force to be planned by Lester Pearson of Canada and Secretary General Hammarskjöld. The British and French backed down, particularly under American pressure. The international peace force was improvised in an amazingly short period of time, and a world conflict was narrowly avoided. The creation of the United Nations Emergency Force, it should be noted, was only possible with at least the tacit consent of the two superpowers. The force was carefully made up of troops volunteered from neutral countries and served successfully as a neutral buffer between the Egyptians and Israelis.

The conflict between colonialism and nationalism so apparent in the Suez crisis was also the dominant tension that caused the Congo crisis. The Belgians had agreed to give the Congo its independence without adequately preparing for their replacement by the Congolese. The situation led to a mutiny against the newly formed native government of the Congo by those who wanted to totally eliminate Belgian interests and influence from the area at once. Belgian troops reentered the Congo to put down the rebellion. Premier Lumumba of the Congo cabled the United States for aid, but soon thereafter claimed that the appeal had been meant as a plea for a United Nations force made up of troops from neutral countries to intervene. Hammarskjöld called an emergency meeting of the Security Council and requested authorization for the formation of a United Nations force to be sent immediately to the Congo. A resolution was passed calling for the withdrawal of Belgian troops from the Congo and authorizing the creation of a United Nations force by the secretary general. However, the Congo crisis quickly became a tool in the warm cold war as the Soviet Union accused the Belgians of armed aggression and the United States of being in collusion with Belgian colonialism. The United Nations force entered the Congo in an atmosphere of great tension between the superpowers.

The superpower consensus supporting the United Nations force broke down, however, when the government of the Congo split into factions, and each superpower supported a different faction. When Andrew Cordier, the executive assistant to Hammarskjöld, shut down the national radio station and closed the Congolese airports in an attempt to cool the enflamed country and prevent civil war, the Soviets claimed that he had destroyed the chances of the faction that they supported, and that the United Nations force was no longer neutral but pro-Western. The Soviets attacked Secretary General Hammarskjöld and called for him to be replaced by a "troika," or three-man secretariat made up of one Westerner, one Easterner, and one neutral. Hammarskjöld, the Soviets claimed, was not neutral nor was it possible for a single individual to be neutral. Soviet Premier Khrushchev asserted that neutral men do not exist. His troika proposal was seen as an attempt to emasculate the secretary general. However, Hammarskjöld responded with eloquent strength, arguing that he was neutral, that the office of secretary general was more important than the man in it, and that he would resign but felt that the Soviets would not approve a successor. He asked for a vote of confidence in the General Assembly and won resoundingly, seventy to zero with eleven abstentions, including the nine Soviet-bloc countries. Following the murder of Patrice Lumumba, the leader of the Soviet-supported faction in the Congo, the Soviets demanded that the United Nations force be withdrawn within a month and said they would no longer recognize Hammarskjöld, whom they linked with Lumumba's murder. In defending himself at a speech at Oxford University, Hammarskjöld described what should be meant by the neutrality of the secretary general:

> The international civil servant must keep himself under the strictest observation. He is not requested to be a neuter in the sense that he has to have no sympathies or antipathies, that there are to be no interests which are close to him in his personal capacity or that he is to have no ideas or ideals that matter for him. However, he is requested to be fully aware of those human reactions and meticulously check himself so that they are not permitted to influence his actions. This is nothing unique. Is not every judge professionally under the same obligation? . . .
>
> This is a question of integrity, and if integrity in the sense of respect for law and respect for truth were to drive him into

Hammarskjöld is greeted by Katanga Premier Moise Tshombe at Elisabethville in 1960 while accompanying a U.N. peacekeeping force. *Wide World photo.*

positions of conflict with this or that interest, then that conflict is a sign of his neutrality and not of his failure to observe neutrality—then it is in line, not in conflict, with his duties as an international civil servant.[12]

Hammarskjöld found himself in a position similar to that of his predecessor Trygve Lie. However, Hammarskjöld refused to back down. He flew to Katanga to bring about a final peace settlement in the Congo, but his plane mysteriously crashed, or was shot down en route. All the bodies were burned except for Hammarskjöld's and a Sergeant Julien. In the secretary general's briefcase were found a shirt, a toothbrush, and twelve pages of his translation into Swedish of Martin Buber's *I and Thou*.

Andrew Cordier told a reporter, "If I had had to shoot down Hammarskjöld's plane I should have done it exactly where it was done." Another United Nations official said, "I'll tell you what I think in ten years."[13] The mystery remains unsolved. Among Hammarskjöld's things was found a diary, *Markings*, with a note giving a friend permission to publish it after his death. He called it "a sort of white book concerning my negotiations with myself—and with God." In that diary he wrote:

> Smiling, sincere, incorruptible—
> His body disciplined and limber.
> A man who had become what he could,
> And was what he was—
> Ready at any moment to gather everything
> Into one simple sacrifice.[14]

II. Principles of World Politics

The Education of Diplomats

Hammarskjöld was a living example of the ideal education and training for a diplomat or international civil servant. He became fluent in several languages and literatures, knowledgeable in philosophy and history, and an expert in economics and political negotiation. Unlike most of the other figures in this book, he had the good fortune to have been born into almost the ideal environment of social facts for developing the personality and the interests suitable for success in a career that would satisfy his highest needs of self-actualization. His family background included dedicated civil servants as well as poets. He benefited greatly from observing his father's experience as prime minister and his dedication to the principles of international law. His mother's interest in religion, literature, and the arts affected him deeply. He became a silent stream combining the warm with the intelligent, the traditional with the pragmatic, and the spiritual with the political. In *Markings* he wrote, "In our era, the road to holiness necessarily passes through the world of action."

In an age when communications, economics, and travel make the world increasingly smaller, it is essential for future diplomats to be fluent in several languages and cultural traditions so they can experience foreign world-views and be able to communicate effectively. Unfortunately in some countries, like the United States, the study of foreign languages is not encouraged but eliminated or replaced by statistics or computer science requirements. Such a trend has many depressing international consequences in terms of human relations, and the implicit chauvinism assumes that all the rest of the world must learn your language if they desire to deal with you. Ethnocentrism waxes as language requirements wane.

Moreover, Hammarskjöld's philosophical knowledge and interests should not go unnoted. Again, in pragmatic cultures like the American, philosophy is often underrated in the educational curriculum and seen more as a luxury of ages past than as a necessity for the present and future. If we remember that philosophy is the study of wisdom, then there has never been a greater need for it than in a century like our own, torn with global, regional and civil wars and violence. Dag Hammarskjöld's ability to charm others with his knowledge of their philosophical and cultural traditions was a great asset in his negotiations. It takes great self-discipline and educational training to understand and participate effectively in another culture.

Part of Hammarskjöld's philosophical wisdom was an effective blending of theory and practice, of international moral ideals combined with economic and political realities. The study of economics and political science is a necessary supplement to a solid educational basis in the philosophy, history, languages, and other liberal arts of the world. Diplomats may never become "Renaissance Men" but they must struggle daily toward that goal if basic human understanding between the many cultures of the world is to be achieved. As poet William Blake observed, our reach must exceed our grasp, otherwise, we will never become fully human.

The Anonymity Principle

One sign of diplomatic wisdom is the art of silence, the use of effective anonymity, and the doing much and taking credit for little. Someone once said, "Diplomacy is the art of letting someone else have your way." Hammarskjöld made brilliant use of the anonymity principle, the strategy of being so effective so quietly that only your successes will eventually become known and your failures will either be foregotten or forgiven because of your enchanting modesty. Such anonymity usually appears in mature individuals of strong character and some philosophical depth. Hammarskjöld wrote "Maturity: among other things—not to hide one's strength out of fear and, consequently, live below one's best" and "to exist for the future of others without being suffocated by their present."[15] He knew that he had been given more than he could ever deserve and devoted himself to selfless service accordingly.

International Law and the United Nations Charter

Hammarskjöld came to represent international law in action. He knew that international law is incapable of preserving world peace unless it can be enforced. Such enforcement, in turn, is dependent upon at least the tacit support of the great powers in the world. Therefore, Hammarskjöld's strategy became to evoke constantly the moral and legal power of the Charter of the United Nations in situations in which the superpowers were not yet involved or in which they were willing not to oppose his efforts to create and maintain conditions of peace between conflicting nation-states.

By carefully adhering to the powers allocated to the secretary general in the Charter of the United Nations and by constantly seeking the advice and support of the Security Council and General Assembly, Hammarskjöld built up confidence in himself as a discreet, trustworthy negotiator and maintained the legitimacy and prestige of the role of secretary general. He had learned from his father the patient, selfless service that is required to make international law work in world politics, particularly for the small nations of the world. Large nations have the military, economic, and political power to make their own laws in many cases. Medium-size and small nations, on the other hand, must rely upon the treaties and agreements that become international law, hoping the great powers will respect such agreements out of deference to world opinion if nothing else.

How the United Nations Works

The United Nations Charter officially documented the founding of the United Nations in San Francisco in 1945. Just as the League of Nations was created in 1919 in the hopes of preventing another World War I, so the United Nations was organized to help prevent another World War II. In each case I think it is fair to argue that the international organization was one war behind the times—like trying to close the barn door after the horse has gone. Neither organization was set up to prepare for the next world war, World War III in this case. The reason for this failure is easily understandable. National elites in power will usually only agree to conditions that will further their present interests in the status quo and prevent past injustices to their prestige from occurring again. Basically politicians are elected for their ability to put out present fires rather than to control all fires that might break out at some vague point in the future. Curiously, nations are much happier to support long-range war and weapon planning than long-range peace planning.

The United Nations, then, was set up largely to preserve the existing status quo following World War II and to create a stable basis for peace. To prevent the pathological idealism which plagued the overambitious planners of the League of Nations, the United Nations planners decided to found a functionally oriented, decentralized international organization that was based upon great power consensus and great power elites. The United States, the Soviet Union, France, England, and China were all given permanent seats on the Security Council to assure that the political actions of the organization would never overreach what the great powers of the world were willing to support at any given moment. It was hoped that by coopting the great powers the organization would never be paralyzed by the absence of a great power, as the League had been, or by a democratic majority that would not take sufficient account of great power privilege and realities, which had also happened in the League.

All that planning can be summed up in one simple principle: the United Nations works only to the extent that the great powers in the world let it work. Each member of the Security Council is allowed to veto any proposal on a "nonprocedural" matter, that is, on any important political action. Since the five great powers were given the only permanent seats on the council, they are the only ones who consistently have the power to veto United Nations action of which they do not approve. For example, by late 1965, 109 vetoes had been cast, 103 by the Soviet Union. Of course sometimes such vetoes can be circumvented by having an agency other than the Security Council carry out the action. Thus, the six vetoes cast by the Soviet Union during the Congo operation were circumvented when the General Assembly passed resolutions almost identical in language to those already vetoed in the Security Council.

In addition to official political vetoes, "hidden" financial vetoes are possible. For example, since the United States has traditionally paid at least a third of the operating cost of the United Nations, the slightest hint that she might withdraw financial support has often sufficed to settle an issue even before it came to a vote in the Security Council.[16] Needless to say, the United States has not hesitated to use this hidden veto in the past, preferring subtle financial pressure to the stigma in world public opinion of an outright political veto in the Security Council. Once again the importance of military and economic superpowers for effective United Nations action becomes clear. In short, the United Nations can only plan effectively for the future to the extent that all of the great powers in the world decide to plan for the future, together.

Of course one should not underestimate the importance of the United Nations in gathering worldwide statistics on the world's greatest problems, on providing an international meeting place on neutral ground for diplomatic discussion, and for doing extremely important work in the functional branches of education, welfare, and human rights. In terms of future world war, however, great power consensus or lack of it is decisive.

The International Civil Servant

Dag Hammarskjöld was the model international civil servant. Coming from a neutral country and with a background of selfless national civil service, he also possessed the ideals, economic, administrative and language skills necessary to become an effective supranational civil servant. Effective service to supranationalism and the United Nations demands unquestionable ethical integrity, political neutrality, and commitment to the welfare of all the people in the world, not just to one's own people, race, or nation.

Moreover in accepting a role in international civil service as important as that of secretary general, it becomes almost mandatory to devote one's whole life to that purpose. Hammarskjöld was not accidentally a bachelor without family responsibilities, which might have distracted him from giving all of his energies to world peace. As André Malraux wrote in his *Antimémoires*, "It is not the role which makes the historical personality, but the vocation."[17]

International Peacekeeping and Self-Help

By watching how international law and the United Nations work through the eyes and actions of Hammarskjöld, one soon sees that international peacekeeping depends heavily upon the tacit consent and consensus of the great powers in the world and that international law will only be respected if it can be enforced. "Self-help" is the restrictive principle of effective international law, which respects the sovereignty of each nation-state officially but can do little if great powers choose to violate the sovereignty of weaker nations. International law and the United Nations act as moral deterrents to aggressive behavior on the part of the great powers with world public opinion the sanction most frequently invoked. If, however, the Soviets choose to invade Czechoslovakia or the Americans the Dominican Republic, there is little international law or the United Nations can do to stop them. Yet these moral deterrents should not be underrated. In the case of the two invasions just mentioned, political scientists Thomas M. Franck and Edward Weisband noted:

> When United States forces invaded the Dominican Republic, Washington arrogantly confronted the Organization of American States with a *fait accompli* more of the era of 1865 than 1965. But when the Warsaw Pact Powers brutally and stupidly suppressed Alexander Dubcek's attempt to impose a human face on socialism, the West was stunned and horrified. Few Western observers noted that the Russians were echoing the very words used by hardheaded realists in Washington to defend America's Latin American policy. By failing to listen to themselves as if they were the enemy speaking, American policy makers had made it easy and cheap for Russia to reassert the

darkest side of its nature. This cannot but be counted a failure of U.S. strategic planning.[18]

Franck and Weisband demonstrated that the great powers of the world tend to mimic each other s rhetoric in justifying their actions and that they often set precedents for each other without being aware of it at the time. Neutral, international peacekeepers can often pinpoint this sort of action in world politics and in some cases make the great powers see how they interact in the situation and thereby avert a confrontation. However, the great powers often make such benevolent intervention by a neutral third-party impossible by taking unilateral actions secretly and swiftly. By the time the issue comes to the international peacekeeper it is almost too late. Alas, the United Nations can do very little about the arrogance of superpower. One can only hope that the superpowers themselves will eventually learn that they actually lose world prestige and power by hot-headed action that fails to take the reaction of others sufficiently into account.

III. Present Implications

The Future of International Law and Morality

Recall again Sigmund Freud's claim that war and chaos can only be prevented if individuals control their instinctual drives or id with their rational ego in accordance with the norms and laws of society, or their superego. Similarly, one can argue that if nation-states are to prevent war and conflict between them, they must control their nationalistic drives through their diplomatic egos in accordance with the norms and agreements of international law. Historically speaking such control has occurred only when the so-called vital interests of the stronger nation-states are not involved in a conflict situation. But since vital interests are often subjective-ly defined and short-term interests often conflict with long-term interests, nation-states must become more civilized and modify their national interests to fit a higher vision of supranational harmony in the world. Otherwise, in a time of increasing scarcity of natural resources and increasing interdependence between nation-states, low-level violence over immediate aims can easily spill over into world war.

Unfortunately, zero-sum thinking and nationalistic antagonism are more apt to dominate the immediate future than variable-sum international cooperation. For even if nation-states adhere to international law, that very law advocates the preservation of national sovereignty and can do little to make large, wealthy nations put their own houses in better human order, much less force them to give a fair share of what they have to the poorer nations in the world. The notion of strict, independent sovereignty is a hopeless anachronism in a century of intercontinental ballistic missiles, multi-national corporations and political interdependence. But people everywhere are still willing to go to war and die for the myth, dressed up as national honor, tradition, pomp and circumstance.

The Power of the United Nations

National sovereignty is the plague of the United Nations as well as of international law. Fundamentally loyalty to national sovereignty is antithetical to loyalty to supranationalism or the United Nations. In Hammarskjöld's case, for example, the tension between national sovereignty and supranational authority became acute in the Congo crisis where the struggle for national liberation from colonialism turned into a civil war. Caught in the middle, the United Nations force could do little. It became increasingly controversial, and its legitimacy and integrity were undermined by nationalistic potshots from all sides. The United Nations was never designed to settle internal disputes; yet many international conflicts border on or lead to civil war. In such ambiguous situations, the United Nations is damned if it does and damned if it doesn't. And the superpowers are not as apt to give the international organization credit as to criticize it for not leaning more in the direction of their own national interests.

The power of the United Nations will continue to depend upon superpower consensus and financial support in major international conflict situations. Unfortunately such superpower support is apt to come only as a last resort, when the superpowers are convinced that they cannot solve the situation with their own diplomats, threats, armies, and power. The phenomenon of superdiplomats like Henry Kissinger representing the superpowers for world peace is apt to become more prevalent than supranational United Nations forces commanded solely by a strong secretary general. The superpowers will strive to maintain as much control of the world situation as they can, using the United Nations when it appears to be a possible instrument to further their own national interests.

In short, the United Nations will maintain its greatest influence as a moral and international symbol of world peace and equality for all human beings. It will continue to provide a neutral meeting place for hostile parties and to give the smaller nations of the world one of the few forums where they can speak to great powers on somewhat equal terms. Individuals from all nations can strengthen its power for world peace and welfare by generously donating their time, money, and services. It will probably be some time before the rich nation-states of the world tax their own peoples heavily enough to adequately finance the United Nations and make it a fully effective force for world peace.

Hammarskjöld's Markings on Tomorrow

The United Nations has been fortunate enough to have had one secretary general who qualified as a hero and a martyr, almost a saint. Such myths and symbolic figures are extremely important in building up loyalty to supranational organizations and objects, just as national heroes of the past have been important in sustaining national loyalties and pride. Recall that international integration refers to the transfer of individual loyalties from national to supranational organizations and objects, as well as to increased international cooperation. On the integration continuum individuals can be expected to move from national to regional to international or global loyalties as their horizons widen and as they identify themselves with the whole human race, as opposed to a particular part of it. The opposite process, international disintegration, which is at least as likely, refers to a regression of individuals back to primitive racial and national loyalties, perhaps even to ethnocentrism and xenophobia.

The progression out of one's ego, from one's family and national loyalties to regional affiliations and finally to the point of embracing the whole world and all of humanity, is an extremely difficult struggle that few people achieve in their lifetime. Hammarsköld clearly did. Toward the end of his journey he wrote in *Markings*:

> Clad in this "self," the creation of irresponsible and ignorant persons, meaningless honors and catalogued acts—strapped into the straight jacket of the immediate.
>
> To step out of all this, and stand naked on the precipice of dawn—acceptable, invulnerable, free: in the Light, with the Light, of the Light. *Whole*, real in the Whole.
>
> Out of myself as a stumbling block, into myself as fulfillment.[19]

Notes

1. As cited in Brian Urquhart, *Hammarskjöld* (New York: Alfred A. Knopf, 1972), p. 19. Other sources for the portrait of Hammarskjöld, but which are not referred to in specific notes, include: Joseph Lash, *Dag Hammarskjöld* (New York: Doubleday & Co., 1961); Henry Van Dusen, *Dag Hammarskjöld: The Statesman and his Faith* (New York: Harper & Row, 1967); Richard Miller, *Dag Hammarskjöld and Crisis Diplomacy* (Dobbs Ferry, N. Y.: Oceana Publications, 1961); Leon Gordenker, *The UN Secretary-General and the Maintenance of Peace* (New York: Columbia University Press, 1967); Joel Larus, ed., *From Collective Security to Preventive Diplomacy* (New York: John Wiley & Sons, 1965); and Andrew Cordier and Kenneth Maxwell, *Paths to World Order* (New York: Columbia University Press, 1967).

2. Ibid., p. 19.

3. Dag Hammarskjöld, *Markings,*, trans. W. H. Auden and Leif Sjöberg (New York: Alfred A. Knopf, 1964), p. 8.

4. Ibid., p. 55.

5. Ibid., p. 66.

6. Urquhart, *Hammarskjöld*, p. 22.

7. As cited in W. H. Auden's "Foreword" to Hammarskjöld, *Markings*, p. viii.

8. Ibid., p. xiv.

9. Statute of the International Court of Justice (1945), Article 38, as cited in William W. Bishop, *International Law: Cases and Materials* (Boston: Little, Brown & Co., 1962), p. 22.

10. Inis Claude, *Swords into Plowshares* (New York: Random House, 1966), p. 285.

11. Dag Hammarskjöld, *Introduction to the Annual Report of the Secretary General on the Work of the Organization, 16 June 1959-15 June 1960* (General Assembly Official Records: Fifteenth Session, Supplement No. 1A [A/4390/Add.I]).

12. Dag Hammarskjöld, "The International Civil Servant in Law and in Fact," (Lecture delivered to Congregation at Oxford University, May 30, 1961) as cited in Michael Barkun and Robert W. Gregg, eds., *The United Nations System and Its Functions* (New York: D. Van Nostrand Co., 1968), p. 228.

13. Emery Kelen, *Hammarskjöld* (New York: G. P. Putnam's Sons, 1966), p. 274.

14. Hammarskjöld, *Markings*, p. 6.

15. Ibid., pp. 67 and 89.

16. John Stoessinger, *The United Nations and the Superpowers* (New York: Random House, 1965). See Chap. 1, "The Security Council: The Veto and the Superpowers," pp. 3-20.

17. André Malraux, *Antimémoires* (New York: Holt, Rinehart & Winston, 1968), p. 103.

18. Thomas Franck and Edward Weisband, *Word Politics: Verbal Strategy Among the Superpowers* (New York: Oxford University Press, 1962), p. vii.

19. Hammarskjöld, *Markings*, p. 152.

CHAPTER 8

Foreign Policy Decision Making in a Nuclear Age — Kissinger

I think of myself as a historian more than as a
statesman. As a historian, you have to be conscious of the fact that every civilization that has
ever existed has ultimately collapsed.
History is a tale of efforts that failed, of aspirations that weren't realized, of wishes that were
fulfilled and then turned out to be different from
what one expected. So, as a historian, one has to
live with a sense of the inevitability of tragedy.
As a statesman, one has to act on the assumption
that problems must be solved.

HENRY KISSINGER

Henry Kissinger refutes the myth that individuals are of little importance in
the world politics of the nuclear age. He has made a great difference in the
possibility of world peace amid the conflict of our times. He has converted a
philosophy of human limitations into incredible political power. Indeed,
history may show that Henry Kissinger was the most powerful individual in
the world in the 1970s.

How long will a democratic country tolerate such individual power and
Kissinger in a high governmental position in the United States at any time in
its history."[1] English reporter Henry Brandon agreed: "Never before in
American history have the intellectual and conceptual views of the world of
one man, who was neither in an elected position nor a member of the
Cabinet, influenced American politics as have those of Dr. Kissinger."[2]
Kissinger has combined the qualities of an intellectual, a scholar, a
European American, and a pragmatic negotiator to become the greatest
secretary of state the United States has ever known.

How long will a democratic country tolerate such individual power and
greatness? Does a nuclear age require superdiplomats to make effective
foreign policy decisions? How does the way Kissinger rose to power in the
United States affect his ideals, strategies, and actions? What can others
learn from his foreign policy principles? What are the consequences of his
blueprint for world peace for the Third World? For the superpowers? For
domestic freedoms? And what is likely to happen when Kissinger is gone?

Henry Kissinger with his wife, Nancy. *David Hume Kennerly,*
Time; © *1974 Time Inc.*

I. Kissinger: A Political Portrait

Escape from Hitler to New World Opportunity

Imagine your grandfather telling you as a child: "Now once upon a time there was a little Jewish boy born in Germany. His mother saved him from the Nazis in the nick of time by urging the family to move to New York. There he squeezed acid from brush bristles by day and studied by night until he was drafted by the army. There he became an interpreter to a general and a teacher. He later went to Harvard where he did brilliantly. After his graduation he taught at Harvard and then went on to serve the American government and become the most powerful man in the world." Upon hearing such a story, you probably would have chided your grandfather for telling such a tall tale. Yet, it is a true story—and not even the half of it.

Among other things, Kissinger is an incredible American success story. In no other country is it really conceivable that a lower-middleclass, Jewish immigrant could rise so swiftly to the top of a national political hierarchy and, once there, be in a position at times almost to rule the world. Of course, it will be some time in the future, with the advantage of historical distance and documents that are presently top secret, before we will be able to see the whole man, both the negative and positive sides. We know a great deal already from his own writing and writing about him, and he provides an illuminating model for individual effectiveness in world politics and for the use of foreign policy principles to advance national interests and world peace in the nuclear era.

Henry Kissinger was born in Fürth, Germany in 1923. His father taught in a high school for girls, his mother was a German Jewish housewife. During his childhood the political environment deteriorated, the Nazis gained ground, and anti-Semitism spread. Finally, his father was fired from his job. Intuiting what was to come, his mother prompted the family to leave Germany for New York in 1938, Kissinger's first stroke of luck.

In the German **Realschule**, the young Kissinger had shown great academic aptitude. At George Washington High School in New York, he confirmed the impression of being a superior student, receiving straight A's. Yet upon graduating in 1941, he found himself in a situation similar to that of many top students whose families could not afford to support their higher education. He therefore enrolled in night courses at City College and continued to work during the day in a Manhattan shaving brush factory, squeezing acid out of brush bristles. He felt as though he spent his days in an industrial factory only to spend his evenings in an educational factory.[3] Soon he was promoted to delivery boy. Then he was drafted, his second lucky break. He was liberated from the repressive factory life by the war. In 1943 he did basic training at Camp Croft, South Carolina, and found the experience to be an exhilarating change from life in New York City. His letters during this period reveal an individual very much alone who carefully looked and listened.[4]

Military Experience and the Normalcy of Change

During the army's regular testing program, Kissinger was discovered to have an IQ high enough to qualify him for a special group of 3,000 men whose minds the army thought might later be useful in the war effort. He was sent at the army's expense to Lafayette College in Easton, Pennsylvania in 1943, where he spent more than six months in a special engineering program. Again, Kissinger was singled out by forces beyond his control to change locations and improve his life chances. His loneliness in youth was marked by constant dislocations, cultural changes, rootlessness, and unpredictable circumstances. It is little wonder that the principle of **indeterminacy** was later to dominate so much of his writing and thinking.

Effective diplomacy in the nuclear age must comprehend the principle of indeterminacy, a relativity of time, space, and measurement that makes certainty impossible in the physical and social sciences yet simultaneously increasing modern man's longing for it. The only constant left is change and the possible limits of the direction of change, at which the diplomat guesses on the basis of his knowledge, past experience, and intuition. Concerning the premises of Kissinger's analytical framework, Graubard wrote, "They all presupposed a philosophical acceptance of indeterminacy. It is no accident that words like ambiguity, irony, paradox, nuance, and tragedy constantly recur in Kissinger's writings. These were not the terms that other foreign policy experts were in the habit of using. Nor were others prepared to give so prominent a place to what Kissinger called psychological factors or elements."[5]

The psychological tension between human needs and social facts for Kissinger was of an unusual and modern sort. The cause of the tension was not his moving from place to place or from position from position. That for him was normal and exhilarating. The tensions that Kissinger found to be unbearable resulted from staying too long in one place or one position and from the false philosophical security of being one thing and one thing only in a particular institutional hierarchy or bureaucracy. Instinctively he knew that truth in the modern nuclear age was more a question of constant change, indeterminacy, and relativity, than of fixed boundaries, roles, and unambiguous situations and positions. Yet, even so, he longed to know the limits of knowledge and his own limits, to know what other philosophers, historians, and great men had found out about the direction of change and human capability in the past. He first tasted that kind of knowledge when he was assigned in 1944 to the Eighty-fourth Infantry Division at Camp Claiborne, Louisiana where he met Fritz Kraemer.

Fritz Kraemer, a thirty-five-year-old German lawyer with two Ph.D.s, was ordered to explain why the United States was in the war to an army unit led by buck Private Kissinger, nineteen years old. Soon thereafter, Kissinger sent Kraemer a note, simple and to the point:[6]

Dear Pvt. Kraemer:

I heard you speak yesterday. This is how it should be done. Can I help you somehow?

Pvt. Kissinger

Human Choice and Limitations

Kissinger and Kraemer soon became inseparable. Not only did Kissinger admire the older man for his knowledge and the high standards of his European educational background, but he was particularly impressed that a German, though not a Jew, had chosen to leave his country for reasons of moral and political conviction, rather than as a result of mere circumstance. The phenomenon of human choice, of men deciding their destinies, fascinated Kissinger, and he greatly respected Kraemer's courage and verve. Kraemer, on the other hand, was only too glad to discover a bright young man who would listen to his theories, a companion who could keep up with his mind.

Using his influence, Kraemer helped to make Kissinger an interpreter in case the Eighty-fourth Division should be sent to Germany. It was, and Kissinger became interpreter for the general. Kissinger's division then took over the city of Krefeld only to discover that the city government had vanished along with the Nazi soldiers. Kraemer suggested that since Kissinger spoke German and was extremely intelligent, he should be placed in charge of reorganizing the government of the city of 200,000 people. In three days Kissinger had the city running smoothly again. Because of his success he was made administrator of the Bergstrasse district, a job he did so well that when he was transferred the German people in the area begged him to stay. After the war, in 1946 Kissinger stayed in Europe as a well-paid instructor at the European Command Intelligence School, where he taught officers of higher rank than his how to root out Nazis who had gone underground. However, Kissinger realized how little he knew and wanted to go home to finish his education. Kraemer advised him that gentlemen did not get their degrees from City College and urged Kissinger to apply elsewhere. Kissinger applied and was accepted at Harvard. There he lived the life of a recluse, making up for all the learning he had missed, a feeling shared by many soldiers returning from the war who went back to school.

He fell under the influence of an exceptional tutor, William Y. Elliott, who gave of himself unstintingly to a handful of undergraduates, on the Oxford model, where he had been a Rhodes Scholar. Among other things, that nutrient relationship resulted in Kissinger's writing a 377-page senior honors thesis entitled "The Meaning of History: Reflections on Spengler, Toynbee and Kant."

In his unusual, wide-ranging thesis, Kissinger was concerned with the phenomenon of historical change and man's role in it. The theories of Oswald Spengler and Arnold Toynbee pointed to a recurring cycle of historical development that went through stages of creation, maintenance, and decay, just as a plant went through the spring of youth, the summer and fall of maturity, and the winter of death. Philosopher Immanuel Kant was, of course, a rigorous ethical philosopher who called upon men to see their responsibilities clearly in history and to treat other human beings as ends, not just as means, within that context. Kissinger wrote; "Though aging in a culture is not analogous to physical decay, it does bear a similarity to another problem of existence, the process of disenchantment. Just as the life of every person exhibits a gradual loss of wonder at the world, so history reveals an increase of familiarity with the environment, a tired groping for a certainty which will obviate all struggles, a quest for a guarantee of man's hopes in nature's mechanism."[7] Kissinger's favorite philosophical theme became man's dilemma of choice in historical uncertainty, particularly in terms of his gradual disenchantment with the world as he grew older and the culture around him decayed.

The tension between Kissinger's needs and the way he viewed the constraints of social and historical facts now revealed itself clearly in terms of his philosophical position. He was neither a determinist nor total advocate of free will. He rejected simplistic engineering theories or technical solutions to human existence, and he mocked all those who would reduce life to formulas. Although he accepted the laws of necessity, he believed that man must use reason to become a responsible individual agent in the process of history. He wrote: "But action derives from an inward necessity, from the personal in the conception of the environment, from the unique in the apprehension of phenomena. Consequently, objective necessity can never guide conduct, and any activity reveals a personality. Reason can help us understand the world in which we live. Rational analysis can assist us in developing institutions which make an inward experience possible. But nothing can relieve man from his ultimate responsibility, from giving his own meaning to life, from elevating himself above necessity . . ."[8]

Like Kant, Kissinger was profoundly aware of the limits of man's reason, of the role of man's emotional and intuitional faculties, and of the terrifying responsibilities life imposes. He saw that life involves suffering and transitoriness, that no person can choose his age or the condition of the time in which he lives. He believed, however, that each responsible person must choose within the environment into which he is born. The personal experience of freedom through the uniqueness that each man imparts to the necessity of his life is the essence of Kissinger's philosophy and underlies all his thinking and political actions.

On the basis of his honors thesis, Kissinger received his bachelor's *summa cum laude*, a sign of true recognition at Harvard. He then decided to do graduate work in international relations, convinced that the future peace of the world and the destiny of mankind depended upon how the relations between states were conducted. Furthermore, he believed one could not separate diplomacy from military policy or domestic politics and that, although the past was never repeated exactly in the future, the study of history could help one to understand the limits of political change between nation-states and within them. Peace, he thought, was not the proper objective of international politics but a necessary by-product of international stability, if that could be achieved. The purpose of international relations, then, was the creation and maintenance of a stable international order. Moreover, he rejected the notion that the explosion of the atomic bomb had also obliterated the revolutionary world order introduced by Napoleon. Throughout his future career he was to argue that we live in a revolutionary age and the problem of world peace is to create a sense of legitimacy to stabilize an equilibrium of the great powers of the world.

Metternich, Legitimacy, and the Balance of Power

William Elliott once told Kissinger that he had the makings of a great philosopher. All of his writings certainly indicate unusual philosophical ability, particularly in everyday diplomatic life. In developing his own theory of international politics, which would later become the basis for his unusually effective foreign policy decisions, Kissinger's choice of a topic for his doctoral thesis was critical. He wrote on the creation and maintenance of the "Metternich system" of balance of power between 1812 and 1822, a thesis which was later published as a book entitled *A World Restored: The Politics of Conservatism in a Revolutionary Age.*

In his thesis Kissinger made the important political distinction between revolutionary and legitimate international orders. He believed that diplomats who could not distinguish between those two basic types of international conditions would make drastic errors. A legitimate international order is one in which the major powers in a region or the world accept certain rules of the game and limits in order to maintain a stable equilibrium called peace from which they can all benefit. A revolutionary world order, on the other hand, includes powerful nation-states with unlimited objectives who are not about to accept the existing status quo over their own national interests. Kissinger examined Metternich's attempts to maintain the legitimacy of the conservative balance of power system in Europe in order to protect Austria's security.* The chief opponent of Metternich was Napoleon, that nationalistic hero with unlimited objectives who sought to

---

*Recall that the details of the balance of power system in Metternich's Europe were given in Chapter Four.

replace the old conservative order with his own revolutionary alternative. In short, Metternich sought to maintain Austria's power in the status quo by using the principle of legitimacy to keep the major European powers—Austria, Prussia, Russia, France, and Britain—in balance. He was a conservative maintenance man who tried to preserve the old European order as long as possible by clever manipulations.

In the end, however, Kissinger rejected Metternich as superficial and as an obsolete leftover from the Enlightenment. He felt that Metternich was misled by his belief in a natural harmony of international affairs, a kind of mechanical clockwork, and because of his faulty world-view, he "failed to achieve final greatness."

In his dissertation Kissinger noted another distinction that is also an important basis of his twentieth-century policy: the distinction between insular and continental powers. As a multinational, continental state, Kissinger pointed out, Metternich's Austria had different interests from Castlereagh's Britain, which was an insular, secure state with a solid national base. As an island power, Britain could advocate noninterference in the domestic affairs of other states. On the other hand, Austrian policy advocated the right to interfere since Austrian security was perceived to rest on the delicate balance of power existing on the continent. The implications of this distinction are important since, at least until the 1950s, the United States behaved rather consistently as an island power. Kissinger, of course, was too sophisticated an academic to make any simple analogies between nineteenth-century models of international politics and twentieth-century political behavior. He pointed out, however, that states are forgetful and often fail to learn from the past. Certainly he bears in mind the limits of what was possible in the nineteenth century in his negotiations in the twentieth century, especially in his disdain for technological solutions to human historical problems.

Bismarck, Women, and Surprise Diplomacy

Kissinger's study of nineteenth-century diplomacy was not limited to the first half of the century dominated by Metternich. He later did a study of the Prussian Otto von Bismarck, the precocious diplomat who first undermined and then overthrew Metternich's balance of power system. He used conservative Prussian nationalism and tactics of surprise and secret alliances to unite Germany and consolidate her power. In his article called "The White Revolutionary: Reflections on Bismarck," Kissinger identified Bismarck as a conservative revolutionary and empathized with the German chancellor's disdain for the bureaucracy and with his flamboyant life-style. When Bismarck left a routine civil service job without giving notice, he said, according to Kissinger:

> I had every prospect for what is called a brilliant career . . .
> had not an extraordinarily beautiful Briton induced me to

change course and sail in her wake for six months without the slightest leave. I forced her to come aside; she lowered the flag, but after possession of two months I lost the booty to a one-armed colonel fifty years of age with four horses and 15,000 dollars revenue.[9]

Kissinger was later an outspoken critic of bureaucratic red tape and cultivated beautiful women in public as a hobby. But like Bismarck, Kissinger viewed women as secondary hobbies. In an interview with Italian journalist Oriana Fallaci during the Vietnam peace negotiations, he ventured that his playboy reputation, far from hurting his negotiating ability, might be an asset in face-to-face talks with other world leaders. He said that he knew how to behave with a diplomat when with a diplomat, and with a girl when with a girl.[10]

Kissinger has been clearly astute in using his reputation with beautiful women as a red herring to lure journalists away from focusing too precisely on the secret diplomatic negotiations at hand. Not only did Kissinger perhaps find in Bismarck a model for his own flamboyant, individualistic style of diplomacy and his tendency to ignore the lower bureaucracies, but he may have learned other things from Bismarck as well. Nora Beloff is undoubtedly on the right track in her perception that Kissinger has used Bismarck's world-view, which was a more flexible one than Metternich's. Bismarck thought that world politics could be stabilized only with a dynamic equilibrium, which was manipulated by diplomats who operated with amoral calculations of power that were marked by secrecy and ambiguity.[11]

Bismarck initially used the existing conservative balance of power system in Europe for his own ends, subverting Metternich's principles within the Prussian Foreign Office with brash memoranda proposing a new basis for Prussian diplomacy. Like Kissinger later, Bismarck was acutely aware of the spirit of his times, an atmosphere of nationalism combined with liberalism. By persuading his countrymen that Prussian nationalism could be based on traditional conservatism rather than liberalism, Bismarck was able to exploit the existing situation to unite Germany's many principalities with Prussian power and force. As soon as he had worked himself up to the top foreign policy-making position, Bismarck used tactics of ambiguity, secrecy, and surprise to accomplish his ends, tactics for which Kissinger is also famous. In fact, Lord Salisbury called Bismarck's strategy of forming secret coalitions "employing one's neighbors to pull out each other's teeth." One must, alas, wait for future histories to be written to see how Kissinger's opponents characterize his clever strategies of coalition.

American Foreign Policy in an Atomic, Revolutionary Era

As a graduate student at Harvard University, Kissinger did not limit himself just to nineteentth-century scholarship even though that was his thesis specialization. He also was a driving force behind the Harvard International Seminar and the creation of a journal called *Confluence*, both with the support and active help of William Elliott.* In organizing the summer Harvard Seminar Kissinger invited many gifted individuals from outside the United States to come to learn and discuss contemporary international issues. Thus, he was brought into contact with members of foreign elites whom he would not otherwise have met and who later helped him further his career. In helping to found *Confluence*, Kissinger became acquainted with influential intellectuals in many disciplines and learned a great deal about publishing.

In 1955 he entered into an association that was even more crucial in his development. Gordon Dean, the former head of the Atomic Energy Commission, in the name of the prestigious and influential Council on Foreign Relations, called together a gifted group of people to discuss the making and implementation of foreign policy in the nuclear age. Not only was Kissinger asked to participate in those discussions, he was asked to join the group as its study director and to write a book growing out of the discussions for which he alone would be responsible. It was clearly a unique opportunity. He had the advantage of experts in and out of government who discussed problems about which he would later write. Furthermore the book was to be published and sponsored by the most prestigious private group of foreign policy advisers in the United States, a group that publishes *Foreign Affairs*, the best-known journal in its field and one for which Kissinger later wrote a good deal.

Most of the books published by the Council on Foreign Relations died, so to speak, upon publication without becoming well known or selling a great number of copies. But not Kissinger's. *Nuclear Weapons and Foreign Policy* became a best-seller in 1957, attracting the attention of statesmen as well as scholars. It was the turning point in Kissinger's career. Indeed, one is reminded of Bismarck's influential memoranda.

Kissinger followed up many of the themes of his dissertation in the book, beginning, for example, with the statement that modern man lives in an age in which Nemesis, the goddess of fate, often punishes him by fulfilling his wishes too completely. In effect he argued that America's nemesis was her technological success. Americans naively believed that technology was the answer to their problems and therefore underestimated the importance of a strategic doctrine, particularly in a nuclear age such as ours.

Moreover, Americans thought they constituted an island power like Great Britain in the nineteenth century. They desired not to be involved where possible, felt disdain for the cynical European political interactions, and did not realize that all politics of national interest are similar, differing only in degree. The result of that insular reserve and belief in nuclear

*The financial influence of the Central Intelligence Agency was also indirectly "behind" the Seminar, although Kissinger claimed not to know about it.

•

technology was the American "more bomb for the buck," all-out total victory defense thinking. Such thinking became increasingly incredible to the Soviet Union, since the Soviets knew that temperamentally and humanistically the Americans were extremely unlikely to use their atomic weapons. As a result of the American incapacity to incorporate atomic power into strategic thinking, Kissinger argued, the United States wasted her nuclear monopoly following the war, by not knowing how to transfer it into actual political power, and allowed the Soviets to make significant gains in Europe under her very nose.

Kissinger went further to argue that American total victory and all-or-nothing psychological rigidity prevented American policymakers from coping with uncertainty and any but unambiguous threats. The reader might recall the results of such psychic rigidity in Wilson and Hitler. Since the basic task of the United States in a revolutionary era such as ours, Kissinger argued, was to preserve her power and secure her interests, it was vital that American policymakers learn how to defend themselves against the nuances, ambiguities, and indeterminacies of international subversion, propaganda, and subtle revolutionary warfare. Clearly Kissinger's European background, upbringing, and philosophical belief in the principle of indeterminacy allowed him to interpret American strategic doctrines in terms of ambiguities and nuances that many native and deeply rooted Americans might well have missed. He suggested that the task of American foreign policy in the nuclear age was to create flexible, tactical nuclear alternatives in order to prevent the single solution of nuclear holocaust. Such alternatives would also wean Americans from crisis decision-making and force them to analyze all levels of threat to American security on a day-to-day basis. Only by accepting and learning to play with the ambiguities and uncertainties of the nuclear diplomatic game could the Americans successfully counter Soviet diplomacy, which they had so clearly failed to do in the past.

Great power diplomats in a revolutionary, nuclear age must increase their decision-making options and defense strategies by learning how to effectively counter ambiguous threats and how to cope with continual uncertainty. A stable international order, or "legitimate" dynamic equilibrium, cannot be created and maintained until "legitimate" big powers learn how to slip into the shoes of revolutionary big and little powers in order to communicate in a non-ideological language of national interest and preserve stability with diversity. Foreign policy decision makers must seek to understand the ambiguities of their opponents and try to cut the costs of uncertainty in terms of their own national interest. They must learn to cope with the logic of the following Jewish anecdote:
"Where are you going?"
"To Minsk."

"Shame on you! You say this to make me think you are going to Pinsk. But I happen to know you ARE going to Minsk."

~o~o~o~o~o~o~o~

Kissinger believed that perceptive, flexible diplomacy was vital if American interests were to be maintained in an era when they were threatened by revolutionary movements on almost all fronts. His philosophy was that of the creative maintenance man, the astute statesman who, like a graceful dancer, makes his entrance, bows, turns, and exits at exactly the right moment, perfectly attuned to the atmosphere and the music and anticipating every movement of his partner. On the sense of timing, Kissinger pointed out in *Nuclear Weapons and Foreign Policy:* "And no conditions should be sought for which one is not willing to fight indefinitely and no advance made except to a point at which one is willing to wait indefinitely. The side which is willing to outwait its opponent—which is less eager for a settlement—can tip the psychological balance, whatever the outcome of the physical battle." Needless to say, this describes almost exactly the psychological strategy that enabled the North Vietnamese to do so well against the much more powerful United States in the Vietnamese war. They simply "outwaited" Western technology and impatience for victory.

Presidential Advising and War in Southeast Asia

Following his success with *Nuclear Weapons and Foreign Policy* and the Council of Foreign Relations Kissinger was appointed as a professor of government at Harvard. However, he was by no means a pure academic, and he later was frustrated with the pettiness of academic life much as Bismarck was contemptuous of the civil service bureaucracy in Prussia. In 1956 Nelson Rockefeller appointed Kissinger as director of a Special Studies Project for the Rockefeller Brothers Fund. The purpose of the project was to define the major problems and opportunities that would challenge the United States in the next fifteen years. It created a lasting relationship between Kissinger and Nelson Rockefeller that later proved to be critical for the two men.

During his fifteen-year academic career, Kissinger wrote four books and numerous articles. His writing analyzed the positive and negative aspects of the foreign policies of Presidents Harry Truman, Dwight Eisenhower, and John Kennedy. About President Lyndon Johnson he had nothing to say, a strong judgment in itself. When he criticized, he always offered alternatives. Kissinger also served as an adviser to Kennedy and Johnson, but not as a chief adviser.

An unusual opportunity appeared when Nelson Rockefeller decided to seek the Republican nomination for the presidency at the last minute in 1968 and chose Kissinger as his foreign policy adviser. As in everything he did, Kissinger gave the campaign all his energy, although it was hopeless because of Rockefeller's late start. After Nixon won the election and even though Kissinger had criticized him publicly, saying that he was not suited to be president, Nixon asked Kissinger, on Rockefeller's recommendation, to be his chief foreign policy adviser and assistant to the president for National Security Affairs. Kissinger accepted, and in his hands the position became unbelievably powerful, even displacing the power of Secretary of State William Rogers, Nixon's longtime friend. Rogers had no real background in foreign affairs, and Kissinger could sell his expertise with the help of his dynamic personality and drive. He organized a large, effective staff, which he worked extremely hard. Soon foreign dignitaries asked to speak to Kissinger rather than to the secretary of state, convinced that he was the more powerful figure with more direct influence upon the president and the making of American foreign policy.

In the political theater of his choice and after a career of unbelievable mobility, Kissinger has obtained the most powerful position available to him, for one must be born an American to become president. All his previous political experience and thinking prepared him for the job of maintaining a decaying nation-state or empire: his military experience, his language skills, his ability to accept change as normal, his studies of nineteenth-and twentieth-century diplomacy, his careful preparations in theories of international politics, and his many influential contacts in and out of government throughout the world. Rarely has a man been so well prepared for an "impossible" job; except, perhaps, Dag Hammarskjöld. The only major weaknesses in his background, which have undoubtedly sown some serious American errors for the future, are his lack of study and experience in economic affairs and in Third World politics. He became the fifty-sixth secretary of state in 1973 without having corrected those weaknesses. C. Fred Bergsten, Kissinger's former expert on international economics, rates Kissinger's record on economic policy matters as "dismal." Commenting upon the observation in an article titled "Henry Kissinger's Non-economics," one journalist wrote: "It may prove unfortunate that Henry Kissinger has become Secretary of State at the moment in history when the crucial issues for American foreign policy are economic. . . . More and more countries tend to define their national interests in economic as much as in political or military power. . . . Many observers tend to agree with Bergsten, who predicts that if Kissinger fails to take economic issues more seriously, he may prove to be an anachronism as Secretary of State."[12]

When Kissinger began working for Nixon as his National Security Adviser, his job was to sort out the best foreign policy options from which Nixon could choose. Naturally, he had a great deal of influence, particularly since the prestige of foreign policy advisers from the social science fields had been rising greatly since World War II. American presidents wanted technological experts who could solve their problems, including their social and political problems. Such deference to expertise was symbolized by the fact that Kissinger was referred to as Dr. Kissinger. Nor did he object.

In 1968, Kissinger knew that the maintenance of American power in the world was threatened by decay. The war in Vietnam had made foreign policy a controversial domestic issue, which in a democratic country means an attack upon the legitimacy of the governing elites, including himself. Like Metternich, he perceived his strategy in that historical situation to be one of maintenance. Maintaining his country's strong position in world politics by balancing other world powers, Russia, China, Japan, and Europe, he played them against one another to maximize American interests. Like Bismarck, however, he knew that it was a dynamic equilibrium he must create and maintain, rather than the predictable, limited clockwork of the eighteenth-century Enlightenment. His was a revolutionary age, and some of the major powers, namely Russia and China, were more revolutionary than legitimate in their unlimited ideological goals.

Kissinger's diplomacy is based upon the assumption that American interests in the world can only be maintained if the powerful revolutionary states of the world can be coaxed, socialized, or forced into accepting the legitimacy of a stable, dynamic equilibrium called peace, which is based on preserving the essentials of the status quo and American status in it. For the United States has the most to lose from a totally revolutionary upset of the status quo in the world today. Kissinger's strategy is to persuade the rest of the world that they will not gain what the United States would lose by a revolutionary change in the rules of the game, that revolutionary chaos would destroy the existing pie for everyone, and that only by cooperating with the United States to keep the economic pie and technological advance developing and expanding will anyone in the world have anything to gain in any future diplomatic negotiations anywhere.

In short, Kissinger saw the Vietnamese war and the general conflict in Southeast Asia as merely one arena for the staging of the stable, dynamic structure of peace towards which the United States would lead the world. The Americans would eventually have to leave Vietnam, since there was nothing to be gained there in terms of political or military objectives. In leaving, however, Kissinger wanted to enforce enough stability to prevent revolutionary chaos in that area of the world, which might threaten his general global scheme.

Of course, to be effective Kissinger's overall blueprint for the world must never come to light. Secrecy was critical. For if it came out, most of the nations of the world would protest that, in effect, the plan was designed to promote and preserve the interest of the rich, Western capitalist countries of the globe, particularly the United States. Such a protest would hit the nail all too squarely on the head, put people on their guard, and block his future actions. Therefore, contrary to his earlier academic speculations, Kissinger's discussions with the press avoid details of his long-range policies and stress the specifics, in an ambiguous and limited way, of whatever issue or negotiation is at hand at the moment. Journalists fall happily into the diversion, for they are wildly in love with gossip about the present and desire to capture the latest little fact before their competition does, regardless of how meaningless it may be in the long run.

In his interview with Oriana Fallaci, Kissinger expressed respect for genuine pacifists, but doubted strongly that their stand was a realistic one. A nation unwilling to fight for its principles would be at the mercy of other nations. But whether or not people agreed with his assessment of the Vietnam war as a necessary one, they had to understand that he was trying to end a particular conflict, not dealing with war as an abstraction.[13] Not long after that interview Kissinger and Le Duc Tho of North Vietnam did negotiate a peace settlement in Vietnam that gave the United States the opportunity to withdraw its forces. Both men thereafter were awarded the Nobel Peace Prize for the accomplishment. The war there continued. So do the prizes.

China, Russia, and the Superbalance

Kissinger's Vietnam activities overlapped with his carefully prepared, secret trip to China in 1971, in which he opened diplomatic relations between the People's Republic and the United States. The world was amazed at the sharp reversal in American policy particularly under President Nixon, who was the traditional conservative and outspoken anti-Communist. Yet, ironically, Nixon was much more enthusiastic about opening relations with China than Kissinger was. The suspense and secrecy of Kissinger's trips, the carefully coordinated press coverage of the fascinating oriental country, and the excitement of uncertainty in regard to the future for everyone made Kissinger into a superstar. Kissinger, himself, has pointed out that he believes the reason for his great, instant popularity in the United States, and perhaps the world, is that he acted alone, a lone ranger out for a good cause who brings home the goods.[14] Americans like a little romantic loneliness and some rugged individualism mixed in with the ambiguity of great political acts in their name. Kissinger keeps them supplied with more of that delicious, heroic individualism, which they so need in such a dehumanized, anti-individualistic age of mass politics.

As for Kissinger, he saw his trips to China and the Soviet Union as mere parts in his larger plan. The critical basis for a stable equilibrium in the nuclear age is for the superpowers to agree on the legitimacy of the rules of the game. Without superpower consensus, all smaller diplomatic endeavors would be hopeless, as we saw in the last chapter on Hammarskjöld. Kissinger would not tolerate an old-fashioned, stodgy nineteenth-century balance of power that was no longer appropriate for the modern age. He sought a strategic triangle composed of the United States, the People's Republic of China, and the Soviet Union. Each would be allowed to play the other two against one another for individual gain according to pre-determined and secret rules of the game, which would not totally upset the status quo.

Kissinger's Style and the Yom Kippur War

In order to maintain his superbalance, to keep the revolutionary middle range and small nations pacified, and to contain conflicts that threatened his blueprint for world equilibrium, Kissinger has developed a uniquely personal style. This style is based upon his acting alone as the world peacemaker and is characterized by secrecy, surprise, ambiguity, promises, and threats. Indeterminacy, more than anything else, describes the fleeting quality of Kissinger's presence and handiwork. Psychologically, he is motivated to establish a structure of peace in the world based upon superpower detente and the containment of all conflict or revolution which might upset the status quo. However, those fundamentally conservative, psychic drives are combined with a deep and tragic sense of history and a lifetime of studying the inevitable decay of social facts, empires, and civilizations. As an historian Kissinger knows he will lose in the future. As a statesman he knows he must do everything that he can to win in the present. Those two opposing intellectual beliefs, the psychic drive for free will against the inevitable decay of social facts, including his own position, give Kissinger a tremendously effective bargaining personality and the aura of a persuasive, pessimistic fortune-teller. Ultimately, Kissinger is a magician who draws one's attention to present details with one hand, while he hides his superpower blueprint and deeper intentions with the other and simultaneously entertains the audience of the world by giving them glimpses into his own dark crystal ball of the future.[15]

Take, for example, the case of the Yom Kippur War of October, 1973, or one should rather say the cases of the Yom Kippur War, since several versions of Kissinger's role in the events of that conflict exist, and the whole truth may or may not eventually come to light in the distant future.[16] Nevertheless, a likely reconstruction of some of the events involving Kissinger is useful here to highlight some aspects of his style.

Recall that in the back of Kissinger's mind were two threats: the undermining of the Nixon Administration's legitimacy, which was due to the revelations in the Watergate scandal and which might include Kissinger's involvement because he had permitted the telephones of members of his own staff to be wiretapped; and the threat of Arab oil cutoffs to the United States if the Nixon-Kissinger policy in the Middle East was too pro-

Israeli. Given his superbalance blueprint, he had to maintain and strengthen his own legitimacy and that of the administration. At the same time he had to create the appearance of an evenhanded policy toward both the Israelis and the Arabs in a situation where he felt the United States must support Israel with weapons and supplies in order to keep American commitments and to counter the Soviet support of the Arabs.

When the fighting first broke out on October 6, Kissinger and many others in the Nixon Administration assumed that the Israelis would quickly win. However, the Israelis were not as ready for war as they could have been, and in a few days it became apparent that they were not doing as well as they expected and were rapidly running out of vital supplies. The Israeli ambassador, Simcha Dinitz, became more and more pressing and desperate in his personal requests to Kissinger for weapons.

From his own perspective, Kissinger found himself in an almost impossible position. If he did not immediately begin to send Israel the needed war supplies, the Israelis could easily make the issue a public one and strong congressional pressure and public opinion would force him to send the supplies and undermine his legitimacy and that of the Nixon Administration in the process. On the other hand, if he gave too many war supplies to the Israelis, too officially and too soon, the United States would appear to be overwhelmingly pro-Israeli, and Israel might again win, take more land, and irreparably humiliate Arab pride, making a Middle East settlement impossible, at least under Kissinger's influence and conditions. So evidence seems to indicate that Kissinger was at first deliberately slow in giving any materiel to the Israelis and then cautious in the amounts and ways he had the materiel delivered. He continually promised the Israeli ambassador that supplies would soon be sent and that the only obstruction was Defense Secretary James Schlessinger at the Pentagon, who did not want the materiel sent. At this point, different versions of events emerge, and it appears likely that Schlessinger was actually not obstructing the shipment at all. He was merely a convenient scapegoat on whom Kissinger could blame reasonable American delays. Thus he prevented supplies from reaching Israel too soon and simultaneously kept the Israeli ambassador sufficiently satisfied not to make the issue public.

Describing such a manipulative diplomatic technique, political analysts Edward N. Luttwak and Walter Laqueur wrote:

> Known in police circles as the "Mutt and Jeff" routine, the technique is intended to undermine the resolve of the victim by creating a false sense of solidarity. While one policeman is friendly and overtly sympathetic, the other is harsh, even brutal. This leads the victim under interrogation to see the friendly policeman as an ally, to the point of confiding in him, especially since the friendly policeman intimates that he is doing all he can to help the victim against his brutal colleague. . . . With their feet

"nailed to the ground" by national (i.e. Kissinger's) policy, Schlessinger and his men . . . played the role of the brutal policeman while Kissinger was the sympathetic cop."[17]

Furthermore, Kissinger's policy appeared to deliberately create a further delay. First he attempted to schedule commercial airlines to carry the war supplies in order to keep a low American profile, but he undoubtedly knew that such an attempt would not succeed, since commercial airlines feared Arab reprisals. By the time all the commercial airlines had been secretly consulted and had turned down the business, Kissinger had delayed a few more days. His style of personal manipulation and secrecy, his determination to have things his own way, and his desire to preserve legitimacy and detente over all else are clearly illustrated by such delays. Indeed, he apparently valued the American-Soviet detente so greatly that he was reluctant to believe that massive Soviet aid was going to the Arabs until intelligence reports and photographs proved it beyond doubt. His reluctance to recognize Soviet actions in the Middle East illustrates his psychological drive to create his own blueprint for a superbalance and a rigid mental image that does not fit the actual deterioration of social facts. Yet the result of that fascinating psychosocial tension is that Kissinger is never deceived for long because of his belief in indeterminacy. Furthermore, because he is willing to sacrifice short-term gains for long-term detente and superbalance, and because he carefully controls all news leaked to the media (except *his own* leaks) he always appears to have succeeded in the end in his policy objectives. In short, Kissinger does not so much create world peace through his style as recreate in his own language and images what has actually happened to fit his personal blueprint. The historical outcome of this personal, philosophical style will consistently be to preserve the superbalance, whatever the cost to middle-range or small nations.

Arab Oil and the Middle East

What could the Third World developing countries do about the budding superbalance that promised to keep the superpowers on top and the rest of the world on the bottom? Blackmail. In 1973, frustrated by their lack of bargaining power in the settlement of the Yom Kippur War, the Arabs agreed to unite in an oil boycott of the rich, Western industrial nations. Since most of the boycotted Western nations were heavily dependent upon the Arabs for an oil supply to keep their industrial production, transportation, and economic success going, they were shocked by such tactics in a group of nations they had always thought powerless. The Arabs had turned potential power into actual power by revolting against the legitimate rules of the global game as espoused by the great powers.

Kissinger with the late King Faisal of Saudi Arabia. *Jerrold L. Schector,*
Time; © *1973 Time Inc.*

Small or revolutionary foreign policy decision makers can turn potential
power into actual power by revolting against the legitimate rules of the
political game of nations as defined by the great powers at certain
opportune moments. Effective revolutionary strategies include economic
blackmail over vital resources needed by the great powers, kidnapping
members of the great power political and business elites for ransom or
political concessions, and coordinated mail bombing and other forms of
terrorism. As Third World countries like India develop nuclear weapons,
the potential violence and power of blackmail and terrorist strategies will
increase. Economist Robert Heilbroner noted: "For if current projections of
population growth rates are even roughly accurate, and if environmental
limitations on the growth of output begin to exert major negative influences
within the next two generations, widespread human deterioration in the
backward areas can be avoided only by a redistribution of the world's
output and energies on a scale immensely larger than anything that has
hitherto been seriously contemplated. Under the best of circumstances such

a redistribution would be exceedingly difficult to achieve. Given the constraints on economic growth that will make their presence felt with increasing severity, such an unprecedented international transfer seems impossible to imagine except under some kind of threat. The possibility must then be faced that the underdeveloped nations with nothing to lose will point their nuclear pistols at the heads of the passengers in the first-class coaches who have everything to lose.'' [18]

~~~~~~~~~~~~~~~~~

In response to economic blackmail and terrorist tactics, Kissinger argues that even the Third World, poorer nations of the globe have a great deal to lose politically and economically if they disrupt international stability and Western economic production. Since the West produces most of the food, products, and technology for the rest of the world, the ultimate effect of immediate violence and blackmail will be to make the whole world worse off for everyone, including the revolutionaries. Yet, clearly the people who benefit first and foremost from world political stability and uninterrupted economic progress are the rich "first-class passengers" in the Western industrial countries.

The Arab oil boycott brought the Arabs tremendous short-term economic gains and increased their political prestige. The era of oil politics had begun. Moreover, ironically, the Western concessions caused by the boycott prepared the way for Israeli flexibility in the Middle East negotiations. Kissinger quickly seized the opportunity and played the neutral third-party arbiter with brilliance to secure temporary settlements of the Egyptian-Israeli and Syrian-Israeli wars. Effectively, however, the global political result was to push Soviet influence momentarily out of the Middle East and greatly increase American influence there as well as to reestablish Kissinger's blueprint for a stable, dynamic equilibrium, or a modified preservation of the status quo. The major long-run benefits of the Kissinger peace settlements in the Middle East will clearly go to the United States and the other great powers of the superbalance. By connecting himself so intimately with American national interests in the world, Kissinger has made himself into an almost irreplaceable institution whose influence can be expected to continue for a long time whether or not he is officially in government.

II. Principles of World Politics

National Security and the National Interest

The principles that Kissinger most represents are national security and the national interest. After going through the trauma of the Watergate scandal and the constant attempts of President Richard Nixon to withhold information in the name of national security, Americans have become increasingly aware that the definition of national security is always subjective and politically loaded. Perhaps more than anything else, the Vietnamese war has persuaded the American public of the necessity of limiting American national interests and policy of national security to her own domestic interests. Yet, the increasing perception of the importance of the interdependence of national economies (best seen after the Arab oil embargo) and runaway worldwide inflation have both alerted Americans to the vital necessity of working toward mutual interests with other nations. Although Americans are beginning to perceive that their national interests and security now depend heavily upon international agreements that often entail certain political risks, they nonetheless would still rather leave high policy issues up to the experts.

Such a situation is, of course, tailor-made for Kissinger. Both his early life and academic experiences were oriented towards making him into an expert on national security affairs. Although skeptical of the possibility that technology alone could be the solution to human problems, Kissinger knew that the political key to our technological era for the individual was the development of a specialty or area of expertise, particularly one that was directly related to contemporary policy formation. Therefore, he wrote prolifically on contemporary foreign policy issues. We live in an age of apolitics, an age governed by an ideology which asserts that technical experts must be relied upon for solutions to our human needs, and that everyday human beings are not really competent to solve major problems or even question the ideology. Kissinger has learned how to use the prestige of the apolitical technocrat without really believing that either he or technology has the answers to all his nation's political problems.

National interest can be defined as objectives or values that work toward satisfying the basic needs of the people who make up a nation. Such needs include physiological, security, love, self-esteem, and self-actualization. National security refers to objectives that serve to satisfy the nation's basic security needs. The problem with a wealthy, post-industrial, and elitist society like the United states is that security needs have come to dominate public politics to the exclusion of the higher-level needs which the nation could, in fact, afford to support. The rich nations of the northern hemisphere like the United States appear to be motivated fundamentally by fear, whereas the poor, less developed nations of the southern hemisphere are motivated by envy. The haves want to secure what they've got with rules and force to back them up. The have-nots want to revolutionize the rules of the game to redistribute the world's goods with all the force they can muster so they, too, can be haves. Politics is the attempt to use social action to solve the tension between human needs and social facts. Diplomacy between the haves and have-nots becomes, therefore, a mutual attempt to solve national tensions over human needs through the give and take of bargaining and negotiation. War is the breakdown of negotiation and eruption of tensions into open conflict.

From the Balance of Power to the Superbalance

Kissinger has insisted upon the legitimacy of American national interests in a balancing game with four other powers: the Soviet Union, China, Japan, and Western Europe. Although higher principles of morality beyond force may be secondary in importance to amoral power calculations for Kissinger, he has nevertheless relied heavily upon two other aspects of Metternich's nineteenth-century balance of power system: the notion of legitimacy and the balance of five major power units. Both these diplomats share one essential in common. As maintenance men threatened by decay, they attempt to reaffirm the legitimacy of the principles that hold their nations and their power together.

The only reason that Kissinger has been able to make use of any of Metternich's principles is that nations with nuclear weapons have thus far tacitly agreed not to employ them. This, in turn, has diminished the importance of Soviet and American nuclear superiority, making the two powers more nearly equal with the other three major powers. Moreover, domestic problems within the United States and the Soviet Union have further restrained the superpowers, tending to make them more comparable to Japan, China, and Western European nations in many day-to-day political and economic interactions.

Even so, the five major powers in Kissinger's era differ much more from one another than did the more closely equal powers of Metternich's Europe. For instance, Japan's power has been largely economic, not military. China's power is based on agriculture, not industry, and upon a large population and a comparatively small nuclear capability. Western Europe is far from united and to become an effective balancing partner it depends upon the constant agreement among the member nations on economic, political, and military matters in a region that is all too proud of national differences. Kissinger himself has said that the differences between his era and that of Metternich make it difficult to draw useful parallels between the two men. He cites the rapidity and ease of travel and communication in the modern world; the disappearance of armies composed of professional soldiers and diplomacy dominated by aristocrats; and the lack of a homogeneous cultural background among states involved in world politics today.[19]

Yet Kissinger does speak in terms of balances, of international stability, and of a structure of peace. He has undoubtedly learned from Metternich, including what to avoid, and has recreated his own blueprint for world balance based upon the reality of nuclear weapons and the dominance of the superpowers. Fundamentally his is a superbalance, despite the constant attentions he must pay to lesser powers in the Middle East, Asia, Europe, and elsewhere.

Bipolarity and Multipolarity

The paradox of Kissinger's complex balancing blueprint is that although militarily the world is bipolar, dominated by two major powers, politically the world is becoming increasingly multipolar, dominated by more than two powers. The United States and the Soviet Union are like two giants who often have too much muscle for their own good. They don't know how to translate their overwhelming military power potential into actual political power in day-to-day policy negotiations. Thus, Kissinger wrote, "In the years ahead, the most profound challenge to American policy will be philosophical: to develop some concept of order in a world which is bipolar militarily but multipolar politically."[20] However, he believes this will not be easy for those brought up in the American tradition of manipulative, pragmatic diplomacy. What is required, Kissinger claims, is a long-term structure of world order or peace that is not a total solution, for there are none today, but a dynamic equilibrium that changes with the revolutionary and technological developments of our age. In short, Kissinger's philosophy is one of existential indeterminacy that assumes that man's basic responsibility is to preserve order and peace in a world of inconceivable changes, even though in the end it may be a losing battle.

Nuclear Strategy and Deterrence

Kissinger's view of nuclear strategy grows out of his bi-multipolar superbalance. In order to deter nations from using nuclear weapons he argues that the superpowers must do everything in their power to prevent nuclear proliferation, or the spread of nuclear capability to more countries. The more powers that have nuclear weapons, the greater the probability of nuclear accidents, blackmail, and world war. The difficulty is that the status of becoming a nuclear power, of joining the nuclear club, has stimulated developing nations like India to create a nuclear capacity and will motivate other nations to do likewise. The more nations that have nuclear power, the more nations that will want it to defend themselves against their neighbors—for countering blackmail.

The principle of deterrence is to create so much potential force or credible threat that the enemy will not be tempted to attack you with his weapons out of fear of retaliation. In the case of the superpowers, however, this principle has only led to a spiraling arms race, making the world more dangerous for everyone. Each superpower perceives its national interest to be the development of the ultimate nuclear weapon before its opponent does in order to maintain a nuclear superiority and to deter its opponent from attacking first. Unfortunately, although nuclear physicists have accepted the principle of indeterminacy, political and military leaders have not. The result is a utopian search for certain security through some mysterious, technological breakthrough or ultimate thermonuclear discovery. Meanwhile, as defense research budgets in the superpower countries expand wildly, contributing to national and worldwide inflation, the majority of the people in the world continue to suffer from malnutrition and starvation. Man's devotion to destructive power is so great that he will let it consume vital energies that would otherwise help to satisfy the real needs of his fellow man. No wonder Kissinger refers to the American foreign policy dilemma as a philosophical one! Americans, alas, have never been much interested in philosophy except for pragmatism and positivism, neither of which has yet developed satisfactory answers to the grave moral, political, or cultural problems of our era.

Limited War and Nuclear Blackmail

In addition to attempting to achieve a superpower military balance and parity or rough equality in nuclear destructive capacity, the superpowers of the world develop tactical nuclear and limited conventional warfare capabilities as well. Beginning with *Nuclear Weapons and Foreign Policy*, Kissinger has argued for a flexible military capability in order to meet all levels of threat and to transform potential nuclear power into actual political power. He has consistently argued that military, foreign, and domestic policies are inseparable. Furthermore, great power legitimacy depends upon superpower ability to enforce it.

Revolutionary powers, on the other hand, will naturally seek to use limited wars of liberation or redistribution to gain their foreign policy objectives. This means that superpowers defending the status quo will have increasingly to deter limited wars before they escalate and to control nuclear blackmail, if they can. The haves of the world will naturally argue that the fundamental problem of our time is to reduce the level of violence and potential for international instability. The have-nots, on the other hand, may well come to view violence as a legitimate means to attain a more equitable redistribution of the world's resources and opportunities. Both sides are right from their own perspective, meaning that a final resolution of the conflict between these positions is highly improbable. As Kissinger is well aware, the contemporary historical situation is essentially tragic and the future unpredictable.

III. Present Implications

The Kissinger Era versus the Third World

The fundamental conflict of the late twentieth century may well be between Kissinger's superbalance blueprint for international stability, on the one hand, and the desire for the satisfaction of basic needs and a redistribution of the world's resources by the Third World developing countries, on the other. Put bluntly, there is likely to be a more or less repressed war between security needs and basic bodily needs, between fear and envy, and between fortification and starvation.

According to the judgment of United Nations experts in 1974, thirty-two countries in the world are so poor and short of food that crop failures and the high prices of grain, fertilizer, and petroleum threaten them with bankruptcy and their people with starvation.[21] Significantly, these countries are located on continents with which Kissinger has been least concerned, Africa, Asia, and Latin America. Vietnam and China were the exceptions that prove the rule, since Kissinger became involved with these nations only to be sure they would not threaten the superbalance blueprint.

Political scientist Frances Hill has gone so far as to claim that Africa is Kissinger's missing continent and that no leader below the Mediterranean fringe of that continent can refer to "our friend Henry." In this regard, Hill noted in 1974: "It would be very simple for the United States to demonstrate its concern with Africa and its peoples when Ethiopia and six West African states are suffering from prolonged drought and famine. The death toll makes this one of the world's major disaster areas, all the more horrifying because the end is not yet in sight. The level of U.S. aid has been almost cynical, the minimum that could be used as evidence of official concern."[22] In short, Kissinger's world is small and personal and he does not understand that Africa matters for his view of world peace.

Although interested in the world's food problem, Kissinger sees that problem and the other problems of Third World countries as global more than American responsibilities, and the thrust of his policy appears to be to persuade other countries of their duties in those areas. Thus, when asked by *New York Times* correspondent James Reston how things would look toward the end of the century Kissinger replied:

> The underdeveloped nations—the now underdeveloped nations—should by then have lost their sense of inferiority and should feel not that they have to extort, but that they should participate. Thus, what I said earlier about the relationship between Western Europe, the United States and Japan should have begun to be institutionalized to embrace at least some of the key countries, and the Soviet Union and China must be related to that.
>
> Take the food problem. I do not believe that over an indefinite future, we can solve the problem of world food reserves if the Soviet Union and Communist China do not accept obligations of their own, or if they simply rely on the rest of the world's production to solve their problems on an annual basis.[23]

In short, Kissinger seems willing to pass the buck in terms of the tragic world food shortage, and he desires to fit all such disruptive Third World problems into the same institutionalized structure of great powers for world peace: Western Europe, the United States, Japan, the Soviet Union, and China. The great contradiction in this approach is, of course, that unless the United States as a major grain producer in the world plays a dominant role of leadership in solving the world food crisis, how are developing countries supposed to "lose their sense of inferiority" and "feel they do not have to extort but participate?" At the moment participation for starving Third World countries means doing anything in their power to begin to feed their people by whatever means are available. Kissinger's policy does not seem aimed at radically changing their status so that they can participate as equals with well-fed countries. As long as this policy of indifference to the Third World continues, Kissinger will perceive developing countries as potentially revolutionary, and they, in turn, will continue to see him as the leading spokesman for a dehumanizing status quo.

Kissinger's success in world politics may be in large part due to his awareness that the principle of indeterminacy is the only guideline that fits our age of rapid change. The result of this awareness is his ability to use ambiguity as a diplomatic concept to bring about momentary peace wherever limited wars erupt. By moving subtly with the flow of change and helping people to get a bit of what they want on both sides of the diplomatic table, Kissinger makes his policies appear inevitable and turns his super-balance blueprint into a series of self-fulfilling prophecies. His extreme concern with secrecy and his careful control of news leaks permit him to create the image of himself that he wants in the media.

The effectiveness of his public relations is even the more amazing, given Kissinger's role in helping to create the cult of secrecy that made the Watergate disaster possible. His secret involvement in approving the Central Intelligence Agency's use of eleven million dollars to "destabilize" the socialist democracy in Chile, where striking workers were paid to help overthrow Salvador Allende, has now come to light. However, President Gerald Ford has officially supported such CIA activity, and Kissinger seems able to manipulate his critics to an amazing extent in a democratic society with a free press. Clearly the use of such secrecy to legitimize his role as the West's most effective conservative maintenance man makes Kissinger the unlabeled King of the Right. Whether he can survive the criticism of the free press and the violence or even assassination attempts of forces to his Left in the world has become the question of the hour. In an individualistic, democratic society which distrusts the centralization of too much power in any one man's hands, a society upset by the arrogance of the European, academic elite that Kissinger sometimes represents, it seems incredible that he has remained in power as long as he has. Yet the key to his future downfall may not lie so much in what he represents as in what he does not know, namely, economics. For the world crises in the late twentieth century appear to be rooted not so much in the balances of strategic military power as in the balances of payments, of monetary exchange, and of economic power, areas in which Kissinger's background, training, and knowledge is known to be inadequate.

Yet, ironically, whether or not Kissinger stays in power, the super-balance model he has lived for is likely to remain. Indeed, if world peace is attainable in our era, it will undoubtedly be based on some of Kissinger's basic principles. Given the unwillingness of the haves of the world to redistribute their wealth and food through foreign aid and other programs to the have-nots, a global consensus on Kissinger's blueprint is unlikely in the near future. Still Kissinger may continue to accumulate immediate successes by appealing to the material desires and greed of the most upwardly mobile have-not nations, dividing them from their poorer brothers by promising them more of the existing economic and political pie. This divide and conquer strategem has proved extremely effective in world politics in the past and there is no reason whatsoever to suppose that it will not be effective in the future if guided by Kissinger's brilliant diplomatic skills. Kissinger can be expected continually to demonstrate to the Third World that diplomacy is the art of letting others have your own way. They will be charmed and seduced into supporting Kissinger's superbalance stability, convinced that only through such stability will they be able to share in the increasing material pie and, perhaps, eventually become haves. The reason that they will be duped is that the odds of have-nots becoming haves are very slim indeed in a world of increasing scarcity of natural resources, population explosion, wild inflation, and recession. As a brilliant existential diplomat, who clearly perceives the reality of the moment, Kissinger can be expected to play the odds astutely as long as his influence lasts.

The Technological Arms Race and Disarmament

A critical aspect of Kissinger's superbalance blueprint has been to dampen the technological arms race and effect arms control through the Strategic Arms Limitations Talks (SALT). By agreeing with the Soviet Union to limit the development of certain kinds of weapons, American policymakers have not only saved themselves millions of dollars, but have actually increased national security. The 1974 Vladivostok agreement between Kissinger and the Soviet Union may finally have put a cap on the strategic arms race, at least symbolically, by putting a ceiling on the number of intercontinental ballistic missiles both sides can produce. However, more extensive agreements in the future depend upon continued mutual trust and mutual international inspection, difficult prerequisites given the extreme ideological differences of both nations. Nevertheless, in the future such ideological differences will undoubtedly seem secondary in importance as the superpowers strive toward a basic agreement on a balance of limited potential violence in order to secure their position in the worldwide status quo. In the future it is likely that more meaningful arms control agreements between the Soviet Union, the United States and even the People's Republic of China will be reached.

Disarmament, however, is another matter. There is a great difference between agreeing to limit the future development of certain kinds of weapons or technologies and agreeing to eliminate what one has already stored away. In an age of indeterminacy where insecurity is the dominant psychological characteristic of the great powers, it is extremely unlikely that meaningful disarmament treaties will be arranged. Furthermore, the unlikelihood of disarmament increases with each new country that develops nuclear weapons, and the trend seems irreversible.

Ambiguity and the Future of American Foreign Policy

Kissinger epitomizes the most probable future trend in American foreign policy. It is that of a lonely, existential odyssey into a threatening world in which a highly educated, technocratic elite attempts to persuade the rest of the world to maintain the status quo and call this international stability and peace. Clearly the task will be an almost impossible one, given the violent conflicts that are apt to emerge from the tensions caused by the population explosion, worldwide inflation, increasing scarcity of resources, nuclear proliferation, and the increasing gap between the rich and the poor. Yet as a great empire in a time of maintenance threatened by decay from within and revolution from without, the United States can be expected to support strong, authoritative maintenance men like Kissinger, regardless of the dangers such a technocratic elite might pose for domestic political freedoms. In the tension between freedom and justice, on the one hand, and the insatiable need for security and the maintenance of a luxurious lifestyle, on the other, the majority of Americans will probably opt for the latter and elect and support maintenance men who represent these basically conservative values. Philosopher George Santayana once said that to be an American is a career. In our day, to be an American has come to mean to preserve a conservative occupation.

The means that will be used to achieve these conservative, maintenance values will stem largely from Kissinger's principle of ambiguity, or the art of using uncertainty to cultivate options that maximize American national interests in the long run, regardless of how benevolent or neutral they appear in the short run. Ambiguity can be used to cut the costs of uncertainty for both individuals and particular nations. The best example of the use of such ambiguity is the number of short-run "peaces" that Kissinger has been piling up in Vietnam and the Middle East. It must always be kept in mind that those "peaces" are, ultimately, pieces of a superbalance blueprint that will primarily attempt to stabilize the world militarily and politically in order to secure the interests of the superpowers and will only secondarily be concerned with equitably redistributing the world's resources or with satisfying human needs everywhere regardless of race, religion, sex, or national origin.

Notes

1. Stephen Graubard, *Kissinger: Portrait of a Mind* (New York: W. W. Norton & Co., 1973), p. ix.

2. Henry Brandon, *The Retreat of American Power: The Inside Story of How Nixon and Kissinger Changed American Foreign Policy for Years to Come* (New York: Doubleday & Co., 1973), p. 23. Other sources for the portrait of Kissinger, but which are not referred to in specific notes, include: Henry A. Kissinger, *A World Restored: The Politics of Conservatism in a Revolutionary Age* (New York: Grosset & Dunlap, 1964); Henry A. Kissinger, *Nuclear Weapons and Foreign Policy* (New York: W. W. Norton & Co., 1969); Henry A. Kissinger, *The Troubled Partnership* (New York: Doubleday & Co., 1966); David Landau, *Kissinger: The Uses of Power* (Boston: Houghton Mifflin Co., 1972); Henry A. Kissinger, *The Necessity for Choice: Prospects of American Foreign Policy* (New York: Harper & Row, 1961); Henry A. Kissinger, ed., *Problems of National Security* (New York: Praeger Publishers, 1965); Henry A. Kissinger, "Reflections on the Political Thought of Metternich," *American Political Science Review* (December 1954); and Henry A. Kissinger, "The Vietnam Negotiations," *Foreign Affairs* (January 1969).

3. Graubard, *Kissinger*, p. 2.

4. Ibid.

5. Ibid., p. 11.

6. Bernard Collier, "The Road to Peking, or How Does This Kissinger Do It?" *New York Times Magazine*, 14 November 1971.

7. As cited in Graubard, *Kissinger*, p. 7.

8. Ibid., p. 8.

9. Henry A. Kissinger, "The White Revolutionary: Reflections on Bismarck," *Daedalus* 97 no. 3 (1968): 893.

10. Oriana Fallaci, "Henry Kissinger: Women, Power, the War" (Interview conducted 4 November, 1972; English version, *New York Post Weekend Magazine*, 23 December, 1972, pp. 1-4.

11. Nora Beloff, "Prof. Bismarck Goes to Washington: Kissinger on the Job," *Atlantic Monthly* (December 1969): 78.

12. "Henry Kissinger's Non-economics," *Business Week* (19 January, 1974): 21.

13. Fallaci, "Henry Kissinger: Women, Power, the War," p. 2.

14. Ibid., p. 4.

15. See Kissinger's interview with James Reston on the state of the Western world and on his role as historian and statesman in it: "Partial Transcript of An Interview with Kissinger on the State of Western World," *New York Times*, 13 October, 1974, pp. 34-35.

16. For different views of Kissinger's role in the Yom Kippur War and the sources of the events as reconstructed here, see Tad Szulc, "Is He Indispensable? Answers to the Kissinger Riddle," *New York Times Magazine*, 1 July, 1974, pp. 33-39; and Walter Laqueur and Edward N. Luttwak, "Kissinger and the Yom Kippur War," *Commentary* 58, no. 3 (September 1974): 33-40; and Bernard Kalb and Marvin Kalb, *Kissinger* (Boston: Little, Brown & Co., 1974).

17. Laqueur and Luttwak, "Kissinger and the Yom Kippur War," p. 36.

18. Robert L. Heilbroner, "The Human Prospect," *New York Review of Books* 20, nos. 21 & 22 (1974): 24.

19. Fallaci, "Henry Kissinger: Women, Power, the War," p. 4.

20. Henry A. Kissinger, *American Foreign Policy: Three Essays* (New York: W. W. Norton & Co., 1969), p. 79.

21. See Boyce Rensberger, "32 Nations Close to Starvation," *New York Times Week in Review*, 20 October, 1974, p. 4.

22. Frances R. Hill, "Kissinger's Missing Continent," *World View* (October 1974): 31. Kissinger's general attitude toward Third World countries that cannot make it on their own may be epitomized by his dismissal of Bangladesh as an "international basket case."

23. Reston, "Partial Transcript of an Interview with Kissinger," p. 34.

Part Five

Individuals and World Politics

Soaked with gasoline, the young Czechoslovak struck a match. Jan Palach became a torch that day, a frail figure of burning flesh in Wenceslaus Square. He had written that he would die to move his conquered countrymen from "the edge of hopelessness." The hope sparked by his protest flashed through Russian-occupied Czechoslovakia. His funeral procession would bring half a million resolute citizens into the streets of Prague.

DOUGLAS PIKE
New York Times

Conclusion

Individuals are the cutting edge of world politics. Nation-states and historical conditions present human beings with opportunities and limitations. But individual willpower and foreign policy decisions make a critical contribution to the outcome and direction of events. Man is conditioned, but at times he can also become a condition. Foreign policy decision making is a crucial focus of world politics since it is in this role that man may have his greatest effect upon international relations, and upon questions of peace and war. As a leader of a nation a man may seek to satisfy not only his own needs and values but those of his people and those of foreign peoples. Where some leaders drop out into the historical background, others will fill the vacuum.

When college student Jan Palach ignited himself with a match to protest the Russian occupation of Czechoslovakia, he focused the attention of millions of people in the world upon the meaning of a single individual in world politics. By deciding to die as a symbol of his people's need for freedom rather than to live as a political slave of a foreign conqueror, Palach brought his people a new spirit of collective hope and purpose. His final act was discussed all over the world.

When Hitler invaded Poland on September 1, 1939, another individual demonstrated the meaning of human willpower in world politics by starting World War II. As the leader of a well-armed and mobilized nation, Hitler had political power much greater than Palach's, and the world felt the consequences accordingly. In a seemingly hopeless historical situation with no apparent opportunity, Palach surprised everyone by becoming a political symbol where few saw the possibility for one. By successfully seizing opportunity after opportunity without significant opposition, Hitler symbolized what an extreme impact an individual can have on world politics if conditions are ripe and he uses his chances. On the other hand, during the 1930s the British and the French passed up many opportunities to stop Hitler by effective individual action.

Of course, individuals alone are not the sole causes or even the main causes of events in world politics. They are merely the tips of massive icebergs of social fact, historical traditions, and political opportunity. But by beginning with individual viewpoints or world-views in approaching the complexities of world politics we can get a feeling for the human meaning and opportunities of historical and contemporary situations that might otherwise appear hopelessly difficult or inevitable. Although a humanist approach to international politics does not guarantee humanistic results, it does begin by focusing upon the needs and values of individual human beings and accents what individual willpower can do in foreign policy making to satisfy a nation's needs or interests in different historical situations.

A World Politics of Human Needs

Politics is social action that attempts to solve the tension between human needs and social facts.[1] International politics is the attempt of certain groups of individuals to solve the tensions between the needs of their own people and the social facts of others and the world.

Such a definition of world politics allows one to analyze the subject where it begins: the interaction of groups of human beings from different cultures, whether it involves an official nation-state, a multinational corporation, a minority terrorist group, or an interracial struggle. All individuals are caught in the beginnings of some kind of international politics. Everyone is born into a certain race, a certain nationality, a certain culture and language. How can he avoid tension or conflict with those from foreign races, cultures, languages or nations, if only on the level of misperception and miscommunication? Such a view of world politics goes further. Every businessman, tourist, or student who travels abroad becomes a miniature ambassador from his cultural group to that of others. He becomes the national image of his country; his faults are its typical weaknesses, his strengths, its virtues. If he is a good diplomat he tries to learn the language of the culture he is visiting and to adapt to its customs while he is there. If he is a bad diplomat, he acts abroad as if he were at home, and his rigid, national habits stand out constantly and conflict with his host country.

Novelist Henry James wrote: "The figures in any picture, the agents in any drama, are interesting only in proportion as they feel their respective situations." Human beings are interesting international agents only when they become aware of the tensions between their own needs and values and foreign social conditions around them and when they feel their way into the human tensions of international relations in order to try to find the proper rhythm of social action to solve them. In the time that it takes you to read this sentence more than four people in the world will have starved to death, and the majority of them will be children. To constantly feel the tension between that fact and your own full stomach is to become a truly international citizen of the world. In late 1974, United Nations experts reported that thirty-two countries in the world were so poor and so short of food that crop failures and the high price of grain, fertilizer, and oil threatened them with bankruptcy and their people with starvation.[2] These are the social facts most relevant to human needs in world politics today. To feel the tension between such needs and facts is to have your international political consciousness raised. To act individually to do something to ease such tensions is to do international politics for human beings.

In terms of basic human needs, the thirty-two starving countries can no longer be called members of the Third World, the developing countries. Rather such massive human deprivation puts them in the Fourth World, the world of undeveloping countries. Suddenly the social class system of nations in world politics becomes unbearably clear. The upper class consists of the richest, most powerful and most self-sufficient nations, like the United States, the Soviet Union, and West Germany. The upper middle class includes faltering Western industrial countries like France, Israel, and Canada, and Eastern countries like Japan and China, and the nouveau riche oil producing countries such as Saudi Arabia, Kuwait, and Iran. Middle-class countries include Western industrial countries that are slipping substantially such as England and Italy, and other countries that are attempting to rise to the upper middle class such as Brazil and Venezuela, and relatively stable and successful countries throughout the world on various levels of development from Kenya to South Africa. The lower middle class consists of poor developing countries of the Third World like Mexico and Morocco, followed by the poorest, starving Fourth World countries, Bangladesh, El Salvador, Ethiopia, Niger, Yemen, and Sri Lanka. Although many countries have been left out of this rough list, it gives a general picture of the social stratification of existing nation-states in terms of class, or what they have of what there is to get, and status, or what others think they have.

As the world economic crisis worsens and food and energy resources become increasingly scarce, the rich may not get richer but the poor will get poorer, and the gap between developed and undeveloping countries will widen to ghastly proportions. Rich nations of similar political culture will tend to cluster together to defend themselves economically and militarily from both other wealthy coalitions and revolutionary Third World and Fourth World terrorism. The United Nations will slowly lose political power as the Third and Fourth World countries outvote the upper-class nations in their attempts to revise the United Nations Charter, which was created to maintain a status quo favorable to the great powers. In terms of social facts, recession, depression, terrorism, starvation, and war will characterize the late twentieth century. On all sides in all classes of states, individuals will mass together and demand strong leadership to defend and promote their human interests and satisfy their needs, in the hope that dynamic leadership might make the crucial difference in their case. In sum, massive deprivations of bodily and security needs on a worldwide scale will make the problems of the elite and the masses within and between nations so acute that people will hysterically call for authoritative, and perhaps authoritarian, world leadership without carefully considering the results.

Leadership in World Politics

How do some people become more international than others? Why do some individuals become international agents who make world politics and world history rather than merely remaining in the backyards of their own culture and nation? What are the prerequisites for international leadership and what motivates such leaders? What are their advantages and disadvantages?

In the preceding chapters we have noted that great world leaders in the twentieth century have often started out like anyone else: Gandhi was a failing lawyer, Mao a revolutionary student, Hitler a drifter, Kissinger a factory worker. Yet none of those men was satisfied with his situation. All became increasingly aware of the tension between their frustrated needs and values and the limits the social facts or conditions imposed upon them. Such awareness is political consciousness. Acting out of such consciousness is politics. All of these individuals were profoundly political men.

Many of the eight leaders had qualities in common in their early development of political consciousness. In building an archetype of a world leader out of these similarities, a personality with the following characteristics emerges:

1. A man
2. Living in a time of great social crisis
3. With an incredible ego and endless motivation
4. With a great interest in history and other world leaders and their lives
5. With a supportive, often religious, mother
6. With a strong-willed father with whom he either experienced intense conflicts or a sense of great identification
7. With a restrained, redirected or nontraditional sex life
8. Who was acutely aware of the needs and tensions of others in his own national community
9. Who constantly worried about how to best communicate with others—particularly with the masses
10. Who developed a certain aloofness or psychological distance between himself and others
11. Who created a coherent *Weltanschauung* or ideological world-view which enabled him to become the interpreter or high priest of the spiritual and political meaning of historical events for his countrymen

12. Who had a tendency towards mental rigidity in his ideological reactions to events and others

13. Who demonstrated great organizational and administrative skills in creating political programs and symbol systems for transmitting and maintaining his *Weltanschauung*.

In sum, great world leaders typically emerge in historical periods of great social crisis. Their perceptions of psychosocial tension intensify to the point where they propose and symbolize an extreme ideological solution in the form of a coherent world-view or *Weltanschauung*—a vision of an ultimate solution for themselves and their people. The personal characteristics of the archetypal world leader merely represent potential power. To actualize that power requires the astute perception and use of roles and role playing appropriate to the historical situation, and subtle strategies and tactics to further the leader's political and ideological cause. In actual political life it is almost impossible to distinguish between a world leader's personal characteristics, role functions, and political strategies and tactics. All of the elements of potential individual power in world politics are blended into an ideological whole. The cause becomes inseparable from the man, both in his own eyes and in the eyes of the masses. In action, the political leader focuses all of his personal, social, and ideological energy into a **Schwerpunkt** or an intense, concentrated point which becomes the razor edge of the leader's program and value system in the eyes of his followers. *Schwerpunkt* is a German term which for our purposes can be translated as the ultimate point of contact.

The ultimate point of contact is the basic means the leader uses to solve the major psychosocial tension that he and his people experience at that historical moment. Gandhi used satyagraha, the nonviolent life force that would satisfy the basic needs of the Indian people and help to bring them self-determination, justice, and peace. For Lenin, the *Schwerpunkt* was an interpretation of Marxism to fit the situation in Russia. For Mao, it was agricultural communism and modernization through guerrilla warfare from the countryside; for Wilson it was national self-determination through international organization; for Hitler it was the superiority of the German race through National Socialism and total war; for de Gaulle it was the recovery of French grandeur through nationalistic bargaining; for Hammarskjöld it was preventive diplomacy through the United Nations; and for Kissinger it was a superbalance of stability and peace for the great powers through American diplomacy. Each of these leaders became totally identified with his ultimate point of contact or *Schwerpunkt*, which alone, more than anything else, explains his behavior in world politics, his great successes, and his final failures. These points of contact represent practical ways or means toward a vision that is ultimately unrealizable, toward a *Weltanschauung* or ideological world-view whose very attractiveness depends upon its utopian quality, upon its call for people to raise themselves to a higher state of perfection, which will never be totally achieved.

The Need for a Human Focus

The basic difficulty with the traditional nation-state and international system approaches to international politics is that they neglect the human or personal prerequisites for effectiveness in world politics and the psychosocial links between those prerequisites and the *Schwerpunkt* and *Weltanschauung* in a particular historical period. The result of such traditional and behavioral studies has been description more than explanation or prediction.[3] In taking the abstract nation-state or international system approach as a point of departure in analysis, one collects data with the object of adequately describing the complexities of world politics in general more than with the purpose of explaining how human beings could or should act in order to bring about certain results or conditions in world politics in particular situations. The result of the trend toward general, global description in the study of international politics has been to dehumanize and overly generalize the discipline.

Students often complete doctoral programs in international politics with a spotty knowledge of world history, except, perhaps, for the nineteenth and twentieth centuries. They have been taught to learn history not for its own sake but for the sake of pulling out a few handy examples that serve to illustrate general theoretical points and add to a framework for holding the whole world in one's head. Moreover, few such students have examined the legitimate human needs that should be satisfied. In trying to become a discipline too quickly, international politics has lost its human focus and become a general, often superficial melting pot for other disciplines. By focusing upon human needs as well as upon the social and historical conditions that frustrate them, international politics can become human and perhaps more of a science. By stressing the nature of the psychosocial tensions between human needs and social facts within and between nations in specific historical periods, we can perhaps derive meaningful explanations and predictions for future human behavior and planning in particular regions of the world.

A Human Focus: The Psychosocial Tension Model

Poet Galway Kinnell speaks of the human focus of international politics in *The Book of Nightmares:*

> My tongue goes to the Secretary of the Dead
> to tell the corpses, "I'm sorry, fellows,
> the killing was just one of those things
> difficult to pre-visualize—like a cow,
> say, getting hit by lightning.[4]

Why do poets seem to be more concerned than political scientists and governments with the way modern men in power dehumanize their psychosocial tensions with technological tools? Is it not because *any* technological means have become perceived to be legitimate for the ends of the modern nation-state? Is it not because experts in international affairs are more concerned with global and nation-state abstractions than with the impact of certain kinds of social facts and technological developments upon human needs? Have we not "scientized" ourselves out of being human in a vain attempt to become marketable technological experts? Is it not time that we recovered a humane philosophy as a basis and guide for our efforts to make a science out of international politics?

Facts are not just facts pure and simple. Facts are pre-selected and pre-interpreted on the basis of certain value assumptions and on the basis of certain human interests. For international politics to become a meaningful social science in human terms it must analyze human needs, social and historical facts, and the tensions between them in order to be able to explain and predict for the future. Mere descriptions of world situations and theoretical abstractions must be turned toward human ends. Otherwise, the massive human problems of malnutrition, starvation, nuclear proliferation, inflation, depression, and the population explosion will never be effectively approached, much less solved.

To point the study of world politics toward human needs one must begin with human needs and with what individuals can and must do to make world politics more humane. This study of eight of the most effective individuals in world politics in our century is just a small beginning. To attempt to analyze world politics with a psychosocial tension model brings the psychology of human needs and values together with the sociology of existing social and political roles, classes, and historical opportunities to explain how individual political behavior relates to national and collective political behavior throughout the world. In short, after analyzing the personal characteristics and ideological world-views of individual political leaders, which formed the bases for their psychological power, we must relate such potential personal power to potential social and national power of the particular historical period to grasp totally their actual power in world politics. Kissinger's political effectiveness, for example, must be explained by considering his psychological mix of indeterminism, intellectuality and willpower, his sociological background of upward mobility, army and academic opportunities, his values as a Jewish German immigrant, his selection as a political adviser and subsequently his appointment as secretary of state. Neither nation-state nor global systems analysis alone would ever reveal how and why Kissinger goes about his world political business as he does. We need a more human and realistic theory that can link significant political individuals to their psychosocial environment and to the position that their nation occupies at that particular historical moment. Universal generalizations at the global or national levels in world politics are useless if they cannot be applied here and now to explain and predict particular individual, and therefore, national, behavior in a specific world problem. My thesis is that it is better to begin such an explanation with the individual and the particular rather than with the universal and the abstract.

In sum, personal power in political situations can be initially explained in terms of personality, social psychology and uses of national ideology in history, such as the *Weltanschauung* and *Schwerpunkt*. Human behavior in world politics must first be seen through human eyes. A particular point of view is inevitable and necessary in social science, as sociologist Max Weber noted. However, personal indicators of political power alone are inadequate if they are not related to social and national roles in the individual's particular historical situation. Individuals never stand alone. They are crucibles of their social class and political culture. As human beings, we always stand in relation to others. In terms of social class and status some of us have more of what there is to get in existing social reality than others. Some of us are in social situations that are better able to satisfy our full range of human needs. In terms of political culture our relation to others depends upon our typical national and cultural values and the rules of the game of human interaction. Rugged individualism and anti-authoritarianism have led Americans to go even above their heads of state to try to stop American involvement in wars abroad, as the anti-war groups did in the Vietnam war, and to negotiate individually to get back family members missing in action. Individuals raised in a different political culture, such as the traditional Japanese, might well perceive such behavior to be ignoble and shocking because of their belief that the individual should sacrifice self-interest for the community whatever the consequences. A Japanese soldier was recently found on an island who believed that he was still defending it for his emperor and that World War II was still being fought, some thirty years after it had ended!

A psychosocial tension model also helps the political analyst to explain and predict the links between individual and mass behavior and to identify probable leaders and followers in different social and historical situations. The great advantage of the psychosocial tension model is that it enables one to anticipate the transfer of potential power into actual power. The psychological aspect leads one to investigate individual personality factors, needs, and motivations. As we have seen in the preceding chapters, when an individual becomes politically aware of what power means for his needs, he increasingly desires to be free to realize himself totally, especially in Western political cultures where self-determination is what freedom means. The eight cases examined in this book demonstrate that great men are origins and agents of self-determining action rather than passive pawns or slaves to others.

Investigating the sociological aspect of psychosocial tension allows one to see what conditions are conducive to success. The sociology of class, political culture, and national historical situation determines the concrete social facts that support or obstruct potential political leaders. Leaders of upper-class cultures at the top of the world in political, military, and economic power will have to adopt an ideology that will enable them to persuade the masses that they exist as agents to maintain the national interest. Leaders of lower-class cultures, on the other hand, will have to adopt more revolutionary ideologies to persuade the masses that they might become effective tools to better satisfy their people's needs. Potential political power only becomes actualized in a particular individual when he accurately channels his psychic motivation into given socioeconomic roles and historical opportunities that are ripe at his moment in his political culture. That is why the concepts of *Weltanschauung* and *Schwerpunkt* are so important. They are useful psychosocial keys that explain how successful political leaders plug into their national historical situations effectively. It was no accident that Lenin, Mao, Kissinger, de Gaulle, Hitler and the others were constant students of history and simultaneously great psychological manipulators of all kinds of media, from words and gestures, literature and ceremonies, to interviews and television. They knew how to make their political dreams into flesh by seizing the moment that was historically and psychologically ripe.

From a sociological perspective, an individual's potential power depends upon his role potency in society, or how many human relationships his decisions affect. The roles with greatest potency in world politics by this criterion are those of heads of state and foreign policymakers, since the decisions concerning war and peace and world economics, which the individuals in these roles make, affect millions of people. Some foreign policymakers have more potent roles than others. Leaders of superpowers such as Henry Kissinger are potentially more powerful than leaders in Luxembourg. Leaders of nations that are rising in world status are potentially more powerful than leaders of decaying empires that are beginning to lose the respect of the world and whose military and economic status is falling. Individuals have roles in nations, nations in the world, and empires in world history. Your potential power sociologically depends upon where you are standing.

Individual power in world politics is nationally based but internationally actualized. Therefore, it is critical for political leaders not just to be sensitive to the opportunities and restrictions provided by the social facts in their own political culture; they must also be sensitive to the social facts and relative power of other nations and their leaders. As we have noted, a nation's status as a superpower varies in different historical periods. For instance, as long as the domination of the world by the United States and the Soviet Union was accepted, the two superpowers could control their respective blocs of nations relatively easily. However, as smaller nations began to rebel in economic and foreign policy, the legitimacy of that domination broke down as well. With the skyjackings and kidnappings of superpower planes, diplomats, and members of the business elite, multipolar disintegration has further eroded the legitimacy of superpower roles in the 1970s. Kissinger has noted that although the world may be bipolar strategically, it has become increasingly multipolar politically. He sees his major task to be the reestablishment of superpower legitimacy in order to maintain a superbalance and to deter and contain revolutionary and terrorist threats by small powers to the international hierarchy of the status quo. Your national power historically depends upon where others can stand against you.

Political Superstars and the Dangers of Hero Worship

Although the thrust of this book has been to demonstrate how great world leaders became great by effectively using certain principles of world politics, its purpose is to show that all individuals can matter to some extent in world politics if they so choose. The heroes of history should be analyzed for their political recipes, not worshiped or taken as ideal models. Indeed, the longing for hero worship can lead to the creation of authoritarian political regimes, and often does, as we have seen.

Professor Lewis Edinger is justified in his concern that nostalgic hero worship of past great political figures may provide support at times of crisis for the emergence of authoritarian political movements in liberal democracies. He notes that "these opposite concepts—Mass Man and Heroic Man—were the stock-in-trade of the authoritarian nationalists who acted as intellectual handmaidens to the grave diggers of liberal democracy in twentieth-century Europe."[5] However, the point that Edinger neglects is that we must understand what makes such authoritarian leaderships and followerships tick, not ignore them. He is certainly correct that many people, seeking models or escapes from present crisis and future shock, look back in a romantic and reactionary way to the good old days when great men strode the earth. A greater danger exists, however. By ignoring history and failing to examine why authoritarian dictatorships and power-mad men succeeded in the past, the world may be forced to repeat that dehumanizing past. Just as many psychologists have learned much about emotional health and normalcy by studying neurotics and psychotics, so political scientists and everyday citizens can learn about healthy and normal political behavior by examining pathological leaders. As poet Theodore Roethke observed, in times of darkness the eye begins to see.

Notes

1. This theory of politics is spelled out in Robert A. Isaak and Ralph P. Hummel, *Politics for Human Beings* (North Scituate, Mass.: Duxbury Press, 1975).

2. Boyce Rensberger, "32 Nations Close to Starvation," *New York Times Week in Review*, 20 October, 1974, p. 4.

3. There are, of course, behavioral approaches not based on systems theory

and, therefore, not as subject to this criticism. For example, see Herbert Kelman, ed., *International Behavior: A Social-Psychological Analysis* (New York: Holt, Rinehart & Winston, 1965).

4. Galway Kinnell, *The Book of Nightmares* (Boston: Houghton Mifflin Co., 1971), p. 43.

5. Lewis J. Edinger, "Where are the Political Superstars?" *Political Science Quarterly* 89, no. 2 (June 1974): 251.

Glossary

ahimsa   Doctrine of nonviolence and refusal to do physical harm to another person's essence, implying love and forgiveness. The ethical basis of Gandhi's ideology in India.

alienation   Disengagement and withdrawal from society out of suffering from perceived paternal and centralized repression by established institutions. There are four types of alienation: (1) *powerlessness*: the feeling that one has no control or influence over one's sociopolitical life or destiny; (2) *meaninglessness*: the belief that life and its sociopolitical forms are made up of mere random activity; (3) *normlessness*: the perception that people's behavior in society is inconsistent with their expressed values or norms; and (4) *isolation*: the belief that the general values of society are unfair and biased, and that one's own values are held by such a minority that one is effectively isolated or alone.

Anschluss   German term for union or annexation, such as Hitler's forced union of Nazi Germany with Austria.

ashram   A tightly knit religious and political community in India striving for self-sufficiency, mutual self-help, and physical and spiritual discipline. Gandhi used what he called "ashrams in motion" as units for political action—communes based on three essentials: prayer, spinning, and writing a diary.

balance of power   The classical eighteenth-century European game of diplomacy in which the members of the elitist club of great powers worked to prevent any of the member states (or any coalition) from becoming strong enough to overwhelm any other state (or coalition), thus preserving the existing status quo and its legitimacy.

Bolsheviks   Name originally applied to the section of the All-Russian Social Democratic Workers party which was founded and led by Lenin. "Bolshevik" literally means Majoritarian and was adopted in 1903 when Lenin's faction received a majority vote at the 2nd Congress of the party against Martov's minority faction, the Mensheviks or Minoritarians.

cartel   An association of private businesses bound by contract to cooperate in regulating production and marketing products and tending to restrict world markets and fix prices.

caste   The Hindu caste system refers to group divisions in India according to rules of descent, rules of marriage, ritual, occupation, ideas about purity and pollution, the Absolute Power, lesser gods and spirits. See *untouchable*.

267

charisma   A social relationship in which a large number of people attribute great spiritual power to one person whom they have come to regard as the solution to their social problems. Thus, the concept refers not just to leadership traits in a personality but to leadership-followership bonding in a social situation usually characterized by crisis.

collective security   An international agreement whereby the leaders of all member states of the system decide to view an attack upon any one of them as an attack upon all of them and to respond accordingly. Both the League of Nations and the United Nations represent largely unsuccessful attempts to create an effective international system of collective security.

collectivism   A politico-economic system characterized by collective control over production and distribution, such as government ownership of wealth in communism or tight one-man, one-party control through the state in fascism.

communism   A system of social organization opposed to private property in which goods are held in common. A doctrine and program based on revolutionary Marxist socialism developed by Lenin and the Bolshevik party. It interprets history as relentless class struggle and war, which eventually results everywhere in the victory of the proletariat, establishing a dictatorship of the proletariat and regulating all social, economic, and cultural activities through an authoritarian party-state. See *dialectical materialism, party-state,* and *dictatorship of the proletariat.*

Communist International or **Comintern**   An international organization that came into being to replace the Second International which Lenin claimed betrayed socialism because most of the leaders of its member parties supported their respective governments at the outbreak of World War I. Founded in Moscow in March, 1919, the organization adopted revolutionary theses drafted by Lenin, Trotsky, Bukharin, and Zinoviev.

détente   An improvement in relations between nations, warmer than accommodation but cooler than rapprochement.

deterrent   A military force or weapons system whose real or feigned strength is capable of forestalling an enemy attack through the threat of devastating retaliation.

dialectic   The theory of the union of opposites used by Hegel and Marx. Hegel's dialectic consisted of a thesis, or affirmation of a proposition, countered by an antithesis, or a negation of the proposition, and the interaction of both resulting in a synthesis, a more perfect union of the best aspects of the thesis and the antithesis. For example, Hegel argued the thesis of "Law" was countered by the antithesis of "Morality," creating the synthesis of "Social Ethics." See *dialectical materialism.*

dialectical materialism   Marx's transformation of Hegel's dialectical idealism into the view of history as an interaction of material economic forces and social classes rather than an interaction of ideas or spirits. See *dialectic*.

dictatorship of the proletariat   Lenin's theory of the need for a trustworthy, enlightened elite, a professional vanguard, to lead the Russian Revolution and become the caretakers of the working class.

Duma   A consultative assembly established by the tsar in Russia in 1905 to appease dissatisfied groups. Although elected by broad suffrage, the Duma was designed to reduce the democratic element through complicated procedures.

economic determinism   The belief associated with Marxism which holds that economic factors are the main or sole causes of political and historical development.

ethnocentrism   The belief in the superiority of one's own people and culture to the point of implicit or explicit disdain for other cultures and peoples.

European Coal and Steel Community (ECSC)   The cooperative organization founded by Robert Schuman, the French foreign minister, to coordinate coal and steel production in six Western European countries after World War II. Later the organization became the basis of the European Common Market (EEC).

finance capitalism   Indirect or direct ownership or control of industries, resources and businesses through capital investments.

Führer   German word for leader. A Nazi decree forbade the use of the word, unless in compounds, except in speaking of Adolf Hitler. It was the usual way of referring to him and had the aura of "his majesty."

functionalist argument   The belief of some integration theorists that political and nonpolitical matters can be separated and that by cooperating on nonpolitical economic and social problems first, political cooperation between nations will then follow. See *spillover thesis*.

geopolitics   The theory of world politics that locates the main determinants of political behavior and strategy in geography or factors of environmental milieu.

historical determinism   The belief that outside, objective causes determine historical events and that man's free will means little if anything.

historical materialism   Dialectical materialism applied to human relations in society. Refers to Marx's philosophy of history which asserts that (1) most basic causes of social life are economic, and (2) these causes operate according to the dialectic principle. See *dialectical materialism*.

home rule   Government of a country, colony, or district by powers vested in the people living within the country, colony, or district. See *self-determination*.

ideology   A set of political beliefs held by a number of people who have fallen in love with certain ideas or explanations that ultimately become the bases of political behavior. See *reification* and *nationalism*.

imperialism   The policy of seeking to extend a nation's or empire's political and economic control over less developed nations in an exploitative fashion.

indeterminacy   The doctrine that events are not strictly determined by antecedent causes and cannot be exactly measured or predicted, implying that man's will is free and that human choice between uncertain alternatives is possible and meaningful. See *historical determinism*.

international politics   The attempt of certain groups of men in nations to solve the tensions between the needs of their own people and the social facts of others and the world. See *politics, needs, social facts*.

Kuomintang   The Nationalist Party in China led by Sun Yat-sen, the Western-oriented, democratic revolutionary in the 1920s.

Lebensraum   German word for living space. Concept used as ideological basis for Hitler's expansion of The Third Reich. See *Reich*.

legal-rational society   A society characterized by means-ends or contractual community relations, specific role structures and achievement-oriented modes of social and political authority. Sociologist Max Weber contrasts modern legal-rational social structures of authority with traditional and charismatic authority patterns. See *traditional society*.

legitimacy   The recognized legal authority to govern over power relationships on a particular territory. Legitimacy often comes from the deference produced by force and awe.

Marxist revisionism   Recent reinterpretations of the thought of Karl Marx such as Marxist humanism, which stresses Marx's early humanistic manuscripts and his focus on alienation rather than the economic determinism of his later works.

Mensheviks   Literally, "the Minoritarians": Martov's minority faction opposing Lenin's Bolsheviks. See *Bolsheviks*.

modernization   The transformation of a traditional society into a more efficient and productive organization of economic, political, and social institutions. Rationalization and bureaucratization to increase the range of choice of the governing elite in order to more effectively satisfy the needs of the people in the society. See *legal-rational society* and *traditional society*.

monopoly capitalism   A stagnant stage of capitalism in Lenin's theory of imperialism in which large monopolies and cartels would divide the world among themselves and expand imperialistically in search of new resources and markets.

multinational corporation   A business firm so large that it is global in scope with manufacturing activities in many countries. Such a firm is characterized by loyalties and interests that go beyond attachments to any particular nation-state.

nation The people who make up the socio-cultural world controlled by the state. See *state, nation-state,* and *legitimacy.*

nationalism The belief that a particular nation-state merits a person's ultimate loyalty and constitutes his ultimate solution. See *nation-state* and *ethnocentrism.*

nation-state A powerful social relationship in which the people who constitute the nation recognize the authority of the state as legitimate. See *nation, state,* and *legitimacy.*

needs The physical, psychological, and social prerequisites for healthy human existence. Representative needs include food, water, air, security, love, self-esteem, and self-actualization. Human needs provide the motivation which makes political action possible.

party-state A state in which the Communist party has succeeded in capturing total control of the government.

Politburo The elitist organ of the Central Committee of the Communist party of the USSR, which, in coordination with the Secretariat, formulates Soviet foreign policy. The Politburo directs the work of the Central Committee between plenary meetings and although it is legally accountable to the Central Committee, there is no further statutory regulation of its activity.

political consciousness Awareness of the tension between human needs and frustrating social facts, which makes political action possible. See *needs* and *social facts.*

politics Social action that attempts to resolve the tension between human needs and social facts. See *needs, social facts,* and *political consciousness.*

Populist Party A Russian party which arose in the 1870s, combining the Western stress on science and education with the Slavophil devotion to the Russian genius in a "Go to the People" movement in which young members of the intelligentsia in homespun clothes went out to live among the peasants to convert them to revolutionary socialism.

purposive-rational action "Modern" political behavior governed by scientific techniques used to convert traditional societies to modern societies by undermining traditional cultural norms through the increase of technologically exploitable knowledge. See *modernization..*

Realschule An alternative to high school following elementary school in Germany which is less difficult and prestigious than high school and does not permit one to go on to the university.

Reich Literally state or empire in German. The First German Reich was the Holy Roman Empire (843-1806), the Second Reich was the German Empire of Bismarck (1871-1918), and the Third Reich was Hitler's (1933-1945).

Reichstag   The Imperial Diet, or legislature, in the Holy Roman Empire;
and the German parliament in the Third Reich. See *Reich*.

reification, fallacy of   The attempt to make something real or concrete
that is not. The word comes from the Latin term for "thing," *res*, and
literally means "thingification." Typically, reification is a belief that a
social relationship (such as a political institution or state) is more real
than the men and women who make it up. Philosopher Alfred North
Whitehead referred to this error as the "fallacy of misplaced con-
creteness," or making abstractions of things real to the extent that one
becomes blind to some of their other aspects or qualities.

relative homogeneity   Relative similarity between a number of characteristics of two nation-states—geographical proximity, culture, ideology, political institutions, economic and diplomatic rules of the game,
etc.—which makes integration or alliances between them possible.

sarvodaya   Gandhi's ideology of Indian socialism, referring to the
welfare of all: a society based on the destruction of class but not on the
destruction of individuals who make up the classes.

satyagraha   Gandhi's concept of "truth force" of principled noncooperation or militant nonviolence. The notion provides for peaceful
resistance to political authority on either an individual or mass basis, its
main thrust being the search for justice.

Schwerpunkt   German word for "point of gravity" or "center of main
effort." Politically it refers to the ultimate point of ideological contact
between the leader and his followers, the psychosocial key to charismatic leadership in a specific historical situation. For example, see
satyagraha.

self-determination   Nationally it refers to the right of the people within
each culture or nation-state to govern their own affairs without outside
interference (see home rule). Individually it refers to the motivation of
each person, particularly in the West, to strive for the freedom to
choose his own destiny, through upward social mobility, political
action, or other means.

self-determinism   The belief that man, not objective historical forces
beyond his control, is the agent of his own destiny. Leaders use the
belief in self-determinism to become the agents of historical action
rather than the pawns of existing social facts or of other people.
Opposite of *historical determinism*.

single factor analysis, fallacy of   The error of explaining social or
political events exclusively in terms of one key element or factor, which
makes one blind to other elements or factors (such as *economic
determinism*). Also see *reification*.

Slavophil   Proponent of the argument that Russia should nurture her
own independent tradition and unique civilization in order to create an
original path of development that is not dependent upon Western
democratic or scientific models.

social facts   Old social acts that have become conditions, which either frustrate or satisfy human needs. Social facts include existing values, personalities, social institutions (such as class and status) political institutions (such as legislatures) and rules of the game (the accepted routines of social and political behavior). See *politics* and *political consciousness*.

sovereignty   The location of legitimacy in a nation-state. In monarchies, monarchs trace sovereignty to themselves; in democracies, democratic elites trace sovereignty to the people. Concept implies national self-determination. See *legitimacy* and *self-determination*.

spillover thesis   The belief that economic and social cooperation will automatically "spill over" into political cooperation between nation-states. The chief assumption of the functionalist school of integration theory. See *functionalist argument*.

state   A social relationship or organization given the legitimacy to govern over power relationships on a particular territory. See *legitimacy*, *nation*, and *nation-state*.

Sturmabteilungen   The "SA": Hitler's private army in Nazi Germany used to threaten politicians with street violence and to build and keep Hitler's power.

subsystem   A small unit of interrelated elements within a larger one (a system). A political party, for example, can be considered a subsystem of a nation-state.

technological society   The stage of development beyond the legal-rational society in which a society has become dominated by applied scientific technology and the purposive-rational action of technocratic elites. See *purposive-rational action*, *legal-rational society*, and *traditional society*.

traditional society   A society based on affective or pre-rational community relationships, diffuse role structures, and ascriptive notions of social and political authority. Compare with *legal-rational society* and *technological society*.

unilateral defense, theory of   A theory based upon one independent state becoming totally capable of defending its own territory all by itself. An outgrowth of the concepts of sovereignty and self-determination rendered problematic in the interdependent world of the nuclear age. See *sovereignty* and *self-determination*.

untouchable   The untouchables or "outcaste" in India are groups of people who, usually over several generations, have "polluted" themselves by becoming involved with any of the following: (1) the destruction of the Life Principle to earn a living (e.g. oil seed crushing has low status while oil selling has high status); (2) occupational association with death or decay (funeral work, for example); (3) occupational work with human waste; (4) killing cows, which are considered sacred by the Hindus, or doing leather work; (5) drinking or selling alcohol; (6) remarriage of widows. See *caste*.

values   Things people want but which may be more than what they need. See *needs*.

variable-sum game   A non-zero-sum or general cooperative game where the sum of the payments received by all players at the end of the game does not add up to zero, often meaning that by cooperating partners can produce more together than either could individually. The European Common Market is a concrete example of a variable-sum game—at least in theory. See *zero-sum game*.

Weltanschauung   A coherent, well-articulated, future-oriented world view that has the potential to become a philosophy of life or an ideology for action. A German concept that is critical for the explanation of leadership and mass movements. See *Schwerpunkt*.

zero-sum game   A game like chess or checkers in which the sum of payments to all players at the end of the game is zero. Whatever one player wins, another player loses. Cooperation in such a logical situation is irrational, implying an ethic of each individual looking out only for himself. See *variable-sum game*.

Annotated Bibliography

Although the notes at the back of each chapter provide the reader with ways to go deeper into some of the topics covered in this book, the following is a short selection of important or provocative readings on central themes. For books on the great leaders themselves, consult the end of the relevant chapter.

Understanding World Politics—Introduction

For creative, humane introductions to world politics, see: Otto Klineberg's *The Human Dimension in International Relations* (New York: Holt, Rinehart and Winston, 1964); Kenneth Waltz's classic *Man, the State and War* (New York: Columbia University Press, 1954); Herbert Kelman's reader *International Behavior: A Socio-Psychological Analysis* (New York: Holt, Rinehart and Winston, 1965); Thomas M. Franck and Edward Weisband's provocative *Word Politics: Verbal Strategy Among the Superpowers* (New York: Oxford University Press, 1972); and David Edwards's *Creating A New World Politics* (New York: David McKay Company, 1973). For a philosophical approach and underrated classic, see F. S. C. Northrop, *The Meeting of East and West* (London: Collier-Macmillan, 1946). The classic "realist" approach focusing on the nation-state and its power: Hans Morgenthau, *Politics Among Nations* (New York: Alfred A. Knopf, 1948) and Machiavelli's *The Prince* (1514) (N.Y.: Bantam Books, 1966); For the most influential systems approach, see Morton Kaplan, *System and Process in International Politics* (New York: John Wiley and Sons, 1957.) For a more recent globalist version: Richard W. Sterling, *Macropolitics* (New York: Alfred A. Knopf, 1974). A classic on the ecological approach: Harold and Margaret Sprout, *The Ecological Perspective on Human Affairs* (Princeton, N.J.: Princeton University Press, 1965). Also see the Sprouts' *Toward a Politics of the Planet Earth* (New York: D. Van Nostrand, Co., 1971). Provocative economic approaches include: David Calleo and Benjamin Rowland, *America and the World Political Economy* (Bloomington, Ind.: Indiana University Press, 1973); and Barbara Ward, *The Rich Nations and The Poor Nations* (New York: W. W. Norton Co., 1962). A short satire on the necessity of the war system to keep industrial states going: Leonard Lewin, *Report from Iron Mountain—On the Possibility and Desirability of Peace* (New York: Dell Publishing Co., 1967). A documentary play on the conflict between the responsibility of the individual (particularly the nuclear physicist) to his country and to humanity as a whole in the nuclear age: Heiner Kipphardt, *In the Matter of J. Robert Oppenheimer*, trans. by Ruth Spiers (N.Y.: Hill and Wang, 1969).

The Needs and Nature of Political Man

For further explanation of the theory of politics and human needs behind this book see Robert Isaak and Ralph Hummel, *Politics for Human Beings* (North

Scituate, Mass.: Duxbury Press, 1975). For a Freudian view, see Sigmund Freud's brilliant short essay *Civilization and Its Discontents* (New York: W. W. Norton Co., 1961, the Strachey translation, orig. 1930). Post-Freudian views include: Colin Wilson, *New Pathways in Psychology: Maslow and the Post-Freudian Revolution* (New York: Taplinger Publishing Co., 1972) and Abraham Maslow, *Motivation and Personality* (N.Y.: Harper and Row, 1954). For empirical evidence supporting Maslow's need-hierarchy as the basis of political behavior see Jeanne Knutson, *The Human Basis of the Polity* (Chicago: Aldine, 1972), Joel Aronoff, *Psychological Needs and Cultural Systems* (New York: Van Nostrand Reinhold, 1967) and Stanley Renshon, *Psychological Needs and Political Behavior* (New York: Free Press, 1974). Also see Amitai Etzioni, "Basic Human Needs, Alienation and Inauthenticity," *American Sociological Review* 33 (1968): 870-885. For recent socio-psychological views, see Elliot Aronson, *The Social Animal* (San Francisco: W. H. Freeman, 1972); Charles Hampden-Turner, *Radical Man: The Process of Psychosocial Development* (Garden City, N. Y.: Doubleday & Co., Anchor Press, 1971); and Henry Kariel, *Open Systems: Arenas for Political Action* (Itasca, Ill.: F. E. Peacock, 1968). On how human beings construct their own social realities, see Peter Berger and Thomas Luckmann, *The Social Construction of Reality* (Garden City, N. Y.: Doubleday & Co., Anchor Press, 1967); Alfred Schutz, *Collected Papers*, Volume I (The Hague: Martinus Nijhoff, 1964); and Kalman Silvert, *Man's Power: A Biased Guide to Political Thought and Action* (New York: Viking Press, 1970). For introductions to "psychohistory" see Robert Jay Lifton and Eric Olson, *Explorations in Psychohistory* (New York: Simon & Schuster, 1975), Bruce Mazlish, "The Psychohistorical Approach" in *In Search of Nixon* (Baltimore, Md.: Penguin Books, 1973); Hans Meyerhoff, "On Psychoanalysis and History," *Psychoanalysis and the Psychoanalytic Review* 49, no. 2 (Summer 1962); and the *History of Childhood Quarterly: The Journal of Psychohistory.*

Elites, Imperialism, and Revolution

Classics on the role of elites in politics include Gaetano Mosca, *The Ruling Class* (New York: McGraw-Hill Co., 1939); Robert Dahl, *Who Governs?* (New Haven, Conn.: Yale University Press, 1961); and Floyd Hunter, *Community Power Structure* (Chapel Hill, N.C.: University of North Carolina Press, 1953). Also see Robert Presthus, *Men at the Top* (New York: Oxford University Press, 1964); Harold Lasswell and Daniel Lerner, *The Comparative Study of Elites* (Stanford, Calif.: Stanford University Press, 1952) and Thomas Dye and L. Harmon Zeigler, *The Irony of Democracy* (North Scituate, Mass.: Duxbury Press, 1975). Classics on imperialism include J. A. Hobson, *Imperialism—A Study*, 1902 (various editions), Rudolf Hilferding, *Finance-capitalism*, 1910 (various editions) and V. I. Lenin, *Imperialism: The Highest Stage of Capitalism*, 1916 (various editions). For a modern interpretation of imperialism applied to the economics of American foreign policy, see Harry Magdoff, *The Age of Imperialism* (New York: Monthly Review Press, 1969). Provocative works on revolution include William Lutz and Harry Brent, eds., *On Revolution* (Cambridge, Mass.: Winthrop, 1971); Kyung-Won Kim, *Revolution and International System* (New York: New York University Press, 1970); Albert Camus, *The Rebel* (New York: Knopf-Random House, 1956); Rollo May, *Power and Innocence* (New York: W. W. Norton Co., 1972); and Thomas Kuhn, *The Structure of Scientific Revolutions* (Chicago: University of Chicago

Press, 1962). The socio-psychology of revolutionary behavior is brilliantly explained in Charles Hampden-Turner, *Radical Man—The Process of Psycho-Social Development* (Garden City, N. Y.: Doubleday & Co., Anchor Press, 1970).

For elitism and imperialism interpreted through multinational corporations, see A. S. Prakash Sethi and Richard Holton, eds., *Management of the Multinationals: Policies, Operations and Research* (New York: Free Press, 1974), Joyce Kolko, *America and The Crisis of World Capitalism* (Boston: Beacon Press, 1974); *Foreign Policy*, Fall and Winter issues, 1973; and especially Richard Barnet and Ronald Müller, *Global Reach: The Power of the Multinational Corporations* (New York: Simon and Schuster, 1975).

Charisma, Limited Warfare, and Modernization

For a standard discussion of charisma and other types of authority, see Max Weber, *The Theory of Social and Economic Organization*, ed. Talcott Parsons (New York: Free Press, 1964), especially Part III, "The Types of Authority and Imperative Co-ordination." Also see Dankwart A. Rustow, ed., "Philosophers and Kings: Studies in Leadership," *Daedalus* 97, no. 3 (1968); and Ralph P. Hummel, "Freud's Totem Theory as Complement to Max Weber's Theory of Charisma," *Psychological Reports*, vol. 35 (October, 1974): 683-686. For the case of Castro's charisma, see Edward Gonzalez, *Cuba Under Castro: The Limits of Charisma* (Boston: Houghton Mifflin Co., 1974). For lucid introductions to theories and problems of modernization, see Lucian W. Pye, *Aspects of Political Development* (Boston: Little, Brown and Co., 1966); Kalman Silvert, *Man's Power* (New York: Viking Press, 1970); and Marion Levy, *Modernization* (N.Y.: Basic Books, 1972). On "limited warfare," see Hans Speier, *Social Order and the Risks of War* (Cambridge, Mass.: M.I.T. Press, 1952), Seymour J. Deitchman, *Limited War and American Defense Policy* (Cambridge, Mass.: M.I.T. Press, 1969) and Raymond Aron, *On War* (Garden City, N.Y.: Doubleday and Co., 1958).

The Nation-State System and Total Peace

For lucid introductions to the nature of the nation-state system and role of the concepts of the balance of power and collective security, see Inis Claude, *Power and International Relations* (New York: Random House, 1966); Inis Claude, *Swords into Plowshares* (New York: Random House, 1959); John Stoessinger, *The Might of Nations* (New York: Random House, 1965) and Robert A. Klein, *Sovereign Equality Among States: The History of An Idea* (Toronto: University of Toronto Press, 1975). A classic history of the balance of power and its assumptions is Edward Gulick's *Europe's Classical Balance of Power* (New York: W. W. Norton and Co., 1967). To probe collective security more deeply, see Joel Larus, ed., *From Collective Security to Preventive Diplomacy* (New York: John Wiley & Sons, 1965). For a short history of the League of Nations and its role in the history of international organization, see Stephen S. Goodspeed, *The Nature and Function of International Organization* (New York: Oxford University Press, 1967), Chapters 1-3. On the meaning of American liberalism and its historical roots, see Louis Hartz's brilliant *The Liberal Tradition in America* (New York: Harcourt, Brace and World, 1955) and H. Mark Roelofs, *The Language of Modern Politics* (Homewood, Ill.: Dorsey, 1967), Chapter 6.

Power, Racism, and Total War

For a classic study on the authoritarian personality and its relationship to power and racism, see T. Adorno, E. Frenkel-Brunswik, D. Levinson, and R. N. Sanford, *The Authoritarian Personality* (New York: Harper and Row, 1950) and R. Christie and M. Jahoda, eds., *Studies in the Scope and Method of The Authoritarian Personality* (Glencoe, Ill.: The Free Press, 1954). An excellent work from the viewpoint of political philosophy is Hannah Arendt, *The Origins of Totalitarianism* (New York: Harcourt Brace Jovanovich, 1973; orig. 1951). A provocative psychological viewpoint is Erich Fromm's *Escape from Freedom* (New York: Holt, Rinehart and Winston, 1941). For experiments demonstrating why human beings are willing to obey authority even to the extent of torturing others to death, see Stanley Milgram, *Obedience to Authority* (New York: Harper and Row, 1969.)

A classic on limited versus total war is Carl von Clausewitz, *On War*, ed. Anatol Rapoport (Baltimore, Md., Penguin Books, 1968, orig. 1832), see especially Rapoport's brilliant long introduction relating von Clausewitz's concept of total war to contemporary war theorists like Herman Kahn. See Herman Kahn's controversial *Thinking About The Unthinkable* (New York: Avon Books, 1962) to understand who would lose least in a thermonuclear war. For a useful summary of recent research on causes of war, see Dean G. Pruitt and Richard C. Snyder, *Theory and Research on the Causes of War* (Englewood Cliffs, N.J.: Prentice-Hall, 1969). For details on the most recent "total war" see Peter Calvocoressi and Guy Wint, *Total War: The Story of World War II* (New York: Pantheon Books, 1972). For a study of the role of individual leaders in helping nations to go to war, see John G. Stoessinger, *Why Nations Go to War* (New York: St. Martin's Press, 1974). Another book focusing on individuals in foreign policy crises that risked or involved war in the past twenty years is Thomas Halper's *Foreign Policy Crises: Appearance and Reality in Decision Making* (Columbus, Ohio: Charles Merrill Publishing Co., 1971).

For tools to understand the neurotic and pathological styles of leaders and others, see David Shapiro's lucid *Neurotic Styles* (New York: Basic Books, 1965); Bert Kaplan, ed., *The Inner World of Mental Illness* (New York: Harper and Row, 1964); and Theodore Millon, ed., *Theories of Psychopathology and Personality* (Philadelphia, Pa.: W. Saunders, 1973). Also see Benjamin Wolman's provocative *Call No Man Normal* (New York: International Universities Press, 1973); Rollo May's *Power and Innocence* (New York: W. W. Norton Co., 1972); and Stanley Renshon's *Personality Theories and Political Analysis* (New York: Free Press, forthcoming).

The most charming introduction to zero-sum and variable-sum thinking in game theory and conflict is still Anatole Rapoport's *Fights, Games and Debates* (Ann Arbor, Mich.: University of Michigan, 1960). A recent collection of experiments on the transformation of destructive zero-sum psychological processes to constructive, variable-sum cooperative processes is Morton Deutsch's *The Resolution of Conflict: Constructive and Destructive Processes* (New Haven, Conn.: Yale University Press, 1973). For a classic on the application of game theory to conflict strategies, see Thomas Schelling, *The Strategy of Conflict* (Cambridge, Mass.: Harvard University Press, 1960). For psychological conformity in groups in foreign policy crisis decisions, see Irving Janis, *Victims of Groupthink: A Psychological Study of Foreign Policy Decisions and Fiascos* (Boston: Houghton Mifflin Co., 1972)

National Bargaining and Regional Integration

On national bargaining in the process of European integration, see John Newhouse, *Collision in Brussels: The Common Market Crisis of 30 June, 1965* (New York: W. W. Norton Co., 1967); F. Roy Willis, *France, Germany and the New Europe* (New York: Oxford University Press, 1968); and Leon Lindberg and Stuart Scheingold, *Europe's Would-Be Polity* (Englewood Cliffs, N. J.: Prentice-Hall, 1970). For a collection of studies relating domestic factors and problems to the European integration process, see Martin Heisler, ed., *Politics in Europe* (New York: David McKay, 1974). For an introduction to the most important theories of international integration, see Ernst Haas, *Beyond the Nation-State* (Stanford, Calif.: Stanford University Press, 1964); Karl Deutsch, *Nationalism and Social Communication* (Cambridge, Mass.: The M.I.T Press, 1967); and especially Leon Lindberg and Stuart Scheingold, eds., *Regional Integration: Theory and Research* (Cambridge, Mass.: Harvard University Press, 1971). For the effects of economic nationalism on European integration and the world economy, see David Calleo and Benjamin M. Rowland, *America and the World Political Economy: Atlantic Dreams and National Realities* (Bloomington, Ind.: Indiana University Press, 1973); and Werner Feld's "Trade Between the U.S. and the European Community" and Robert A. Isaak's "America and the World Economic Crisis", both in the *Journal of International Affairs* 28, 1, (1974).

International Law and The United Nations

For classic approaches to international law, see J. L. Brierly, *The Law of Nations*, 6th ed. (Oxford: Oxford University Press, 1963) and William W. Bishop, *International Law: Cases and Materials* (Boston: Little, Brown and Co., 1962). Also see K. W. Deutsch and S. Hoffmann, eds., *The Relevance of International Law* (Cambridge, Mass.: Schenkman, 1968); R. A. Falk, ed., *The Vietnam War and International Law* (Princeton, N.J.: Princeton University Press, 1968); R. A. Falk and S. H. Mendlovitz, eds., *International Law*, 4 vols. (New York: World Law Fund, 1966); and R. E. Osgood and R. Tucker, *Force, Order and Justice* (Baltimore, Md.: Johns Hopkins Press, 1967).

Lucid introductions to the United Nations, its history and effectiveness include the following: Inis Claude, *Swords Into Plowshares* (New York: Random House, 1966); John Stoessinger, *The United Nations and the Superpowers* (New York: Random House, 1965); Robert Gregg and Michael Barkun, *The United Nations System and its Functions* (Princeton, N. J.: D. Van Nostrand Co., 1968); and Joel Larus, ed., *From Collective Security to Preventive Diplomacy* (New York: John Wiley & Sons, 1965). For a private, poetic view of the inner thoughts of a secretary general of the United Nations, see Dag Hammarskjöld, *Markings*, trans. Leif Sjöberg and W. H. Auden (New York: Alfred A. Knopf, 1964).

Nuclear Weapons and Foreign Policy Decision Making

On the role of nuclear weapons in modern diplomacy, see Henry Kissinger, *Nuclear Weapons and Foreign Policy* (New York: Harper and Row, 1957); John H. Herz, *International Politics in the Atomic Age* (New York: Columbia University Press, 1962); Adam Yarmolinsky, *The Military Establishment* (New York: Harper and Row, 1971); Richard Barnet, *The Economy of Death* (New York: Atheneum, 1969); Robert J. Lifton, *Death in Life: Survivors of Hiroshima* (New York: Random House, 1967). For a fascinating documentary account of the responsibility of scientists in atomic diplomacy, see Heinar Kipphardt's play, *In the Matter of J. Robert Oppenheimer* (New York: Hill and Wang, 1969). For an account in poetry, see Gregory Corso, *The Happy Birthday of Death* (New York: New Directions, 1960).

For psychological approaches to foreign policy decision making, see Joseph de Rivera, *The Psychological Dimension of Foreign Policy* (Columbus, Ohio: Charles Merrill Co., 1968); Ole Holsti et al, *Enemies in Politics* (Chicago: Rand McNally Co., 1967); Otto Klineberg, *The Human Dimension in International Relations* (New York: Holt, Rinehart and Winston, 1964); Irving Janis, *Victims of Groupthink* (Boston: Houghton Miffllin Co., 1972); Thomas Halper, *Foreign Policy Crises: Appearance and Reality in Decision-making* (Columbus, Ohio: Charles Merrill, 1971); and Graham T. Allison, *Essence of Decision: Explaining the Cuban Missile Crisis* (Boston: Little, Brown and Co., 1971). For a simulation approach, see Charles Hermann, *Crises in Foreign Policy: A Simulation Analysis* (New York: The Bobbs-Merrill Co., 1969). An excellent collection of different historical accounts of American foreign policy is Jerold A. Combs, *Nationalist, Realist and Radical: Three Views of American Diplomacy* (New York: Harper and Row, 1972). On the role of Congress in foreign policy, see James A. Robinson, *Congress and Foreign Policy-making* (Homewood, Ill.: The Dorsey Press, 1967). On American educational and cultural policy abroad, see Charles Frankel, *The Neglected Aspect of Foreign Affairs* (Washington, D.C.: The Brookings Institute, 1966). For the viewpoint of those inside the foreign policy-making process in the United States, see George Kennan, *Memoirs* (New York: Bantam Book, 1969) and Lincoln Bloomfield, *In Search of American Foreign Policy: The Humane Use of Power* (New York: Oxford University Press, 1974). For military aspects of foreign policy-making, see Townsend Hoopes, *The Limits of Intervention* (New York: David McKay, 1969); Morton Halperin, *Defense Strategies for the Seventies* (Boston: Little, Brown and Co., 1971); and Herman Kahn, *On Escalation* (New York: Praeger Publishers, 1965). For ethnocentrism as an American problem in foreign relations, see Stephen Spender, "Americanization," *Partisan Review* 39, no. 2 (1972). On the possibility of a new cold war between the United States, as the world's largest surplus food producer, and the hungry nations, see Walter Falcon and C. P. Timmer, "Food: War on Hunger or New Cold War?" in *The Stanford Magazine* 2, no. 2 (1974). On the future economic and political implications for the United States of the redistribution of the world's wealth because of the organization of oil producers, see Paul Lewis's incisive article, "Getting Even," *The New York Times Magazine*, 15 December, 1974.

Individuals and World Politics

To approach world politics from the viewpoint of the individual is, in general, a radically new departure from the traditional nation-state or global system approaches to the field. In this light, the assumptions behind this book were first analyzed in Robert A. Isaak, "The Individual in International Politics: Solving the Level-of-Analysis Problem," *Polity* 2, no. 2 (1974). This article, in turn, was influenced heavily by the theory of politics developed in Robert A. Isaak and Ralph P. Hummel, *Politics for Human Beings* (North Scituate, Mass.: Duxbury Press, 1975).

In terms of the sociology of knowledge, the following works are representative of the kind of thinking that made *Individuals and World Politics* possible: Alfred Schutz, *Collected Papers*, Vol. 1 (The Hague: Martinus Nijhoff, 1964); Peter Berger and Thomas Luckmann, *The Social Construction of Reality* (Garden City, N.Y.: Doubleday & Co., Anchor Press, 1967); Kalman Silvert, *Man's Power* (New York: Viking Press, 1970); Abraham Maslow, *Motivation and Personality* (New York: Harper and Row, 1954); Kenneth Boulding, "Learning and Reality-Testing Process in the International System," in John C. Farrell and Asa P. Smith, eds., *Image and Reality in World Politics* (New York: Columbia University Press, 1968); Kyung-Won Kim, *Revolution and International System* (New York: New York University Press, 1970); Robert White, ed., *The Study of Lives* (Chicago, Ill.: Aldine-Atherton, 1963); Erik Erikson, *Gandhi's Truth* (New York: W. W. Norton Co., 1969); Kenneth Boulding, *The Image: Knowledge in Life and Society* (Ann Arbor, Mich.: University of Michigan, 1964); and Albert Camus, *The Rebel* (New York: Knopf-Random House, 1956). And, perhaps most of all, the here and now of the concrete individual experience of world politics and the dangers of abstract technological rationality came to me in the favorite analogy of Zen: to point at the moon a finger is needed, but woe to those who take the finger for the moon.

Appendix I

Wilson's Fourteen Points *

The Fourteen Points are as follows:

1. Open convenants of peace, openly arrived at, after which there shall be no private international understandings of any kind, but diplomacy shall proceed always frankly and in the public view.

2. Absolute freedom of navigation upon the seas, outside territorial waters, alike in peace and in war, except as the seas may be closed in whole or in part by international action for the enforcement of international convenants.

3. The removal, so far as possible, of all economic barriers and the establishment of an equality of trade conditions among all the nations consenting to the peace and associating themselves for its maintenance.

4. Adequate guarantees given and taken that national armaments will be reduced to the lowest point consistent with domestic safety.

5. A free, open-minded, and absolutely impartial adjustment of all colonial claims, based upon a strict observance of the principle that in determining all such questions of sovereignty the interests of the populations concerned must have equal weight with the equitable claims of the government whose title is to be determined.

6. The evacuation of all Russian territory and such settlement of all questions affecting Russia as will secure the best and freest co-operation of the other nations of the world in obtaining for her an unhampered and unembarrassed opportunity for the independent determination of her own political development and national policy and assure her of a sincere welcome into the society of free nations under institutions of her own choosing; and, more than a welcome, assistance also of every kind that she may need and may herself desire. The treatment accorded Russia by her sister nations in the months to come will be the acid test of their good will, of their comprehension of her needs as distinguished from their own interests, and of their intelligent and unselfish sympathy.

7. Belgium, the whole world will agree, must be evacuated and restored without any attempt to limit the sovereignty which she enjoys in common with all other free nations. No other single act will serve as this will serve to restore confidence among the nations in the laws which they have themselves set and determined for the government of their relations with one another. Without this healing act the whole structure and validity of international law is forever impaired.

8. All French territory should be freed and the invaded portions restored, and the wrong done to France by Prussia in 1871 in the matter of Alsace-Lorraine, which has unsettled the peace of the world for nearly fifty years, should be righted, in order that peace may once more be made in the interest of all.

9. A readjustment of the frontiers of Italy should be effected along clearly recognizable lines of nationality.

10. The peoples of Austria-Hungary, whose place among the nations we wish to see

*As they appear in Frank P. Chambers, *This Age of Conflict* (N.Y.: Harcourt, Brace and World, 1962), pp. 832-833.

safeguarded and assured, should be accorded the freest opportunity of autonomous development.

11. Rumania, Serbia, and Montenegro should be evacuated; occupied territories restored; Serbia accorded free and secure access to the sea; and the relations of the several Balkan states to one another determined by friendly counsel along historically established lines of allegiance and nationality; and international guarantees of the political and economic independence and territorial integrity of the several Balkan states should be entered into.

12. The Turkish portions of the present Ottoman Empire should be assured a secure sovereignty, but other nationalities which are now under Turkish rule should be assured an undoubted security of life and absolutely unmolested opportunity of autonomous development, and the Dardanelles should be permanently opened as a free passage to the ships and commerce of all nations under international guarantees.

13. An independent Polish state should be erected which should include the territories inhabited by indisputably Polish populations, which should be assured a free and secure access to the sea, and whose political and economic independence and territorial integrity should be guaranteed by international covenant.

14. A general association of nations must be formed under specific covenants for the purpose of affording mutual guarantees of political independence and territorial integrity to great and small states alike.

Appendix  II

The Covenant of the
League of Nations *†

The High Contracting Parties

In order to promote international co-operation and to achieve international peace and security

by the acceptance of obligations not to resort to war,
by the prescription of open, just and honourable relations between nations,
by the firm establishment of the understandings of international law as the actual
    rule of conduct among Governments,
and by the maintenance of justice and a scrupulous respect for all treaty obligations
    in the dealing of organised peoples with one another,
Agree to this Covenant of the League of Nations.

Article 1

1. The original Members of the League of Nations shall be those of the Signatories which are named in the Annex to this Covenant and also such of those other States named in the Annex as shall accede without reservation to this Covenant. Such accession shall be effected by a Declaration deposited with the Secretariat within two months of the coming into force of the Covenant. Notice thereof shall be sent to all other Members of the League.

2. Any fully self-governing State, Dominion or Colony not named in the Annex may become a Member of the League if its admission is agreed to by two-thirds of the Assembly, provided that it shall give effective guarantees of its sincere intention to observe its international obligations, and shall accept such regulations as may be prescribed by the League in regard to its military, naval and air forces and armaments.

3. Any Member of the League may, after two years' notice of its intention so to do, withdraw from the League, provided that all its international obligations and all its obligations under this Covenant shall have been fulfilled at the time of its withdrawal.

Article 2

The action of the League under this Covenant shall be effected through the instrumentality of an Assembly and of a Council, with a permanent Secretariat.

Article 3

1. The Assembly shall consist of Representatives of the Members of the League.

*As it appears in Inis Claude, *Swords Into Plowshares* (N.Y.: Random House, 1964), pp. 409-417.

†The texts printed in italics indicate amendments adopted by the League.

2. The Assembly shall meet at stated intervals and from time to time as occasion may require at the Seat of the League or at such other place as may be decided upon.

3. The Assembly may deal at its meetings with any matter within the sphere of action of the League or affecting the peace of the world.

4. At meetings of the Assembly, each Member of the League shall have one vote, and may have not more than three Representatives.

Article 4

1. The Council shall consist of Representatives of the Principal Allied and Associated Powers, together with Representatives of four other Members of the League. These four Members of the League shall be selected by the Assembly from time to time in its discretion. Until the appointment of the Representatives of the four Members of the League first selected by the Assembly, Representatives of Belgium, Brazil, Spain and Greece shall be members of the Council.

2. With the approval of the majority of the Assembly, the Council may name additional Members of the League whose Representatives shall always be Members of the Council; the Council with like approval may increase the number of Members of the League to be selected by the Assembly for representation on the Council.

2. *bis. The Assembly shall fix by a two-thirds majority the rules dealing with the election of the non-permanent Members of the Council, and particularly such regulations as relate to their term of office and the conditions of re-eligibility.*

3. The Council shall meet from time to time as occasion may require, and at least once a year, at the Seat of the League, or at such other place as may be decided upon.

4. The Council may deal at its meetings with any matter within the sphere of action of the League or affecting the peace of the world.

5. Any Member of the League not represented on the Council shall be invited to send a Representative to sit as a member at any meeting of the Council during the consideration of matters specially affecting the interests of that Member of the League.

6. At meetings of the Council, each Member of the League represented on the Council shall have one vote, and may have not more than one Representative.

Article 5

1. Except where otherwise expressly provided in this Covenant or by the terms of the present Treaty, decisions at any meeting of the Assembly or of the Council shall require the agreement of all the Members of the League represented at the meeting.

2. All matters of procedure at meetings of the Assembly or of the Council, including the appointment of Committees to investigate particular matters, shall be regulated by the Assembly or by the Council and may be decided by a majority of the Members of the League represented at the meeting.

3. The first meeting of the Assembly and the first meeting of the Council shall be summoned by the President of the United States of America.

Article 6

1. The permanent Secretariat shall be established at the Seat of the League. The Secretariat shall comprise a Secretary-General and such secretaries and staff as may be required.

2. The first Secretary-General shall be the person named in the Annex; thereafter the

Secretary-General shall be appointed by the Council with the approval of the majority of the Assembly.

3. The secretaries and staff of the Secretariat shall be appointed by the Secretary-General with the approval of the Council.

4. The Secretary-General shall act in that capacity at all meetings of the Assembly and of the Council.

5. *The expenses of the League shall be borne by the Members of the League in the proportion decided by the Assembly.*

Article 7

1. The Seat of the League is established at Geneva.

2. The Council may at any time decide that the Seat of the League shall be established elsewhere.

3. All positions under or in connection with the League, including the Secretariat, shall be open equally to men and women.

4. Representatives of the Members of the League and officials of the League when engaged on the business of the League shall enjoy diplomatic privileges and immunities.

5. The buildings and other property occupied by the League or its officials or by Representatives attending its meetings shall be inviolable.

Article 8

1. The Members of the League recognise that the maintenance of peace requires the reduction of national armaments to the lowest point consistent with national safety and the enforcement by common action of international obligations.

2. The Council, taking account of the geographical situation and circumstances of each State, shall formulate plans for such reduction for the consideration and action of the several Governments.

3. Such plans shall be subject to reconsideration and revision at least every ten years.

4. After these plans have been adopted by the several Governments, the limits of armaments therein fixed shall not be exceeded without the concurrence of the Council.

5. The Members of the League agree that the manufacture by private enterprise of munitions and implements of war is open to grave objections. The Council shall advise how the evil effects attendant upon such manufacture can be prevented, due regard being had to the necessities of those Members of the League which are not able to manufacture the munitions and implements of war necessary for their safety.

6. The Members of the League undertake to interchange full and frank information as to the scale of their armaments, their military, naval and air programmes and the condition of such of their industries as are adaptable to warlike purposes.

Article 9

A permanent Commission shall be constituted to advise the Council on the execution of the provisions of Articles 1 and 8 and on military, naval and air questions generally.

Article 10

The Members of the League undertake to respect and preserve as against external aggression the territorial integrity and existing political independence of all Members of the League. In case of any such aggression or in case of any threat or danger of such aggression, the Council shall advise upon the means by which this obligation shall be fulfilled.

Article 11

1. Any war or threat of war, whether immediately affecting any of the Members of the League or not, is hereby declared a matter of concern to the whole League, and the League shall take any action that may be deemed wise and effectual to safeguard the peace of nations. In case any such emergency should arise, the Secretary-General shall, on the request of any Member of the League, forthwith summon a meeting of the Council.

2. It is also declared to be the friendly right of each Member of the League to bring to the attention of the Assembly or of the Council any circumstance whatever affecting international relations which threatens to disturb international peace or the good understanding between nations upon which peace depends.

Article 12

1. The Members of the League agree that if there should arise between them any dispute likely to lead to a rupture they will submit the matter either to arbitration *or judicial settlement* or to enquiry by the Council, and they agree in no case to resort to war until three months after the award by the arbitrators *or the judicial decision* or the report by the Council.

2. In any case under this article the award of the arbitrators *or the judicial decision* shall be made within a reasonable time, and the report of the Council shall be made within six months after the submission of the dispute.

Article 13

1. The Members of the League agree that whenever any dispute shall arise between them which they recognise to be suitable for submission to arbitration *or judicial settlement*, and which cannot be satisfactorily settled by diplomacy, they will submit the whole subject-matter to arbitration *or judicial settlement*.

2. Disputes as to the interpretation of a treaty, as to any question of international law, as to the existence of any fact which, if established, would constitute a breach of any international obligation, or as to the extent and nature of the reparation to be made for any such breach, are declared to be among those which are generally suitable for submission to arbitration *or judicial settlement*.

3. *For the consideration of any such dispute, the court to which the case is referred shall be the Permanent Court of International Justice, established in accordance with Article 14, or any tribunal agreed on by the parties to the dispute or stipulated in any Convention existing between them.*

4. The Members of the League agree that they will carry out in full good faith any award *or decision* that may be rendered, and that they will not resort to war against a Member of the League which complies therewith. In the event of any failure to carry out such an award *or decision*, the Council shall propose what steps should be taken to give effect thereto.

Article 14

The Council shall formulate and submit to the Members of the League for adoption plans for the establishment of a Permanent Court of International Justice. The Court shall be competent to hear and determine any dispute of an international character which the parties thereto submit to it. The Court may also give an advisory opinion upon any dispute or question referred to it by the Council or by the Assembly.

Article 15

1. If there should arise between Members of the League any dispute likely to lead to a rupture, which is not submitted to arbitration *or judicial settlement* in accordance with Article 13, the Members of the League agree that they will submit the matter to the Council. Any party to the dispute may effect such submission by giving notice of the existence of the dispute to the Secretary-General, who will make all necessary arrangements for a full investigation and consideration thereof.

2. For this purpose, the parties to the dispute will communicate to the Secretary-General, as promptly as possible, statements of their case with all the relevant facts and papers, and the Council may forthwith direct the publication thereof.

3. The Council shall endeavour to effect a settlement of the dispute, and if such efforts are successful, a statement shall be made public giving such facts and explanations regarding the dispute and the terms of settlement thereof as the Council may deem appropriate.

4. If the dispute is not thus settled, the Council either unanimously or by a majority vote shall make and publish a report containing a statement of the facts of the dispute and the recommendations which are deemed just and proper in regard thereto.

5. Any Member of the League represented on the Council may make public a statement of the facts of the dispute and of its conclusions regarding the same.

6. If a report by the Council is unanimously agreed to by the members thereof other than the Representatives of one or more of the parties to the dispute, the Members of the League agree that they will not go to war with any party to the dispute which complies with the recommendations of the report.

7. If the Council fails to reach a report which is unanimously agreed to by the members thereof, other than the Representatives of one or more of the parties to the dispute, the Members of the League reserve to themselves the right to take such action as they shall consider necessary for the maintenance of right and justice.

8. If the dispute between the parties is claimed by one of them, and is found by the Council, to arise out of a matter which by international law is solely within the domestic jurisdiction of that party, the Council shall so report, and shall make no recommendation as to its settlement.

9. The Council may in any case under this article refer the dispute to the Assembly. The dispute shall be so referred at the request of either party to the dispute provided that such request be made within fourteen days after the submission of the dispute to the Council.

10. In any case referred to the Assembly, all the provisions of this article and of Article 12 relating to the action and powers of the Council shall apply to the action and powers of the Assembly, provided that a report made by the Assembly, if concurred in by

the Representatives of those Members of the League represented on the Council and of a majority of the other Members of the League, exclusive in each case of the Representatives of the parties to the dispute, shall have the same force as a report by the Council concurred in by all the members thereof other than the Representatives of one or more of the parties to the dispute.

Article 16

1. Should any Member of the League resort to war in disregard of its convenants under Articles 12, 13 or 15, it shall, *ipso facto*, be deemed to have committed an act of war against all other Members of the League, which hereby undertake immediately to subject it to the severance of all trade or financial relations, the prohibition of all intercourse between their nationals and the nationals of the Covenant-breaking State, and the prevention of all financial, commercial or personal intercourse between the nationals of the Covenant-breaking State and the nationals of any other State, whether a Member of the League or not.

2. It shall be the duty of the Council in such case to recommend to the several Governments concerned what effective military, naval or air force the Members of the League shall severally contribute to the armed forces to be used to protect the covenants of the League.

3. The Members of the League agree, further, that they will mutually support one another in the financial and economic measures which are taken under this article, in order to minimise the loss and inconvenience resulting from the above measures, and that they will mutually support one another in resisting any special measures aimed at one of their number by the Covenant-breaking State, and that they will take the necessary steps to afford passage through their territory to the forces of any of the Members of the League which are co-operating to protect the convenants of the League.

4. Any member of the League which has violated any covenant of the League may be declared to be no longer a Member of the League by a vote of the Council concurred in by the Representatives of all the other Members of the League represented thereon.

Article 17

1. In the event of a dispute between a Member of the League and a State which is not a member of the League or between States not members of the League, the State or States not members of the League shall be invited to accept the obligations of membership in the League for the purposes of such dispute, upon such conditions as the Council may deem just. If such invitation is accepted, the provisions of Articles 12 to 16 inclusive shall be applied with such modifications as may be deemed necessary by the Council.

2. Upon such invitation being given, the Council shall immediately institute an enquiry into the circumstances of the dispute and recommend such action as may seem best and most effectual in the circumstances.

3. If a State so invited shall refuse to accept the obligations of membership in the League for the purposes of such dispute, and shall resort to war against a Member of the League, the provisions of Article 16 shall be applicable as against the State taking such action.

4. If both parties to the dispute when so invited refuse to accept the obligations of membership in the League for the purposes of such dispute, the Council may take such measures and make such recommendations as will prevent hostilities and will result in the settlement of the dispute.

Article 18

Every treaty or international engagement entered into hereafter by any Member of the League shall be forthwith registered with the Secretariat and shall, as soon as possible, be published by it. No such treaty or international engagement shall be binding until so registered.

Article 19

The Assembly may from time to time advise the reconsideration by Members of the League of treaties which have become inapplicable and the consideration of international conditions whose continuance might endanger the peace of the world.

Article 20

1. The Members of the League severally agree that this Convenant is accepted as abrogating all obligations or understandings *inter se* which are inconsistent with the terms thereof, and solemnly undertake that they will not hereafter enter into any engagements inconsistent with the terms thereof.

2. In case any Member of the League shall, before becoming a Member of the League, have undertaken any obligations inconsistent with the terms of this Covenant, it shall be the duty of such Member to take immediate steps to procure its release from such obligations.

Article 21

Nothing in this Covenant shall be deemed to affect the validity of international engagements, such as treaties of arbitration or regional understandings like the Monroe doctrine, for securing the maintenance of peace.

Article 22

1. To those colonies and territories which as a consequence of the late war have ceased to be under the sovereignty of the States which formerly governed them and which are inhabited by peoples not yet able to stand by themselves under the strenuous conditions of the modern world, there should be applied the principle that the well-being and development of such peoples form a sacred trust of civilisation and that securities for the performance of this trust should be embodied in this Covenant.

2. The best method of giving practical effect to this principle is that the tutelage of such peoples should be entrusted to advanced nations who, by reason of their resources, their experience or their geographical position, can best undertake this responsibility, and who are willing to accept it, and that this tutelage should be exercised by them as Mandatories on behalf of the League.

3. The character of the mandate must differ according to the stage of the development of the people, the geographical situation of the territory, its economic conditions and other similar circumstances.

4. Certain communities formerly belonging to the Turkish Empire have reached a stage of development where their existence as independent nations can be provisionally recognised subject to the rendering of administrative advice and assistance by a

Mandatory until such time as they are able to stand alone. The wishes of these communities must be a principal consideration in the selection of the Mandatory.

5. Other peoples, especially those of Central Africa, are at such a stage that the Mandatory must be responsible for the administration of the territory under conditions which will guarantee freedom of conscience and religion, subject only to the maintenance of public order and morals, the prohibition of abuses such as the slave trade, the arms traffic and the liquor traffic, and the prevention of the establishment of fortifications or military and naval bases and of military training of the natives for other than police purposes and the defence of territory, and will also secure equal opportunities for the trade and commerce of other Members of the League.

6. There are territories, such as South West Africa and certain of the the South Pacific Islands, which, owing to the sparseness of their population, or their small size, or their remoteness from the centres of civilisation, or their geographical contiguity to the territory of the Mandatory, and other circumstances, can be best administered under the laws of the Mandatory as integral portions of its territory, subject to the safeguards above mentioned in the interests of the indigenous population.

7. In every case of mandate, the Mandatory shall render to the Council an annual report in reference to the territory committed to its charge.

8. The degree of authority, control or administration to be exercised by the Mandatory shall, if not previously agreed upon by the Members of the League, be explicitly defined in each case by the Council.

9. A permanent Commission shall be constituted to receive and examine the annual reports of the Mandatories and to advise the Council on all matters relating to the observance of the mandates.

Article 23

Subject to and in accordance with the provisions of international Conventions existing or hereafter to be agreed upon, the Members of the League:

(a) will endeavor to secure and maintain fair and humane conditions of labour for men, women and children, both in their own countries and in all countries to which their commercial and industrial relations extend, and for that purpose will establish and maintain the necessary international organisations;

(b) undertake to secure just treatment of the native inhabitants of territories under their control;

(c) will entrust the League with the general supervision over the execution of agreements with regard to the traffic in women and children, and the traffic in opium and other dangerous drugs;

(d) will entrust the League with the general supervision of the trade in arms and ammunition with the countries in which the control of this traffic is necessary in the common interest;

(e) will make provision to secure and maintain freedom of communications and of transit and equitable treatment for the commerce of all Members of the League. In this connection, the special necessities of the regions devastated during the war of 1914-1918 shall be borne in mind;

(f) will endeavour to take steps in matters of international concern for the prevention and control of disease.

Article 24

1. There shall be placed under the direction of the League all international bureaux already established by general treaties if the parties to such treaties consent. All such international bureaux and all commissions for the regulation of matters of international interest hereafter constituted shall be placed under the direction of the League.

2. In all matters of international interest which are regulated by general Conventions but which are not placed under the control of international bureaux or commissions, the Secretariat of the League shall, subject to the consent of the Council and if desired by the parties, collect and distribute all relevant information and shall render any other assistance which may be necessary or desirable.

3. The Council may include as part of the expenses of the Secretariat the expenses of any bureau or commission which is placed under the direction of the League.

Article 25

The Members of the the League agree to encourage and promote the establishment and co-operation of duly authorised voluntary national Red Cross organisations having as purposes the improvement of health, the prevention of disease and the mitigation of suffering throughout the world.

Article 26

1. Amendments to this Covenant will take effect when ratified by the Members of the League whose Representatives compose the Council and by a majority of the Members of the League whose Representatives compose the Assembly.

2. No such amendments shall bind any Member of the League which signifies its dissent therefrom, but in that case it shall cease to be a Member of the League.

Appendix **III**

The Charter of the United Nations*

NOTE: The Charter of the United Nations was signed on 26 June 1945, in San Francisco, at the conclusion of the United Nations Conference on International Organization, and came into force on 24 October 1945. The Statute of the International Court of Justice is an integral part of the Charter.

Amendments to Articles 23, 27 and 61 of the Charter were adopted by the General Assembly on 17 December 1963 and came into force on 31 August 1965. The amendment to Article 109, adopted by the General Assembly on 20 December 1965, came into force on 12 June 1968.

The amendment to Article 23 enlarges the membership of the Security Council from 11 to 15. The amended Article 27 provides that decisions of the Security Council on procedural matters shall be made by an affirmative vote of nine members (formerly seven) and on all other matters by an affirmative vote of nine members (formerly seven) including the concurring votes of the five permanent members of the Security Council.

The amendment to Article 61 enlarges the membership of the Economic and Social Council from 18 to 27.

The amendment to Article 109, which relates to the first paragraph of that Article, provides that a General Conference of Member States for the purpose of reviewing the Charter may be held at a date and place to be fixed by a two-thirds vote of the members of the General Assembly and by a vote of any nine members (formerly seven) of the Security Council. Paragraph 3 of Article 109, which deals with the consideration of a possible review conference during the tenth regular session of the General Assembly, has been retained in its original form in its reference to a "vote of any seven members of the Security Council," the paragraph having been acted upon in 1955 by the General Assembly, at its tenth regular session, and by the Security Council.

WE THE PEOPLES
OF THE UNITED NATIONS
DETERMINED

to save succeeding generations from the scourge of war, which twice in our lifetime has brought untold sorrow to mankind, and

to reaffirm faith in fundamental human rights, in the dignity and worth of the human person, in the equal rights of men and women and of nations large and small, and

to establish conditions under which justice and respect for the obligations arising from treaties and other sources of international law can be maintained, and

to promote social progress and better standards of life in larger freedom,

*From the *Yearbook of the United Nations* Vol. 24, 1970, United Nations Publications, pp. 1001-1013.

AND FOR THESE ENDS

to practise tolerance and live together in peace with one another as good neighbors, and

to unite our strength to maintain international peace and security, and

to ensure, by the acceptance of principles and the institution of methods, that armed force shall not be used, save in the common interest, and

to employ international machinery for the promotion of the economic and social advancement of all peoples,

HAVE RESOLVED TO COMBINE OUR EFFORTS TO ACCOMPLISH THESE AIMS

Accordingly, our respective Governments, through representatives assembled in the city of San Francisco, who have exhibited their full powers found to be in good and due form, have agreed to the present Charter of the United Nations and do hereby establish an international organization to be known as the United Nations.

Chapter I
PURPOSES AND PRINCIPLES

Article 1

The Purposes of the United Nations are:

1. To maintain international peace and security and to that end: to take effective collective measures for the prevention and removal of threats to the peace, and for the suppression of acts of aggression or other breaches of the peace, and to bring about by peaceful means, and in conformity with the principles of justice and international law, adjustment or settlement of international disputes or situations which might lead to a breach of the peace;

2. To develop friendly relations among nations based on respect for the principle of equal rights and self-determination of peoples, and to take other appropriate mea-

sures to strengthen universal peace;

3. To achieve international co-operation in solving international problems of an economic, social, cultural, or humanitarian character, and in promoting and encouraging respect for human rights and for fundamental freedoms for all without distinction as to race, sex, language, or religion; and

4. To be a centre for harmonizing the actions of nations in the attainment of these common ends.

Article 2

The Organization and its Members, in pursuit of the Purposes stated in Article 1, shall act in accordance with the following Principles.

1. The Organization is based on the principle of the sovereign equality of all its Members.

2. All Members, in order to ensure to all of them the rights and benefits resulting from membership, shall fulfil in good faith the obligations assumed by them in accordance with the present Charter.

3. All Members shall settle their international disputes by peaceful means in such a manner that international peace and security, and justice, are not endangered.

4. All Members shall refrain in their international relations from the threat or use of force against the territorial integrity or political independence of any state, or in any other manner inconsistent with the Purposes of the United Nations.

5. All Members shall give the United Nations every assistance in any action it takes in accordance with the present Charter, and shall refrain from giving assistance to any state against which the United Nations is taking preventive or enforcement action.

6. The Organization shall ensure that states which are not Members of the United Nations act in accordance with these Principles so far as may be necessary for the maintenance of international peace and security.

7. Nothing contained in the present Charter shall authorize the United Nations to intervene in matters which are essentially within the domestic jurisdiction of any state or shall require the Members to submit such matters to settlement under the present Charter; but this principle shall not prejudice the application of enforcement measures under Chapter VII.

Chapter II
MEMBERSHIP

Article 3
The original Members of the United Nations shall be the states which, having participated in the United Nations Conference on International Organization at San Francisco, or having previously signed the Declaration by United Nations of 1 January 1942, sign the present Charter and ratify it in accordance with Article 110.

Article 4
1. Membership in the United Nations is open to all other peace-loving states which accept the obligations contained in the present Charter and, in the judgment of the Organization, are able and willing to carry out these obligations.

2. The admission of any such state to membership in the United Nations will be effected by a decision of the General Assembly upon the recommendation of the Security Council.

Article 5
A Member of the United Nations against which preventive or enforcement action has been taken by the Security Council may be suspended from the exercise of the rights and privileges of membership by the General Assembly upon the recommendation of the Security Council. The exercise of these rights and privileges may be restored by the Security Council.

Article 6
A Member of the United Nations which has persistently violated the Principles contained in the present Charter may be expelled from the Organization by the General Assembly upon the recommendation of the Security Council.

Chapter III
ORGANS

Article 7
1. There are established as the principal organs of the United Nations: a General Assembly, a Security Council, an Economic and Social Council, a Trusteeship Council, an International Court of Justice, and a Secretariat.

2. Such subsidiary organs as may be found necessary may be established in accordance with the present Charter.

Article 8
The United Nations shall place no restriction on the eligibility of men and women to participate in any capacity and under conditions of equality in its principal and subsidiary organs.

Chapter IV
THE GENERAL ASSEMBLY

Composition
Article 9
1. The General Assembly shall consist of all the Members of the United Nations.

2. Each Member shall have not more than five representatives in the General Assembly.

Functions and Powers
Article 10
The General Assembly may discuss any questions or any matters within the scope of the present Charter or relating to the powers and functions of any organs provided for in the present Charter, and, except as provided in Article 12, may make recommendations to the Members of the

United Nations or to the Security Council or to both on any such questions or matters.

Article 11

1. The General Assembly may consider the general principles of co-operation in the maintenance of international peace and security, including the principles governing disarmament and the regulation of armaments, and may make recommendations with regard to such principles to the Members or to the Security Council or to both.

2. The General Assembly may discuss any questions relating to the maintenance of international peace and security brought before it by any Member of the United Nations, or by the Security Council, or by a state which is not a Member of the United Nations in accordance with Article 35, paragraph 2, and, except as provided in Article 12, may make recommendations with regard to any such questions to the state or states concerned or to the Security Council or to both. Any such question on which action is necessary shall be referred to the Security Council by the General Assembly either before or after discussion.

3. The General Assembly may call the attention of the Security Council to situations which are likely to endanger international peace and security.

4. The powers of the General Assembly set forth in this Article shall not limit the general scope of Article 10.

Article 12

1. While the Security Council is exercising in respect of any dispute or situation the functions assigned to it in the present Charter, the General Assembly shall not make any recommendation with regard to that dispute or situation unless the Security Council so requests.

2. The Secretary-General, with the consent of the Security Council, shall notify the General Assembly at each session of any matters relative to the maintenance of international peace and security which are being dealt with by the Security Council and shall similarly notify the General Assembly, or the Members of the United Nations if the General Assembly is not in session, immediately the Security Council ceases to deal with such matters.

Article 13

1. The General Assembly shall initiate studies and make recommendations for the purpose of:

  a. promoting international co-operation in the political field and encouraging the progressive development of international law and its codification;

  b. promoting international co-operation in the economic, social, cultural, educational, and health fields, and assisting in the realization of human rights and fundamental freedoms for all without distinction as to race, sex, language, or religion.

2. The further responsibilities, functions and powers of the General Assembly with respect to matters mentioned in paragraph 1(b) above are set forth in Chapters IX and X.

Article 14

Subject to the provisions of Article 12, the General Assembly may recommend measures for the peaceful adjustment of any situation, regardless of origin, which it deems likely to impair the general welfare or friendly relations among nations, including situations resulting from a violation of the provisions of the present Charter setting forth the Purposes and Principles of the United Nations.

Article 15

1. The General Assembly shall receive and consider reports from the other organs of the United Council; these reports shall include an account of the measures that the Security Council has decided upon or taken to maintain international peace and security.

2. The General Assembly shall receive

and consider reports from the other organs of the United Nations.

Article 16

The General Assembly shall perform such functions with respect to the international trusteeship system as are assigned to it under Chapters XII and XIII, including the approval of the trusteeship agreements for areas not designated as strategic.

Article 17

1. The General Assembly shall consider and approve the budget of the Organization.

2. The expenses of the Organization shall be borne by the Members as apportioned by the General Assembly.

3. The General Assembly shall consider and approve any financial and budgetary arrangements with specialized agencies referred to in Article 57 and shall examine the administrative budgets of such specialized agencies with a view to making recommendations to the agencies concerned.

Voting

Article 18

1. Each member of the General Assembly shall have one vote.

2. Decisions of the General Assembly on important questions shall be made by a two-thirds majority of the members present and voting. These questions shall include: recommendations with respect to the maintenance of international peace and security, the election of the non-permanent members of the Security Council, the election of the members of the Economic and Social Council, the election of members of the Trusteeship Council in accordance with paragraph 1(c) of Article 86, the admission of new Members to the United Nations, the suspension of the rights and privileges of membership, the expulsion of Members, questions relating to the operation of the trusteeship system, and budgetary questions.

3. Decisions on other questions, in-

cluding the determination of additional categories of questions to be decided by a two-thirds majority, shall be made by a majority of the members present and voting.

Article 19

A Member of the United Nations which is in arrears in the payment of its financial contributions to the Organization shall have no vote in the General Assembly if the amount of its arrears equals or exceeds the amount of the contributions due from it for the preceding two full years. The General Assembly may, nevertheless, permit such a Member to vote if it is satisfied that the failure to pay is due to conditions beyond the control of the Member.

Procedure

Article 20

The General Assembly shall meet in regular annual sessions and in such special sessions as occasion may require. Special sessions shall be convoked by the Secretary-General at the request of the Security Council or of a majority of the Members of the United Nations.

Article 21

The General Assembly shall adopt its own rules of procedure. It shall elect its President for each session.

Article 22

The General Assembly may establish such subsidiary organs as it deems necessary for the performance of its function.

Chapter V
THE SECURITY COUNCIL

Composition

Article 23[1]

1. The Security Council shall consist of fifteen Members of the United Nations.

[1]Amended text of Article 23 which came into force on 31 August 1965.

(The text of Article 23 before it was amended read as follows:

The Republic ot China, France, the Union of Soviet Socialist Republics, the United Kingdom of Great Britain and Northern Ireland, and the United States of America shall be permanent members of the Security Council. The General Assembly shall elect ten other Members of the United Nations to be non-permanent members of the Security Council, due regard being specially paid, in the first instance to the contribution of Members of the United Nations to the maintenance of international peace and security and to the other purposes of the Organization, and also to equitable geographical distribution.

2. The non-permanent members of the Scurity Council shall be elected for a term of two years. In the first election of the non-permanent members after the increase of the membership of the Security Council from eleven to fifteen, two of the four additional members shall be chosen for a term of one year. A retiring member shall not be eligible for immediate re-election.

3. Each member of the Security Council shall have one representative.

1. The Security Council shall consist of eleven Members of the United Nations. The Republic of China, France, the Union of Soviet Socialist Republics, the United Kingdom of Great Britain and Northern Ireland, and the United States of America shall be permanent members of the Security Council. The General Assembly shall elect six other Members of the United Nations to be non-permanent members of the Security Council, due regard being specially paid, in the first instance to the contribution of Members of the United Nations to the maintenance of international peace and security and to the other purposes of the Organization, and also to equitable geographical distribution.

2. The non-permanent members of the Security Council shall be elected for a term of two years. In the first election of the non-permanent members, however, three shall be chosen for a term of one year. A retiring member shall not be eligible for immediate re-election.

3. Each member of the Security Council shall have one representative.

Functions and Powers

Article 24

1. In order to ensure prompt and effective action by the United Nations, its Members confer on the Security Council primary responsibility for the maintenance of international peace and security, and agree that in carrying out its duties under this responsibility the Security Council acts on their behalf.

2. In discharging these duties the Security Council shall act in accordance with the Purposes and Principles of the United Nations. The specific powers granted to the Security Council for the discharge of these duties are laid down in Chapters VI, VII, VIII, and XII.

3. The Security Council shall submit annual and, when necessary, special reports to the General Assembly for its consideration.

Article 25

The Members of the United Nations agree to accept and carry out the decisions of the Security Council in accordance with the present Charter.

Article 26

In order to promote the establishment and maintenance of international peace and security with the least diversion for armaments of the world's human and economic resources, the Security Council shall be responsible for formulating, with the assistance of the Military Staff Committee referred to in Article 47, plans to be submitted to the Members of the United Nations for the establishment of a system for the regulation of armaments.

Voting

Article 27[2]

1. Each member of the Security Council shall have one vote.

[2]Amended text of Article 27 which came into force on 31 August 1965.

(The text of Article 27 before it was amended read as follows:

2. Decisions of the Security Council on procedural matters shall be made by an affirmative vote of nine members.

3. Decisions of the Security Council on all other matters shall be made by an affirmative vote of nine members including the concurring votes of the permanent members; provided that, in decisions under Chapter VI, and under paragraph 3 of Article 52, a party to a dispute shall abstain from voting.

Procedure

Article 28

1. The Security Council shall be so organized as to be able to function continuously. Each member of the Security Council shall for this purpose be represented at all times at the seat of the Organization.

2. The Security Council shall hold periodic meetings at which each of its members. may, if it so desires, be represented by a member of the government or by some other specially designated representative.

3. The Security Council may hold meetings at such places other than the seat of the Organization as in its judgment will best facilitate its work.

Article 29

The Security Council may establish such subsidiary organs as it deems necessary for the performance of its functions.

Article 30

The Security Council shall adopt its own rules of procedure, including the method of selecting its President.

1. Each member of the Security Council shall have one vote.

2. Decisions of the Security Council on procedural matters shall be made by an affirmative vote of seven members.

3. Decisions of the Security Council on all other matters shall be made by an affirmative vote of seven members including the concurring votes of the permanent members; provided that, in decisions under Chapter VI, and under paragraph 3 of Article 52, a party to a dispute shall abstain from voting.)

Article 31

Any Member of the United Nations which is not a member of the Security Council may participate, without vote, in the discussion of any question brought before the Security Council whenever the latter considers that the interests of that Member are specially affected.

Article 32

Any Member of the United Nations which is not a member of the Security Council or any state which is not a Member of the United Nations, if it is a party to a dispute under consideration by the Security Council, shall be invited to participate, without vote, in the discussion relating to the dispute. The Security Council shall lay down such conditions as it deems just for the participation of a state which is not a Member of the United Nations.

Chapter VI
PACIFIC SETTLEMENT OF DISPUTES

Article 33

1. The parties to any dispute, the continuance of which is likely to endanger the maintenance of international peace and security, shall, first of all, seek a solution by negotiation, enquiry, mediation, conciliation, arbitration, judicial settlement, resort to regional agencies or arrangements, or other peaceful means of their own choice.

2. The Security Council shall, when it deems necessary, call upon the parties to settle their dispute by such means.

Article 34

The Security Council may investigate any dispute, or any situation which might lead to international friction or give rise to a dispute, in order to determine whether the continuance of the dispute or situation is likely to endanger the maintenance of international peace and security.

Article 35

1. Any Member of the United Nations

may bring any dispute, or any situation of the nature referred to in Article 34, to the attention of the Security Council or of the General Assembly.

2. A state which is not a Member of the United Nations may bring to the attention of the Security Council or of the General Assembly any dispute to which it is a party if it accepts in advance, for the purposes of the dispute, the obligations of pacific settlement provided in the present Charter.

3. The proceedings of the General Assembly in respect of matters brought to its attention under this Article will be subject to the provisions of Articles 11 and 12.

Article 36

1. The Security Council may, at any stage of a dispute of the nature referred to in Article 33 or of a situation of like nature, recommend appropriate procedures or methods of adjustment.

2. The Security Council should take into consideration any procedures for the settlement of the dispute which have already been adopted by the parties.

3. In making recommendations under this Article the Security Council should also take into consideration that legal disputes should as a general rule be referred by the parties to the International Court of Justice in accordance with the provisions of the Statute of the Court.

Article 37

1. Should the parties to a dispute of the nature referred to in Article 33 fail to settle it by the means indicated in that Article, they shall refer it to the Security Council.

2. If the Security Council deems that the continuance of the dispute is in fact likely to endanger the maintenance of international peace and security, it shall decide whether to take action under Article 36 or to recommend such terms of settlement as it may consider appropriate.

Article 38

Without prejudice to the provisions of Articles 33 to 37, the Security Council may,

if all the parties to any dispute so request, make recommendations to the parties with a view to a pacific settlement of the dispute.

Chapter VII
ACTION WITH RESPECT TO THREATS TO THE PEACE, BREACHES OF THE PEACE, AND ACTS OF AGGRESSION

Article 39

The Security Council shall determine the existence of any threat to the peace, breach of the peace, or act of aggression and shall make recommendations, or decide what measures shall be taken in accordance with Articles 41 and 42, to maintain or restore international peace and security.

Article 40

In order to prevent an aggravation of the situation, the Security Council may, before making the recommendations or deciding upon the measures provided for in Article 39, call upon the parties concerned to comply with such provisional measures as it deems necessary or desirable. Such provisional measures shall be without prejudice to the rights, claims, or position of the parties concerned. The Security Council shall duly take account of failure to comply with such provisional measures.

Article 41

The Security Council may decide what measures not involving the use of armed force are to be employed to give effect to its decisions, and it may call upon the Members of the United Nations to apply such measures. These may include complete or partial interruption of economic relations and of rail, sea, air, postal, telegraphic, radio, and other means of communication, and the severance of diplomatic relations.

Article 42

Should the Security Council consider that measures provided for in Article 41 would be inadequate or have proved to be inadequate, it may take such action by air, sea, or land forces as may be necessary to maintain or restore international peace and security. Such action may include demonstrations, blockade, and other operations by air, sea, or land forces of Members of the United Nations.

Article 43

1. All Members of the United Nations, in order to contribute to the maintenance of international peace and security, undertake to make available to the Security Council, on its call and in accordance with a special agreement or agreements, armed forces, assistance, and facilities, including rights of passage, necessary for the purpose of maintaining international peace and security.

2. Such agreement or agreements shall govern the numbers and types of forces, their degree of readiness and general location, and the nature of the facilities and assistance to be provided.

3. The agreement or agreements shall be negotiated as soon as possible on the initiative of the Security Council. They shall be concluded between the Security Council and Members or between the Security Council and groups of Members and shall be subject to ratification by the signatory states in accordance with their respective constitutional processes.

Article 44

When the Security Council has decided to use force it shall, before calling upon a Member not represented on it to provide armed forces in fulfilment of the obligations assumed under Article 43, invite that member, if the Member so desires, to participate in the decisions of the Security Council concerning the employment of contigents of Member's armed forces.

Article 45

In order to enable the United Nations to take urgent military measures, Members shall hold immediately available national air-force contingent for combined international enforcement action. The strength and degree of readiness of these contin-

gents and plans for their combined action shall be determined, within the limits laid down in the special agreement or agreements referred to in Article 43, by the Security Council with the assistance of the Military Staff Committee.

Article 46

Plans for the application of armed force shall be made by the Security Council with the assistance of the Military Staff Committee.

Article 47

1. There shall be established a Military Staff Committee to advise and assist the Security Council on all questions relating to the Security Council's military requirements for the maintenance of international peace and security, the employment and command of forces placed at its disposal, the regulation of armaments, and possible disarmament.

2. The Military Staff Committee shall consist of the Chiefs of Staff of the permanent members of the Security Council or their representatives. Any Member of the United Nations not permanently represented on the Committee shall be invited by the Committee to be associated with it when the efficient discharge of the Committee's responsibilities requires the participation of that Member in its work.

3. The Military Staff Committee shall be responsible under the Security Council for the strategic direction of any armed forces placed at the disposal of the Security Council. Questions relating to the command of such forces shall be worked out subsequently.

4. The Military Staff Committee, with the authorization of the Security Council and after consultation with appropriate regional agencies, may establish regional sub-committees.

Article 48

1. The action required to carry out the decisions of the Security Council for the maintenance of international peace and

security shall be taken by all the Members of the United Nations or by some of them, as the Security Council may determine.

2. Such decisions shall be carried out by the Members of the United Nations directly and through their action in the appropriate international agencies of which they are members.

Article 49

The Members of the United Nations shall join in affording mutual assistance in carrying out the measures decided upon by the Security Council.

Article 50

If preventive or enforcement measures against any state are taken by the Security Council, any other state, whether a Member of the United Nations or not, which finds itself confronted with special economic problems arising from the carrying out of those measures shall have the right to consult the Security Council with regard to a solution of those problems.

Article 51

Nothing in the present Charter shall impair the inherent right of individual or collective self-defence if an armed attack occurs against a Member of the United Nations, until the Security Council has taken measures necessary to maintain international peace and security. Measures taken by Members in the exercise of this right of self-defence shall be immediately reported to the Security Council and shall not in any way affect the authority and responsibility of the Security Council under the present Charter to take at any time such action as it deems necessary in order to maintain or restore international peace and security.

Chapter VIII
REGIONAL ARRANGEMENTS

Article 52

1. Nothing in the present Charter precludes the existence of regional arrangements or agencies for dealing with such matters relating to the maintenance of international peace and security as are appropriate for regional action, provided that such arrangements or agencies and their activities are consistent with the Purposes and Principles of the United Nations.

2. The Members of the United Nations entering into such arrangements or constituting such agencies shall make every effort to achieve pacific settlement of local disputes through such regional arrangements or by such regional agencies before referring them to the Security Council.

3. The Security Council shall encourage the development of pacific settlement of local disputes through such regional arrangements or by such regional agencies either on the initiative of the states concerned or by reference from the Security Council.

4. This Article in no way impairs the application of Articles 34 and 35.

Article 53

1. The Security Council shall, where appropriate, utilize such regional arrangements or agencies for enforcement action under its authority. But no enforcement action shall be taken under regional arrangements or by regional agencies without the authorization of the Security Council, with the exception of measures against any enemy state, as defined in paragraph 2 of this Article, provided for pursuant to Article 107 or in regional arrangements directed against renewal of aggressive policy on the part of any such state, until such time as the Organization may, on request of the Governments concerned, be charged with the responsibility for preventing further aggression by such a state.

2. The term enemy state as used in paragraph 1 of this Article applies to any state which during the Second World War has been an enemy of any signatory of the present Charter.

Article 54

The Security Council shall at all times be

kept fully informed of activities undertaken or in contemplation under regional arrangements or by regional agencies for the maintenance of international peace and security.

Chapter IX
INTERNATIONAL ECONOMIC AND SOCIAL CO-OPERATION

Article 55

With a view to the creation of conditions of stability and well-being which are necessary for peaceful and friendly relations among nations based on respect for the principle of equal rights and self-determination of peoples, the United Nations shall promote:

a. higher standards of living, full employment, and conditions of economic and social progress and development;
b. solutions of international economic, social, health, and related problems; and international cultural and educational co-operation; and
c. universal respect for, and observance of, human rights and fundamental freedoms for all without distinction as to race, sex, language, or religion.

Article 56

All Members pledge themselves to take joint and separate action in co-operation with the Organization for the achievement of the purposes set forth in Article 55.

Article 57

1. The various specialized agencies, established by intergovernmental agreement and having wide international responsibilities, as defined in their basic instruments, in economic, social, cultural, educational, health, annd related fields, shall be brought into relationship with the United Nations in accordance with the provisions of Article 63.

2. Such agencies thus brought into relationship with the United Nations are hereinafter referred to as specialized agencies.

Article 58

The Organization shall make recommendations for the co-ordination of the policies and activities of the specialized agencies.

Article 59

The Organization shall, where appropriate, initiate negotiations among the states concerned for the creation of any new specialized agencies required for the accomplishment of the purposes set forth in Article 55.

Article 60

Responsibility for the discharge of the functions of the Organization set forth in this Chapter shall be vested in the General Assembly and, under the authority of the General Assembly, in the Economic and Social Council, which shall have for this purpose the powers set forth in Chapter X.

Chapter X
THE ECONOMIC AND SOCIAL COUNCIL

Composition

Article 61[3]

[3]Amended text of Article 61, which came into force on 31 August 1965.

(The text of Article 61 before it was amended read as follows:

1. The Economic and Social Council shall consist of eighteen Members of the United Nations elected by the General Assembly.

2. Subject to the provisions of paragraph 3, six members of the Economic and Social Council shall be elected each year for a term of three years. A retiring member shall be eligible for immediate re-election.

3. At the first election, eighteen members of the Economic and Social Council shall be chosen. The term of office of six members so chosen shall expire at the end of one year, and of six other members at the end of two years, in accordance with arrangements made by the General Assembly.

4. Each member of the Economic and Social Council shall have one representative.)

1. The Economic and Social Council shall consist of twenty-seven Members of the United Nations elected by the General Assembly.

2. Subject to the provisions of paragraph 3, nine members of the Economic and Social Council shall be elected each year for a term of three years. A retiring member shall be eligible for immediate re-election.

3. At the first election after the increase in the membership of the Economic and Social Council from eighteen to twenty-seven members, in addition to the members elected in place of the six members whose term of office expires at the end of that year, nine additional members shall be elected. Of these nine additional members, the term of office of three members so elected shall expire at the end of one year, and of three other members at the end of two years, in accordance with arrangements made by the General Assembly.

4. Each member of the Economic and Social Council shall have one representative.

Functions and Powers
Article 62
1. The Economic and Social Council may make or initiate studies and reports with respect to international economic, social, cultural, educational, health, and related matters and may make recommendations with respect to any such matters to the General Assembly, to the Members of the United Nations, and to the specialized agencies concerned.

2. It may make recommendations for the purpose of promoting respect for, and observance of, human rights and fundamental freedoms for all.

3. It may prepare draft conventions for submission to the General Assembly, with respect to matters falling within its competence.

4. It may call, in accordance with the rules prescribed by the United Nations, international conferences on matters falling within its competence.

Article 63
1. The Economic and Social Council may enter into agreements with any of the agencies referred to in Article 57, defining the terms on which the agency concerned shall be brought into relationship with the United Nations. Such agreements shall be subject to approval by the General Assembly.

2. It may co-ordinate the activities of the specialized agencies through consultation with and recommendations to such agencies and through recommendations to the General Assembly and to the Members of the United Nations.

Article 64
1. The Economic and Social Council may take appropriate steps to obtain regular reports from the specialized agencies. It may make arrangements with the Members of the United Nations and with the specialized agencies to obtain reports on the steps taken to give effect to its own recommendations and to recommendations on matters falling within its competence made by the General Assembly.

2. It may communicate its observations on these reports to the General Assembly.

Article 65
The Economic and Social Council may furnish information to the Security Council and shall assist the Security Council upon its request.

Article 66
1. The Economic and Social Council shall perform such functions as fall within its competence in connexion with the carrying out of the recommendations of the General Assembly.

2. It may, with the approval of the General Assembly, perform services at the request of Members of the United Nations and at the request of specialized agencies.

3. It shall perform such other functions as are specified elsewhere in the present Charter or as may be assigned to it by the

General Assembly.

Voting
Article 67
1. Each member of the Economic and Social Council shall have one vote.
2. Decisions of the Economic and Social Council shall be made by a majority of the members present and voting.

Procedure
Article 68
The Economic and Social Council shall set up commissions in economic and social fields and for the promotion of human rights, and such other commissions as may be required for the performance of its functions.

Article 69
The Economic and Social Council shall invite any Member of the United Nations to participate, without vote, in its deliberations on any matter of particular concern to that Member.

Article 70
The Economic and Social Council may make arrangements for representatives of the specialized agencies to participate, without vote, in its deliberations and in those of the commissions established by it, and for its representatives to participate in the deliberations of the specialized agencies.

Article 71
The Economic and Social Council may make suitable arrangements for consultation with non-governmental organizations which are concerned with matters within its competence. Such arrangements may be made with international organizations and, where appropriate, with national organizations after consultation with the Member of the United Nations concerned.

Article 72
1. The Economic and Social Council shall adopt its own rules of procedure, including the method of selecting its President.
2. The Economic and Social Council shall meet as required in accordance with its rules, which shall include provision for the convening of meetings on the request of a majority of its members.

Chapter XI
DECLARATION REGARDING NON-SELF-GOVERNING TERRITORIES

Article 73
Members of the United Nations which have or assume responsibilities for the administration of territories whose peoples have not yet attained a full measure of self-government recognize the principle that the interests of the inhabitants of these territories are paramount, and accept as a sacred trust the obligation to promote to the utmost, within the system of international peace and security established by the present Charter, the well-being of the inhabitants of these territories, and, to this end:
a. to ensure, with due respect for the culture of the peoples concerned, their political, economic, social, and educational advancement, their just treatment, and their protection against abuses;
b. to develop self-government, to take due account of the political aspirations of the peoples, and to assist them in the progressive development of their free political institutions, according to the particular circumstances of each territory and its peoples and their varying stages of advancement;
c. to further international peace and security;
d. to promote constructive measures of development, to encourage research, and to co-operate with one another and, when and where appropriate, with specialized international bodies

with a view to the practical achievement of the social, economic, and scientific purposes set forth in this Article; and

e. to transmit regularly to the Secretary-General for information purposes, subject to such limitation as security and constitutional considerations may require, statistical and other information of a technical nature relating to economic, social, and educational conditions in the territories for which they are respectively responsible other than those territories to which Chapters XII and XIII apply.

Article 74

Members of the United Nations also agree that their policy in respect of the territories to which this Chapter applies, no less than in respect of their metropolitan areas, must be based on the general principle of good-neighbourliness, due account being taken of the interests and well-being of the rest of the world, in social, economic, and commercial matters.

Chapter XII
INTERNATIONAL TRUSTEESHIP SYSTEM

Article 75

The United Nations shall establish under its authority an international trusteeship system for the administration and supervision of such territories as may be placed thereunder by subsequent individual agreements. These territories are hereinafter referred to as trust territories.

Article 76

The basic objectives of the trusteeship system, in accordance with the Purposes of the United Nations laid down in Article 1 of the present Charter, shall be:

a. to further international peace and security;
b. to promote the political, economic,

social, and educational advancement of the inhabitants of the trust territories, and their progressive development towards self-government or independence as may be appropriate to the particular circumstances of each territory and its peoples and the freely expressed wishes of the peoples concerned, and as may be provided by the terms of each trusteeship agreement;

c. to encourage respect for human rights and for fundamental freedoms for all without distinction as to race, sex, language, or religion, and to encourage recognition of the interdependence of the peoples of the world; and

d. to ensure equal treatment in social, economic and commercial matters for all Members of the United Nations and their nationals, and also equal treatment for the latter in the administration of justice, without prejudice to the attainment of the foregoing objectives and subject to the provisions of Article 80.

Article 77

1. The trusteeship system shall apply to such territories in the following categories as may be placed thereunder by means of trusteeship agreements:

a. territories now held under mandate;
b. territories which may be detached from enemy states as a result of the Second World War; and
c. territories voluntarily placed under the system by states responsible for their administration.

2. It will be a matter for subsequent agreement as to which territories in the foregoing categories will be brought under the trusteeship system and upon what terms.

Article 78

The trusteeship system shall not apply to territories which have become Members of the United Nations, relationship among which shall be based on respect for the principle of sovereign equality.

Article 79

The terms of trusteeship for each territory to be placed under the trusteeship system, including any alteration or amendment, shall be agreed upon by the states directly concerned, including the mandatory power in the case of territories held under mandate by a Member of the United Nations, and shall be approved as provided for in Articles 83 and 85.

Article 80

1. Except as may be agreed upon in individual trusteeship agreements, made under Articles 77, 79, and 81, placing each territory under the trusteeship system, and until such agreements have been concluded, nothing in this Chapter shall be construed in or of itself to alter in any manner the rights whatsoever of any states or any peoples or the terms of existing international instruments to which Members of the United Nations may respectively be parties.

2. Paragraph 1 of this Article shall not be interpreted as giving grounds for delay or postponement of the negotiation and conclusion of agreements for placing mandated and other territories under the trusteeship system as provided for in Article 77.

Article 81

The trusteeship agreement shall in each case include the terms under which the trust territory will be administered and designate the authority which will exercise the administration of the trust territory. Such authority, hereinafter called the administering authority, may be one or more states of the Organization itself.

Article 82

There may be designated, in any trusteeship agreement, a strategic area or areas which may include part or all of the trust territory to which the agreement applies, without prejudice to any special agreement or agreements made under Article 43.

Article 83

1. All functions of the United Nations relating to strategic areas, including the approval of the terms of the trusteeship agreements and of their alteration or amendment, shall be exercised by the Security Council.

2. The basic objectives set forth in Article 76 shall be applicable to the people of each strategic area.

3. The Security Council shall, subject to the provisions of the trusteeship agreements and without prejudice to security considerations, avail itself of the assistance of the United Nations under the trusteeship system relating to political, economic, social, and educational matters in the strategic areas.

Article 84

It shall be the duty of the administering authority to ensure that the trust territory shall play its part in the maintenance of international peace and security. To this end the administering authority may make use of volunteer forces, facilities, and assistance from the trust territory in carrying out the obligations towards the Security Council undertaken in this regard by the administering authority, as well as for local defence and the maintenance of law and order within the trust territory.

Article 85

1. The functions of the United Nations with regard to trusteeship agreements for all areas not designated as strategic, including the approval of the terms of the trusteeship agreements and of their alteration or amendment, shall be exercised by the General Assembly.

2. The Trusteeship Council, operating under the authority of the General Assembly, shall assist the General Assembly in carrying out these functions.

Chapter XIII
THE TRUSTEESHIP COUNCIL

Composition
Article 86

1. The Trusteeship Council shall consist of the following Members of the United Nations:

a. Those Members administering trust territories;

b. such of those Members mentioned by name in Article 23 as are not administering trust territories; and

c. as many other Members elected for three-year terms by the General Assembly as may be necessary to ensure that the total number of members of the Trusteeship Council is equally divided between those Members of the United Nations which administer trust territories and those which do not.

2. Each member of the Trusteeship Council shall designate one especially qualified person to represent it therein.

Functions and Powers
Article 87

The General Assembly and, under its authority, the Trusteeship Council, in carrying out their functions, may:

a. consider reports submitted by the administering authority;

b. accept petitions and examine them in consultation with the administering authority;

c. provide for periodic visits to the respective trust territories at times agreed upon with the administering authority; and

d. take these and other actions in conformity with the terms of the trusteeship agreements.

Article 88

The Trusteeship Council shall formulate a questionnaire on the political, economic, social, and educational advancement of the inhabitants of each trust territory, and the administering authority for each trust territory within the competence of the General Assembly shall make an annual report to the General Assembly upon the basis of such questionnaire.

Voting
Article 89

1. Each member of the Trusteeship Council shall have one vote.

2. Decisions of the Trusteeship Council shall be made by a majority of the members present and voting.

Procedure
Article 90

1. The Trusteeship Council shall adopt its own rules of procedure, including the method of selecting its President.

2. The Trusteeship Council shall meet as required in accordance with its rules, which shall include provision for the convening of meetings on the request of a majority of its members.

Article 91

The Trusteeship Council shall, when appropriate, avail itself of the assistance of the Economic and Social Council and of the specialized agencies in regard to matters with which they are respectively concerned.

Chapter XIV
THE INTERNATIONAL COURT
OF JUSTICE

Article 92

The International Court of Justice shall be the principal judicial organ of the United Nations. It shall function in accordance with the annexed Statute, which is based upon the Statute of the Permanent Court of International Justice and forms an integral part of the present Charter.

Article 93

1. All Members of the United Nations are *ipso facto* parties to the Statute of the

International Court of Justice.

2. A state which is not a Member of the United Nations may become a party to the Statute of the International Court of Justice on conditions to be determined in each case by the General Assembly upon the recommendation of the Security Council.

Article 94

1. Each Member of the United Nations undertakes to comply with the decision of the International Court of Justice in any case to which it is a party.

2. If any party to a case fails to perform the obligations incumbent upon it under a judgment rendered by the Court the other party may have recourse to the Security Council, which may, if it deems necessary, make recommendations or decide upon measures to be taken to give effect to the judgment.

Article 95

Nothing in the present Charter shall prevent Members of the United Nations from entrusting the solution of their differences to other tribunals by virtue of agreements already in existence or which may be concluded in the future.

Article 96

1. The General Assembly or the Security Council may request the International Court of Justice to give an advisory opinion on any legal question.

2. Other organs of the United Nations and specialized agencies, which may at any time be so authorized by the General Assembly, may also request advisory opinions of the Court on legal questions arising within the scope of their activities.

Chapter XV
THE SECRETARIAT

Article 97

The Secretariat shall comprise a Secretary-General and such staff as the Organization may require. The Secretary-General shall be appointed by the General Assembly upon the recommendation of the Security Council. He shall be the chief administrative officer of the Organization.

Article 98

The Secretary-General shall act in that capacity in all meetings of the General Assembly, of the Security Council, of the Economic and Social Council, and of the Trusteeship Council, and shall perform such other functions as are entrusted to him by these organs. The Secretary-General shall make an annual report to the General Assembly on the work of the Organization.

Article 99

The Secretary-General may bring to the attention of the Security Council any matter which in his opinion may threaten the maintenance of international peace and security.

Article 100

1. In the performance of their duties the Secretary-General and the staff shall not seek or receive instructions from any government or from any other authority external to the Organization. They shall refrain from any action which might reflect on their position as international officials responsible only to the Organization.

2. Each Member of the United Nations undertakes to respect the exclusively international character of the responsibilities of the Secretary-General and the staff and not to seek to influence them in the discharge of their responsibilities.

Article 101

1. The staff shall be appointed by the Secretary-General under regulations established by the General Assembly.

2. Appropriate staff shall be permanently assigned to the Economic and Social Council, the Trusteeship Council, and, as required, to other organs of the United Nations. These staffs shall form a

part of the Secretariat.

3. The paramount consideration in the employment of the staff and in the determination of the conditions of service shall be the necessity of securing the highest standards of efficiency, competence, and integrity. Due regard shall be paid to the importance of recruiting the staff on as wide a geographical basis as possible.

Chapter XVI
MISCELLANEOUS PROVISIONS

Article 102

1. Every treaty and every international agreement entered into by any Member of the United Nations after the present Charter comes into force shall as soon as possible be registered with the Secretariat and published by it.

2. No party to any such treaty or international agreement which has not been registered in accordance with the provisions of paragraph 1 of this Article may invoke that treaty or agreement before any organ of the United Nations.

Article 103

In the event of a conflict between the obligations of the Members of the United Nations under the present Charter and their obligations under any other international agreement, their obligations under the present Charter shall prevail.

Article 104

The Organization shall enjoy in the territory of each of its Members such legal capacity as may be necessary for the exercise of its functions and the fulfilment of its purposes.

Article 105

1. The Organization shall enjoy in the territory of each of its Members such privileges and immunities as are necessary for the fulfilment of its purposes.

2. Representatives of the Members of the United Nations and officials of the Organization shall similarly enjoy such privileges and immunities as are necessary for the independent exercise of their functions in connexion with the Organization.

3. The General Assembly may make recommendations with a view to determining the details of the application of paragraphs 1 and 2 of this Article or may propose conventions to the Members of the United Nations for this purpose.

Chapter XVII
TRANSITIONAL SECURITY ARRANGEMENTS

Article 106

Pending the coming into force of such special agreements referred to in Article 43 as in the opinion of the Security Council enable it to begin the exercise of its responsibilities under Article 42, the parties to the Four-Nation Declaration, signed at Moscow, 30 October 1943, and France, shall, in accordance with the provisions of paragraph 5 of that Declaration, consult with one another and as occasion requires with other Members of the United Nations with a view to such joint action on behalf of the Organization as may be necessary for the purpose of maintaining international peace and security.

Article 107

Nothing in the present Charter shall invalidate or preclude action, in relation to any state which during the Second World War has been an enemy of any signatory to the present Charter, taken or authorized as a result of that war by the Governments having responsibility for such action.

Chapter XVIII
AMENDMENTS

Article 108

Amendments to the present Charter shall come into force for all Members of the

United Nations when they have been adopted by a vote of two thirds of the members of the General Assembly and ratified in accordance with their respective constitutional processes by two thirds of the Members of the United Nations, including all the permanent members of the Security Council.

Article 109[4]

1. A General Conference of the Members of the United Nations for the purpose of reviewing the present Charter may be held at a date and place to be fixed by a two-thirds vote of the members of the General Assembly and by a vote of any nine members of the Security Council. Each Member of the United Nations shall have one vote in the conference.

2. Any alteration of the present Charter recommended by a two-thirds vote of the conference shall take effect when ratified in

[4]Amended text of Article 109 which came into force on 12 June 1968.

(The text of Article 109 before it was amended read as follows:

1. A General Conference of the Members of the United Nations for the purpose of reviewing the present Charter may be held at a date and place to be fixed by a two-thirds vote of the members of the General Assembly and by a vote of any seven members of the Security Council. Each Member of the United Nations shall have one vote in the conference.

2. Any alteration of the present Charter recommended by a two-thirds vote of the conference shall take effect when ratified in accordance with their respective constitutional processes by two thirds of the Members of the United Nations including all the permanent members of the Security Council.

3. If such a conference has not been held before the tenth annual session of the General Assembly following the coming into force of the present Charter, the proposal to call such a conference shall be placed on the agenda of that session of the General Assembly, and the conference shall be held if so decided by a majority vote of the members of the General Assembly and by a vote of any seven members of the Security Council.)

accordance with their respective constitutional processes by two thirds of the Members of the United Nations including all the permanent members of the Security Council.

3. If such a conference has not been held before the tenth annual session of the General Assembly following the coming into force of the present Charter, the proposal to call such a conference shall be placed on the agenda of that session of the General Assembly, and the conference shall be held if so decided by a majority vote of the members of the General Assembly and by a vote of any seven members of the Security Council.

Chapter XIX
RATIFICATION AND SIGNATURE

Article 110

1. The present Charter shall be ratified by the signatory states in accordance with their respective constitutional processes.

2. The ratifications shall be deposited with the Government of the United States of America, which shall notify all the signatory states of each deposit as well as the Secretary-General of the Organization when he has been appointed.

3. The present Charter shall come into force upon the deposit of ratifications by the Republic of China, France, the Union of Soviet Socialist Republics, the United Kingdom of Great Britain and Northern Ireland, and the United States of America, and by a majority of the other signatory states. A protocol of the ratifications deposited shall thereupon be drawn up by the Government of the United States of America which shall communicate copies thereof to all the signatory states.

4. The states signatory to the present Charter which ratify it after it has come into force will become original Members of the United Nations on the date of the deposit of their respective ratifications.

Article 111

The present Charter, of which the Chinese, French, Russian, English, and Spanish texts are equally authentic, shall remain deposited in the archives of the Government of the United States of America. Duly certified copies thereof shall be transmitted by that Government to the Governments of the other signatory states.

In faith whereof the representatives of the Governments of the United Nations have signed the present Charter.

Done at the city of San Francisco the twenty-sixth day of June, one thousand nine hundred and forty-five.

Index